THE UNI...

LONG DRUMS & CANNONS

WITHDRAWN FROM
THE LIBRARY

UNIVERSITY OF
WINCHESTER

D1462860

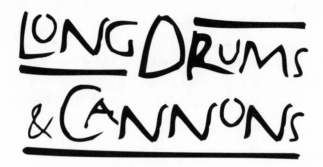

LONG DRUMS & CANNONS

NIGERIAN DRAMATISTS
AND NOVELISTS
1952–1966

Margaret Laurence

Edited with an Introduction by
Nora Foster Stovel

The University of Alberta Press

Published by
The University of Alberta Press
Ring House 2
Edmonton, Alberta, Canada T6G 2E1

Copyright © *Long Drums and Cannons* by Margaret Laurence's estate.
Originally published by Macmillan and Co. Ltd., London, Melbourne, Toronto, 1968.

Copyright © "Tribalism As Us Versus Them" by Margaret Laurence's estate.
The original paper can be found in the York University Archives and Special
Collections.

Copyright © new materials in this edition by The University of Alberta Press 2001

ISBN 0–88864–332–2

National Library of Canada Cataloguing in Publication Data

Laurence, Margaret, 1926–1987.
   Long drums and cannons

   Includes bibliographical references and index.
   ISBN 0–88864–332–2

   1. Nigerian literature (English)—History and criticism. 2. Nigerian literature
(English) I. Title.
PR9387.L38 2001   820.9   C2001–910257–7

All rights reserved.

No part of this publication may be produced, stored in a retrieval system, or
transmitted in any forms or by any means, electronic, mechanical, photocopying,
recording, or otherwise, without the prior permission of the copyright owner.

Printed on acid-free paper. ∞

Printed by Hignell Book Printing Ltd., Winnipeg, Manitoba.

Printed and bound in Canada.

The University of Alberta Press gratefully acknowledges the support received for its
publishing program from The Canada Council for the Arts. In addition, we also
gratefully acknowledge the financial support of the Government of Canada through
the Book Publishing Industry Development Program for our publishing activities.

THE CANADA COUNCIL | LE CONSEIL DES ARTS
FOR THE ARTS | DU CANADA
SINCE 1957 | DEPUIS 1957

UNIVERSITY OF WINCHESTER

03036022

CONTENTS

Long Drums and Cannons

FOREWORD

Douglas Killam

MARGARET LAURENCE'S *Long Drums and Cannons: Nigerian Dramatists and Novelists 1952–1966* was the first full-length study of Nigerian literature in English. Although it has been superceded since its publication in 1968, it has lost none of its validity as a way into understanding the literature that was produced between 1952, the date of Amos Tutuola's *The Palm-Wine Drinkard*, and 1966, the date of Achebe's *A Man of the People* and Ekwensi's *Iska*.

Long Drums and Cannons is a study of the first wave of Nigerian writing in English. The novelists and playwrights she includes, who were, by the time she wrote, already on the world stage—Soyinka, Achebe, Clark, Tutuola, Ekwensi—plus several promising new voices—Aluko, Amadi, Nwankwo, Nwapa, Nzekwu and Okara—all (with the exception of Nzekwu, who published no fiction after *Highlife for Lizards*) validated her attention in their subsequent literary careers. They were subsequently joined by a number of gifted writers from Nigeria, many of whom have since achieved an international reputation. Had *Long Drums and Cannons* received the recognition it deserved, Laurence might well have revised it, taking into account this subsequent explosion of writing. She averred as much in the early 1970s.

Laurence's interest in this body of writing obviously proceeds from her personal experience of living in Africa—first in Somalia and then in the Gold Coast. Her novel, *This Side Jordan* (1961), and collection of short stories, *The Tomorrow-Tamer* (1963), about what would, in 1957, become Ghana, reflect her interest in those exciting years in West Africa. Stories such as "A Gourdful of Glory," with Mammii Ama's cry of "Free-Dom" in the closing lines of *The Tomorrow-Tamer*, convey that excitement vividly. As a literary person, Laurence was aware of what was being done by West African writers, and it was clear to her, as *Long Drums and Cannons* reveals, that an exciting literature was being produced in Nigeria. She suggests many reasons why this was so, including the creation in 1948 of the University College of Ibadan, with the creation of the MBARI Club and its associated publication venture under Ulli Beier and Gerald Moore, assisted by gifted undergraduates at the University of Ibadan—Achebe, Clark, Nwapa, Amadi, Nzekwu, and, a year or two later, Nwankwo and Okara.

Laurence was very partisan about this first wave of African writing from West Africa. In *The Prophet's Camel Bell* she stated that she was opposed to imperialism, and this sympathy with colonized African peoples was produced by her awareness, as a Canadian, of the degree to which national autonomy was compromised by links with Westminster. Thus, she understood the impulse in Nigerian writers to set the record of history straight—to do what Achebe claimed was the purpose of his first novel: to show his people what they had lost during the years of the imposition of imperial-colonial rule in Nigeria. Laurence understood the connection between the artistic aims of literature and its social and political function. She was, in fact, a forerunner of "cultural studies."

Her discussion of the writers under review reveals her interest in the culture of the various communities represented by these writers: the Yoruba of Soyinka and Aluko, the Ibo of Achebe, Ekwensi, Nwapa and Nwankwo, and the Ijaw-Ijekere of J.P. Clark[-Bekederemo]. Laurence takes pains to provide the cultural background to the writers whose works she discusses: we learn about the religious customs of the Yoruba, which, as outsiders to that culture, we need to understand in order to make sense of Soyinka's complex dramas. The same may be said of the writing of Clark, where the religious beliefs of the Ijaw shape his *Song of a Goat*, *The Masquerade* and *Ozidi*. Similarly, Laurence brings her experience of the volatile night life of Accra to her discussion of Ekwensi's Lagotian tale, *People of the City*, and *Jagua*

Nana. And her experience of the Somalian desert doubtless shaped her understanding of Ekwensi's work dealing with the Hausa-Igbo difficulties in *Iska* and *Burning Grass.* Only a reader who had personal experience of these cultures could write about their products with such insight.

Margaret Laurence cared passionately about this literature, and she wrote about it with a perceptivity that is still valuable today. *Long Drums and Cannons* could be described as a "writerly" book—a commentary by an author who is not primarily a literary critic, but who has a unique literary sensibility to bring to the material. Achebe once said that, in his view, no one who was not an African had written with the perceptivity and sensitivity of Margaret Laurence. But she was also diffident about her involvement in Africa and said, after she had completed her five African texts, that she could no longer hear the voices of Africa and therefore would write about the country whose voices she could hear: Canada.

In the early 1970s, Margaret was prepared, with characteristic diffidence, to visit classes I was teaching at York University and talk about the writers under review—primarily those whom she had written about in *Long Drums and Cannons.* She was always sensitive to students' views, even when they had failed to grasp what a writer was trying to convey. But she could be firm in describing situations that the students had misunderstood. Remember, these were days when Africa was not much on the minds of Canadian students, eager as some of them were to know and understand those cultures. But there were some students who had been with CUSO in West Africa and whose accounts of their experiences and encounters with aspects of those cultures added zest to group discussions. Margaret was always willing to linger after the end of a class when the enthusiasm had spilled over. On a panel for the Ontario Association of Secondary School teachers that included a Nigerian Professor, Dr. Unachukwu Mezu, she explained why it was important to include African writing in the secondary school syllabus in order to introduce Canadian students to other cultures.

At a meeting of the Royal Society at the University of Guelph in 1985, Margaret was reunited with her old friend Chinua Achebe, who was then Senior Commonwealth Practitioner at the University. The meeting was memorable. Margaret was in the early stages of what became a terminal illness. She, like Achebe, was having trouble with "writer's block." Their two heads were together for the whole of the evening, and the formalities of the occasion were entirely lost on them. But Achebe reported that his discussion with Margaret that evening helped him revitalize the writing of his "own problematic novel," *Anthills of the Savannah*, and Margaret reported that their discussion helped to overcome her writer's block.

Margaret's interest in Africa never abated. She kept in touch with the literature that was coming out of Africa, especially Nigeria. Whenever we met, we consulted each other about the new developments in that literature.

Long Drums and Cannons never reached the audience it deserved for various reasons: it was poorly and indifferently marketed, and so its sales were slow and low. The original publisher was not interested in producing an inexpensive edition until the cased edition sold out—which it never did. When James Currey, then responsible for publishing the series of critical studies accompanying the Heinemann African Writers Series, enquired about obtaining the rights from Macmillan, he was not successful. Had he been, *Long Drums and Cannons* would have joined a list of distinguished African studies and been used by scholars wherever African writing was attracting attention.

This new edition from the University of Alberta Press will doubtless correct this situation. Although published in the 1960s, *Long Drums and Cannons* is still a source of enduring insight into early Nigerian writing—one that places the writing in its particular cultural context and reveals its connections with problems inherent in the post-colonial era—the principal concern of the writers included in *Long Drums and Cannons*.

PREFACE

Christian Riegel

*L*ONG *DRUMS AND CANNONS: NIGERIAN DRAMATISTS AND NOVELISTS 1952-1966*, Laurence's only book of literary criticism, forms a significant contribution to the long list of her literary achievements, establishing her as a post-colonial writer and reinforcing our recognition of the multi-faceted nature of her literary achievement. The success of Laurence's five Canadian fictions, collectively known as the Manawaka cycle, and of her two fictional texts set in Africa, has long overshadowed the critical acuity she demonstrates in *Long Drums and Cannons* (1968).

Long Drums and Cannons clarifies the importance that Africa had in her developing intellectual and literary sensibility. Laurence's passionate interest in Nigerian literature in the 1960s followed closely upon her earlier commitment to translating the Somali folk literature that she published in her first book, *A Tree for Poverty* (1954). Together, these two texts establish Laurence's place in the vanguard of appreciation of African literature by Western writers. In *Long Drums and Cannons* Laurence demonstrates an acute awareness of the importance of Nigerian literature, and she does so, remarkably enough, while still in the shadow of an only recently dismantled colonial structure. What makes Laurence a rarity amongst her peers is her awareness of her ambiguous position as a white writer who, whether she was a willing supporter or not, was nevertheless a representative of the British colonial regime wherever she traveled and lived in Africa, if only by virtue of the fact that her engineer husband, Jack Laurence, worked for the British Government—first in the British Protectorate of Somaliland (now Somalia) and then in the Gold Coast (later Ghana). Indeed, her recognition of the complexity of Nigerian literature is a testament to her struggle to break free from the paternalistic attitudes of European imperialism. While Nigerian literature did not *need* Margaret Laurence to *exist*, it was usefully served by her decision to take up the task of making it known to a larger audience.

Long Drums and Cannons, Laurence's fifth and final African text—following upon her fictional works, *This Side Jordan* and *The Tomorrow-Tamer*, and her nonfiction books, *A Tree for Poverty* and *The Prophet's Camel-Bell*—contributes significantly to our understanding of the importance of her African experience. *Long Drums and Cannons* establishes Laurence as a post-colonial writer and signals her role as an observer of the changes that accompanied the shift from a colonial country to a post-colonial, ultimately independent, Nigerian nation. In her critique, she examines Nigerian writers, not as mere products of imperialism, but rather as products of an indigenous culture. She recognizes that Nigerian writers are reflective of individual tribal cultures, independent of the so-called civilizing missions of British imperialists. Her African writing has been viewed as apprentice work, as the place where Laurence learned her craft and where she perfected the sensibility that made her Canada's best-loved novelist. But it is also essential to read her African texts as the expression of a writer acutely aware of the injustice and hypocrisy of imperialism. Moreover, it is important to see her African experience as the source of the post-colonial perspective that distinguishes her Canadian fiction.

The urgent need for a new and updated edition of *Long Drums and Cannons* was first drawn to my attention by Tracy Ware of Queen's University, whose own work on Canadian and post-colonial topics made him acutely aware of the points of intersection of these areas. I approached Glenn Rollans, then Director of the University of Alberta Press—who had demonstrated his sense of Laurence's continuing importance by publishing my own edition, *Challenging Territory: The Writing of Margaret Laurence* (1997)—with the idea that a new edition was imperative and that such an edition would need to place Laurence within a historical and a contemporary context. Encouraged by his enthusiasm for the project, I approached Nora Foster Stovel, my then Ph.D. Supervisor, to decide on how best to proceed to make this important text available once again.

Dr. Foster Stovel undertook to negotiate with the Laurence Estate for permission to republish *Long Drums and Cannons*, as well as Laurence's previously unpublished paper on "Tribalism As Us Versus Them," written the following year as an afterword to *Long Drums and Cannons*. In addition, she wrote a substantial Introduction, clarifying the origins, reception and influence of Laurence's critique and examining the influences that Nigerian writing had on her Canadian fiction. She involved some of her graduate students in annotating Laurence's original manuscript and updating the biographies and bibliographies of the Nigerian authors. She invited her colleague, Dr. G.D. Killam, to write a reminiscence, recreating the impact of the original publication of *Long Drums* and recalling the context of his friendship with Margaret Laurence. At the suggestion of the Press's editor, Mary Mahoney-Robson, Dr. Abdul-Rasheed Na'Allah was invited to write a commentary discussing the development of Nigerian literature since the sixties and re-evaluating the importance of *Long Drums* from the perspective of Nigerian writers today.

This new edition re-establishes *Long Drums and Cannons* as a significant element in Laurence's long list of literary accomplishments. With the addition of this text, Laurence's only critical book, her literary achievement can be fully appreciated and the importance of her place in Canadian and world literature can be fully understood.

ACKNOWLEDGEMENTS

First and foremost, I wish to thank Jocelyn and David Laurence for permission to republish Margaret Laurence's 1968 text of *Long Drums and Cannons*, as well as her previously unpublished essay, "Tribalism As Us Versus Them." I also wish to acknowledge Dr. Christian Riegel, my colleague and former doctoral student, for suggesting this project to me; Glenn Rollans, former Director of the University of Alberta Press, for encouraging the project; Leslie Vermeer, Managing Editor of the Press, for completing the contract negotiations; Carol Dragich, for designing the book; and, last but not least, Mary Mahoney-Robson, Editor, for her expert copy-editing.

I also wish to thank Charlotte Stewart-Murphy, Carl Spadoni and the Special Collections staff of the Mills Memorial Library at McMaster University for furnishing photocopies of Margaret Laurence's typescript of *Long Drums and Cannons*, and Kent Haworth and the Archives and Special Collections staff of the Scott Memorial Library at York University for providing Laurence's unpublished essay "Tribalism As Us Versus Them."

I would like to acknowledge the assistance of several of my graduate students. In editing this text, I followed the method that I employed in editing two volumes of Margaret Laurence's early writings for my colleague Dr. Juliet McMaster's Juvenilia Press, whereby students are educated in the editing process. Accordingly, I invited former students to participate in annotating chapters and providing bibliographies and biographies for each writer discussed in *Long Drums and Cannons*: Kim Solga for Chapter 1 on Wole Soyinka, Krissy Lundberg for Chapter 2 on John Pepper Clark, Lisa Grekul for Chapter 3 on Chinua Achebe, Robyn Fowler for Chapter 4 on Amos Tutuola, Tracy Wright for Chapter 5 on Cyprian Ekwensi, and Jun Ling Khoo for Chapter 6 on Other Voices. Special thanks are due to Laura Taylor and Kathryn Holland, who both revised the biographies and bibliographies to make them sound more like one voice, as well to Kathryn Holland, again, for compiling the Glossary and Appendix II and III and to Jan Olesen for revising the index. Thanks are also due to Tobi Kozakewich, Jennifer Prestash, Laura Taylor, Micaela Brown, Jan Olesen and Kathryn Holland for proofreading the text at various stages. Theresa Daniels was helpful in nego-tiating technical problems in translating computer programs.

I also wish to thank Dr. Christian Riegel for writing the Preface, Dr. G.D. Killam for contributing the Foreword, Dr. Abdul-Rasheed Na'Allah for contributing a piece on Nigerian literature since the time of the composition of Laurence's text, and Dr. Ronald Ayling for his encouragement and advice.

As always, I wish to thank my husband, Dr. Bruce Stovel, and my children, Dr. Laura Stovel and Grant Foster Stovel, for their constant support.

Note on the Text

IN EDITING MARGARET LAURENCE'S *LONG DRUMS AND CANNONS* FOR THIS new publication, I adhered precisely to the original text published by Macmillan in 1968. In the case of clearly unintentional typographical errors, I respected Laurence's opinions regarding editors who fail to correct unintentional errors, as she expresses them in her discussion of Tutuola's texts, and corrected them silently. Wherever any doubt occurred about Laurence's intentions, I consulted her original typescript in the Special Collections at McMaster University. In annotating the text, we noted any major changes and omissions, quoting the version in her original typescript, with page refer-ences. Pagination of this typescript is rather misleading, however, since Laurence paginated each chapter separately and frequently changed the order of pages.

— Nora Foster Stovel

TALKING DRUMS & DANCING MASKS

Introducing Margaret Laurence's
Long Drums and Cannons:
Nigerian Dramatists and Novelists 1952–1966

Nora Foster Stovel

CANADIAN WRITER MARGARET LAURENCE (1926–1987) COMPOSED *Long Drums and Cannons: Nigerian Dramatists and Novelists 1952–1966* (1968), the first full-length study of Nigerian literature, to bring this new Nigerian literature in English to the attention of the Western reader. In a draft of an unpublished Introduction, superceded by the Preface, she states that "Nigeria, more than any other African country in which the *lingua franca* is English, has produced in a short space of time an astonishing number of interesting writers" (1). She devotes one chapter to each of five outstanding Nigerian writers of fiction and drama: "Voices of Life, Dance of Death," celebrates the plays of Wole Soyinka; "Rituals of Destiny" focusses on the plays of poet John Pepper Clark; "The Thickets of Our Separateness" praises the novels of Chinua Achebe; "A Twofold Forest" explores the fiction of Amos Tutuola; "Masks of the City" examines the novels of Cyprian Ekwensi; and "Other Voices" introduces six promising new writers: T.M. Aluko, Elechi Amadi, Nkem Nwankwo, Flora Nwapa, Onuora Nzekwu, and Gabriel Okara. Her typescript includes an apologia: "I should make clear that this book is not intended as a comprehensive survey of contemporary Nigerian writing. I have not included all Nigerian writers, although I have certainly included the most significant ones. I admit to having been guided in my choice of material only by personal preference" (1).

Referred to as a pioneering study by reviewers such as Alistair Niven, who judges it "perhaps the best book relating to Nigerian literature in English that has been produced," and John Povey, who concludes, "Within its selected area it is as useful and informative as any study yet published in the field of African literature," *Long Drums and Cannons* is still relevant over thirty years later. In *Into Africa with Margaret Laurence* (1992), Fiona Sparrow judges: "*Long Drums and Cannons* is still a valuable work and essential reading for those embarking on a study of Nigerian literature since it explains its beginnings with thoroughness and sensitivity" (163).

Laurence of Africa

Margaret Laurence, called "Canada's most successful novelist" by Joan Coldwell in *The Oxford Companion to Canadian Literature*, is most famous for her Canadian fiction set in her mythical microcosm of Manawaka. Canadians do not think of her as an author of African texts, although she does deserve that title, for the fame of her Canadian fiction has overshadowed her earlier African work. While she wrote five fictions set in Canada, she wrote an equal number of books set in Africa. Her first published book, *A Tree for Poverty* (1954), was the first ever translation or publication of Somali folk literature. Her first novel, *This Side Jordan* (1960), her first collection of short stories, *The Tomorrow-Tamer* (1963), her first memoir, *The Prophet's Camel Bell* (1963), and her first and only critical study, *Long Drums and Cannons: Nigerian Dramatists and Novelists, 1952–1966*, were all written out of Africa, where she lived from 1950 to 1957.

In 1950 she moved to Somalia with her husband, Jack Laurence, an engineer who built *ballehs* or reservoirs in the desert. Margaret found her own form of conservation in translating the Somali folk literature that she published in *A Tree for Poverty* and in writing the diaries that were to form the basis for her African journal, *The Prophet's Camel Bell*, called *New Wind in a Dry Land* in the American edition. Next, the Laurences lived from 1952 to 1957 in the Gold Coast, where Jack was building the port at Accra—the setting for her novel, *This Side Jordan*, and short story collection, *The Tomorrow-Tamer*—as it moved towards independence as the nation of Ghana.

In an essay titled "Margaret Laurence and Africa," Canadian critic and teacher Craig Tapping recalls that introducing himself as a Canadian to a university class in Eastern Nigeria in 1979 was greeted by an enthusiastic chant—"Canada, Canada." When he asked the source of the enthusiasm, a student explained that "one Canadian had done more than any other person to promote Nigerian writing internationally and, in so doing, had examined the crucial role writers play in building a culture. And that Canadian was Margaret Laurence in her book *Long Drums and Cannons*" (66).

Long Drums and Cannons

Long Drums and Cannons, hailed on the cover as a "pioneer in its field," as the first full-length study of Nigerian literature, was part of a surge of books on African culture in the 1960s that included George Moore's pioneering work *Seven African Writers* (1962), Ezekiel Mphalele's *The African Image* (1962), Anne Tibble's *African/English Literature: A Survey and Anthology* (1965), John Ramsaran's *New Approaches to African Literature* (1959), Judith Gleason's *This Africa* (1969) and Jahnheinz Jahn's *Literary History of Neo-African Literature* (1969), as well as Ulli Beier's *Introduction to African Literature*—many of which Laurence cites in her study.

Long Drums and Cannons covers the period from 1952 to 1966—"the fifteen years in which Nigerian writers created a kind of Renaissance," as Laurence claims. In her Preface, she states that "Nigerian literature in English, although its roots go demonstrably far back into the country's cultural past, is of comparatively recent vintage" (11). She dates this literary renaissance from 1952, when Amos Tutuola's *The Palm-Wine Drinkard* was the first novel in English by a Nigerian to be published outside Nigeria and widely read in the West. She explains: "Since then there has been an outpouring of plays and novels, a kind of renaissance, the flourishing of a new literature which has drawn sustenance both from traditional oral literature and from the present and rapidly changing society" (11). "Why this sudden upsurge?" she asks rhetorically in her typescript. "One can only guess" (2). In the Preface, she locates the origins of this literary renaissance in the new Nigerian universities, especially the University of Ibadan, founded in 1948, and the MBARI writers' and artists' club, founded in 1954, as well as literary journals such as *Black Orpheus*, founded in 1957 and edited by such distinguished people as Ulli Beier, Janheinz Jahn, Wole Soyinka, Ezekiel Mphalele and Ronald Dathorne (11). She concludes her study with Soyinka's experimental novel *The Interpreters*, Clark's *Ozidi*, Ekwensi's *Iska* and Achebe's *A Man of the People*, all published in 1966—some of them, especially Achebe's novel, reflecting the conflict that was already beginning in Nigeria.

Laurence establishes her focus in her subtitle: *Nigerian Dramatists and Novelists*. As a novelist herself, whose fiction is intensely dramatic, this is a natural selection. In the draft Introduction, she explains, "I have dealt with the plays of Wole Soyinka and John Pepper Clark largely as literature rather than theatre, because I have seen only a few of them performed and have experienced the others through the printed page. I realize that this view is necessarily a limited one, but perhaps it will provide some background to Nigerian theatre today. It is to be hoped that more of these plays will soon be performed in England and America" (1). In her Preface, she explains, "This book does not deal with contemporary Nigerian poetry, for this field is now extensive enough to require a separate commentary" (13). But, in fact, she pays particularly close attention to the poetic quality of some of these dramatists and novelists, especially Soyinka and Clark.

Laurence says her purpose is "to show that Nigerian prose writing in English has now reached a point where it must be recognised as a significant part of world literature" (13): "Modern Nigerian literature interprets Africa, both past and present, from the inside. Africa was interpreted and misinterpreted by outsiders for long enough. Now its own writers are engaged in reassessing their past, in rediscovering their inheritance, in interpreting themselves both to their own people and to the rest of the world.... To people outside Africa, the work of these West African writers has made accessible for the first time a picture in depth" (12). Laurence writes *Drums* as an outsider, a white Western woman, facilitating that process of introducing Nigerian literature to the rest of the world. As Fiona Sparrow concludes in *Into Africa with Margaret Laurence*: "Laurence locates each new text within its regional context, but she never denies it a place within a wider field of reference, within a world where boundaries are recognized, but only because they can be crossed" (204).

Laurence is true to her purpose in *Long Drums and Cannons* of publicising the new Nigerian writing in English and of educating a Western readership unfamiliar with that literature or with the traditions that nourished it. This dual purpose accounts for both the strengths and weaknesses of her study. Her guide to Nigerian literature is basic, but useful: she introduces each author with a brief biography, as well as information about the cultural background of the works that might be unknown to Western readers: for example, she explains the significance of the Yoruba *abiku* and the Ibo *ogbanje*, the talking drums and masquerade dances, to an audience unfamiliar with tribal traditions. She provides a commentary on the major works of each author that is clearly intended to introduce a reader to new material, for it consists primarily of summaries that are studded with insights, as she comments intepretively and contextually on the artistry of these writers. As Craig Tapping concludes, "She gets it right every time, and with each writer she discusses" (70).

Origins

Long Drums and Cannons began with a request to write four scripts on Nigerian literature for the BBC, which wanted an impression of Nigeria as seen through the eyes of its contemporary writers (King 220). Laurence, who had taken a passionate interest in African affairs since her seven years living in Somalia and Ghana and had already published four texts out of Africa, embraced this project enthusiastically. Residing in England from 1962 to 1972—the first year in Hampstead, London, and the remaining years in Elm Cottage in Penn, Buckinghamshire—she was able to take advantage of the cultural opportunities in London. The 1965 Commonwealth Festival gave her the opportunity to see plays by Soyinka and Clark. As her Macmillan editor Alan Maclean recalls, Laurence had an affair with Jamal, an ambassador from an African country to the court of St. James (Duncan 15)—a married man with seven children, whom she dubbed "the old lion" (King 224)—who introduced her to African artists. In her memoir she recalls, "I had met a number of young Nigerian writers, including Wole Soyinka and the poet Christopher Okigbo, through mutual friends in London, and had begun to read other works by Nigerians" (*Dance* 185). Laurence's African library, including 148 texts, many of them annotated, now housed in the Mills Memorial Library at McMaster University, bears witness to her familiarity with African literature. On 16 January 1966, she writes to her friend, fellow Canadian novelist Adele Wiseman:

> After about 4 months reading and thinking about Nigerian
> writing, traditional and contemporary, I feel I've taken a do-it-
> yourself course in contemporary African writing, and I have so
> much material it nearly breaks my heart, as there isn't anything I
> can do with it, but maybe I'll write a book, which would be no
> hell critically as I am no academic critic and don't even know the
> jargon, but it might be interesting in an amateur way. (King 220)

She resolved to collect her scripts on Nigerian writers into a book, writing to Wiseman on 7 July 1966, "I want to know about Africa," and "I've always wanted to do some really close literary criticism" (Lennox 210–11); on 2 May 1967, she reports, "I finished the *final* work on the Nigeria book yesterday, and handed it over last night to Alan Maclean" (Lennox 216). As she recalls in her memoir, "I continued [in 1967] to work on a survey I was writing of contemporary Nigerian writers. *Long Drums and Cannons* was never intended to be a deep analysis. It was, rather, a survey and an interpretation, from the viewpoint of a reasonably skilled reader who stood outside the culture and who hoped to make these works better known and more accessible" (*Dance* 185).

Laurence was a novelist, not an academic, and she was often apologetic about her limitations as critic and scholar. In her typescript of *Long Drums and Cannons*, she acknowledges: "I do not delude myself that this is a work of literary criticism. It is a commentary, written from the point of view of a reader and a writer." This perspective is both an advantage and a disadvantage. The advantages include the insights she offers into Nigerian writers' creative processes and artistic achievements, as well as in the readability of a study that eschews jargon. Disadvantages include a lack of theoretical context and scholarly research that could have reinforced her aim of introducing Nigerian literature to the rest of the world. But this aim was foiled by the outbreak of civil war.

Nigerian Civil War: "Africa's Wounded Giant"

She records: "The book was published by Macmillan in England in 1968, and a year later by Praeger in America. By the time it came out, however, Nigeria was in the throes of a civil war that split the country and caused unbelievable suffering. Wole Soyinka went to jail and Chris Okigbo was killed. The lines from his poem seemed cruelly ironic" (*Dance* 185). In a 1969 article entitled "Ten Years' Sentences," she explains that Nigerian writers created a renaissance by "drawing upon their cultural past and relating it to the present, seeking links with the ancestors and the old gods in order to discover who they themselves were. This exploration and discovery ended abruptly with the first massacre of the Ibo in the north, some two years ago" (Woodcock 30). Later she laments, "How much everything can change in a couple of years! Chris Okigbo is dead, fighting for Biafra. Wole Soyinka, undoubtedly the best writer that English-writing Africa has yet produced, and one of the best anywhere, has been in a Federal jail in Kaduna for more than a year. Chinua Achebe, that excellent and wise novelist, isn't writing for himself these days—he's doing journalism for Biafra, and all one can hope at the moment is that he manages to survive" (Woodcock 31). "Africa's wounded giant," she notes in her draft Introduction, is the way Nigeria was recently described by a journalist (1).

Laurence was devastated by the war and deflated by the irrelevance of her study of Nigerian literature—given that the nation was torn apart by civil war and some of its writers imprisoned or killed. She confides to George Woodcock 18 September 1968: "I've got a book on contemporary Nigerian literature coming out in England next month, but I feel a total lack of interest in it, owing to the terrifying situation now in Nigeria. The book seems at this point quite irrelevant to what is going on there now." On 26 September, she writes: "Thank you so much for your reassurance re: my book on Nigerian writing. Yes, I guess it is possible that some relevance will return, although it is difficult to believe so, at the moment, at least within the next generation" (Wainwright 219).

So Laurence's *Long Drums and Cannons* was, ironically, outdated even before it was published by the outbreak of civil war in Nigeria and the secession of Biafra in 1967. The irony of this timing is exemplified by the epigraph for the study, which is also the source of its title—"long drums and cannons: / The spirit in the ascent"—a quotation from Christopher Okigbo's poem *Heavensgate*. Laurence appended a note to her Preface, when the study was already in press, lamenting the death of Okigbo and the cruel irony of her title (13). In fact, Laurence wished to revise her study later, in the 1970s, when the conflict had ended, but Macmillan declined to republish it. They also refused to sell the rights to James Currey, who wanted to republish it. In 1969, the year after her book was first published, she gave a lecture titled "Tribalism As Us Versus Them" at London's Institute of Commonwealth Studies. In a subsequent introduction to the essay—which was probably intended to follow the African essays in *Heart of a Stranger*, her 1976 collection of travel articles—she explains that "I took the opportunity to update my thinking in view of the war." Her lecture begins with a statement— "Tribalism [is] central to the present civil war in Nigeria and Biafra"—and poses a question: "How does tribalism appear in the writing of Nigerian novelists and dramatists in the period between 1952 and 1966, when Nigerian literature experienced a tremendous upsurge?" (*Drums* 223). She discusses the conflict between traditional Nigerian tribalism and modern European individualism. This previously unpublished essay on tribalism forms, in effect, an afterword to *Long Drums and Cannons*; for that reason, it is included in this new edition.

Critical Reception

Unfortunately, *Long Drums and Cannons* did not receive the circulation or the recognition that it deserved, although Chinua Achebe singled it out for special praise in his 1975 study, *Morning Yet on Creation Day* (18). It is interesting to speculate on the reasons for this neglect. Apart from the irony of timing already mentioned, the study was published only in England and America, not Africa or Canada, where interest in both Nigerian literature and Margaret Laurence might have made it more successful. Macmillan declined to produce a paperback edition until the original hard copy printing sold out, and, since it never did, perhaps as a result of poor publicity, an inexpensive edition was never published. Had McClelland and Stewart, Laurence's Canadian publishers, for example, published it along with her other African books, it might have been far more influential.

The critics who reviewed it most enthusiastically were Canadian—probably as a result of Laurence's reputation in Canada as a novelist, since she had published her first Manawaka novels—*The Stone Angel* (1964) and *A Jest of God* (1966), which won a Governor General's Gold Medal—before she published *Long Drums and Cannons* in 1968. Moreover, many Canadian readers may have been less familiar with African literature and cultural studies. Clara Thomas, in *Canadian Literature*, concludes that "*Long Drums and Cannons* is an important guidebook and commentary on Nigerian literature" (92); James Dale of McMaster University, which purchased the draft of *Long Drums and Cannons* in 1969, judges that "Laurence has done a great service in making Nigerian literature better known...for this is much the best and fullest account yet provided of Nigerian prose writing in English." Librarians emphasise its usefulness: *Library Journal* concludes: "This is a basic work for literature collections, public, or academic" (1148); *Choice* judges: "If...a student is reading a Nigerian work in his 'World Lit' class and requires lucid critical guidance, this is by far the best book that a librarian could recommend." "Ways into Africa" in the *Times Literary Supplement* states in 1969 that Laurence "eminently succeeds in her aim: even those who have had little knowledge of Nigerian writers before reading her book will be convinced by her perceptive analysis, that this is indeed now a significant part of world literature."

Some reviewers appreciate Laurence's "writerly" approach to literary criticism: Piquefort, in *Canadian Forum*, judges that "Laurence, quite rightly, has kept to a simple format; she presents what one might term writer's criticism: more concerned with what the writers are saying than with forms or influences or theories of techniques." He concludes: "The newcomer to this part of the jungle will find her an intelligent and understanding guide; her own fans will find in this study an explanation for some of the depths of *The Stone Angel*" (249). David Carroll, in *The University of Toronto Quarterly*, opines that "Laurence's great virtue as a critic is that she is sympathetic, down-to-earth, and refuses to be ingenious or theoretical.... One feels that she respects her fellow-writers' works and has no desire to stand between them and their rightful audience" (360).

International reviewers—including Lewis Nkosi, who deems it "a modest book written with admirable clarity and simplicity" (70), in "A Question of Literary Stewardship" in *Africa Report*, and Eric Sellin, who considers it most valuable for the novice in *Journal of Modern Literature*—are naturally more critical, although John Povey judges, in *Journal of Asian and African Studies*:

> If I had to advise a reader or student of one book that would be the most useful introduction to this new writing I think it would be Margaret Lawrence's [*sic*] volume. I would recommend it for the precise and commonsense explanations it gives concerning writings which have too often been treated by critics not as works of literature but as anthropological, linguistic or political evidence of contemporary African conditions. Margaret Lawrence [*sic*] brings us back to the recognition that these are authors as well as racial and national spokesmen and it is a valuable and healthy reminder. (110)

The most balanced reviews come, not surprisingly, from Canadian critics who specialise in African or Commonwealth (as it was then termed) literature: Anthony Boxhill and Douglas Killam are fully aware of Laurence's advantages and disadvantages as a critic of Nigerian literature. Boxhill commends Laurence's "writerly," nonacademic approach, as it perceives the universal appeal of Nigerian literature, but concludes that she is "too kind a critic" in that she tends to avoid negative criticism of works like Ekwensi's *Burning Grass*. He values the study's dual significance: "Quite apart from its content, this book is very significant because it is written by a Canadian about Nigerian writing. As a Canadian it is easier for her to be disinterested than a Nigerian critic, or a British critic, whose countrymen were the colonizers mentioned in so much of the writing" (106). G.D. Killam, in *The Journal of Commonwealth Literature*, applauds Laurence's study, affirming: "Her arguments are exact and convincing" (110).

Recently, Canadian critics have re-evaluated *Long Drums and Cannons*. Fiona Sparrow judges: "the value of her work as a pioneering analysis is considerable, and her line by line commentary is not without many well-argued and perceptive judgements, which, more than twenty years later, have lost none of their point and value" (162). Craig Tapping asserts: "*Long Drums and Cannons* cannot but astonish the reader granted the hindsight of the present. The book is historically significant.... What is striking is just how exact and scrupulous, and therefore undated, Laurence's judgements, insights and explanations are" (70).

Renewed Relevance
Three decades later, Laurence's study of Nigerian literature has significance for a contemporary reader, but its significance has changed or even reversed. No longer does a Western reader need any introduction to Nigerian writers, especially Chinua Achebe and Wole Soyinka, who have long since achieved international acclaim, as the 1986 awarding of the Nobel Prize for Literature to Soyinka eloquently illustrates. Rather, Laurence's "writerly" critique illuminates not so much the Nigerian literature that provides its focus as the author's own perspective. *Long Drums and Cannons* now has reflexive value not only as an historical document chronicling the perspective of a Western writer, but also as a key to Laurence's own artistry, for a consideration of what she values in Nigerian writing can illuminate her own creative values in her Canadian, as well as her African, works.

Canadian critics have noted this very point. Craig Tapping judges: "The book is historically significant, and sheds further light on Laurence's literary mission in Manawaka and environs," for "the critical terms with which Laurence describes Achebe's early achievement prefigure her own Manawaka cycle of novels" (70–73). James King concludes, in *The Life of Margaret Laurence*: "*Long Drums* is a good critical book, especially if it is seen as the work of a professional writer of fiction passing judgment on the works of her peers and, in the process, revealing to herself and her readers some of the controlling ideas in her own writing," for "It is obvious that in the work of Wole Soyinka, Chinua Achebe, Amos Tutuola, Flora Nwapa and their contemporaries Margaret Laurence also saw reflected many of her own themes" (221). Patricia Morley agrees: "Because [Laurence] feels a sympathetic identification with many Africans, her comments on their work reveal many of her own attitudes towards writing" (35).

It is especially relevant that Laurence wrote *Long Drums and Cannons* in the middle of the decade in which she composed her Manawaka cycle. Clara Thomas judges, "She was particularly influenced then, I believe, by her recent work in *Long Drums and Cannons* on the Nigerian writers, especially Achebe, Soyinka and Okigbo" (Woodcock 104). Craig Tapping articulates the relevance of *Long Drums and Cannons* to Laurence's Manawaka cycle: "the critical terms with which Laurence describes Achebe's early achievement prefigure her own Manawaka cycle of novels.... [for] Laurence's critical endeavours on behalf of African literature determine what it is she will attempt on returning to Canada" (73). As Laurence recalls in her memoir, "I found it exciting that African writers were producing what I thought I and many Canadian writers were producing: a truly non-colonial literature" (*Dance* 185).

Artistic Values

Laurence emphasises the commitment of Nigerian writers, especially Achebe and Soyinka, to creating *characters* who are living individuals. In "A Place to Stand On," the first article in her collection of travel essays, *Heart of a Stranger* (1976), she affirms the paramount importance of character to her own writing. In fact, she calls herself a "Method writer" (New 157), because she is possessed by her protagonists—almost like the dancers who are possessed by the spirits of the ancestors in Nigerian masquerade drama. She says, "I write...what I would call a Method novel. Like a Method actor, you get right inside the role. I take on, for the time I'm writing, the *persona* of the character..." (Cameron 102). She recalls that writing *The Stone Angel* was like taking dictation: "The novel poured forth. It was as if the old woman was actually there, telling me her life story, and it was my responsibility to put it down as faithfully as I could" (*Dance* 156).

She also emphasises the centrality of what she terms the character's *dilemma* or inner conflict. She explains dilemma as "the individual's effort to define himself, his need to come to terms with his ancestors and his gods, his uncertainties in relation to others, his conflicts in the face of his own opposed loyalties, the dichotomy of his longing for both peace and war, his perpetual battle to free himself from the fetters of the past and the compulsions of the present" (*Drums* 181). For Nigerian writers, the conflict includes "the clash between generations, the social and individual disturbances brought about by a period of transition, the slow dying of the destructive aspects of tribalism, the anguish and inadequacy of uncompromising individualism as an alternative to tribalism" (12).

Laurence sees the ancestral past haunting the present in Nigerian writing as well as in her own work, for she believes "the past and the future are both always present" (New 157) and both affect the future. In *Heart of a Stranger*, she discusses the "attempt to understand one's background and one's past, sometimes even a more distant past which one has not personally experienced" (1). She explains: "This sort of exploration can be clearly seen in the works of contemporary African writers, many of whom re-create their people's past in novels and plays in order to recover a sense of themselves, an identity and a feeling of value from which they were separated by two or three generations of colonialism and missionizing. They have found it necessary, in other words, to come to terms with their ancestors and their gods in order to be able to accept the past and be at peace with the dead, without being stifled or threatened by their past" (2). This is precisely Laurence's own approach:

> Oddly enough, it was only several years ago, when I began doing research into contemporary Nigerian writing and its background, that I began to see how much my own writing had followed the same pattern—the attempt to assimilate the past, partly in order to be freed from it, partly in order to try to understand myself and perhaps others of my generation, through seeing where we had come from. (2)

Similarly, she says that when she constructed her first Canadian heroine, Hagar Currie of *The Stone Angel*, she had to return to an ancestral past that she had not personally experienced: "I had to begin approaching my background and my past through my grandparents' generation," because Hagar "incorporates many of the qualities of my grandparents' generation. Her speech is their speech, and her gods their gods" (3–4). Interestingly, Achebe also began with his grandparents' generation in his first novel *Things Fall Apart* (1958), indicating the close connections between these two writers.

Laurence sees the recovery of the ancestral past as the central theme in Nigerian literature:

> Certain themes recur throughout contemporary Nigerian writing.
> There is a strong desire to reassess the historical past, to revalue
> the life of the village and the traditional forms of society, to

rediscover roots which were severed. Many Nigerian writers
have been concerned with an attempt, both personal and general,
to reunite with a past which was for several generations lost or
despised. No writer of any quality has viewed the old Africa in
an idealised way, but they have tried to regain what is rightfully
theirs—a past composed of real and vulnerable people, their
ancestors, not the figments of missionary and colonialist
imaginations. (*Drums* 178)

Orphaned before the age of ten and raised in her patriarchal grandfather's
home, Laurence was also haunted by the past, and she views her own writing
as "the attempt to assimilate the past, partly in order to be freed from it,
partly in order to try to understand [it]" (*Heart* 2). For Nigerians, she says,
"the work of writers such as Chinua Achebe and Wole Soyinka [has] done
much to restore a true sense of their own past, a knowledge of a tribal society
which was neither idyllic, as the views of some nationalists would have it, nor
barbaric, as many missionaries and European administrators wished and
needed to believe" (*Drums* 12). We can see similar conflicts recreated in
Laurence's African fiction, especially *This Side Jordan*, where her central
character, Nathaniel Amegbe, is torn between the tribal past of his father, the
village drummer, and his present as a schoolmaster teaching history at the
Futura Academy. Amegbe hopes that the future will resolve the conflicts
between past and present in the person of his newborn son, as he exhorts him
to "Cross Jordan, Joshua" (282). Later, in her Manawaka cycle, the need to
respect the ancestors, while freeing oneself of the past in order to go forward
into the future, can be seen in all her Canadian heroines.

Laurence asserts, "My writing, then, has been my own attempt to come to
terms with the past. I see this process as the gradual one of freeing oneself
from the stultifying aspect of the past, while at the same time beginning to see
its true value" (*Heart* 5). The theme of freedom, then, is closely connected to
the importance of recovering the past, for one must appreciate the past while
freeing oneself from its fetters. She explores Nigerian writers' progress
toward independence in this light.

Freedom is central to her own fiction: *This Side Jordan* employs epigraphs
drawn from the Akan proverb, "'Oh God, there is something above, let it
reach me," as well as "Slogans from African 'mammy-lorries'"—"The Day
Will Come," "Authority Is Never Loved," "Flee, Oh Ye Powers Of Darkness,"
and "Rise Up, Ghana"—while *The Tomorrow-Tamer* ends with Mammii
Ama chanting "Free-Dom" in the final story "A Gourdful of Glory" (242). In
her Canadian fiction, all her female protagonists seek freedom from the

shackles of the past—from Hagar who realizes on her deathbed that she has been chained by her own pride, to Vanessa, who hopes, "if I sounded all my trumpets loudly enough, [Grandfather Connor's] walls would quake and crumble" (172).

Clearly, the theme of communication is closely related to that of freedom. In *Long Drums and Cannons*, Laurence asserts that "Achebe's writing also conveys the feeling that we must attempt to communicate, however imperfectly, if we are not to succumb to despair or madness" (112). G.D. Killam quotes that same statement in introducing *A Jest of God* (1966), for he asserts the need for (and difficulty of) communication as the central concern of her own fiction: "Of these writers she obviously feels the greatest affinity with the Nigerian novelist Chinua Achebe, and she might be talking about her own novels—including those set in Canada as well as in Africa—when she stresses his preoccupation with communication..." (n.p.). Recalling her subsequent friendship with Achebe in her memoir, Laurence writes, "Knowing that, in our different ways, Achebe and I have been trying to do much the same sort of thing all our writing lives, I recognized that communication [between African and Western writers] could be possible" (*Dance* 153).

Laurence believes that "The best of these [Nigerian] writers have also chosen themes which are at once universal and able to carry their particular experience" (*Drums* 178). She praises Nigerian literature for "the insight it gives not only into immediate and local dilemmas but, through these, into the human dilemma as a whole" (*Drums* 13). She believes that, in order to achieve that universality, literature "must be planted firmly in some soil" (*Drums* 13). She admires writing that is rooted in real landscapes, both rural and urban, writing that paints the forests and swamps of Nigeria as vividly as her own writing portrays the Canadian Prairies. Nigerian characters are often torn between a rural past and an urban present, and Laurence, who loathed Toronto, which she called the "Vile Metropolis," or "V.M." for short (*Dance* 180), represents that conflict in her African and Canadian fiction. She insists, "Writing, for me, has to be set firmly in some soil, some place, some outer and inner territory which might be described in anthropological terms as 'cultural background'" (*Heart* 6). That "territory" generates a rich lode of symbolism in Nigerian writing, as well as in her own fiction.

Laurence praises the symbolic richness of Nigerian writers, especially Soyinka. She is particularly interested in his use of drumming and masquerade dances in his drama. Both are important to her own creative writing: her first published short story, "The Drummer of All the World" (1954), provided the introduction for her collection of stories, *The Tomorrow-Tamer* (1963), set in the emergent nation of Ghana. Metaphorical masks pervade her work, notably in the story "The Mask of the Bear," so central to her collection of Canadian stories, *A Bird in the House* (1970), where she writes of "the Bear Mask of the Haida Indians": "before it became a museum piece, the mask had concealed a man" (74). Water symbolism is the undercurrent that flows through all her fiction: just as the mother offering the cup of water first to her infant on the desert of the Haud during the Jilal was indelibly printed on Laurence's memory when she wrote *The Prophet's Camel Bell* (66), so the cup of water that Hagar wrests from the nurse at the end of *The Stone Angel* (302) is her final act of independence and of redemption. "The river [that] flowed both ways" (11) throughout *The Diviners* is "the river of life" (Kroetsch 50) itself, as Laurence asserts in an interview with Canadian writer Robert Kroetsch.

Laurence praises Nigerian writers' adaptation of English to communicate an African reality—from the eloquence of Soyinka through the quirkiness of Ekwensi to the irony of Achebe:

> Soyinka's ability to translate into English words the rhythms and the beliefs of Yoruba drumming and mask dancing; J.P. Clark's terse and formal lines which are so effective in dealing with the rituals he is exploring; Okara's use of Ijaw speech patterns in order to create a prose which is also a kind of poetry; Ekwensi's knack of catching the tone of the city dweller's speech with its jazziness like highlife music; the precision of Aluko's writing when he mimics a newspaper article which is a hybrid English, combining Yoruba oratory with mission-school sloganizing—all these are ways in which Nigerian writers have made of English a language which is specifically their own. (*Drums* 178)

Laurence quotes Achebe's essay on "English and the African Writer": "The African writer should aim to use English in a way that brings out his message best without altering the language to the extent that its value as a medium of international exchange will be lost. He should aim at fashioning out an English which is at once universal and able to carry his peculiar experience" (177). Laurence's own fiction is distinguished by her ability to capture her characters' individual idiom—from the child Vanessa through the harried housewife Stacey to the matriarch Hagar. She asserts:

> the main concern of a writer remains that of somehow creating the individual on the printed page, of catching the tones and accents of human speech, of setting down the conflicts of people

who are as real to him as himself. If he does this well, and as truthfully as he can, his writing may sometimes reach out beyond any national boundary. The best of these Nigerian plays and novels reveal something of ourselves to us, whoever and wherever we are. (*Drums* 13)

Nigerian Dramatists and Novelists

Laurence discusses in depth the works of five outstanding Nigerian writers—Wole Soyinka, John Pepper Clark, Chinua Achebe, Amos Tutuola, and Cyprian Ekwensi—demonstrating how these authors, by writing skilfully about their own place and people, convey universal messages that reach beyond geographical boundaries to speak to all people in any place or time.

Wole Soyinka: "Voices of Life, Dance of Death"

Laurence devotes the first and by far the longest chapter of *Long Drums and Cannons* to a discussion of the writings of Wole Soyinka that some original reviewers termed "masterful." Judging from her praise of Soyinka's work, Laurence felt an affinity with this versatile writer, and exploring the aspects of his artistry that she most admires can illuminate her own creativity.

In "Voices of Life, Dance of Death," Laurence emphasises Soyinka's dramatic presentation of the conflict between past and present—the core of her own writing—between the old tribal customs and the new Western ways, between Yoruba rites and Christian rituals. He combines traditional Yoruba masquerade drama, with its talking drums and dancing masks, with classical and modern European models of drama in order to convey "themes which are universal" (16), for he believes the role of the artist is to maintain the relationship of the community with its gods and ancestors:

> This, then, is Wole Soyinka's inheritance and background—the mask dramas of *Egungun*, the Yoruba pantheon of gods, the praise-songs and the rituals of the festivals, the ever-present drums which convey both words and emotions, the Yoruba mythology and proverbs, the folk opera with its chanted songs and its quick-paced and often violent action. He has drawn material from all these sources, transforming it into something rich and strange and new, and adding to it his own ability to create individual character and his own way of seeing. (21)

Still in his thirties when Laurence composed her critique, Soyinka had already produced ten plays, six of which had been published, as well as one novel. She offers detailed interpretations of the novel and six of the plays, emphasising many facets that are featured in her own fiction. She begins with two early comedies. First, she praises *The Lion and the Jewel* (1959), a comedy that satirises the manners and morals of both the old and new Africa with a delightfully light touch. She discusses *The Trials of Brother Jero* (1960), a "shyster-prophet," that satirizes evangelists, prophets and other religious impostors who fleece the gullible in a comedy that parallels and may have inspired her own portraits of shysters in *The Tomorrow-Tamer and Other Stories* (1963). She is less enthusiastic about *The Swamp Dwellers* (1958), a serious play in which Soyinka abandons his Yoruba background for the swamps of the Eastern Niger Delta inhabited by the Ijaw people.

Following these early comic plays, Soyinka's drama becomes more tragic in its preoccupation with death, especially voluntary human sacrifice, which combines the Yoruba scapegoat with the Christian martyr motifs in threnodies that feature messianic figures who manipulate the martyrs. In *The Strong Breed*, Eman, a young teacher in a village that is not his own, is revealed through flashbacks to be the scion of a family known as "the strong breed," whose role it is to carry away the sins of their village. While the motifs of the scapegoat, sacred grove and river are drawn from African religions, the play reflects the Christian myth of the son as martyr and redeemer.

Laurence sees Soyinka's drama as increasingly imbued with the "desire to die" (30), reflecting the Freudian death-wish. She emphasises the figure of the Half Child, the *abiku*, the child born with death in its soul, in *A Dance of the Forests*. Commissioned for Nigeria's Independence Day celebrations in 1960, this play, with in its fantastical elements, satirises the old ways as much as it does the new, prophesying that independence will not necessarily bring Nigeria peace. *The Road* exemplifies the death wish in Professor's spiritual journey in quest of the essence of death, a quest that is dramatized in the dance of death by the possessed mask of Ogun, god of war and iron (as well as Soyinka's muse), who is revered by drivers and all who travel the road of life.

Laurence concludes with Soyinka's first novel, *The Interpreters* (1965), a complex work that follows five young intellectuals, educated abroad, who return home to Nigeria to find themselves exiles in their own land—a motif that Laurence explores in her own writing—in a comic satire that prophesies the conflict that was about to break out. The messianic and martyr themes, embodied by Lazarus and Noah, reflect those of *The Road*, concluding this celebration of Soyinka's dance of death.

As always, Laurence praises Soyinka for his ability to create living characters who speak in their own individual idiom, as well as in poetic prose—all
features of Laurence's own writing:

> Soyinka's writing is life-filled, overflowing with energy, capable of
> realising human personalities and catching the sound of one
> particular voice, at times intensely comic, coloured with rhythm
> and dance, with drums and masquerade. But underneath, there is
> a concern with the inner territory of the spirit, a painful appraisal
> of the usually hidden parts of the mind. This strong undercurrent
> in his writing places him, ultimately, among the chroniclers of the
> areas of darkness within us all. (69)

Certainly, Laurence's admiration for Soyinka's artistry has been borne out
by subsequent decades in which he has emerged as Africa's paramount playwright and as an artist whose creative work has had profound political
influence. In recognition of his contribution to the world of letters, Soyinka
was awarded the Nobel Prize for Literature, the only African writer to be so
honoured, in 1986—the last full year of Laurence's life before her death on
Epiphany Sunday, 1987.

John Pepper Clark: "Rituals of Destiny"

Although John Pepper Clark's plays demonstrate striking parallels with
Greek drama, Laurence suggests that his real sources lie in the Ekine drama
of the Ijaw people of the Eastern Niger Delta—a tribal society that Laurence
suggests parallels Attic culture, just as its epic dramas associated with religious festivals parallel Greek drama. Destiny, central to Greek drama,
provides the focus of Clark's plays, as he debates "how much the individual
chooses his own fate and how much is decided for him by forces (external or
internal) beyond his knowledge and control" (87). In debating such conflicts,
he also explores the relation between the conscious and unconscious mind in
terms that relate to the traditional Ijaw belief in the *biomgbo* and the *teme*,
the personal soul and the immortal soul, as well as to modern psychological,
especially Freudian, theories of personality. She distinguishes the themes that
characterize his strongest plays, *Song of a Goat* and *Ozidi*—"the theme of
lineage, the concern with blood honour, the curse laid on an entire house, the
son obliged to act out a fate begun by his father, the destiny-deciding *teme*
catapulting a man into situations not of his conscious choosing, the different
parts of the individual soul working in opposition to one another" (87)—in
terms that recall the drama of Sophocles and Aeschylus.

John Pepper Clark had published four plays when Laurence composed her critique—*Song of a Goat, The Masquerade, The Raft,* and *Ozidi*—and she addresses each of them in detail. *Song of a Goat,* his first play, is also, in Laurence's opinion, his best. Drawing on traditional Ekine themes of lineage, impotence and incest, exemplified in the downfall of the house of Zifa, *Song of a Goat* also explores the relation between the individual and the community. Zifa, the impotent fisherman, attempts a ritual cleansing by sacrificing a goat and stuffing its severed head into an earthen vessel, causing the miscarriage of his wife, Ebiere, pregnant from an incestuous relationship with Zifa's younger brother Tonye. Laurence highlights the scapegoat motif noted in Soyinka's drama, contrasting it with symbolism of the leopard. Zifa's failure to observe due rights sanctioned by the community, ancestors and gods, by taking fate into his own hands and offending the gods through his hubris, results in the carnage typical of classical Greek, as well as Renaissance, tragedy.

The Masquerade—which forms a strange sequel to *Song of a Goat,* since the bridegroom Tufa is Ebiere's son by Tonye, a child that the previous play indicated was aborted—involves the theme of lineage as well. But Laurence judges that "*The Masquerade* seems much too frail a craft to bear the weight of the tragedy with which it is overloaded" (79), for characters are undeveloped, actions are unmotivated, and speeches are "little more than sentimental clichés" (79). Her typescript makes it clear that she saw both plays performed at the 1965 Commonwealth Festival by the Eastern Nigerian Theatre Group and that, while *Song of a Goat* proved a stageworthy play, the weaknesses of *The Masquerade* were even more apparent on stage than on paper.

The Raft, an allegory about destiny, employing the existentialist allegory of four men adrift on a raft afloat on a river, interests Laurence primarily because of its evocation of landscape—or, rather, waterscape—for the river, as she observes, is effective not only because it is an ancient symbol, but because it is convincing "on the level of physical reality, simply as a river" (82). Laurence readers will recall the significance of "The river [that] flowed both ways" (11) in *The Diviners* (1974).

Ozidi, a series in five parts, is based on an Ijaw epic, a masquerade serial play told in seven days, accompanied by dance, music, and mime. Laurence's typescript reveals that she read this play in manuscript before its publication. Clark made a film version—*Tides of the Delta: The Saga of Izidi,* released in 1975—and translated the entire epic—from the Ijaw recitation by poet Okabou Ojobolo, published as *The Ozidi Saga* in 1977. *Ozidi* has much in common with *Song of a Goat,* including the curse on the house, the figure of the prophetess, the scapegoat and leopard motifs, the failure to observe traditional rituals, and the attempt by the protagonist, Ozidi, to take his fate into his own hands in a hubristic manner that offends the spirits and, ironically, causes his own death. Laurence concludes that "Clark's rendering of this Ijaw epic shows the complexity of his traditional sources and the ways in which he has drawn—in all his plays—upon forms and concepts of Ekine masquerade drama, extending these and using them as a means of expressing conflicts which are both contemporary and universal" (87).

Laurence compares the plays of John Pepper Clark with those of Wole Soyinka to the detriment of the former, judging that Clark does not have Soyinka's gift for creating character or his ability to make scenes work on both symbolic and realistic levels. She concludes that his plays suffer from an insufficient knowledge of theatre, with too much reliance on off-stage action, stilted speeches, and declamation rather than dramatization of events. She praises his poetic language, but criticizes his grandiose rhetoric tending to pomposity, lacking the "saving humour" (79) that distinguishes Soyinka's drama. Indeed, she toned down her criticism considerably, omitting scathing comments from her typescript. Nevertheless, she commends Clark's study of the individual's fate in relation to his lineage and community, gods and ancestors—his exploration of "the rituals of destiny" (87).

Chinua Achebe: "The Thickets of Our Separateness"

Laurence has nothing but praise for Chinua Achebe, whose novels have such affinity with her own. Indeed, the two novelists were colleagues who shared a mutual admiration and who enjoyed the occasional meetings that occurred throughout their careers at conferences and celebrations. She claims that Achebe's consummate craftsmanship, his commitment to the theme of communication, his ability to create memorable and living characters and to recreate the locale in convincing detail "place him among the best novelists now writing in any country in the English language" (89).

She praises his command of the history of the Ibo people and the complexities of colonisation. The British administrative system was directly opposed to traditional Ibo society, which was an individualistic tribal society that did not acknowledge inherited kings or chiefs. Rather, the village group, the *egwugwu* or elders, and the ancestors, which spoke through oracles or ancestral masks, formed a loosely-structured authority. But the Christian missions severed two generations of Africans from their past and caused "untold psychological harm" (97), in Laurence's view.

Achebe had published four novels by the time Laurence composed *Long Drums and Cannons*—*Things Fall Apart* (1958), *No Longer at Ease* (1960),

Arrow of God (1964), and *A Man of the People* (1966)—and she discusses each of them in detail. She particularly admires his ability to convey the three eras of Ibo history—the pre-mission and pre-colonial era of his grandparents' generation, the mission-oriented era of his parents' generation, and the emancipated but troubled era of his own generation—as he does in his first two historical novels, *Things Fall Apart* and *Arrow of God*. On the individual level, she admires his ability to create living characters whose tragedy it is to be caught between the old ways and the new—no longer able to adhere to the traditional ways entirely, but unable to reject them totally in order to adapt fully to the new ones. We see the same dilemma recreated in the character of Nathaniel Amegbe in her first novel *This Side Jordan*, but the conflict between past and present is central to both her Canadian and African fiction. While Achebe sets out to correct the warped view of African history refracted by outsiders' perspectives, he never idealises the old Ibo society or condemns the European. Rather, his is "the method of the genuine novelist," whose "gift of character portrayal" is his greatest talent (*Drums* 111), for "He portrays the Ibo society of the late 1800's in *Things Fall Apart* and then of the 1920's in *Arrow of God* by re-creating that society" (111) in terms of real people and places, Laurence asserts.

In his first novel, *Things Fall Apart*, Achebe recreates the first impact of European invasion on the old Ibo society, setting his novel in the late 1800s immediately prior to European colonisation. As the Christian mission gains influence in protagonist Okonkwo's village of Umuofia, his son Nwoye is rechristened Isaac by the mission, placing Okonkwo in the biblical role of the patriarch Abraham, who sacrifices his son. Father and son are separated and can find no bridge between them, no means of communication. Obierika says the white man "has put a knife on the things that held us together and we have fallen apart" (*Drums* 95)—reflecting Achebe's title, which echoes the line "Things fall apart" from Yeats's vision of chaos in "The Second Coming." Achebe "portrays this failure of communication at both a personal and a social level, in a prose which is plain and spare and at all times informed with his keen sense of irony" (97), Laurence claims. Rather than idealising the Ibo or condemning the colonialists, he portrays the destruction of the old Ibo society "both by inner flaws and outer assaults" (96) and presents the conflict between Africans and Europeans "for the heartbreakingly complicated affair it must have been" (97).

Okonkwo is a tragic figure whose flaw is his pride in his strength and his inability to express love for fear of appearing weak. Interestingly, Laurence begins her Manawaka cycle by harking back to her grandparents' generation in creating Hagar, heroine of *The Stone Angel*, affirming that "Her speech is their speech and her gods their gods" (*Heart* 4). Like Okonkwo, Hagar is unable to express love for fear of appearing weak, realizing on her deathbed that "Pride was my wilderness, and the demon that led me there was fear" (292). Okwonkwo's tragedy lies in his division from his *chi*, his personal god or conscience—although Laurence prefers the Freudian term the "unconscious" or the Ijaw term *teme*, the guardian of the soul—for his *chi* prompts a gentleness that is ignored by Okonkwo, whose pride in his strength leads him to acts of violence—acts that cause him to be outcast by his community and that also "do violence to his own spirit" (94), resulting ultimately in his suicide.

Achebe's second novel, *No Longer at Ease* (1960), about contemporary Nigeria, forms a sequel to the first, as Obi Okonkwo is the son of Isaac and grandson of Okonkwo from *Things Fall Apart*. As the title, drawn from T.S. Eliot's "Journey of the Magi," suggests, Obi—his name a reversal of Ibo—rejects the traditional religion in favour of the missions' Christianity. Educated in England, he develops a deeply anti-African attitude, referring to the old Ibo society as "the days of darkness." But "the past and the present are fated to do battle in Obi's life" (99), as Laurence observes. Obi becomes a tragic figure when his love for an educated girl, a nurse from an outcast group called the *osu*, leads him to take bribes to pay for her abortion. He discovers that "the chains of external bondage can be broken more easily, in the end, than the chains of love" (100), for achieving an "inner independence" is the hardest form of emancipation. "Achebe does not spare us from the knowledge that Obi's dilemma, torn between what is expected of him and what he himself believes, bound by the subtle but inescapable chains of love, is in some way our own" (100).

Achebe's third novel, *Arrow of God* (1964), which deals with the early 1920s, is his best, in Laurence's view, as well as one of the best novels of the decade. Ezeulu is the priest of Ulu, the guardian deity of the village of Umuaro: his tragedy is to be caught between the forces of the past Ibo religion and the new Christian mission and British administration. While he tries to enforce the power of the god, he discovers that "He was no more than an arrow in the bow of his god" (103). "Caught in the outer web of the white man's disruptions and the divided village, and in the inner web of pride," Ezeulu goes mad. The individual tragedy is that of "Ezeulu, man and priest, god's man, like Oedipus and like Lear" (106), "broken by the violence of both the inner and the outer forces" (105–6), but "The greatest tragedy is that of man's lack of comprehension of the reality of others, his lack of comprehension of the validity of differences" (105)—a tragedy that informs Laurence's own fiction, especially her first Manawaka novel, *The Stone Angel*.

In his fourth novel, *A Man of the People* (1966), Achebe portrays a corrupt politician, Chief Nanga, a Minister of Culture, opposed to university education, through the eyes of the idealistic young school-teacher Odili, who conveys through his first-person narrative his disenchantment with the village teacher whom he idolised as a boy. Appalled by Nanga's corruption, Odili runs against him and is crushed by his party machine. Ironically, the unrest caused by the election leads to an army coup that Laurence views as a *"deus ex machina"* invoked to resolve the plot, but also as a prophesy illustrating "life's imitation of art" (110). "What begins as a comic novel ends as an incisive social satire, written in scalding prose, the purpose of which is to cauterise" (110).

Laurence concludes that Achebe's dominant theme is communication, the central theme of her own work, as it "seeks to send human voices through the thickets of our separateness" (113).

Amos Tutuola: "A Two-Fold Forest"

Laurence emphasises Tutuola's Yoruba roots, as he draws on the myths and folk tales that are so rich in magic charms and fantastical creatures: "The tone of Tutuola's writing also resembles that of many Yoruba tales, for it is both humorous and poetic, and it fluctuates between a portrayal of beauty and lightness and a portrayal of grotesque ugliness" (114). Unlike Soyinka, who shares his Yoruba roots, Tutuola lacks the formal education of many of his fellow Nigerian writers. Consequently, his books, which are not novels in the conventional sense, but rather the episodic sagas found in all cultures, do not unite African and European, traditional and modern elements in the intellectual manner of Achebe and Soyinka. "Tutuola's method is poetic and intuitive" (121), rather than intellectual, Laurence claims, as he combines past and present cultures in fantastical figures, such as the Television-Handed Ghostess, and unites Christian rituals with the old religion in monstrous creatures, such as Rev. Devil. Tutuola writes out of his imagination or unconscious, "the forests of the mind" (131), for he remains true to "an inner sight which perceives both the dazzling multicoloured areas of dream and the appalling forests of nightmare" (114).

Laurence views Tutuola's themes as dark, even grim, with strong sadomasochistic elements in odysseys of pain which are filled with grotesque images of horror that recall Grimms's fairy tales: "Amos Tutuola has a way of combining the macabre and the beautiful, the horrifying and the humorous, the familiar and the mysterious" (130), for, "under the lightness and humour, under the descriptions of enchanted places, there lies the continuing theme of pain, dreaded and yet sought."

Laurence admires Tutuola's writing for the sheer vitality of his imaginative and idiosyncratic style. After quoting a passage from his first novel, she exudes, "For music, for rhythm, for a sense of life, for the vibrant sound of the story-teller's voice, that passage would be hard to beat" (130). She might be describing her own writing when she says that "He succeeds best with a first-person narration, as though he were able in this way to get inside the personality of the central character and to write with the unfailingly true sound of a human voice" (122). She particularly admires his idiosyncratic language, his "knack of using English in an original way" (125), for this "spontaneous newness of language is one of Tutuola's gifts" (126): "What Tutuola captures here is the living sound of the narrator's voice speaking in an English adapted and changed by the thought-patterns and constructions of Yoruba speech underneath. The result, as in so much of Tutuola's writing, is a phraseology which is both fresh and precise without in any sense straining to be either" (125).

In fact, Tutuola's rendering of Pidgin English in his characters' idiom has been perceived by Western readers as a charming quirkiness, although some of that false quaintness results from poor editing on the part of his publishers. Laurence the novelist waxes highly indignant on this subject:

> It is difficult here to see the publishers' justification for printing Tutuola's manuscript errors of spelling.... It would have been a great editorial mistake to alter any of Tutuola's imagery and phraseology.... Spelling is an entirely different matter.... The correction of such errors is common editorial practice, and the fact that it has not been done here seems to give weight to the feeling that many West Africans have had about Tutuola's work— that it was read in Europe and America only so that its language could be ridiculed. (126)

Tutuola's first novel, *The Palm-Wine Drinkard* (1952), was "the first novel written in English by a West African to gain world-wide attention" (114), Laurence claims. It was followed by *My Life in the Bush of Ghosts* (1954), *Simbi and the Satyr of the Dark Jungle* (1955), *The Brave African Huntress* (1958), and *Feather Woman of the Jungle* (1962)—each of which Laurence discusses in detail—followed by *Ajaiyi and His Inherited Poverty* (1967), *The Witch Herbalist of the Remote Town* (1981), and *Pauper,*

Brawler and Slanderer (1987), as well as collections of stories—*Yoruba Folktales* (1986) and *The Village Witch Doctor and Other Stories* (1990).

Laurence deems Tutuola's first novel, *The Palm-Wine Drinkard*, "his masterpiece"—"a classic journey" (115) found in every culture's myths, such as the adventures of Orpheus and Odysseus:

> It takes the form of an odyssey, a journey into the underworld
> which the hero undertakes in order to prove himself. It is really a
> journey of the spirit, in which the hero meets the monster-
> creations of his own mind, suffers torments, wins victories and
> finally returns to his own country, able now to rule it because of
> the wisdom his experiences have given him and because of the
> power he has gained through the terrors he has overcome. (115)

Laurence cites Gerald Moore's theory that "'all his heroes or heroines follow out one variant or another of the cycle of the heroic monomyth, Departure—Initiation—Return'" (115). This classic framework offers Tutuola an ideal opportunity to incorporate the monstrous creatures, reminiscent of the visions in the Book of Revelation, who inhabit his imagination, as his hero, the Drinkard, sets out on a perilous quest for his dead palm-wine tapster, who dwells in the Town of the Deads. The Drinkard is rewarded for his bravery by the gift of a Magic Egg that will fulfil all his wishes. The Magic Egg feeds his people, long in the grip of a famine, until it is accidentally broken. When the Drinkard sacrifices to Heaven, "Heaven, thus recognised as superior to Earth, is appeased," as Laurence explains: "Rain falls and the famine is over" (117).

The feature that interests Laurence is "the White Tree, where lives the Faithful Mother. This tree in mythological terms is the Tree of Life and its goddess is the archetypal earth-mother" (116). She cites Gerald Moore's interpretation of the seniority of Heaven as an indication that "'...from henceforth the supreme deity will be the male Sky God and not the old Female Earth Goddess, protectress of matriarchy'" (118). In a passage that predicts her statement of faith in the female principle as part of the Holy Spirit in her memoir, *Dance on the Earth* (14–15), Laurence writes:

> The Yoruba myth is paralleled in the myths of many cultures, for
> it represents a transfer of affiliation which did in fact take place in
> innumerable religions at one time or another—the decision that the
> heavenly deity was superior to the gods of earth. In many places
> this change took the form of a rendering of chief homage to a
> male deity—Our Father which art in heaven—instead of the earth

mother with which most religions began, and this shift in emphasis often paralleled a similar social move away from matriarchy. (118)

Laurence is not as impressed with Tutuola's second novel, *My Life in the Bush of Ghosts*, although she is intrigued by its grotesquerie. An initiation tale or rite of passage, in which the boy-hero is lost from his home and enters the Bush of Ghosts, the story represents "a journey into the depths of the subconscious" (119), wherein dwell gruesome creatures and painful torments. The boy thinks of his own mother, but encounters repulsive mother figures like the Flash-Eyed Mother, that dreadful matriarch, and eventually marries the Super-Lady. Laurence is intrigued by Tutuola's "'born and die'" (119) children, who remind her of the Yoruba *abiku*, the child born to die.

Tutuola's third book, *Simbi and the Satyr of the Dark Jungle*, is not as strong as his first two, in Laurence's opinion, partly because it is his only novel not written in the first person. This novel features a female protagonist, Simbi, who has been brought up in luxury and perversely longs to experience poverty and punishment. And she does when she encounters the Satyr of the Dark Jungle, who traps her in a Hall of Music, chains her to a rock and beats her with a cudgel of bones. But Tutuola's descriptions of Simbi's dancing in the Hall of Music, with its walls made of song, are delightful. Ultimately, Simbi outwits and kills the Satyr by magic means, but the emphasis on torment undermines the humour and vitality of Tutuola's tale in Laurence's opinion.

Tutuola's fourth book, *The Brave African Huntress*, is less imaginative than his first three, in Laurence's view. Adebisi, another female hero, sets out with her "inherited ju-ju compass" (124) to rescue her brothers, who are imprisoned in the Jungle of the Pigmies. Although she ultimately triumphs and liberates her brothers, she must first endure cruel tortures by the sadistic Pigmies. Laurence concludes, "as in everything Tutola has ever written, the goal of peace and fulfilment can only be reached by the path of 'endless punishments'" (124).

The Feather Woman of the Jungle is structured as a series of stories, ten nights' entertainments narrated by an ageing chief about his life's adventures that draw on Yoruba folk tales. In the first tale, the hero and his brother Alabi set off in adolescence on a quest for adventure, but encounter torments in true Tutuola fashion. Enchanted by the hideous Feather Woman, they are eventually liberated by their sister Ashabi, who bravely breaks the ostrich eggs in the magic pit and defeats the witch and dissolves all her evil spells in a story that parallels European fairy tales. In the case of the tale of "The Treacherous Queen and the King in the Bush of Quietness," Laurence judges that "this tale expresses the theme of the male subconscious fear of woman as an emasculating force, a creature both infinitely desirable and infinitely dangerous" (128). She concludes that in this latest book the hero's goal can be "achieved only through pain and humiliation" (129).

Laurence concludes that "His forests are certainly and in detail the outer ones but they are, as well, the forests of the mind, where the individual meets and grapples with the creatures of his own imagination. These creatures are aspects of himself, aspects of his response to the world into which he was born, the world to which he must continue to return if he is to live as a man" (131).

Amos Tutuola's writing has been both praised and criticised since the publication of his highly acclaimed *The Palm-Wine Drinkard* in 1952. Although critics are, in Charles Lawson's words, "a little less awed now than they were in the early 1950's," Tutuola's works continue to draw critical attention. Thirty years later, *The Witch-Herbalist of the Remote Town* (1981) was widely reviewed, although critics remained divided about his imaginative narrative and his use of English language. Ultimately, Tutuola is an individual, in Laurence's view: "He is in a sense an epic poet who as a man belongs nowhere, and this isolation is both his tragedy and his artistic strength" (114).

Cyprian Ekwensi: "Masks of the City"

"Cyprian Ekwensi's world is largely the city world of right-this-minute. His idiom is that of the city streets and the beat of the highlife music" (133), Laurence claims. She admires his ability to capture the people of the city realistically and sympathetically, although she notes that "Ekwensi's women come alive and step from the printed page much more often than his men do, and he has created a few really memorable women characters" (133). While most of his novels are set in the city, they all contain country episodes, in which, Laurence says, "there is a strong undercurrent of anti-tribalism" (134) —an attitude she finds sympathic, as we can see in her essay on "Tribalism As Us Versus Them." She notes that his career in fiction began with writing 'Onitsha market books'—popular stories, such as his *Where Love Whispers*. At his worst, his fiction recalls this superficial and sentimental style of popular journalism.

Ekwensi published five novels—*People of the City* (1954), *Jagua Nana* (1961), *Burning Grass* (1962), *Beautiful Feathers* (1963), and *Iska* (1966), as well as the collection, *Lokotown and Other Stories* (1966)—each of which Laurence discusses in detail in "Masks of the City."

People of the City made an impact as the "first truly contemporary novel by a West African to be widely read throughout the English-speaking world"

(134). The hero, Amusa Sango, a crime reporter for the *West African Sensation* and leader of a jazz band in The All Language Club in Lagos, becomes involved with a series of girls. Laurence judges that, while the surface realism of the night life and street scenes are lively, the construction of the novel is weak, the plot diffuse, the writing sentimental and banal, and the characters stereotyped (135). She quotes passages to convey his brisk style: "Girls ripen quickly in the city—the men are so impatient" (136). She concludes: "The city's atmosphere of exhilarating newness, with its undertones of isolation and uncertainty, is portrayed well in *People of the City*, but the novel is now of interest principally because it was the first of its kind. Its weakness of organisation and frequent falsity of tone prevent its being considered an important novel in itself" (136).

Laurence takes a very different view of his second novel, *Jagua Nana*: "Ekwensi is a long way from being the best writer in Nigeria, but he has written one of the best single novels to have come out of the whole of West Africa so far" (136). The protagonist, a middle-ageing prostitute in love with a younger man, is a character calculated to appeal to Laurence, for she suggests her own Stacey Cameron, the middle-ageing heroine of *The Fire-Dwellers*: "In *Jagua Nana* he has created a magnificent and fully alive character" (136–37) who will "remain alive for a long time" (140).

Laurence labels Ekwensi's third novel, *Burning Grass*, a story of the Fulani, a nomadic cattle-herding tribe, "a B-grade Western set in Northern Nigeria" (141), for it is "unbroken melodrama" (141) in her opinion. Mai Sunsaye, head of a family, who is infected by the *sokugo* or wandering sickness, wanders with his three sons in a series of bizarre adventures that may have inspired her own picaresque children's narrative, *Jason's Quest* (1970). She judges that *Burning Grass* is not so much a novel as a modern folktale containing all the qualities of traditional African stories—"magical occurrences, mysterious and seductive women, acts of phenomenal heroism, and swift-paced adventure" (142)—and that it belongs with Ekwensi's popular Onitsha market books.

Beautiful Feathers "belongs in the mainstream of his writing but it falls very far short of the standard he set himself in *Jagua Nana*" (142), Laurence concludes. Concerned with politics, which is not Ekwensi's forte, the novel is about Wilson Iyari, a Logos pharmacist who is the new leader of the Nigerian Movement for African and Malagasy Solidarity. The title is from an Ibo proverb that says, "a man not respected in his own house is like a bird with beautiful feathers—wonderful on the outside, but ordinary within" (142)—a saying that applies to Wilson, for his wife, Yaniya, angry at his neglect, has an affair with Gadson Salifas. While Laurence sympathises with Yaniya's plight, she fears she becomes "a cardboard figure speaking cardboard conventionalities" (144). Wilson's "thundering denunciations of painted women toll like sermons" (142): they seem satirical, but are not so. Laurence judges, "*Beautiful Feathers* seems to represent a desire to preach rather than any need to write a novel. The writing is stilted, stiffly bristling with maxims pertaining to the solid bourgeois virtues. Wilson speaks platitudes and is himself indistinguishable from them" (144).

Laurence considers that the value of the short stories collected in *Lokotown and Other Stories* lies in the fact that some of them contain the origins of Ekwensi's later novels. "Glittering City," for example, about Fussy Joe, a trumpet-player with a jazz band, who pretends to be a reporter on the *West African Sensation*, is probably the embryo of Ekwensi's first novel, *People of the City*.

Laurence has unqualified praise for Ekwensi's latest novel, *Iska*, which she considers "his best since *Jagua Nana* and perhaps in some ways his best so far" (145). Like *Jagua Nana*, *Iska* has a female protagonist: Filia, nick-named Iska, meaning wind, represents "Africa's wind of change" (149), as she drifts from man to man, each representing an aspect of Nigerian life, until her death:

> The characters in this novel *are* the themes, and the themes are given individual voices with each character. The different men in Filia's life represent different aspects of present-day Nigeria's upheaval, and yet this novel is emphatically not propaganda and its characters are never abstractions. Taken together, however, these men illustrate both the agony and the hope that Ekwensi feels towards his torn land. (146)

The main theme of *Iska* is tribalism, especially the Ibo-Hausa riots in the north. Ekwensi portrays the conflict eloquently through Filia Enu, who is, like Ekwensi himself, an Ibo from the north. Laurence admires his dramatization of this war-torn country:

> Written with greater restraint than any of Ekwensi's previous novels, *Iska* is probably his most moving work. Filia does not give out sparks like Jagua, but the novel as a whole burns with the painful love of a country in which individuals are caught up in lunatic ferocities not of their own making, forced to make choices which no one should have to make—the cruel choices imposed by a situation perilously close to civil war. (149)

Ekwensi is writing about events as they happen. He has always been a chronicler of right-now, and in this novel he reaches a new maturity in that role. Some day *Iska* will be read as an historical novel. But then, as now, it will present events as no textbook can—in terms of the truly felt pain of real people. (150)

Laurence's prophesy proved true, as her subsequent essay on "Tribalism As Us Versus Them" indicates.

Other Voices

While Laurence devotes a chapter to five Nigerian writers who have produced a considerable body of work of a high standard, notably Chinua Achebe and Wole Soyinka, she includes in the last chapter six promising new writers who have written an excellent first novel, like Elechi Amadi, Nkem Nwankwo, Gabriel Okara and Flora Nwapa. These are voices that will reach out, in Laurence's opinion—an opinion that was, in most cases, proved correct.

T.M. Aluko

Timothy Mofolorunso Aluko, a Yoruba from Western Nigeria, educated in Nigeria and England as a civil engineer (like Jack Laurence) and town planner, is thus well equipped to compare the old and new ways from the inside, and he does so in each of the three novels that Laurence discusses—*One Man, One Wife* (1959), *One Man, One Matchet* (1964), and *Kinsman and Foreman* (1966)—in which he aims "to set down the ways in which the generations are apart, and to explore the almost impossible problems created by this enormous gap between a tribally oriented way of thought and an individually oriented, scientific way of thought" (158). Laurence admires Aluko's ironical voice in his first novel, *One Man, One Wife*, which satirises both Christian and African religious views of polygamy. She judges that his second novel, *One Man, One Matchet*, which focusses on the treatment of diseased cocoa trees—pitting a university-educated Nigerian named Udo Akpan, recently appointed District Officer, and labelled "'the black white man'" (155), against a young nationalist named Benjamin Benjamin, a political advisor to the Oba, or king, of Ipaja—"should be required reading for every European or American technician and teacher involved in aid schemes in Africa, as well as for every African government official dealing with development projects, for Aluko sees clearly the heart-breaking difficulties which such projects inevitably entail, and he manages to make comprehensible the genuinely held and diametrically opposed views of the old chiefs and the new young men of government" (153). Consequently, Laurence prophesies that, "for its incisive irony, perceptive social analysis and convincing character portrayals, *One Man, One Matchet* will remain worth reading for a long time to come" (157). *Kinsman and Foreman*, focussing on a Nigerian, Titus Oti, who returns from university in England to take up a post as engineer with the Public Works Department in his own village, conveys the same conflict of values between traditional tribal and modern scientific methods as his previous novels, but it presents the conflict in a more organized structure that lacks "the fiery life and human chaos" (158) of his earlier works, in Laurence's view. Although his fiction contains many flaws, Laurence admires the analytical intelligence and subtle irony that informs it. Aluko proceeded to publish five more novels and was awarded the Order of the British Empire in 1964, fulfilling Laurence's prophesy.

Elechi Amadi

Amadi is unique in chronicling the African village during the pre-colonial era when the tribal system was still intact. This gives his fiction an authenticity that univeralises its ideas, in Laurence's view, for Amadi's theme is "man's struggle with fate itself, his perpetual attempt to placate and therefore to control his gods" (158). Laurence focusses on Amadi's first novel, *The Concubine*, which centres on Ihuoma, a beautiful woman who is beloved by various men, but who is also loved by the god of the sea, who kills any man who seeks to marry her; she can be a concubine, therefore, but never a wife. The novel displays a tragic inevitability, what Laurence terms "the mystery at the centre of being" (163), in presenting "the age-old conflict of man with his gods" (163). "*The Concubine* contains some of the best descriptions of a village in all of Nigerian writing" (162), she concludes. Laurence's praise for Amadi's first novel is borne out by his publication of three more novels, three plays and other works that have been admired for their depiction of pre-colonial Nigeria.

Nkem Nwankwo

Laurence praises Nwankwo's first novel, *Danda* (1964), which centres on a comic character named Danda, a clown who wears bells and loves to dance, drink palm-wine and make love with the young wives of old men in his village. Nicknamed 'Rain' for his "musical wayward nature" (164), Danda is an Ibo anti-hero, "the classic rebel of comedy" (164). Despite its disjointed, episodic quality, Laurence admires Nwankwo's novel for its vibrant character and energetic prose style. Indeed, *Danda* was made into a musical by

Nwankwo, who wrote numerous radio plays, as well as short stories, another novel, and various critical articles in his subsequent academic career.

Flora Nwapa

Flora Nwapa is the only woman writer whom Laurence includes in *Long Drums and Cannons* for the simple reason that she was the only Nigerian woman to publish a novel or play before Laurence wrote her book. *Efuru* (1966) chronicles the life of an intelligent, independent woman who defies the custom of her Ibo village by choosing her own husband. While she is successful in her professional career as a trader, she is less successful in her personal life, for both her husbands leave her, and her only child dies. Although she is an excellent wife who nearly "kills her husbands with kindness" (167), Laurence notes that Efuru, unwittingly, has an emasculating effect on both: "Efuru's tragedy is partly that she cannot permit herself the mistakes of ordinary people, and partly that she does not marry a man with enough inner assurance to be able to bear her intelligence and efficiency" (168). Efuru appears to be a modern woman in a traditional society, but there is more to the story: Efuru believes she has been chosen to be a worshipper of the goddess Uhamiri, whose worshippers are barren. Laurence compares her fate to that of Ihuoma, in Amadi's *The Concubine*, for "both are women of high character who suffer in ways which apparently have nothing to do with their own actions. Both are fated not to achieve the happiness they deserve, and both are unluckily connected with a deity in ways unsought by themselves" (167). She notes that "*Efuru* takes place almost totally within the minds and society of women" (169), and she praises Nwapa for catching the exact tone of the women's voices: "These women do not 'know book', but they...possess both shrewdness and tenacity" (169). Consequently, she judges that, "although Flora Nwapa's women belong in an Ibo village, they convey insights which are valid anywhere" (169). Again, Laurence's enthusiasm is validated, for Flora Nwapa went on to a distinguished career both as an author of novels, stories and children's books, and as an academic administrator.

Onuora Nzekwu

Onuora Nzekwu, teacher and editor, published three novels—*Wand of Noble Wood* (1961), *Blade Among the Boys* (1962) and *Highlife for Lizards* (1965)—which Laurence sees as concerned with the dilemma of a man caught between old values and new. In *Wand of Noble Wood*, the hero, Peter Obiesie, becomes engaged to Nueka, who is under a curse, which Peter views ambivalently. His dilemma is "reminiscent of Tutuola, whose work also reflects the battle of gods within a man's heart and mind" (170). Unlike Tutuola, however, who conveys this painful conflict compellingly, Nzekwu presents a "formal argument rather than a true fictional creation of individual dilemmas" (170). *Blade Among the Boys* focusses on the conflicts within Patrick, an Ibo boy, who fails to become a priest when he gets a girl pregnant. Laurence judges that the novel becomes a lecture in old-fashioned mission morality, while presenting traditional Ibo beliefs in a patronising manner.

She considers Nzekwu's third novel, *Highlife for Lizards*, his most successful, perhaps because it features the kind of spirited and independent heroine that Laurence admires: "Intelligent and passionate, Agom marries a man who is basically weaker than herself—a pattern which seems to be a recurring one in Nigerian fiction" (171). She judges, "*Highlife for Lizards* does not reach beyond its own time and place, but within those limits it creates several convincing characters and sets down dilemmas which are unquestionably real" (171). Unlike most of Laurence's other new voices, Nzekwu did not publish more novels, but pursued his career as a civil servant.

Gabriel Okara

Best known as a poet in his own right, as well as a translator of Ijaw poetry, Okara has written one powerful novel, *The Voice* (1964). Laurence defines its theme as "an individual's questioning of the established values, his need to relate the inner truth to the outer reality" (171)—a definition that applies to her own novels. The hero, Okolo, whose name means "the voice," one of Laurence's favourite terms, is searching for *it*—an essential truth and genuine contact with others. Okolo's questioning of the order of things in his tribal society—what Laurence frequently refers to as "the Establishment"—leads to his banishment and eventual martyrdom. A "Jesus figure" (173), Okolo is primarily a "truth-seeker," a teacher who has a mission "to speak the heart's truth" (173) and to plant *it* in the hearts of his people. But the people are not ready for his truth, so he leaves only one disciple, who promises, "'Your spoken words will not die'" (173).

Laurence admires Okara's prose-poetry—"its accomplished simplicity, the precision of its imagery, its strong underlying sadness" (172)—in which he employs parables and metaphors from Ijaw mask drama, especially in his use of the leopard and goat symbols to suggest the slayer and the victim, as John Pepper Clark did in *Song of a Goat*. She also commends his use of Ijaw speech patterns that can express his meaning vividly in English. She concludes, "Although it is set within a tribal society, *The Voice* contains a voice which reaches out" (175)—as do all her "Other Voices."

Conclusion

Long Drums and Cannons has value not only as a pioneering study of Nigerian literature that illuminates its subject; it also has value as an historical document chronicling the perspective of a Western woman writer long before post-colonial studies became current. Moreover, it has reflexive value as a reflection of the influence of Nigerian literature on one of Canada's foremost writers of fiction, as we have observed, for, in introducing the voices of African authors to Western readers, Laurence also discovered her own voice.

In the Forewords to her memoir, Laurence laments, "How long, how regrettably long it took me to find my true voice as a woman writer" (*Dance* 5). In an introduction to *Long Drums and Cannons* that was never published, Laurence explains:

> My own first novel and a subsequent book of short stories were set in Ghana, where I lived for a number of years. I began to realize, however, that if I wanted to go on as a novelist, I could really only write about people whom I knew from the inside, my own people who came out of the same background as myself— Scots Presbyterian, in a Canadian prairie town—people who were (as Muslims say about Allah) closer to me than my own neck-vein. For myself, this was the only possibility. Everything else was tourism. It might be a fairly subtle tourism. It might even be an understanding tourism, but it was tourism all the same. It could not go deeply enough. It was probably fortunate that I came to this conclusion—a conclusion which did not relate to all the literature of Africa but only to my own writing—at the moment when I did, for in fact the time for outsiders to write about Africa was then nearly over. (1)

Later, in *Heart of a Stranger*, she affirms, "I always knew that one day I would have to stop writing about Africa and go back to my own people, my own place of belonging" (3). When she did return to Canada in her writing, however, it was with the knowledge gained from her experience of living in and writing about Africa. Canadian critics have noted how Laurence's African experience informs her Canadian fiction. Craig Tapping asserts, "Canadian literature is the sleeping giant behind the description of Nigerian literature in *Long Drums and Cannons*" (73). Patricia Morley, in *Margaret Laurence: The Long Journey Home*, claims: "The way to Manawaka lay through Ghana, Nigeria, and the searching desert sun" (39), for "Africa was catalyst and crucible for much of Laurence's work" (44). She concludes, "Her ability to write great fiction is due to her imaginative comprehension of the Other, an ability nurtured by her African experience" (52).

In her Foreword to *Heart of a Stranger*, Laurence writes:

> for a writer of fiction, part of the heart remains that of a stranger, for what we are trying to do is to understand those others who are our fictional characters, somehow to gain entrance to their minds and feelings, to respect them for themselves as human individuals, and to portray them as truly as we can. The whole process of fiction is a mysterious one, and a writer, however experienced, remains in some ways a perpetual amateur, or perhaps a perpetual traveler, an explorer of those inner territories, those strange lands of the heart and spirit. (*Heart* vii)

Thus, *Long Drums and Cannons* can not only illuminate Nigerian literature and reflect Laurence's post-colonial perspective; it can also illuminate that mythical microcosm we call Manawaka and light our journey into those strange lands of the heart and spirit we call the Manawaka Cycle.

Works Cited

Achebe, Chinua. *Morning Yet On Creation Day*. London: Heinemann, 1975.

Booklist 66 (1 Oct. 1969): 171.

Boxhill, Anthony. *Fiddlehead* 80 (1969): 105–6.

Carroll, David. "Letters in Canada: 1970. Literary Studies." *The University of Toronto Quarterly* 40 (1970–71): 359–60.

Choice 7 (May 1970): 394.

Cameron, Donald. "Margaret Laurence: The Black Celt Speaks of Freedom." *Conversations with Canadian Novelists*. Toronto: Macmillan, 1973. 96–115.

Coger, Greta, Ed. *New Perspectives on Margaret Laurence*. Westport: Greenwood, 1996.

Coldwell, Joan. "Margaret Laurence." *The Oxford Companion to Canadian Literature*. Ed. W. Toye. Toronto: Oxford UP, 1983. 434.

Dale, James. "Valuable addition to the Mac library." *Hamilton Spectator*, 8 March 1969: 26.

Duncan, Isla. "Interview with Alan Maclean." *Margaret Laurence Review* 9 (1999): 13–17.

Godfrey, Dave. "Piquefort's Column." *Canadian Forum*, Feb. 1969: 249.

Kertzer, Jon. *Margaret Laurence and Her Works*. Toronto: ECW Press, n.d.

Killam, Douglas. "On African Writing." *The Journal of Commonwealth Literature* 9 (1970): 109–13.

King, James. *The Life of Margaret Laurence*. Toronto: Knopf, 1997.

Kroetsch, Robert. "A Conversation with Margaret Laurence." In *Creation: Robert Kroetsch, James Bacque, Pierre Gravel: Including the Authors' Conversations with Margaret Laurence, Milton Wilson, J. Raymond Brazeau*. Ed. Robert Kroetsch. Toronto: New Press, 1970: 53–63.

Laurence, Margaret. *A Bird in the House*. Toronto: McClelland & Stewart, 1970.

———. *A Jest of God*. Toronto: McClelland & Stewart, 1966.

———. *A Tree for Poverty: Somali Poetry and Prose*. Toronto: ECW, 1993.

———. *Dance on the Earth*. Toronto: McClelland & Stewart, 1989.

———. "Gadgetry or Growing: Form and Voice in the Novel." *A Place to Stand On: Essays by and about Margaret Laurence*. Ed. George Woodcock. Edmonton, NeWest Press, 1983. 80–89.

———. "Geography—Outer or Inner?" Unpublished essay, Fo341, 1980–001, Box 22, File 155, Canadian Literary Papers, York University Archives.

———. *Heart of a Stranger*. Toronto: McClelland & Stewart, 1976.

———. *Long Drums and Cannons*. London: Macmillan, 1968.

———. *Long Drums and Cannons*. Ed. Nora Foster Stovel. Edmonton: U of Alberta P, 2001. Citations are to this new edition.

———. "Ten Years' Sentences." *Margaret Laurence*. Ed. William New. Toronto: McGraw-Hill Ryerson, 1977. 17–23.

———. *The Diviners*. Toronto: McClelland & Stewart, 1974.

———. *The Fire-Dwellers*. Toronto: McClelland & Stewart, 1969.

———. *The Prophet's Camel Bell*. Toronto: McClelland & Stewart, 1963.

———. *The Stone Angel*. Toronto: McClelland & Stewart, 1964.

———. *The Tomorrow-Tamer*. Toronto: McClelland & Stewart, 1963.

———. *This Side Jordan*. Toronto: McClelland & Stewart, 1960.

———. "Tribalism As Us Versus Them." Previously unpublished essay, FO341, 1980–001/023, File 156, plus a probable first draft in 1980-001/022, File 155, and a probable second draft in 1980-001/023, File 156, Canadian Literary Papers, York University Archives and Special Collections.

Lennox, John and Panofsky, Ruth, Eds. *Letters of Margaret Laurence and Adele Wiseman*. Toronto: U of Toronto P, 1997.

Library Journal 94 (15 March 1969): 1148.

Mannoni, O. *Prospero and Caliban: The Psychology of Colonization*. New York: Praeger, 1950.

Morley, Patricia. *Margaret Laurence*. Twayne's World Authors. Boston: Twayne, 1981.

New, William, Ed. *Margaret Laurence*. Toronto: McGraw, 1977.

Nicholson, Colin, Ed. *Critical Approaches to the Fiction of Margaret Laurence*. Vancouver: UBC P, 1990.

Niven, Alastair. *The Legon Observer* (Legon, Ghana) 6 June 1969: 15–17.

Nkosi, Lewis. "A Question of Literary Stewardship." *Africa Report* 14.5–6 (1969): 69–71.

Povey, John F. *Journal of Asian and African Studies* 8, 1–2 (1973): 109–10.

Riegel, Christian, Ed. *Challenging Territory: The Writing of Margaret Laurence*. Edmonton: U of Alberta P, 1997.

Sellin, E. "Neo-African and Afro-American Literatures." *Journal of Modern Literature* 1.2: 249–53.

Sparrow, Fiona. *Into Africa with Margaret Laurence*. Toronto: ECW Press, 1992.

Tapping, Craig. "Margaret Laurence and Africa." *Crossing the River: Essays in Honour of Margaret Laurence*. Ed. Kristjana Gunnars. Winnipeg: Turnstone Press, 1988. 65–80.

Thomas, Clara. *The Manawaka World of Margaret Laurence*. Toronto: McClelland & Stewart, 1976.

———. "Ascent and Agony." *Canadian Literature* 42 (1969): 91–93.

Verduyn, Christl, Ed. *Margaret Laurence: An Appreciation*. Peterborough: Broadview, 1988.

Wainwright, J.A.W., Ed. *A Very Large Soul: Selected Letters from Margaret Laurence to Canadian Writers*. Dunvegan: Cormorant, 1995.

"Ways into Africa." *Times Literary Supplement*, 2 Jan. 1969: 8.

Woodcock, George, Ed. *A Place to Stand On: Essays by and about Margaret Laurence*. Edmonton: NeWest Press, 1983.

NIGERIAN LITERATURE THEN & NOW

Abdul-Rasheed Na'Allah

DRUMS ANNOUNCE THE FLOURISHING SPIRIT OF THE NIGERIAN ARTIST IN Margaret Laurence's *Long Drums and Cannons*. Africa had been denied its history, named the Dark Continent, and depicted as beastly, as it is in Conrad's *Heart of Darkness*.[1] Without Joyce Cary's *Mister Johnson*, Chinua Achebe might not have written *Things Fall Apart*. Without European primitivists, Nigritude and Tigritude might not have existed.[2] Yet Margaret Laurence found Okigbo's drums in "Heavensgate" irresistible.[3]

Laurence's *Long Drums and Cannons* is one of the rare books in which a Western writer celebrates African culture. From as early as 1966, Laurence worked toward becoming the first Western writer to affirm the truth about Africa's past as well as the strengths and weaknesses of its present. This was the first time a Westerner viewed Nigerian literature through the lens of Nigerian culture. Laurence's study meant more than a mere critique to Nigerian writers and scholars, for *Long Drums* acknowledges Nigeria's cultural influences from the past and envisions its role in the future.

The first paragraph of Laurence's Preface sets out her agenda and exhumes lies about African culture. She affirms that, although modern Nigerian literature may be written in English, its birth mother is African, with roots in indigenous Nigerian traditions. She discusses literature "which had drawn sustenance both from traditional oral literature and from the present and rapidly changing society" (*Drums* 11). Her recognition seemed profound to African writers who were accustomed to hearing Eurocentric critics accuse Nigerian writers of copying European literature.[4] No wonder Chinua Achebe isolated Laurence's humane critique when he was challenging "colonialist criticism" and identifying racism in Conrad's *Heart of Darkness*. The Canadian Laurence became the antithesis of the Polish Conrad with regard to African culture. Achebe notes Conrad's own account of his encounter with a black person: "A certain enormous buck nigger encountered in Haiti fixed my conception of blind, furious, unreasoning rage, as manifested in the human animal to the end of my days. Of the nigger I used to dream for years afterwards" (Achebe "Image" 13). Conrad's shocking statement demonstrates his vast distance from Laurence's humane critical position.

While reviewing Western interpretations of African culture, Achebe noted Laurence's recognition of African writers' perspective, quoting her statement in *Long Drums* (12): "No writer of any quality has viewed the old Africa in an idealized way, but they have tried to regain what is rightly theirs—a past composed of real and vulnerable people, their ancestors, not the figments of missionary and colonialist imaginations" (Achebe "Colonialist Criticism" 81).[5]

Laurence's book resurfaces amidst contemporary emphases on post-colonial discourses and cultural studies, as well as the romantic notion of the world as a 'global village.' Africa and the world can now celebrate the achievement of the Nigerian writers that Laurence praised in *Long Drums and Cannons*. Indeed, Laurence anticipated the recognition of many literary awards for Nigerian writers and their roles in reshaping the world's literary culture. She eagerly promoted the importance of multicultural communities in the New World. G.D. Killam recalls in his Foreword Laurence's efforts to introduce African Literature to Toronto high schools as an example of her interest in bringing this exciting work to the attention of Western readers.

Nora Foster Stovel's Introduction claims Laurence wants the world to see that individual experience in Nigerian literature also represents universal human experience. Laurence constantly sees herself, a typical Westerner, through the Nigerian authors' eyes. Whenever a Nigerian author talks about post-colonial experiences, Laurence reflects on Nigerian ideas through her own post-colonial background. This type of interpretation displays a kind of post-colonialism that operated without convenient abstraction.[6]

Long Drums and Cannons displays three important qualities—most of which satisfy an *Elaloro*, or indigenous Yoruba concept, of critical discourse[7]— that reveal Laurence as a humane writer and critic. The first of these qualities is the contextual framework of Laurence's analysis. She does not uproot writers from their African traditions or superimpose foreign critical criteria on them. Laurence constantly reflects on sociopolitical situations in Nigeria and provides readers with relevant information on Nigerian traditions. She invites readers to understand the literature from the perspective of its own cultural reality. Despite her humility in stating that she is really more of a writer than a critic, she sets an important standard for cross-cultural paradigms in criticism by avoiding the dominant Eurocentric approach. Laurence bases her approach on her respect for literature as she creates her own masterpieces.

While Laurence may not be concerned with theories, her insights into Nigerian literature will benefit scholars of world literature and critical theory for centuries. No other book written by a Western author about African literature has surpassed Laurence in returning modern African literature to African culture. The second quality that *Long Drums* displays involves the way that Laurence relates issues in Nigerian literature to universal human experiences. As Stovel explains in her Introduction, Laurence recognizes that the features of African literature "are valid anywhere." In Laurence's own African fiction, she creates human connections where others have claimed African barbarism. With every writer she discusses, she looks for answers from within African traditions, rather than simply assuming a European influence.

The third quality is what Lewis Nkosi describes as the "admirable clarity and simplicity" in Laurence's language (*Drums* xxv). Laurence does not try to mesmerize readers or to prove to Nigerian writers that her mother tongue is a mystical wand. In the Nigerian colonial mentality, difficult constructions were chosen over clarity, yet Laurence presents Nigerian literature to readers with the clearest explanations possible.[8]

As Laurence anticipated, the number of Nigerian writers working in English continues to grow. By 1971, Bruce King writes,

> We are now used to Nigerian writers winning international
> literary prizes; we expect their plays to be performed in London
> and Dakar as well as Lagos and Ibadan; we are not surprised
> when their poems are analyzed in serious critical journals. This
> was not always so. It is easy to forget that Nigerian literature in
> English is a recent phenomenon. While there is still a long and still

undocumented tradition of Nigerian writers in English, it was only
in the early 1950's that authors emerged who are worthy of
serious literary attention. (1)

Like Laurence, King refers to Amos Tutuola's *The Palm-Wine Drinkard*
(1952) as the beginning, although he later identifies Chinua Achebe's *Things
Fall Apart* (1958) as the start of "the real tradition of Nigerian literature in
English" (3). Since then, there have been many critical books examining
Nigerian literature. From King's *Introduction to Nigerian Literature* (1971)
to Bernth Lindfors's *Critical Perspectives on Nigerian Literatures* (1976),
Oladele Taiwo's *Culture and the Nigerian Novel* (1976), Claudia Baldwin's
Nigerian Literature: A Bibliography of Criticism, 1952–1976 (1980), James
Booth's *Writers and Politics of Nigeria* (1981), Bernth Lindfors's *Early
Nigerian Literature* (1982), and more on individual Nigerian writers.
However, despite all the new critical works, *Long Drums and Cannons*
retains its first and forever relevant position to the cross-cultural paradigm
encouraged in Elaloro discourse.

Nigerian writers have validated Laurence's claims: many first-generation
Nigerian writers have made headlines at home and abroad, Soyinka and
Achebe being the kings of Nigerian writing. Powerful female Nigerian writers
include Flora Nwapa, Zulu Sofola, Zaynab Alkali, and Buchi Emecheta. Ben
Okri, Niyi Osundare, and Tanure Ojaide continually draw applause from
Africa, Europe, and America.

Laurence claimed that Nigerian poetry was "extensive enough to require
a separate commentary" (13). A few constantly mentioned poets include
Catherine Acholonu, Odia Ofeimun, Harry Garuba, Molara Ogundipe, Ada
Ugha, Emevwo Biakolo, Okinba Launko, Ezenwa-Ohaeto, Sesan Ajayi, and
Remi Raji. Playwrights Femi Osofisan, Kola Omotoso, Tess Onwueme, Olu
Obafemi, and Tunde Fatunde deserve mention. Noted novelists include
Isidore Okpewho, Festus Iyayi, Adaora Ulasi, Ibrahim Tahir, Ifeoma Okoye,
and Abubakar Gimba.

Today, outlets for Nigerian literature have multiplied. One of these outlets
is traveling theater, whose icons include Hubert Ogunde, Ade Love, Baba
Sala, Duro Ladipo, Kola Ogunmola, Jimoh Aliu, Oyin Adejobi, Lere Paimo
and Isola Ogunsola.[9] Nigerian campuses experiment with community theater
projects, such as "Wasan Manoma" at the Ahmadu Bello University. Ola
Rotimi, Wole Soyinka, and several other Nigerian dramatists organized
theater groups. Electronic media and performing theaters have formed an
exciting alliance. Radio presentations developed into gramophone records,
television, and films. Publishing houses for Nigerian literature include

Heinemann Educational Books (Nigeria), Malthouse Press, Onibonoje Press, and Kraft Books Limited. With Niyi Osundare and Ken Saro-Wiwa's successful newspaper platforms, more Nigerian newspapers now dedicate several pages to poetry and critical essays.[10]

Literature is extremely popular among Nigerian scholars. Nigerian universities remain the strongest factor in developing Nigerian writing. In the 1950s and 1960s, Ulli Beier's *Black Orpheus* at the University of Ibadan was the center of literary productivity (*Drums* 11). Nigeria now has over fifty universities active in producing young writers. Creative writers' groups, literary journals, and branches of the Association of Nigerian Authors (ANA), started by Achebe, are on virtually every campus.[11]

Nigeria's sociopolitical situations have, ironically, encouraged writers. Chinua Achebe predicted the military take-over in *A Man of the People*, and the Nigerian civil war almost ended the fragile Nigerian Union. The Nigerian civil war became the most important theme in Nigerian literature written in English from 1967 to the 1980s (Amuta 83–84). Many publications mirrored the African Writers Series and the popular James Hardy Chase romances, causing a revolutionary surge in reading Nigerian novels; school children in particular now have more books that appeal to their interests.

Achebe once predicted that it would not be all roses for Nigerian literature.[12] Okigbo was killed in the Nigerian civil war, and Ken Saro-Wiwa was murdered by the Abacha military regime. Achebe almost lost his life on a Nigerian roadway, which he had earlier condemned Nigerian rulers for neglecting (*The Trouble with Nigeria*). Soyinka and several other Nigerian writers escaped from dictators' death chambers by fleeing abroad after many of them had spent time in prison. But Nigerian writers are resilient.

Nigerian writers have been inspired to write by their political situation. As Laurence explains in her analysis, Nigerian writers became preoccupied with their alignment with politicians as partners in nation building after Independence in 1960. However, most Nigerian writers realized that the politicians with whom they had fought wars for liberation had a different plan for Nigeria. Politicians stirred ethnic and religious sentiments in order to gain and hold power. Politicians appealed to regional solidarity and weakened Nigerian national alliance. Nigerian natives were surpassing foreign looters in reducing economic resources. As Nigerian writers became more critical of politicians, more and more writers found themselves in jail. Ironically, such opposition actually inspired Nigerian writing.

Laurence's insistence that Nigerian literature be perceived through the lens of Nigerian culture demands that notice also be taken of current trends in indigenous language literature. Laurence did not include in *Long Drums and Cannons* any discussion of the long tradition of writing in indigenous Nigerian languages perhaps because she was not conversant with those languages; however, the significance of this literature has long been recognized. The earliest Christian missionaries in West Africa developed Roman orthographies for many Nigerian languages in order to convert Africans to Christianity and to teach Africans to read the Bible in their own languages. Reverend J.F. Schön produced a Hausa dictionary around 1843 and, with the help of a freed Hausa slave named Dorugu, developed a Hausa reader titled *Maganan Hausa* in 1866 (Skinner 163–64). Works in Hausa have emerged in colonial Nigeria, sometimes still using an Arabic script called *Ajami* which had been flourishing from as far back as the thirteenth century. Many colonial works from northern Nigeria focus on cultural and religious issues and are written for *boko*[13] textbooks, *boko* being the Hausa name for Roman script.

More serious *boko* writing in Hausa did not occur until much later. From 1929, the colonial administration founded a project to produce books written in Hausa. Mr. Whitting and R.M. East mobilized Hausa book writing and assisted the Translation Bureau, which became the Literature Bureau and then the Northern Nigerian Publishing Corporation. A missionary press was established in Jos, and, in 1939, R.M. East founded a Hausa newspaper called *Gaskiya Ta fi Kwabo*. Earlier Hausa *boko* writers include Mallam Bello, Abubakar Imam, Abubakar Tafawa Balewa, Saadu Zungur, Akilu Aliyu, Mudi Sipikin, Aliyu'dan Sidi, Na'ibi Wali, and Muazu Hadeja. Contemporary Hausa writers include Ibrahim Yaro Yahya, Mohammed Dalhatu, Bala Funtua, and Yusuf Muhammed Adamu.

Literature in Roman script in Igbo and Yoruba began much earlier, with more influence from missionaries and Western education. D.O. Fagunwa was perhaps the earliest popular writer in Yoruba, and Akinwuni Isola has carried the genre into the twenty-first century. The most popular Nigerian written literature may be the Onitsha market pamphlets (Obiechina 1973) that Laurence mentions. Onitsha literature, which may be on any subject and can appeal to difference age groups, is available in English, Igbo, and Nigerian pidgin English (Lindfors *Popular* 23–33).

Even the *Norton Anthology of World Literature* now feels incomplete without Nigerian authors. Students of comparative, world, post-colonial, and commonwealth literature have to know some Nigerian literature. From the five major dramatists and novelists that Laurence discusses to the six writers she refers to as "Other Voices," a few have died, but their works continue to be read. Important voices that have been silenced since the publication of

Laurence's study include Flora Nwapa, Amos Tutuola, Gabriel Okara, and Ola Rotimi.[14]

What is the best way to understand Nigerian literature? This question is answered in Laurence's *Long Drums and Cannons*. Readers can understand Nigerian literature through the context of Nigerian culture and by studying the oral traditions that gave birth to contemporary Nigerian writing. A humane critic does not impose external criteria, but understands that literature is based on real human experience. Ethnic origin, linguistic choice, and place of composition do not determine the greatness of a work. When Laurence's melodious drums beat for Nigerian writing, our rhythmic steps roll across her Canadian prairie into the world's scholarly spaces.

---

1. Read Chinua Achebe's response to Joseph Conrad's *Heart of Darkness*.

2. Nigritudinists [also spelled Negritudinists] are African and African Diaspora writers led by Sengor and Cesaire who responded to European propaganda by singing "I am Black and Proud," and Tigritudinists are their twin sisters, led by Soyinka, saying "the tiger doesn't have to proclaim its tigritude." Read more in Soyinka (1970) and Chinwezu, et al.

3. Laurence uses this poem in which Okigbo characteristically celebrates African rituals and spirit of his people as epigraph to *Long Drums*, and she takes a line from it as her book's title.

4. Read Chinwezu, et al.

5. Mongo Beti's *The Poor Christ of Bomba*, for example, exposes the figments of missionary and colonial imagination to which Laurence refers.

6. One interesting issue in post-colonial discourse into the twenty-first century is that many critics wonder about the relevance of the post-colonial paradigms to Canadian (or Australian, or New Zealand's) situations. However, perspectives such as Laurence's show that there are areas of common experience between a Canadian and a Nigerian!

7. "*Elaloro*" was given at the first ICLA congress held in Africa, Pretoria, August 2000.

8. A commonplace was the Nigerian élites' obsession with difficult and tongue-scrolling English, and it became a hallmark of excellence and popularity even in the political arena, especially during the first Nigerian republic. It was therefore quite striking that Laurence preferred the simplicity of the English language when Nigerian élites were obsessed with its complexity.

9. See Biodun Jeyifo (1984) for a detailed discussion of the Yoruba travelling theatre. Jeyifo listed 115 troups of the Yoruba travelling theatre as at 1984 (200-203).

10. Osundare's poems were common in newspapers, especially in his popular column in the *Nigerian Tribune* and Ken Saro-Wiwa on *Vanguard*. Others include *The Guardian*'s Literary Series, and *The Herald*'s, *New Nigerian*'s and the *Punch*'s Arts pages.

11. The Association of Nigerian Authors was started by Chinua Achebe. See "Postcolonial Nigeria, African Literature and the Twenty-First Century: An Interview with Chinua Achebe." *Neohelicon* XXVI.1 (1999).

12. "Postcolonial Nigeria." 185, 191.

13. The Western school is Makarantar Boko.

14. Laurence does not include this last writer.

Works Cited

Achebe, Chinua. "An Image of Africa: Racism in Conrad's *Heart of Darkness*." In *Hopes and Impediments: Selected Essays*. New York: Doubleday, 1989. 1–20.

———. "Colonialist Criticism." In *Hopes and Impediments: Selected Essays*. New York: Doubleday, 1989. 68–90.

———. *The Trouble with Nigeria*. London: Heinemann, 1984.

Amuta, Chidi. "The Nigerian Civil War and the Evolution of Nigerian Literature." *Contemporary Nigerian Literature*. Ed. Hal Wylie, et al. Washington, D.C.: Three Continents Press, Inc., 1983. 83–93.

Baldwin, Claudia. *Nigerian Literature: A Bibliography of Criticism, 1952–1976*. Boston: G.K. Hall & Co., 1980.

Beti, Mongo. *The Poor Christ of Bomba*. London: Heinemann, 1971.

Booth, James. *Writers and Politics in Nigeria*. New York: African Publishing Company, 1981.

Jeyifo, Biodun. "The Yoruba Popular Travelling Theatre of Nigeria." Lagos *Nigeria Magazine*, 1984.

King, Bruce. "Introduction." *Introduction to Nigerian Literature*. Ed. Bruce King. Lagos: U of Lagos and Evans Brothers Limited, 1971. 1–11.

Laurence, Margaret. *Long Drums and Cannons*. Ed. Nora Foster Stovel. Edmonton: U of Alberta P, 2001.

Lindfors, Bernth. *Early Nigerian Literature*. New York and London: Africana Publishing Company, 1982.

———. *Popular Literatures in Africa*. Trenton: Africa World Press, 1991.

Na'Allah, Abdul-Rasheed. "*Elaloro*: An Indigenous African Theory for Critical Discourse." Paper given at the ICLA Congress, Pretoria, South Africa, August 2000.

———. "Postcolonial Nigeria, African Literature and the Twenty-First Century: An Interview with Chinua Achebe." *Neohelicon* XXVI.1 (1999). 185–92.

Obiechina, Emmanuel. *An African Popular Literature: A Study of Onitsha Market Pamphlets*. Cambridge: Cambridge UP, 1973.

Skinner, Neil. *An Anthology of Hausa Literature*. Zaria: Northern Nigerian Publishing Company, 1980.

Taiwo, Oladele. *Culture and the Nigerian Novel*. New York: St. Martin's Press, 1976.

Long Drums
& Cannons

Long Drums & Cannons

Nigerian Dramatists and Novelists
1952–1966

Margaret Laurence

I have visited, the prodigal...
in palm grove,
long drums and cannons:
the spirit in the ascent.

Christopher Okigbo: *Heavensgate*

Acknowledgements

I WOULD LIKE TO EXPRESS MY GRATITUDE TO DENNIS DUERDEN, of the Transcription Centre, London, for the help he gave me in finding background material dealing with Nigerian traditional literature and religions; to Gillian Shears, of Dillon's University Bookshop, London, who unfailingly managed to obtain for me the works of Nigerian writers, even those which were not readily available in England; and to C.J. Martin, of the B.B.C. African Service, who discovered for me several books which I had despaired of being able to find.

Contents

Preface

Nigerian literature in English, although its roots go demonstrably far back into the country's cultural past, is of comparatively recent vintage. In 1952 Amos Tutuola's *The Palm-Wine Drinkard* was published. It was the first novel in English by a Nigerian to be published outside Nigeria and widely read. Contemporary Nigerian literature really dates from that time. Since then there has been an outpouring of plays and novels, a kind of renaissance, the flourishing of a new literature which has drawn sustenance both from traditional oral literature and from the present and rapidly changing society.

It is impossible to know why Nigeria should have produced more writers than any other African country in which English is used as the common language. A contributing factor may have been the Nigerian universities. The University of Ibadan, especially, seems to have encouraged many young writers. *Black Orpheus*, the literary journal founded in 1957 and edited by such able and enthusiastic men as Ulli Beier, Janheinz Jahn, Wole Soyinka, Ezekiel Mphahlele and Ronald Dathorne, has also done much to stimulate new writing, as has the MBARI writers' and artists' club.

Nigerian writers, unlike their counterparts in French-writing Africa, have never been much concerned with the concepts of negritude. Wole Soyinka's remark—does a tiger have to be concerned with its tigritude?—has probably been quoted too often, but it remains a concise summing-up of the often-expressed views of Nigerian writers on this subject. This is not to say that colonialism left no scars—it did, and many of them can be seen outlined with bitter clarity in the novels of such writers as Chinua Achebe. But although Nigerians during the colonial period lost their autonomy and became for several generations disconnected from their own past, they never lost their land, for there were no white settlers as there were, for example, in Kenya. Whether or not this may have assisted them in maintaining some kind of inner strength and self-faith, it is impossible to know. At any rate, the writers of Nigeria seem to have been able to by-pass the negritude phase, which is essentially a means of restoring self-faith by proclaiming the worth and even (with extreme negritudinists) the superior worth of being black. Nigerian writing is concerned with an examination of the psychological damage done during the colonial period, but this is usually portrayed in social, cultural and religious terms, hardly ever in purely racial terms.

Modern Nigerian literature interprets Africa, both past and present, from the inside. Africa was interpreted and misinterpreted by outsiders for long enough. Now its own writers are engaged in reassessing their past, in rediscovering their inheritance, in interpreting themselves both to their own people and to the rest of the world. This process has been of enormous value, both inside and outside Africa. To several generations of West Africans, educated in mission schools and brought up with a view of Africa which was superimposed upon them from the outside, the work of writers such as Chinua Achebe and Wole Soyinka must surely have done much to restore a true sense of their own past, a knowledge of a tribal society which was neither idyllic, as the views of some nationalists would have had it, nor barbaric, as many missionaries and European administrators wished and needed to believe. To people outside Africa, the work of these West African writers has made accessible for the first time a picture in depth. Most Nigerian writers have in some way or other made an attempt to restore the value of the past, without idealising it and without being shackled by it. Present conflicts in an independent Nigeria have been dealt with too, by nearly all writers. They are not disengaged from the events and problems of their own times—the clash between generations, the social and individual disturbances brought about by a period of transition, the slow dying of the destructive aspects of tribalism, the anguish and inadequacy of uncompromising individualism as an alternative to tribalism.

Perhaps the most enduringly interesting aspect of Nigerian literature, however, as of literature everywhere, is the insight it gives not only into immediate and local dilemmas but, through these, into the human dilemma as a whole. Literature can only do this in very specific and detailed ways. It must be planted firmly in some soil. Even works of non-realism make use of spiritual landscapes which have been at least partially inherited by the writer. Despite some current fashions to the contrary, the main concern of a writer remains that of somehow creating the individual on the printed page, of catching the tones and accents of human speech, of setting down the conflicts of people who are as real to him as himself. If he does this well, and as truthfully as he can, his writing may sometimes reach out beyond any national boundary. The best of these Nigerian plays and novels reveal something of ourselves to us, whoever and wherever we are.

This book does not deal with contemporary Nigerian poetry, for this field is now extensive enough to require a separate commentary. Principally, these essays are an attempt to show that Nigerian prose writing in English has now reached a point where it must be recognised as a significant part of world literature.

Note

This book was written before the outbreak of civil war in Nigeria and the secession of Biafra. Although Nigeria was originally formed by almost arbitrary boundaries devised in the colonial era, these boundaries represent the country which was being written about by novelists and dramatists in the past fifteen years. There is now no Nigeria in that form, but the writing survives and may even provide some clues to the present tragic situation.

Some of the biographical material in this book is now out of date. News of these writers is scant at the moment, so it is not possible to amend these sections. The lives of Nigerian and Biafran writers are in continuing danger, and some have already been lost. Christopher Okigbo, one of Africa's finest poets, was recently killed. The title of this book, taken many months ago from one of his poems, now seems cruelly ironic.

January 1968   M.L.

ONE

Voices of Life, Dance of Death

Wole Soyinka

WOLE SOYINKA'S WRITING often seems like a juggling act. He can keep any number of plates—and valuable plates, at that—spinning in the air all at the same time. He is able to handle many themes simultaneously without ever endangering the reality of his characters. His people are never ciphers or symbols, always persons speaking in their own voices. He is a volatile writer, and he achieves in his work an almost unbelievable amount of vitality. He is well known as a poet, and he has written one novel, but it is as a playwright that he has done his major work so far.

Still only in his thirties, Soyinka has written ten plays—*The Swamp Dwellers, The Lion and the Jewel, The Invention, The Strong Breed, The Detainee, The Trials of Brother Jero, Camwood on the Leaves, A Dance of the Forests, The Road,* and *Kongi's Harvest.* Six of these have been published. He has produced and directed his own plays in Lagos and Ibadan, and has virtually founded contemporary theatre in Nigeria. His two theatre groups are 'The 1960 Masks', in Lagos, and 'Orisun Theatre' in Ibadan. *The Road* was produced at the Commonwealth Arts Festival, London, 1965, and won a prize at the Darkar Festival of the Negro Arts in 1966, where also *Kongi's Harvest* was performed by both theatre companies acting as one group. *The Lion and the Jewel* was performed by the Ijinle Theatre Company at the Royal Court Theatre in London, 1966.

Born in 1934 in Isara, Ijebu Remo, Soyinka is a member of the Yoruba, the largest tribal group in Western Nigeria. He attended the University of Ibadan and in 1954 went to England where he studied at the University of Leeds. After gaining a degree in English literature at Leeds, he went to work with the Royal Court Theatre in London as a play-reader. In 1960 he returned to Nigeria to do research in traditional African drama at the University of Ibadan. He then became lecturer in English literature at the University of Ife. He has also taught African literature at the University of Lagos, and is now Head of the School of Drama, University of Ibadan.

In his work Soyinka enriches and gives dramatic emphasis to modern themes by drawing upon the religion, the mythology and the poetry of the African past. Yoruba gods inhabit his plays, and he uses the Yoruba drums, including the talking drums, as they have been used for centuries to heighten and define rituals. He also makes use of the dance and mask idiom which are an integral part of traditional Yoruba drama. He combines these elements with contemporary settings and with themes which are universal, and the results are sometimes electrifying.

Soyinka himself has remarked that some Yoruba play-goers have criticised him for being 'too European', while some Europeans have told him that they felt they missed many of the allusions and that a Yoruba audience must surely get much more out of the plays. The fate of innovators is to be looked at dubiously from all sides. Of course it is not necessary to be Yoruba to appreciate Soyinka's plays any more than it is necessary to be Greek to care about the plays of Euripides. Generally speaking, Soyinka's plays contain everything necessary to understand his references to Yoruba gods or cults. Nevertheless, because Soyinka's background is so wide, and includes influences both from the European theatre (Brecht, Dürrenmatt and Arden have all been said to have influenced him) and from African traditional drama, and because his frame of reference includes a double mythology, Yoruba and Christian, it is necessary to see his plays in context and to realise that his writing, both in form and content, owes as much to African sources as it does to European.

Traditional Yoruba Drama

The oldest forms of drama in Nigeria—forms which are still very much alive—were not performed on stages or in theatres. Their theatre was the street, the market-place and the temple. Art was associated with religion, just as it was in classical Greece or medieval Europe. The function of the artist was to help maintain the close and necessary relationship with the ancestors and gods, and to try to ensure the benevolence of gods who were neither totally good nor evil but simply powerful. These pageants were, and are, complex productions, requiring the combined talents of the carvers who created the elaborate masks, the masquerade dancers and the drummers.

The basic concept, or world-view, behind West African tribal societies is that the prime reality is a spiritual one. Every tree and river has its indwelling spirit, and when a plant has the power of healing a wound, it is not chemical acting upon flesh but spirit acting upon spirit. Perhaps this dominance of the spiritual partly explains what now seems in many traditional rituals to be the great amount of attention paid to human psychological needs, through the opportunities which are given to express and externalise the inner life— the hates, the irrational fears, the resentments, the overwhelming desire for reassurance about death and immortality, the impulse to rejoice or to mourn.

Among the Yoruba in Western Nigeria *Egungun* was one form which religion took when it combined with art. *Egungun* is a cult of the ancestors. The word 'cult', with its somewhat esoteric connotations, tends to be misleading. In Yoruba society various cults each owe allegiance to a particular deity or to the spirits of earth or the watchful dead. This is only to say that each interprets the mysteries of creation and death in its own way. The religious cults of the Yoruba are no more esoteric than the religious cults of Methodist or High Anglican—all are a particular people's way of viewing themselves in relation to their world, past and present, and in relation to their god or gods. In most tribal societies, including the Yoruba, the present generations of living do not stand entirely alone, nor is the individual ever abandoned entirely to the limits of his own powers, for the dead ancestors continue to watch over and guide their descendents. The *Egungun* society is the special custodian of the ancestral spirits. Basically it is an attempt to reassure people about an individual immortality and to diminish the fear of death through the dramatic appearance of the ancestral spirits within the world of men.

When a particular ancestor is selected for worship, a mask is carved to him. Once a year, at the times of festivals, the *Egungun* masks come out and dance through the streets of the town. When the masqueraders appear and dance to the appropriate drumming—for the Yoruba talking drums speak lines of poetry and set the theme for the dancers—the townspeople gather and accompany the procession. They will not, however, venture too close, for it is considered dangerous to come too near to an *Egungun*. The dancers under the masks speak in assumed voices. Naturally everyone knows that a human is under the mask, and probably many people know which townsman, but this is not acknowledged openly.

The *Ifa* society, a cult of divination, decides which dead are to have masks dedicated to them. If a man is advised to worship a particular ancestor, he will order the mask to be carved, and he will pay for it, but he will never dance under it. A member of the *Egungun* society is secretly appointed to be the mask's keeper and dancer.

Some masks are carved to cover the face, while others have a carving on top of the head and a face covering made of leather or raffia. Carvings are sharply symbolic in the strongly gashed lines, pared down to the spiritual bone, which are the great talent of West African carvers. The *Egungun* masks are rarely named for the ancestor in whose honour they have been carved. Usually a type-name is found—Andu, a royal prince; Atere, the slender one; Gbajero, hanger of witches, a grotesque mask whose wearer used to be responsible for executing people found guilty of performing the forbidden rites of black magic.

Masks are a tangible means of connection with the other world. They are regarded with reverence and at the same time provide a near-touching of the revered object—god become flesh—for in the act of possession of the dancer by the spirit of the mask, dancer and mask merge in a union of the mortal and the immortal. When an *Egungun* dances, the state of possession frequently takes place and at this moment the ancestral spirit is believed to be actually and perceptibly present. The dancer's own spirit is suspended, held in abeyance, and when he becomes subservient to the spirit of the mask, he is often able to perform with a skill greater than his own. The ancestral spirit is like the Yoruba gods, neither totally good nor evil, but possessing enormous power. It must therefore be treated in the proper ritualistic manner so that it will be kindly disposed towards the human community.

The poetry which accompanies the *Egungun's* dance is expressed not only verbally but also rhythmically through the voices of the drums and the physical response of the dancers to the drums. The talking drums instruct the dancers and provide the theme of the whole ritual, and in consequence they are more important than the spoken word.

The Yoruba festival which has the closest bearing on the work of Soyinka is the Festival of Ogun, which is still celebrated each year. Ogun is the Yoruba god of war and of iron. He is the protector god of hunters and carvers and all who work with iron. His followers nowadays include taxi drivers and a great many of the brotherhood of the road, the drivers of buses and lorries and the famous West African mammy-wagons which will carry anything from passengers to dried fish and will dare any road, however hazardous. In the plays of Soyinka, Ogun takes on new dimensions and acquires meanings which are psychological and symbolic, but it is important to remember that for many of Soyinka's characters, just as for many Yoruba drivers and mechanics, Christian or otherwise, Ogun is believed in literally.

Perhaps a semantic difficulty lies at the core of some religious battles. Many Christians would reject the Yoruba concept of protector gods such as Ogun, while at the same time professing with no apparent sense of disparity their own belief in patron saints. The late Dr J.B. Danquah, of Ghana, said in his book *The Akan Doctrine of God*, 'If we are to pay due compliments to one another's gods, we should call them by none but their proper names.' He was objecting, with justification, to people who referred to the Akan supreme deity, Nyame, as 'the Sky God'. He claimed that this patronising name gave an impression of *naïveté* to a concept which was no more naïve in fact than the Heavenly Father of Christian doctrine. The respect which Dr Danquah advocated towards one another's gods might well be borne in mind when considering Ogun, for Soyinka is talking about a god who is real.

The Festival of Ogun begins with a public prayer to beg the god's prevention of fatal motor accidents. Then, in the procession, the worshippers of Ogun take part—the Ogun priests, the drivers, mechanics, blacksmiths, cycle repair men—all in fancy dress. Some of the worshippers carry images of the god from their shrines, and masqueraders appear in splendidly carved masks. Praise-songs are chanted to the god. This one, for example, is the priests' incantation:

> *God forbid that Ogun*
> *Should weep in my presence*
> *For when Ogun weeps*
> *He sheds blood....*

In contrast, there is this hectic one from the drivers:

> *The die is cast*
> *Fire and hell are let loose*
> *Everyone should run for his life!*

The drumming, the dancing, the chanting of praise-songs—all this goes on for a number of days and culminates in the sacrifice of a dog, Ogun's sacrificial animal.

Yoruba Folk Opera

Traditional religious masquerade is not the only form of Yoruba drama which has had an influence on the plays of Wole Soyinka. A popular theatre, with plays performed in Yoruba, had its origins in the Christian Church, and particularly with such sects as the Apostolic Church and the Seraphim and Cherubim. These sects, some thirty years ago, began to produce biblical plays which can be compared with the European medieval passion plays and mortality plays, strong-lined and simply motivated. About twenty years ago, Hubert Ogunde developed a secular theatre which took politics and social satire as its themes. Later Ogunde's colleague, I.E. Ogunmula, developed a form of Yoruba drama which drew on these sources but also incorporated folk tales and fantasy.

The most recent and perhaps the most exciting development in Yoruba theatre has been the folk operas of Duro Ladipo. A man with very little formal education, Ladipo began to compose church music for All Saints' Church in Oshogbo, his home town. In 1962 he began to write the music and libretti for his own secular folk operas. He used historical subjects, adapting them freely. His opera, *Oba Koso*, was first performed in Nigeria in 1963. It has since been performed in both Berlin and London. He has produced three operas—*Oba Koso* (The King Does Not Hang), *Oba Moro* (The Ghost-Catcher), and *Oba Waja* (The King Is Dead). These have been published in English translations by Ulli Beier. Ladipo has founded his own company, the Duro National Theatre, in Oshogbo, Western Nigeria. He not only writes the plays and the music; he also directs his operas and acts in them himself.

In Ladipo's operas an element of the traditional Yoruba mask drama can be seen in the use of the talking drums to underline and accompany the main theme. For a Yoruba audience, this provides a reverberating commentary on the entire drama, and even for non-Yoruba the drums indicate mounting tension and tellingly foreshadow the crucial events of the play. Some non-Yoruba would undoubtedly disagree; when *Oba Koso* was produced in London at the Commonwealth Arts Festival in 1965, one reviewer did not mention the drums at all but wrote plaintively of the singing that it seemed coarse and monotonous although fortunately one tune had reminded him faintly of 'Yes,

We Have No Bananas'. In fact, the drums are of equal importance with the music in *Oba Koso*, the talking drum having the ability to speak lines of poetry and the *dundun* drum having a range of a full octave. The music itself is based on the tonal system of the Yoruba talking drums.

Each of Ladipo's operas is in some way about a king, or *Oba*. The Yoruba were at one time empire-builders whose ancient kingdoms included Oyo, Ife and Benin. The king was believed to possess mystical powers and was a link between the people and the gods. His person was sacred, and he did not die—he went away. He was not, however, all-powerful, nor was the title of *Oba* an inherited one. A king was elected from the royal lineage, by a council of elders drawn from all the religious cults. A king could be deposed, and when this grave step was taken he was expected to commit suicide. In Duro Ladipo's opera *Oba Koso* many of these elements of sacred kingship can be seen. The opera is based on the legendary founder of the Oyo kingdom, Alafin Sango, who, after his death, was deified and became the Yoruba god of thunder and lightning.

The Yoruba gods, or *orisha*, are seen as aspects of the supreme god, Olorun, who is not worshipped directly. Each god represents some archetypal personality. Sango is seen as powerful, dramatic, lusty, violent in rage, unpredictable, generous, disliking liars and thieves. In *Oba Koso*, the character of Sango closely corresponds to this concept. When the opera was performed at the Commonwealth Arts Festival, Ladipo himself took the role of Sango. Bearded and hugely authoritative, fantastically garbed in a glittering gold and black costume, and wearing a swirling cloak embroidered with pearl-like cowrie shells, he might almost have been a reincarnation of Sango himself.

This, then, is Wole Soyinka's inheritance and background—the mask dramas of *Egungun*, the Yoruba pantheon of gods, the praise-songs and the rituals of the festivals, the ever-present drums which convey both words and emotions, the Yoruba mythology and proverbs, the folk opera with its chanted songs and its quick-paced and often violent action. He has drawn material from all these sources, transforming it into something rich and strange and new, and adding to it his own ability to create individual character and his own way of seeing.

The Lion and the Jewel

Irony, in this comedy, is used with a delicate touch. The manners and customs of both the old Africa and the new are satirised, but lightly, never with the bitter vigour that marks Soyinka's social commentaries in his later plays. All the protagonists in this play are treated affectionately. Lakunle, the pompous young school-teacher with his blanco-white tennis shoes and his determined faith in progress is an absurd and yet highly sympathetic figure. He is starch-charactered for much of the time, but he is not presented only in one light. He can occasionally yield to gaiety, even though it goes against his principles, and he is not beyond pinching the bottom of a nubile village girl. Similarly, Baroka, the old chief or Bale, the 'Lion of Ilujinle' and the representative of the ancient traditions, emerges as an enormously appealing figure—a man of both guile and real wisdom, a man who, in his illiteracy and his mud palace, possesses a degree of sophistication undreamed of by Lakunle. Lakunle's idea of living it up is a week-end in the nightclubs at Ibadan, doing the waltz and foxtrot with a high-heeled girl, and he is scornful of what he believes to be Baroka's uncouth ways. But Baroka, in fact, could have walked with no trouble at all into the court of the Sun King in France or on to the yacht of some Greek shipping magnate. Baroka is a master of intrigue, and he never for an instant forgets his long-term aims. Poor Lakunle, in his innocent and well-meaning clerkdom, can have no idea what he is up against, in having Baroka as rival for the affections of the 'Jewel of Ilujinle', the lissom Sidi.

Sidi, in the beginning, is admittedly naïve, but she has an inkling of her own potentialities and she is not a girl to be ordered about. Lakunle does not feel that he is ordering her about, of course. He believes he is trying to educate his loved one, to raise her from her bush background, to make a Lagos lady out of her. For her own good, therefore, he tells her she must not carry a bucket on her head, for that is primitive. And she must not expose what he euphemistically calls her 'shoulders', because to do so is common and vulgar. Sidi finds all this moral talk very boring, but she says she will marry him—

> ...Today, next week
> Or any day you name.
> But my bride-price must first be paid.

Here is the snag. Lakunle refuses to pay any bride-price, which he believes to be 'a savage custom, barbaric, out-dated, rejected, denounced, accursed—' and as many more damning adjectives as he can muster with the aid of the Shorter Companion Dictionary.

Sidi's first real glimpse of her own beauty, and therefore her own power, comes when she learns that the pictures taken in the village shortly before by a visiting photographer have now appeared in a magazine, and her own picture is on the cover. Sidi is entranced at the sight of her own image, and in an exuberant outburst she declares that she is more important than the Bale. When she receives an invitation from Baroka, the Bale, to have supper with him, she refuses haughtily, saying he is too old and she has no intention of becoming another of his many wives. This is no fate for the jewel of Ilujinle.

Old Sadiku, Baroka's chief wife, returns to tell the Bale of Sidi's refusal. He is at first angry, then dejected. Because Sadiku is his senior wife, he tells her something he has told no one—his manhood has ended, and he had hoped, with the beautiful young Sidi, that 'my failing strength would rise and save my pride'. Sadiku, far from keeping her lord's sad secret, gloats to herself and then rushes off to whisper in Sidi's ear. Sidi decides to visit Baroka after all, in order to mock him.

The scene between Sidi and Baroka is a delight—Sidi, believing herself to be much cleverer than the old chief, and Baroka allowing her to believe it, leading her on with calculated gradualness to what he finally maintains is the real reason he has asked her to his palace. He is all in favour of progress, he says, and the first step will be for the village to print its own stamps. Would Sidi consent to having her picture on the stamps of Ilujinle? Not for nothing has he been called the Fox as well as the Lion. When Sidi returns to Lakunle and her friends, it is in a pandemonium of tears and tantrums. Baroka, of course, has not lost his manhood at all. He lied to Sadiku, knowing the old woman would not keep the secret, and Sidi has been neatly caught in the trap, as he planned and as she richly deserved.

Lakunle is outraged, but at the same time tries to turn the situation to his own advantage. Nobly, he offers to marry Sidi just the same, but naturally there can be no question of any bride-price now, 'Since you no longer can be called a maid'. But Sidi fools everyone, perhaps even herself—everyone, that is, except the cunning old Baroka. She could not possibly marry Lakunle now, she declares.

> Why, did you think that after him,
> I could endure the touch of another man?
> I who have felt the strength,
> The perpetual youthful zest
> Of the panther of the trees?

So Sidi will become the newest of Baroka's wives, and nobody could feel sorry for her. He will do very well by her. They will not cheat one another. They may turn to hate some day, but that is a different story—the story told by Sadiku, who was once Baroka's favourite woman.

The tone is airy and subtle throughout, and the play has many of the elements of true farce, for themes which are serious and even frightening are dealt with in a flutter of comparative manners and highly plotted intrigues, so that we are enchanted (in both senses of the word) by the shimmering quality of the thing, its swiftness and its barbs. Only afterwards do we suspect how protective our laughter may have been, for the themes in actuality have been those of impotence and the fear of impotence, and woman's sexual malice. But Soyinka softens his themes deliberately here, and prevents that brittleness which is often found in farce, by interweaving the sexual themes with social ones—that is, by holding up to a not-unkind ridicule the foibles of both traditionalists and progressives. He views all his characters tolerantly and bestows upon them the saving grace of paradox. Lakunle is ludicrous in his stilted concept of social virtues and his total dismissal of the past, but there is something brave and moving, as well, about his earnestness and his endeavour. Baroka is wily and unscrupulous, yet he is also perceptive and he cares enough about his people to hope that social progress will not obliterate their vitally alive variety:

> But the skin of progress
> Masks, unknown, the spotted wolf of sameness.

Sidi, vain as she is, has a certain radiance about her, and although she goes to Baroka's palace out of high-spirited spite, there is something pathetic as well as comic in the ease with which she is taken in by the Bale. Even Sadiku no doubt has her reasons for rejoicing so cruelly over Baroka's imagined impotence, and although she is a gruesome old hag in some ways, there is an earthy practicality about her which saves her from becoming a one-dimensional figure.

Dance and masquerade, used so extensively by Soyinka in his later plays, are used to a lesser extent but very effectively in *The Lion and the Jewel*. In the first scene the village girls and Lakunle stage the dance of the lost traveler, to show how the photographer came to the village. Four girls crouch on the floor, miming the four wheels of a car; Lakunle acts the part of the driver; the drums supply the appropriate rhythms and sounds, and—as Soyinka explains in the stage directions— 'the "trees" perform a subdued and unobtrusive dance'. Among other dance sequences is a masked dance in which mummers act out the tale of the Baroka's famed virility and rumoured defeat, and Sadiku joins in among the masqueraders and dances as though possessed by some spirit of female vengeance at last given release against her domineering lord.

The Trials of Brother Jero

This short comedy is a take-off or send-up of the many evangelists, prophets and other religious curiosities who flourish and milk money from the gullible along the beaches of Lagos. It has the simplest structure of all Soyinka's plays, and in fact the entire plot hangs on the well-worn device of concealed identity.

Brother Jero, shyster-prophet, has bought a gorgeous white velvet cloak from a trader woman and has neglected to pay for it. The woman is in constant pursuit of Brother Jero, and even camps on his doorstep, demanding her one pound, eight shillings and ninepence. Meantime, Chume, Brother Jero's assistant, has been having trouble with his nagging wife, and pleads with the prophet for permission to beat her. Brother Jero steadfastly and virtuously cautions Chume against the sin of wife-beating, until he learns that Chume's wife is none other than Amope, the trader woman who sold him the cloak. Soyinka gives this old chestnut a slightly new gloss by introducing a few gimmicks at the end—Chume, having discovered the prophet's real reason for changing his mind and sanctioning his disciple's wife-beating, grows suspicious that Brother Jero may have been Amope's lover as well as her debtor. He creates a loud disturbance, until Brother Jero takes the under-hand way of having him locked up as a lunatic.

The situation is thin and at times implausible, but what saves this play from being a mere skit is Soyinka's sharp ear for the cadences of human speech. The crowds at the revivalist beach meetings; Brother Jero praying like thunder for help against his one weakness, 'this lust for the daughters of Eve', and the excited Chume praying with him and slipping unconsciously into pidgin English, 'Help 'am, God. Help 'am, God. I say make you help 'am. Help 'am quick quick...'—the voices here come across as marvelously alive. This quality places *The Trials of Brother Jero* as a direct forerunner of *The Road*, in which the speech of drivers and thugs is handled with the same certainty of touch, the same authenticity.

Brother Jero himself, although he is an uncomplicated conman, in some ways foreshadows Professor, the main protagonist and word-enchanted leader of drivers and layabouts, in *The Road*. The beginnings can be seen here of Professor's oratory, at once comic and tragic, a combination of the shrewd and the visionary, in Jero's less lofty but still energetically fluent style of speech. At the play's opening, Jero introduces himself:

I am a Prophet. A prophet by birth and by inclination. You have
probably seen many of us on the streets, many with their own
churches, many inland, many on the coast, many leading
processions, many looking for processions to lead, many curing
the deaf, many raising the dead. In fact, there are eggs and there
are eggs. Same thing with prophets. I was born a Prophet.

Brother Jero does not approach Professor in terms of being a fully realised
character, but he, too, has his dreams of glory, dreams which are so firmly
rooted in fantasy that they cannot fail to move us because of the dreamer's
great need.

They will look at my velvet cape and they will think of
my goodness. Inevitably, they must begin to call me...
the Velvet-hearted Jeroboam. Immaculate Jero, Articulate
Hero of Christ's Crusade—

That fascination with the power of the word, with the lengthiness and
rhythm of words, comes out here as it does so strongly later on in Professor.
'Immaculate Jero, Articulate Hero—'.

The Swamp Dwellers

Soyinka leaves his usual Yoruba background and sets this play in a village in
the swamps. No more definite *local* is mentioned, but one can assume that
the swamp-dwellers are Ijaw people who live in the tidal mangrove swamps
of the Eastern Niger Delta. The background and beliefs which emerge in the
play are recognisably Ijaw. The 'water people' or gods of the swamp and
creeks are believed by Ijaw villagers to appear sometimes in the guise of a
python, and in Soyinka's play the Serpent of the Swamps is the god who must
constantly be propitiated through his priest Kadiye, so that floods will not
destroy the meagre crops nor the uncertain soil return to the swamp.

Igwezu, a young man, has just returned to his parents' home after a time
in the city, where he had gone to find his twin brother, long missing. He
found his brother—and found a changed man, an unscrupulous low-dealer
and cash-worshipper who not only fiddled Igwezu's money away but also
contrived to steal his wife. Now, arriving back at his village, Igwezu learns
that the crops have been totally destroyed by heavy rains. Disillusioned and
bitter, Igwezu turns his anger against Kadiye, sleek priest of the Swamp
Serpent, well-fed even in times of famine.

Into the situation arrives a stranger, a Muslim from the north, a blind man who has spent most of his life as a beggar. This instrument of fate reveals that he, growing up in a land which suffers almost perpetual drought, had once after a season of unusually ample rains tried to become a farmer, only to have his ripening crops fall to the locusts. He has come to this place because he never wants to live in a dry land again, and he offers to become Igwezu's bondsman and to care for the land in the young man's absence. Igwezu, having threatened his own safety by his hard words to the priest—'If I slew all the cattle in the land and sacrificed every measure of goodness, would it make any difference to our lives, Kadiye?'—stumbles off into the night. The beggar remains, enigmatically saying 'I shall be here to give account'.

This play does not seem to hang together. The central irony—Igwezu's crops destroyed by water, while the northerner's crops were either blighted by drought or devoured by locusts—is well enough balanced, and it rings true. But when it comes, finally, to Igwezu's long denunciation of the Swamp Serpent's priest, two separate threads appear to have become snarled. If Igwezu has changed, as he makes clear he has, and no longer believes in the efficacy of the priest's rituals to protect the people, why blame Kadiye or the gods for the rotted harvest? True, it is often unbelievers who curse a god whom they believe to be non-existent, and if Soyinka had made Igwezu's outburst a clear symptom of this dichotomy, this undirected grief seeking something and someone to blame, the structure of the play would have held. But he does not do so. Igwezu's confusion is not presented as confusion but as some kind of liberation. The beggar says, almost in adulation, 'Master—master—slayer of serpents'. But Igwezu does not appear to have slain very many serpents in his own mind. A more solid fatalism might have been expected from the beggar, a Muslim who is presented as a man of some wisdom. As an uncompromising monotheist, he would have been opposed to the Swamp Serpent, no doubt, but surely he would have pointed out to Igwezu that the drought and the rain alike represented the incomprehensible will of Allah.

The matter of the priest's corpulence is quite a different one. Had Igwezu only blamed the priest for growing fat on the offerings to the god, or even if—from a position of disbelief—he had blamed Kadiye for contracting to do what he was unable to do, namely to stop the rains, then the semi-heroic stance in which Igwezu is shown at the end might have had a greater justification.

The Strong Breed

A young man, Eman, has been working as a teacher in a village which is not his own, assisted by an educated village girl, Sunma, who has fallen in love with him. As the play opens, Sunma is trying to get Eman to leave the village, even for a few days. He refuses, and finally it becomes clear that Sunma is really attempting to get him away before the forthcoming festival of the new year, partly because she does not wish him to see the rites, which she describes as evil, and partly because she fears for Eman's safety. She reminds him that he is a stranger here and is therefore potentially in danger. But Eman stubbornly refuses to leave, and when the rites begin, a half-witted boy, Ifada, who is also a stranger, is seized by the priest and elders but escapes and runs to Eman for protection. The elders follow, and Eman learns that the idiot boy has been tolerated only so that he may be used as 'carrier'—that is, a scapegoat who carries on his shoulders all the sins and evil of the village, sins which are piled on him symbolically (and also actually, in the villager's view) by his being reviled and whipped and cursed. The culmination of the rites— the driving of the carrier away for ever—purges the village, the people believe, and permits them to begin the new year cleansed. No carrier may return to the village, or else he will be stoned to death.

Eman objects to the rites and refuses to let the boy be taken. The elders tell him he cannot possibly understand the local customs, and they resort to threats when Eman is still unmoved. Eman tells them that he understands very well the custom of carrier who bears away the sins of all, but '. . in my home we believe that a man should be willing'. He tells them that the act can have no meaning if the carrier is terrified and has no grasp of the significance of what he is doing.

From flashbacks, we learn that Eman comes from what is known as 'the strong breed' and that the traditional role of the men of his family has been to carry the sins of their village down to the river each year in a boat and to get rid of them in this way. Although the function of carrier, as practiced by Eman's father and grandfather, was essentially the same as it is in Sunma's village, the concept of what a carrier should be was quite different. The strong breed were raised to understand the nature of their duty. The spiritual weight of the evil-laden boat would naturally have been gigantic to anyone who believed in it, but although the burden weighed heavily on the men of Eman's family, they undertook it willingly. Only Eman himself refused the role, telling his father, 'I am unfitted for your call'. Eman's young wife died giving birth to a son, for each time one of the strong breed was born, the mother died. Eman was determined to leave his village. His father, when he could not persuade Eman to stay, prophesied that 'your own blood will betray you, son, because you cannot hold it back'.

Now Eman's heritage draws him irresistibly to offer himself as carrier in place of the half-wit boy. The elders accept him, but they are suspicious and afraid of his strangeness. He comprehends too much, and they cannot understand his willingness to offer himself up to pain and humiliation. Jaguna, Sunma's father, predicts that 'the year will demand more from this carrier than we thought'. Eman is accordingly whipped and driven from the village, but he returns for a drink of water. This is refused him, and he sets off for the river. The elders are now determined that Eman must die. Because the rites have not been performed in the usual way, and the carrier has unforgivably returned to the village, nothing less than a human sacrifice will appease the gods. Learning where Eman is headed, they set a trap for him. On his way to the river, Eman has a vision of his father, who tells him to go the other way. But Eman says, 'Father, I am your son and I am coming with you'. He walks on into the forest, falls into the elders' trap, and is hanged upon the sacred tree. The elders, discussing Eman's death, reveal the fact that the villagers 'looked up at the man and words died in their throats'. No one was able to curse him after all.

There are strands of both traditional religion and Christianity in this play. The elders and priest, the sacred grove, the carrying of the year's evils to the river—these are drawn from African religions. But the whole play in a sense is a parallel with the Christian passion story—the man who must ultimately act the role demanded of him as his father's son, the temptation to evade the role, the final facing of the role of the redeemer who takes upon himself the sins of all, the death on the cross (the sacred tree).

Soyinka is exploring the nature both of human sacrifice, where the victim is unwilling, and of a type of martyrdom where the victim offers himself. There are several aspects to Eman's acceptance of the role of carrier. Partly, he seems to be motivated by his heritage, by the fact that he was born to be one of the strong breed. Partly, he offers himself in order to redeem others. This is his means of expressing love—and perhaps his only way, for he tells Sunma that 'Love comes to me more easily with strangers', and although he is gentle with Sunma, as he is with everyone, he has obviously never had any intention of marrying her and he tries tactfully to make her realise this. Partly, also, Eman seems to be drawn towards suffering and even death simply for its own sake. He does not actually need to return to the village. He is pulled back to it as much by his memory of his child-wife's death as he is by his physical need for water. There is a certain degree of masochism in his reaction to the beating given him by the villagers. One of the elders says of him, 'I think he is the kind who would let himself be beaten from night until dawn and not utter a sound. He would let himself be stoned until he dropped dead.' And in his death there are various elements—a desire to serve, a desire to give meaning to his own life, and finally a desire to die.

The Strong Breed is an exceedingly compact play. In a relatively short space, Soyinka has managed to convey and contrast concepts relating to figures found in many societies and many religions. Man's recurring need to provide himself with scapegoats is perhaps more closely related to his need to seek redeemers than we would like to believe.

A Dance of the Forests

A Dance of the Forests is Soyinka's most intricate play. Among many other things, it contains some extremely vitriolic comments on corrupt politicians and a number of pointed warnings about the dangers which face a newly independent country. It was first performed—amazingly enough—as part of the Nigerian Independence celebrations in 1960. Either the authorities of that period were more liberal-minded than they subsequently became, or else they did not understand what *A Dance of the Forests* was all about. If some of Soyinka's barbs passed by unnoticed, it would not be surprising. The play has been criticised for its obscurity, and it is true that parts of it are difficult and open to more than one interpretation. It is a play which is likely to be around for some time, however, and like many works which are thought to be obscure when they first appear, it may seem perfectly plain to the next generation of readers and play-goers. The action is rapid—sometimes almost too rapid; the themes are never dealt with singly but always more than one at a time; the idiom is frequently unfamiliar; the poetic imagery is sometimes bewildering. Nevertheless, a great deal does come across, even on a first contact with this play.

As the play opens, the gathering of the tribes is about to take place—that is, Independence, although this word is never used and the time is never definitely stated. The people have sought to invite some of the dead to the celebration. They have hoped for glorious ancestors, ancestors who could verify the splendour of the lost empires. But the Dead Man and Dead Woman who turn up are repulsive in appearance, stumbling and apologetic in speech, altogether embarrassing. Yet, having once been conjured up, they refuse to go away. The past, however it fails us, cannot be got rid of so easily. Three humans find themselves in the forest with the Dead Man and Dead Woman— Demoke the carver, who has just finished carving the splendid totem for the gathering of the tribes; Rola, a beautiful prostitute; and Adenebi, a counsellor. A fourth man announces himself as Obaneji, a filing clerk for the courts, but in reality he is Forest Head, or the supreme deity, in disguise. Admittedly, the plot thickens almost before it has begun, but this is Soyinka's method. Obaneji, or Forest Head, has led the three into the forest in order to reveal themselves to themselves. Subtly and with irony, Forest Head questions the living and makes them show what they are under the surface.

Adenebi the counsellor has taken bribes in exchange for altering the number of passengers allowed on lorries, and as a result an overloaded lorry has crashed and burned, and many people have been killed. Rola is revealed as cruel and heartless. Several of her lovers have fought over her and are now dead, yet she disclaims any responsibility. Indeed, she does not even seem very interested. She is called Madame Tortoise, after a legendary figure, and the Tortoise is a common symbol of a prostitute. Both Adenebi—obtuse and pompous—and Rola—brash, cold and sly—utterly deny Forest Head's implications when he brings up the subject of their guilt.

Demoke the carver is different. We see from the beginning that he is a man haunted by the awareness of his own guilt. He is the most talented carver in the land. Obaneji (Forest Head) says to him, of the totem, 'It was the work of ten generations. I think your hands are very old. You have the fingers of the dead.' It may be worthwhile noting that the carver, as representing the creative artist, is a natural choice here. Yoruba woodcarvers have always been of prime importance in Western Nigeria. Their carvings of gods and the followers of gods have been described and analysed fascinatingly by such authorities on Yoruba culture as Ulli Beier, who says of Yoruba temple carvings, 'They help the worshippers to achieve the calm state of receptiveness that is necessary if the god is to manifest himself during the ceremonies.' (*Black Orpheus* 4, 1958). Of the carvers themselves, Ulli Beier says 'The Yoruba carver represents this heightened state, this intensified experience which is the purpose of *orisha* worship. The final impression of harmony which the carver achieves is the result of controlled tension, of rigid form imposed on the pressure which seems to come from inside the carving' (*Black Orpheus* 4). Again, in *Art In Nigeria*, 1960, Beier says 'To the African the act of creation is the important thing. It is an attitude that keeps the art alive instead of prolonging the life of the object.' Slightly idealised as this view may be in relation to art elsewhere (it is not only African artists for whom the act of creation is the important thing), these comments serve to underline the importance and skill of Yoruba carvers. This was Demoke's heritage, and it has to be understood to some extent before Demoke himself becomes comprehensible. He is a sculptor in wood, inheritor of a long tradition with which he feels a direct and vitalising connection, and his work obsesses him.

Despite Demoke's devotion to his art, he has no head for heights. He is terrified and cannot go above a certain level. When he carved the totem, it was done on a tree sacred to *Oro*. The *Oro* cult, among the Yoruba, used to be responsible for killing those found guilty of practising witchcraft. In *A Dance of the Forests*, Oro seems to represent not only a cult god but also the punitive principle, or blind vengeance. Demoke had to have the top cut off the *araba* tree, in order to carve it, but he was unable to do so himself. Oremole, a follower of Oro, and Demoke's apprentice, climbed to the top and mocked Demoke for his inability. Demoke, infuriated, pulled Oremole down and he fell to his death. Then, possessed by his god Ogun, patron god of carvers, Demoke cut the top off the tree and carved the totem. Now, however, he bears the guilt for his apprentice's death, for having sacrificed a human life in the cause of his art and for the sake of his own pride. Demoke is not at any point forced or even persuaded to confess. He does so, out of his own need, but the process takes some time to bring about.

Rola admires Demoke for beheading the tree, and Obaneji (Forest Head) says 'It is the kind of action that redeems mankind, don't you think?' This probing has the effect of making Demoke irritated and nervous, but he does not speak yet about the thing that is really troubling him. Obaneji asks Demoke what kind of death he would prefer. God's questions—or our own deepest questions to ourselves—are always leading ones, and always the ones we would prefer to evade. Demoke replies—quickly, almost as though speaking the genuine truth without thinking—'A fall from a great height'. He feels it necessary then to explain. If he could climb to the top of the tree, the very top, he would willingly fall to his death afterwards. But this seems the rational or logical reason found afterwards by someone who has voiced a portion of his own truth without fully comprehending it. Demoke seems to be both afraid of heights and to be fascinated by them. In the midst of his great need to create there also exists a strong thread of self-destruction. Forest Head admits that he is trying to uncover their death wishes, for he questions Adenebi the counsellor, who refuses to reply, and then says to Rola, 'Since the Orator won't tell us his death-wish, perhaps you will.' It is perhaps a little unfortunate that Soyinka felt he had to introduce psychological jargon at this point. Demoke's dual nature would have been sufficiently defined without it.

The course of the play is moving inexorably towards Demoke's confession. The Dead Woman and Dead Man reappear, and the Dead Man says 'When I died, I fell into the understreams....beneath the great ocean—'. Demoke immediately becomes anxious and asks 'Did you meet Oremole the bonded carver? Does he accuse me?' Forest Head tells Demoke that he need not speak, but Demoke must now face what he has done, and speak it aloud.

> Down, down I plucked him, screaming on Oro,
> Before he made hard obeisance to his earth
> My axe was executioner at Oro's neck.

Having pulled his apprentice down, Demoke was able to cut the top off the tree and to carve the totem.

> ...and I
> Demoke, sat on the shoulders of the tree,
> My spirit set free and singing, my hands,
> My father's hands possessed by demons of blood
> And I carved three days and nights till tools
> Were blunted, and these hands, my father's hands
> Swelled big as the tree-trunk. Down I came
> But Ogun touched me at the forge, and I slept
> Weary at his feet.

The interesting factor here is Demoke's sense of exhilaration. Soyinka is no liberal humanist. He is not dealing with man in any idealised sense. He is dealing with the violence which is the other side of the coin of every personality, even the gentlest. It has been possible for Demoke, true artist and carver as he is, committed to the celebration of life, to be released into his greatest creative effort not by love but by rage and pride. Soyinka is always reminding us of the inconvenient terrors of the human spirit. The process of art is seen partly in terms of possession by the god and partly in terms of Demoke's necessity to face within himself the existence of the opposing forces of creation and destruction. Demoke is constantly torn two ways. He has humility towards his art, even feeling that he himself is not entirely the originator of his skill, 'my hands, my father's hands...', and yet he has enormous self-pride, 'I, Demoke, sat on the shoulders of the tree, my spirit set free and singing...' He needs to create, but he is also capable of the destruction both of others and of himself.

The forest spirits, including Murete the tree imp and Aroni the Lame One, have entered, unknown to the people, and have discussed the presence of the two un-illustrious dead. Murete says to Aroni, 'They asked Forest Father for illustrious ancestors and you sent them accusers.' But after Demoke's self-facing in the form of the admission of the acts, Ogun his protector god enters as though to prevent the dead from becoming accusers in the way Murete means. Ogun, a strong and sympathetic figure, tries to exonerate Demoke.

> The crime, if crime it was, lies on my head...I killed
> The proud one, who would not bow araba's head
> When the gifted hands of Demoke, son and son
> To carvers would pass his spirit into wood.

Ogun says that he will not desert Demoke, and seeks to take all the responsibility on to himself. But the unfolding of the bond between past and present cannot be prevented by either naïve men or naïve gods. Ogun is a god, and he wishes to protect Demoke, who is his man, but this does not prove to be possible.

The human community next tries to prevent the unfolding of the past. Demoke's father, and Agboreko—Elder of Sealed Lips, whose pompously reiterated byword is 'Proverb to bones and silence'—enter together, and Demoke's father plans to get rid of the dead pair by getting a beat-up lorry nicknamed the Chimney of Ereko to drive through the forest, shedding smoke and petrol fumes. Demoke's father, sadly uncertain of himself, disillusioned with the ancestors, says, 'The guests we were sent are slaves and lackeys. They have only come to undermine our strength. To preach to us how ignoble we are.'

And Adenebi, the counsellor, pathetic in his stupidity, says, 'I had thought how splendid it would all be. Purple robes, white horses dressed in gold—By the way, I really ought to tell you how disappointed I was with your son's handwork. Don't you think it was rather pagan?' Adenebi wants the unreal splendours of the past, but cannot see the present splendour of Demoke's carving, any more than he can see the true nature of the Dead Woman and Dead Man, who will turn out to be not as shabby as he thinks. Adenebi's view has been so corrupted by his own greed that when the gods offer him honesty in any form he cannot even see what he is being offered.

The dead are moving into an increasingly important position. Their true roles have not yet been revealed, but omens are cast now. Masked dancers enter, almost as though they were *Egungun* bearing the ancestors' spirits, and a dirge-man chants the refrain, 'Leave the dead some room to dance.'

Agboreko, prototype of the village elder, wise yet self-congratulating, dignified yet not beyond being flustered by the unexpected, consults the divining methods of the board and kernels and says—hopefully, or perhaps whistling in the dark— 'If they are the dead and we are the living, then we are their children. They shan't curse us.'

But the reeking old lorry, the Chimney of Ereko, thunders into the forest. Demoke's father says, in primly idiotic explanation, 'I sent for it. For fumigation.' Humour is never very far away in Soyinka's writing, and it can combine strangely and yet rightly with the grotesque, the grave, the sinister. Agboreko, knowing more, says 'Will you never believe that you cannot get rid of ancestors with the little toys of children?' The past is within. We put our faith in the external, in mechanisms which look as though they might bulldoze even ghosts. But the ghosts rise to confront us once again after the petrol fumes have evaporated. The lorry crashes and smokes through the forest, and the forest creatures and spirits are driven out, a weird crew, holding leaves to their noses against the stench.

At this moment, with everything shaken, even Adenebi, the dense counsellor, is at last propelled into some revelation of his inner self— 'I have always lived in mortal fear of being lost.' And yet when Forest Head, still probing, asks *who* was responsible for the burning lorry and the lives lost, and *who* took the bribes, Adenebi says, very movingly, 'I—do not wish to know you. I want to be left alone.' Adenebi is irretrievably corrupt, but he is still a man whose pain is real. His tragedy is that he cannot face either God or himself.

Forest Head (now increasingly seen in his true role as supreme deity) majestically leads Demoke, Rola and Adenebi deeper into the forest, saying he is taking them to 'the welcoming of the dead'. Neither men nor gods can now stop the past revealing itself in order to reveal to the present its own face. But Demoke the carver is the only one who is really open to the revelation. Fear has closed Adenebi and Rola. Whatever words are spoken, these two will not be able to hear.

A Dance of the Forests is divided into two parts. As Part II opens, Eshuoro enters. Eshuoro is described as 'the wayward flesh of Oro', which seems a vague definition, but the spirit himself comes across so vividly that no one could possibly have any difficulty in identifying his purpose or personality. In fact, Soyinka has here combined two Yoruba cult gods—Oro, punitive and revengeful, and Eshu, who is the Yoruba trickster god, the embodiment of uncertainty, caprice, trouble, the inexplicable malice of fate. Eshuoro talks to Murete, and it is clear he hopes to spoil what he calls 'Aroni's harmless little ceremony. His welcoming of the dead.' Eshuoro, who is a nasty bit of work, is angry at the lopping off of Oro's tree, and he intends to create whatever confusion and trouble he can. He says, 'Aroni means to let the humans judge themselves', and 'He means to let them go afterwards.' Aroni is acting as Forest Head's right-hand spirit, in an attempt neither to judge nor to punish the living but to bring them to some greater awareness. But Eshuoro is determined that the humans will not escape from this drama without punishment and suffering—not even deserved suffering, just suffering, for Eshuoro would like to see them squirm. Murete the tree imp says 'Eshuoro, you wouldn't dare.' Eshuoro replies—showing, perhaps, more awareness of the situation than Ogun has done, for if the devil is nothing else, he is always clever— 'Not by my hand. But if the humans, as always, wreak havoc on their own heads, who are we to stop them? Don't they always decide their own lives?' The struggle now begins to take on the proportions of a battle of gods. Forest Head wants to direct the humans towards self-awareness, but although he is the supreme deity, his powers cannot be absolute, for he is not interested in puppets who are manipulated. Eshuoro wants to drive men into the deepest slavery, which is to make them for ever prey to their own violence and their own fear. But at least some of the gods know something that the humans do not—living men are ultimately responsible for their own lives. This is reminiscent of Ogun's great and yet unavailing effort to take all of Demoke's responsibility on his own head. However much God cares about men, he cannot bear all the responsibility for men's actions, for man is a free agent and yet at the same time linked to and dependent upon the gods and the ancestors.

Eshuoro, in a particularly threatening speech, reveals his own power which is basically the power of fear.

> Oro is the nothing that the eye beholds,
> Spirits of the dead eat and drink of me...

And again,

> Demoke, son and son again to pious carvers,
> Have you lost fear? Demoke, renegade, beware
> The slanted eye of night...

If Demoke has lost fear, then he is free and cannot be harmed by Eshuoro, the turbulent spirit of destruction, violence and malevolence. But has Demoke really lost fear? He has faced certain things in himself. He has accepted his ability to create and his tendency towards violence. But how will he react to the revelation of the past?

The past is presented as a play within the play. The Forest Crier announces it with the striking of a gong and with the words:

> Sons and subjects of Forest Father, and all
> That dwell in his domain, take note, this night
> Is the welcome of the dead, when spells are cast
> And the dead invoked by the living, only such
> May resume their body corporeal as are summoned
> When the understreams that whirl them endlessly
> Complete a circle.

Among those watching are Forest Head, now appearing as himself and no longer in disguise, and his helper Aroni. Present also are Adenebi the counsellor, Rola the whore, and Demoke the carver. The scene which is re-created for this audience is the court of Mata Kharibu, 'about eight centuries back'. Aroni comments ironically, 'One of their great empires. I forget which.'

It becomes clear that we are witnessing archetypes. The same basic characters go on and are reborn into each successive generation. Whatever individual forms they may take, they hark back to forgotten ancestors. Madame Tortoise, the unscrupulous and self-seeking woman, lacking tenderness and filled only with ambition, is the ancestress of Rola. Eight centuries back she was the wife of the emperor Mata Kharibu. The court poet was Demoke in a previous life. The Historian, speaking only what his master wishes to hear, was of course Adenebi. The Soothsayer was Agboreko, Elder of Sealed Lips. All these, in their past selves, have their present characters and characteristics. The poet lets his novice fall to his death in rescuing the queen's canary from the roof-top. This particular parallel is inadequate—it does not measure up at all to Demoke's agonised slaying of his mocking apprentice Oremole, and in consequence it seems strained. The court poet despises the queen, Madame Tortoise, but although he refers to her in asides as a slut, he permits himself to be ordered utterly by her, the bitch goddess, because at heart his own violence is satisfied by the novice's death coupled with the sexual overtones of the queenly command.

But the real revelation of the past is yet to come. Demoke, Rola and Adenebi are seen in their past roles as essentially their present selves, although the Demoke of the past seems entirely a more naïve and less inner-knowing man. But then we see that these three are not the only present-day beings to appear in the drama of the past. The Dead Man, the shabby ancestor, has in fact been a Captain of genuine integrity. Mata Kharibu, representative of the kingly past, whose grandeur, such as it was, was based on ruthlessness, says

'Do you dare to question my words?' And the Warrior (the Dead Man) replies, 'No, terrible one, only your commands.' The Warrior refuses to command his men to fight a frivolous and unjust war, comparable to the Trojan war, over the possession of Madame Tortoise, whom Mata Kharibu stole from a rival king. The physician at the court tries to dissuade the Warrior from his stand, implying that history will not appreciate the actions of a man of integrity. The Warrior knows this only too well, for he says, 'Unborn generations will, as we have done, eat up one another.' The physician pleads with the Warrior to release his men from allegiance to him. Suddenly, then, the Warrior understands. His men are loyal more to him, personally, than they are to Mata Kharibu. He sees that the Establishment is actually afraid. 'You are afraid. Mata Kharibu is afraid.' The physician says, 'For heaven's sake, do not speak so loudly.' The Warrior replies, 'But I am right. Perhaps I have started a new disease that catches quickly.' Soyinka is not talking about one country only, or one era. The 'new disease', essentially, can only be the release from fear, the inner freedom which permits men to take responsibility for their own actions and to say *No* to leaders who would make them believe that they are powerless.

The Historian (Adenebi, as unctuous and self-deceptive as he is in the present) advises his master, Mata Kharibu, about the fate of the rebellious Warrior—'This renegade must be treated as a slave.' The emperor agrees—'Sell that man down the river.' And so it is. The man who questions authority is sold as a slave. Before his final departure, Madame Tortoise approaches him. She tries to persuade him to overthrow Mata Kharibu and take her as his queen. The Warrior refuses. Madame Tortoise brings in the Warrior's pregnant wife (the present-day Dead Woman) and says she does not intend to be spurned by a common soldier. The Warrior's wife begs for mercy, but Madame Tortoise has the Warrior made into a eunuch.

In the audience of gods who are watching the re-creation of the past, Eshuoro, Ogun and Aroni discuss what they have seen and its relationship to the present. Ogun wants to protect Demoke; Eshuoro wants to destroy him. Forest Head is trying to teach not only men but gods. Ogun still maintains 'He has no guilt. I, Ogun, swear that his hands were mine in every action of his life.' But Forest Head replies, 'Will you all never rid yourselves of these conceits?' The gods are not and cannot be totally responsible for human actions.

A Questioner appears, accompanied by the Dead Woman. She is asked about her ever-pregnant state— 'What made you deaf! To the life that begged within you? Had he no claim?' Forest Head tells her '...there is no choice but one of suffering.' The Dead Woman's child is to have considerable significance in the settling of Demoke's fate, but no clue is yet given as to what that significance will be. The Dead Man (Warrior) now reveals that after his castration he was sold as a slave for a flask of rum. This must be one of the very few places in contemporary Nigerian literature in which the question of the slave trade is mentioned. Either it is too far back in the past, or else there is some deep reluctance to look at it. Soyinka here deals with the guilt of the old African empires who sold their own people as slaves. The Questioner says:

> Three hundred rings have formed
> Three hundred rings within that bole
> Since Mulieru went away, was sold away
> And the tribe was scattered.

One searing effect of the slave trade lay in the fact that it was not only a wound inflicted from the outside. It was also a self-inflicted wound, and Soyinka seems to be saying here that the responsibility for this part of it must be examined, looked at. The result of the slave trade, of course, was a rending of the whole fabric of society— 'The tribe was scattered.'

The Questioner asks about the Warrior, 'What did he prove?' saying that the Warrior's refusal to play the game of Mata Kharibu and Madame Tortoise was 'surely the action of a fool'. But the Questioner proves to be Eshuoro's jester, and his outlook is therefore loaded against man.

Forest Head now commands that the Dead Woman be relieved of her child, saying '...let the tongue of the unborn, stilled for generations, be loosened.'

A complicated masquerade now begins, to introduce what will finally prove to be Demoke's partial choice of his own fate. Demoke, Rola and Adenebi appear in symbolic roles, wearing masks, as the Dead Woman enters with the Half Child. Each of the human three becomes possessed and speaks, in the manner of humans possessed by the spirit of the masks. This elaborate masquerade scene very nearly collapses under the strain of too many whirling symbols. The Spirit of the Palm, the Spirit of Darkness, the Spirit of Precious Stones, the Spirit of the Pachyderms, the Spirit of the Sun—all express in intense poetry the violation of nature by man.

Basically, however, it is the Half Child who will soon be the central figure in this scene. He expresses his plight and enables the audience to see what manner of being he is.

> I who flee from womb
> To branded womb, cry it now

I'll be born dead
I'll be born dead.

He is an *abiku*, a child born with death in its soul. The Yoruba, like many other West African peoples, have a belief that the children who die at birth or in infancy are always the same children, born time and time again only to die, for they long for their companions in the spirit world and will not stay with their earthly families. Here Soyinka uses this figure of the *abiku* both in the traditional Yoruba way and as a symbol of that death-in-the-soul which is a portion of every man. Ulli Beier, in an article about *A Dance of the Forests*, says that the *abiku* 'symbolises man's incomprehensible fascination for causing extinction in his own image' (*Black Orpheus* 8).

But there are further diversions before the role of the Half Child is fully revealed. The Ants enter with a precise and clear warning for the leaders of mankind. They represent what is usually called the masses or the common people, the pawns of fate, the cannon fodder, those who suffer most from the wars of the leaders and from political tribulations not of their own making. One of the Ants says:

I thought, staying this low
They would ignore me. I am the one
That tried to be forgotten.

The Ants' refrain is an old old one, a voice which Soyinka makes certain will be heard at the Gathering of the Tribes—

We are the headless bodies when
The spade of progress delves.

And again,

We are the ever legion of the world,
Smitten, for—'the good to come'.

Soyinka rejects here the philosophy that the end justifies the means. There is in the scene with the Ants a deep compassion for the unspeaking, the inchoate, the individuals who live as a crowd but who are *not* a crowd, those who are powerless because they believe themselves to be so.

The masquerade continues with the entry of the Triplets, who are abstractions in irony. The first says, 'Has anyone found the Means? I am the End that will justify it.' The second says, 'I am the Greater Cause—excusing the crimes of today for tomorrow's mirage.' The third says, 'I find I am Posterity. Can no one see on what milk I have been nourished?' Here Soyinka seems merely to be reinforcing unnecessarily the point he has already made with the Ants.

The focal point of the masquerade is reached when Ogun (the creative force) and Eshuoro (the destructive force) fight for the Half Child. The culmination of the play takes place with the intense Dance of the Half Child, in which the Mother (Dead Woman) and Demoke are also protagonists. The Dead Woman says,

> Child, your hand is pure as sorrow
> Free me of this endless burden,
> Let this gourd, let this gourd
> Break beyond my hearth—

In her role as Mother, she wants to relinquish her child to the world of the living and also to be rid of the burden of the death-in-the-soul, yet she feels ambiguously about it, for she does not want to relinquish the child entirely. In her role as Ancestress, she wants the living to take responsibility for that part of themselves which longs for self-destruction, yet she is still not quite able to set the living free to follow totally their own course.

There are two possible endings for *A Dance of the Forests*, although both add up to much the same thing. The original ending had to be modified for the production of the play by Soyinka's company, The 1960 Masks, because the first version of the Dance of the Half Child proved too difficult to stage. As originally written, the Half Child is tossed from the Triplets to Eshuoro, and is finally taken by Demoke, in whose hands the decision lies—will the *abiku* join the world of the living or will it be returned to the Dead Woman, to be born over again? Demoke, in a gesture of instinctive human warmth, returns the child to its mother. Forest Head, deeply troubled, asks Demoke if he knows the meaning of his act. But Demoke goes ahead. The Half Child is returned, and Eshuoro shouts in triumph.

In its modified version, the Half Child is wearing an *ibeji* figure on one wrist, a carved figure worn by twins. It is the carved figure, not the actual child, that is snatched away and tossed around from god to god. The advantage of this version in production is plain, unless there happened to be a cast of skilled acrobats and a child whose off-stage mother did not worry unduly about him. The Half Child himself clings to Demoke, and Forest Head asks Demoke if he knows the meaning of his act, that is, the meaning of what Demoke must now decide. The *ibeji* figure is returned by Demoke to the Half Child. Ogun and Eshuoro clash, but not conclusively. Demoke is exhausted and sinks to his knees. The Dead Woman then retrieves her child.

Ulli Beier, writing of this play in *Black Orpheus* 8, says of the ending, 'Demoke...is the protagonist among the human group of characters. Being the only creative person he is the only one worthy of redemption and he is the centre of the struggle between Ogun and Eshuoro. Demoke hesitates a while with the Half Child in his arms. Finally he goes and returns it to its Mother....Demoke returns the Half Child because he does not wish to live under the compulsion of old ideas perpetually reborn. It is for Demoke that the vision of a new life is opened at the end.' This interpretation of the play's ending is questionable. What about Eshuoro's shout of triumph? And Forest Head's asking if Demoke really understands the meaning of his action? It is hard to avoid the conclusion that the wrong decision has been taken by Demoke.

Una Maclean, in an article on 'Soyinka's International Drama' in *Black Orpheus* 15, sees the Half Child as the means by which Demoke finds peace, by shielding the child from the wrath of Ogun. The Half Child, she says, is 'the new child or nation...born from the warrior who was the one man of integrity from the past. But without the protection of the artist the child remains in danger of destruction.' Una Maclean's article is an illuminating study of Soyinka's work, but this interpretation of the play's ending does not seem satisfactory. Demoke does not shelter the Child from the wrath of Ogun. Ogun, after all, is Demoke's own protector, and it is Eshuoro who represents the forces of destruction. Also, to see the Half Child as 'the new nation', going steadily onward and upward with the 'protection of the artist', seems to be wishful thinking.

With both endings of *A Dance of the Forests*, although there are subtle differences as well as the obvious difference of the use of the *ibeji* figure instead of the actual child in the dance, the main point centres around the fact that the Half Child is the *abiku*, the child born with the will to die in its soul, or in slightly different terms, with the death wish. Eshuoro wants the Half Child to be returned to its mother, the Dead Woman, because this means that the old pattern will begin all over again—the never-ending cycle, the desire for oblivion born again into each soul, rarely recognised or admitted openly and therefore a part of our portion of fear, that fear of the unknown which creates external demons in the shape of internal ones. In the end, Demoke has been able to face a great deal within himself—the never-to-be-understood need to create, something which remains mysterious to him, the violence and ruthlessness which represents the other side of his nature, the guilt which he bears for the destructive acts he has done. In some areas Demoke accepts the responsibility for his own actions; he accepts the knowledge that he is capable of destruction or corruption, that he is not apart from mankind but is fallible like everyone else. But he is not totally freed from fear. What he cannot face is his own urge towards self-destruction. Innocently, or in some conventional way (a child should go to its mother) he returns the child born-to-die to the Dead, to the ancestors, from whence it will be re-born and re-born. It is a concept not yet to be faced openly by Demoke—that we may with our hands and hearts desire to create, but still have to grapple with the other, the unacknowledged darkness, the desire to make a final end, to fall from the elusive heights, to cease to have to bear the burden of the ancestors who are incessantly re-born within ourselves. Demoke is a man caught in tensions which do not admit any immediate solution and may not ever admit any solution at all. But these tensions do not make it impossible for him to live as a man and a carver. Demoke can go on, not knowing everything about himself, but at least able to live with the knowledge of what he does know, able to come to some terms with his past, able to face a future which must always remain uncertain but which does not totally sever him from his known world. His act, in returning the Half Child to the world of the dead, whence it will continue to re-enter the human community harmfully, is only in one sense done in innocence. In another sense, it is the act of someone who has faced as much as he can and who must accept that it is man's fate to carry along with him some of the anguish of the past, some of the unsolved mysteries at the core of his own heart.

In terms of social themes, Soyinka seeks to establish a relationship with the past which will neither stifle and dominate man nor sever him from his roots. In terms of psychological or spiritual themes, Soyinka seeks to make us look at those aspects of ourselves which we would rather not see, to induce us to examine them and at least admit their existence.

A crucial speech is that of Forest Head, just before the Dance of the Half Child. This is the supreme deity speaking about man and free will, and the concepts here have strongly Christian undertones, combined with the writer's highly individual view of the deity and of mankind.

> ...I must persist, knowing that nothing is ever altered. My secret is my eternal burden—to pierce the encrustations of soul-deadening habit, and bare the mirror of original nakedness—knowing full well, it is all futility. Yet I must do this alone, and no more, since to intervene is to be guilty of contradiction, and yet to remain altogether unfelt is to make my long-rumoured ineffectuality complete; hoping that when I have tortured awareness from their souls, that perhaps, only perhaps, in new beginnings....

Man has been created with free will, and however much God may break His heart over the acts of His creatures, they must continue to act by themselves, for 'to intervene is to be guilty of contradiction'. Yet, 'to remain altogether unfelt' is to give men cause to believe that they have created God in their own image only out of weakness and fear. Forest Head's view, which he tries to communicate to the other gods who are aspects of himself, seems to be that the dilemma of gods is that however much they may love or hate mankind, in the end it is men themselves who decide their own fates, not in any theoretical way, not in a state of vacuum, but with deep emotional reference to their fathers and their gods. Maybe at some point our ancestors and our gods will be free of us. But not quite yet.

There are some parts of *A Dance of the Forests* which seem overloaded. There are moments when the multiplicity of themes creates the feeling that there are a few too many plates spinning in the air—some of them speed by without being properly seen, and some crash down. But these are minor flaws in a work of enormous richness. The characters of Demoke the carver, Rola the whore, Adenebi the corrupt counsellor, Agboreko the elder, all come alive, as do the gods Ogun and Eshuoro and the forest spirits Murete and Aroni. The use of the mask and dance idiom reinforces the splendid vividness of the play and heightens the sense of mystery which is essential to the 'welcoming of the dead'. Humour and poetry exist side by side in this play in ways that might be disastrous but never are.

A Dance of the Forests is pertinent not only to Africa and to newly independent countries there, but also to any and every man's relationship with his past, with his gods and with the concealed parts of his own heart.

The Road

In *The Road*, Soyinka deals with fewer themes than he does in *A Dance of the Forests*. The central theme is stated unambiguously in a note to the producer which prefaces the published play, where Soyinka speaks of '...the part psychic, part intellectual grope of Professor towards the essence of death'. In the play itself this theme is developed windingly and with a great many apparent detours, but in fact the main road is never lost sight of, and the end of Professor's bizarre spiritual journey has an unquestionable inevitability about it.

Although there is much more humour in *The Road* than in *A Dance of the Forests*, the tone of the play as a whole is more sombre. Perhaps this is because in *A Dance of the Forests*, Demoke's dilemma is a spiritual one, but one which is thoroughly grasped by himself at a verbal level. In *The Road*, although Professor verbalises constantly his own situation, the equally central conflict of the driver Kotonu takes place at an emotional level—he sees only glimpses of his own truth; he suspects or half suspects what may be at the core of the mystery, but for the most part he is afraid and in despair, and these feelings are communicated directly and movingly.

No more contemporary characters could be imagined than the drivers, thugs and layabouts who move through *The Road*. Yet the play makes use of sources which go very far back in Yoruba culture, and the characters themselves show the clashing and blending of past and present. In particular, the Festival of Ogun, mentioned earlier in this chapter, is used by Soyinka with tremendously dramatic effect, for Ogun is the patron god of drivers and the heart of this play's meaning lies in an event which took place at the last drivers' festival.

Once more, as in *A Dance of the Forests*, Soyinka uses drums to underline his meaning and to heighten whatever emotion is the dominant one in a scene. He uses masks as well, but here his use of this traditional drama form has narrowed and deepened. Unlike *A Dance of the Forests*, in *The Road* the maskers are never used for any broad spectacular effects. A group of masked dancers enters once, in a flashback which takes us to the Festival of Ogun. But chiefly, the use of masks is limited to one particularly significant mask, and in this play the whole concept of possession by the spirit of the mask is explored minutely, in both religious and psychological terms.

With the traditional Yoruba *Egungun*, the state of possession can take place only with the proper ritual, at the time of festival, and with the accompaniment of the drums which speak the key phrases and establish the pattern and pace of the entire procedure. The state of possession may be self-hypnosis, but even if it is, this does not make it any less genuine. When the wearer of an *Egungun* mask experiences possession, he performs the ritual dance with a skill beyond his usual. His own spirit has momentarily departed, or is held in some hiatus, and the ancestral spirit has taken over. In *The Road* Soyinka uses the word '*Egungun*' to refer to the mask and its wearer, together, in various stages of possession. The mask by itself, when not being worn by its true wearer, is simply 'the mask', a thing, a carved object. When the only man who can rightfully wear it puts it on, together they become the *Egungun*.

Professor runs a kind of flophouse-bar for drivers, mainly those who are unemployed or who have become thugs or layabouts, the rejects of the road.

It is situated near the church where Professor used to be the Sunday school teacher, lay reader and chief pillar. Now Professor earns his living by forging drivers' licences and by salvaging bits from crashes and wrecked vehicles, and then selling them as spare parts.

Samson and Kotonu have come to Professor's place because Kotonu has lost his nerve and will not drive any more. Samson has been driver's tout, that is, he has worked with Kotonu to rustle up business for their passenger lorry. Samson will not desert his friend, and keeps hoping that he can persuade Kotonu to go back on the road. As the play opens, Samson mocks Salubi, who has a uniform but no job or driver's licence. Salubi, none too bright but always willing to join in a game, says 'As I am standing so, I am fit to drive the Queen of England,' and the wisecracking Samson replies, 'One look at you and she will abdicate.' Soyinka is often at his best in scenes where humour and compassionate irony combine, as in this scene in which Samson and Salubi, both jobless, dream of what they would do if they were millionaires. Samson has no difficulty in deciding— 'Me, I will buy all the transport lorries in the country, then make Kotonu the head driver.' All through the play, Samson's deep affection for Kotonu is brought out with humour and sadness, without ever falling into the trap of sentimentality.

Professor returns with a road sign (BEND) which has obviously and recently been ignored, for he has picked it up at the scene of an accident. Professor, we soon realise, spends only half his time running his dual business. The other half is spent in searching for the Word. For much of the play we are not quite certain just how mad Professor is, or whether in fact he is mad at all. He talks obscurely, sometimes confusedly, and often at cross-purposes with others, who fail to understand him, but his obsession is single-minded and very clear to him. At this point, all we see of him is that his pursuit of the Word is some undefined quest for meaning. He is excited by the sign he has found— 'God God God but there is a mystery in everything. A new discovery every hour...' Samson, on the table, still wearing the paraphernalia of his millionaire act (the tablecloth and Professor's glasses) tries to tell Professor that this is not the right place and that Professor has lost his way. Professor pretends to believe Samson's simple deception—and yet, because he is always looking for signs and omens, he is also made genuinely anxious by Samson's telling him that 'you must have missed your way', for Professor is never content with interpreting words on one level only. Kotonu, in order to allow Samson a way of ending his amateurish charade, offers to accompany Professor, and Professor tells Kotonu that he has a new wonder to show him— 'a madness where a motor car throws itself against a tree—Gbram!

And showers of crystals flying on broken souls.' Samson enquires with alarm if there has been an accident, and Professor, with the enigmatic sternness he so often shows to those around him, says 'Are you ignorant of the true path to the Word? It is never an accident.' Kotonu has been involved in an accident, and Samson wants to protect him against the sight of another. But Professor, who habitually sleeps in the nearby church graveyard, says 'My bed is among the dead, and when the road raises a victory cry to break my sleep, I hurry to a disgruntled swarm of souls full of spite for their rejected bodies.' He seeks out road accidents in no simple way. We catch a whiff of necrophilia, perhaps, but the souls of the violently departed are of greater interest to Professor than their broken bodies. He ponders meanings at the scene of every accident he finds—and, because he possesses some cold shrewdness under his mystical-oratorical manner, he also takes the opportunity of collecting whatever salvage can be scavenged. He tells Samson, in words whose meaning does not really penetrate our consciousness until much later in the play, 'The Word may be found companion not to life but to Death.'

After Professor has gone out with Kotonu, Salubi reveals to Samson that Kotonu plans to take over the Accident Store, that part of Professor's Bar which deals in the spare parts gleaned from crashes. Until recently the Store has been managed by Sergeant Burma, who also used to do most of the salvaging of wrecks, but Burma has died himself in an accident not long ago. Samson is horrified that Kotonu, one of the best-known drivers on the road, could even contemplate taking over such a vulture's profession.

Samson is a semi-educated man, wise in some ways of the world, utterly naïve in others, acting mainly out of emotional pressures such as his desire to protect Kotonu and restore him to a driver's job. Samson frequently denies his belief in traditional Yoruba religion, the old 'superstitions', yet some aspects of the old gods are so much a part of him that he takes them for granted, hardly realising they are there. Anxious now about Kotonu, Samson says that Kotonu has foolishly always refused to kill a dog. 'Why, I ask him, why? Don't you know a dog is Ogun's meat? Take warning, Kotonu. Before it's too late take warning and kill us a dog.'

When Kotonu arrives back from the accident, with motor parts, the layabouts sing in Yoruba the Drivers' Dirge, accompanied by the drums. Soyinka uses Yoruba throughout the play for the drum songs, partly no doubt because only the Yoruba words would fit the drum rhythms, but in the published play he gives translations of the Yoruba songs. Part of the translation of the Drivers' Dirge is:

It's a long long road to heaven
It's a long road to heaven, Driver
Go easy a-ah go easy driver
It's a long long road to heaven
My Creator, be not harsh on me—

This song sets the tone of the entire play, and it is used on several occasions as a refrain.

When Samson accuses Kotonu of taking over Sergeant Burma's business and deserting his own calling as a driver, Kotonu says, 'A man gets tired of feeling too much.' Kotonu is not inarticulate, we see, although he is silent so much of the time. He is a man so disturbed that he frequently cannot make the effort to speak and try to explain, a man who thinks all the time about his crisis but who understands it only in fragments. He cannot bear to go back on to the road. Whatever happened to him, it has almost destroyed him. In a magnificent speech he mourns the lost drivers and drivers' touts, not those who were rejects of the road, but those who were its kings—and its victims.

> Where is Zorro who never returned from the North without a
> basket of guinea-fowl eggs? Where is Akanni the Lizard? I have
> not seen any other tout who would stand on the lorry's roof and
> play the samba at sixty miles an hour. Where is Sigidi Ope?
> Where is Sapele Joe who took on six policemen at the crossing
> and knocked them all into the river?

Soyinka has a remarkable ability to bring his characters to life. Apart from anything that is going on under the surface, the open plain of this play is filled with characters who come across so directly that it is a pleasure simply to listen to them being themselves. The crooked politician, Chief-In-Town, exchanges a greeting with one of the drivers, Say Tokyo Kid, a greeting that is almost a replica of a drum salute.

> *Say Tokyo:* Chief-In-Town!
> *Chief:* The Captain!
> *Say Tokyo:* Chief-In-Town!
> *Chief:* Say Tokyo Kid!
> *Say Tokyo:* No dirty timber, thas me Chief.

Say Tokyo Kid is captain of the thugs, and is addicted to hemp. He sells his services for any kind of dirty work, but he is also a man of belief where the old gods are concerned. He drives a vehicle which hauls the big timber. Ogun is his god, and the road is synonymous with Ogun. Say Tokyo feels that the only reason he has not yet been in an accident is that he understands and treats properly the spirits within the timber, for timber, as he knows, is not a dead load.

> Dead! You think a guy of timber is dead load. What you talking kid? You reckon you can handle a timber lorry like you drive your passenger truck. You wanna sit down and feel that dead load trying to take the steering from your hand. You kidding? There is a hundred spirits in every guy of timber trying to do you down cause you've trapped them in, see? There is a spirit in hell for every guy of timber. You reckon a guy just goes and cuts down a guy of timber. You gorra do it proper man or you won't live to cut another log. Dead men tell no tales kid. Until that guy is sawn up and turned to a bench or table, the spirit guy is still struggling inside it, and I don't fool around with him see....Why ain't I cut and bruised like all those guys? Cause timber don't turn against her own son see? I'm a son of timber.

Brash and flippant though he is, Say Tokyo Kid has within him a fearful reverence which in the end will make him an instrument of the gods and one of the chief protagonists in this play. His outlook is a mixture of the old religions with Christianity. The spirits within the timber—this is the traditional belief that none of the external world is essentially inanimate; everything has its indwelling spirit. The 'spirit in hell' has a peculiarly Christian ring. West African religions admitted the continuing existence of the spirits, who could turn nasty if not properly propitiated, but they did not generally assign them to an eternity of fiery furnaces. 'You gorra do it proper' is a traditional belief in the efficacy of the proper ritual—in fact, a belief in the disastrous consequences which attend the non-observance of proper ritual. It will turn up again in this play, and with the same character, Say Tokyo Kid. Soyinka introduces this theme here, only to return to it under much more intense circumstances.

Soyinka now begins to use to an even greater degree the method he has employed with Say Tokyo. He throws out clues, engages our interest and curiosity, then moves on, as though saying—remember this, for it will come up again, more significantly, later on. Nearly every writer does this, of course, and it would not be worth mentioning except for the fact that Soyinka does it a very great deal, and many of the meanings which are adumbrated early on in the play are totally mystifying at the time. This kind of foreshadowing is sometimes overworked by Soyinka, because the memory of the reader or audience is severely taxed in retaining a multitude of details which will later prove meaningful. Salubi, for example, prepares a meal for himself, and Samson discovers that the food consists of stockfish. Samson is thrown into consternation and tosses Salubi out. We sense some relation to Kotonu's fears here, and we realise that Samson is once again trying to protect Kotonu, but only much later on do we learn that Kotonu's father died in a crash which involved a lorry carrying a load of stockfish. There are perhaps too many threads like this, which have to be held on to mentally until Soyinka ties them into some revelation of meaning.

Samson continues to try to persuade Kotonu to return to the road. Kotonu, however, can only reply, 'It could have been us at the bridge.' They have recently come very close to an accident, and this has been the last straw to Kotonu, for the lorry that narrowly overtook them was the one that crashed through the rotten wood of the bridge. Kotonu seems bewildered and even cheated— 'But why they and not us? Their names weren't carved on the rotten wood.' Whose name, we begin to wonder, did Kotonu imagine *was* carved on the rotten wood? But when Professor returns to the Bar, Kotonu has dropped the question of the accident and seems anxious only about the appearance of Murano the palm-wine tapper.

Murano comes each evening with fresh palm-wine for Professor and his men, and Samson is worried that Kotonu, like so many derelict drivers, will become a drunk. 'Murano has become his evensong.' Samson reveals that it was he who paid for Kotonu's driving licence, although he has never complained because 'It was a good investment. Was.' And Kotonu says, 'Yes, was. Until this.' Kotonu then—surprisingly and shockingly—pulls out an Ogun mask from the Accident Store, and speaks of it.

> It has to stay with me.
> My humble quota to the harvest of the road.

Kotonu is very disturbed, and Samson cannot fully understand, or cannot bear to. But the tension is broken by a comic interchange between Professor and Salubi, who says he will commit suicide if Professor doesn't supply him with a forged driver's licence. Professor becomes inexplicably furious, calling Salubi 'false contractor to death', and Salubi, desperate for the licence, and willing to abase himself in any idiotic way that Professor apparently desires, promises 'Never say die—that is my motto from now on.' Samson, unable to resist testing the poor clown, chips in with such comments as 'Ten like you and soap factories close down,' to which the prostrate Salubi can only reply, 'Never say die.' Soyinka has the ability to mix comedy scenes like this one with the anguish of Kotonu and Professor's mysterious search for the Word, without any sense of jarring.

They are still waiting for Murano, and Professor now reveals that he found Murano 'in the back of a hearse' and looked after him when he was 'like a dog whose legs have been broken by a motor car'. The reference here to the dog (Ogun's sacrificial animal) cannot be accidental. We can sense, rather than see, that we are beginning to approach the core of the mystery.

The two questions really are these: why is Kotonu so afraid of the road, and what is Professor searching for in the elusive Word?

Professor tells Kotonu, 'You grope towards Murano, the one person in this world in whom the Word reposes.' But Murano is a mute. Such people, Professor maintains, 'have slept beyond the portals of secrets'. He points out that one of Murano's legs is shorter than the other and that he has one leg in each world. He says that the left foot is the one that 'rests on the slumbering chrysalis of the Word'. The reference here appears to be to the Yoruba Ogboni society, a cult whose god is Ile, the Earth, which they say existed before the other gods, just as Ogboni existed before the law. In the forms of worship prominence is given to the left side, a fact which is believed by Peter Morton-Williams to suggest 'that they perceive that they cannot reject one side of themselves, but must accept the unclean, that which is hidden and knowledge which is forbidden'. ('Yoruba Responses to the Fear of Death', *Africa*, 1960, vol. xxx). This description of the Ogboni cult expresses accurately what Professor is trying to do—to discover and accept knowledge believed by many to be forbidden.

It is not only the Ogboni who try to gain knowledge and perceptions of themselves which many people prefer to evade. The plays of Soyinka can be viewed through either the eyes of the traditional religions or those of contemporary psychology. Perhaps the two sets of concepts are more similar in essence than they appear to be, semantically and ritually. Professor's comments indicate a mind which seeks to know beyond the limits of defined and socially accepted knowledge. This seems to be a brave although foolhardy path. Is it, though? What does it really entail? The only thing we can confidently expect from Soyinka is that things will not turn out as anyone might on the surface expect them to do.

When Professor advises Samson to 'Find the Word' and tells him to ask Murano, Samson objects that Murano cannot talk. Professor, either in madness or cunning, replies, 'You see. They know what they are doing.' The gods, presumably, are guarding their own secrets. Murano is not a mute for nothing.

Deciding that the time has finally come for Salubi's driving licence, Professor takes Kotonu's licence and alters it to Salubi's name. Samson, in pain and alarm, protests, but Professor gently tells him, 'Lion-hearted Samson with an ass's head, can you not see that your friend will never drive again?' He explains that when he took Kotonu out to the scene of the accident this morning, Kotonu was forced past the point of return.

Samson tries persuasion by recounting as much of Kotonu's history as he knows—how Kotonu was born in the back of a lorry, and how his father had a push-truck. But the story gets out of hand, and it is Kotonu himself who reveals how his father died— 'of a lorry in his back. It beat his spine against a load of stockfish.' To Kotonu, 'Torn bodies on the road all smell of stockfish, have you noticed?' He wants desperately to escape and yet he finds himself increasingly shackled by these memories which now seem to relate to his own fate.

The layabouts return to the haven, and Professor is harsh with them. 'I offer you a purpose but you take unmeaning risks which means I, I must wait and hope that you return alive to fulfil the course I have drawn for you.'

This begins to sound sinister. 'The course I have drawn for you,' and 'I, I must wait…' As though he were justified in drawing a course for others? As though *his* having to wait was not to be borne? For the first time, the messianic aspect of Professor is revealed, or at least, the messianic quality he has in his own eyes. The victims from the bridge accident are being brought in, for funeral rites at the nearby church. Professor says of Kotonu and Samson, 'You were so near—perhaps in that is contained a promise. But I feel cheated just the same. Such a prodigal hearse and not one of you within it.' Why does he feel cheated? Does he want his small and un-select flock to die? Perhaps he does, yet it is impossible to believe in him as a figure of indifference or absolute cruelty. He is not that. He cares about his followers. What we do not yet know is *in what way* he cares about them.

As Part II opens, Professor is preparing Samson and Kotonu's statement to the police, regarding the bridge accident. Kotonu admits, 'Even before the bridge, I saw what was yet to happen.' Professor writes that the other lorry was 'pregnant with stillborns'. For Kotonu, the nightmare situation was heightened by the fact that the people had no faces. Samson explains that the lorry was from the north and had been going through heavy dust, so the people had put cloth over their faces. But the whole scene, in Kotonu's mind, has been changed by his own fears until he believes the other lorry carried a load of stockfish.

His terror becomes unbearable and breaks into a flashback of the bridge crash, where we see him, horrified, knowing the death was not meant for him and yet unable to understand why it was not, because of the guilt he bears for something else he has done, some event we do not yet know about. The drivers at the edge of this flashback scene, watching it from the present moment, begin to chant the Drivers' Dirge, as Samson— in a speech that expresses anguish half in terms of fearful belief, half in terms of mockery—pleads with Kotonu:

> Kill us a dog Kotonu, kill us a dog. Kill us a dog before the
> hungry god lies in wait and makes a substitute of me...Dog's
> intestines look messy to me he says—who asked him to like it?
> Ogun likes it that's all that matters. It's his special meat. Just run
> over the damned dog and leave it there, I don't ask you to stop
> and scoop it up for your next dinner. Serve Ogun his tit-bit so the
> road won't look at us one day and say Ho ho you two boys you
> look juicy to me. But what's the use? The one who won't give
> Ogun willingly will yield heavier meat by Ogun's designing.

As the flashback ends, Samson sees the layabouts returning from the funeral, and says, 'May we never walk when the road waits famished.' But Professor is angry and upset when he hears this. He claims that Samson has spoken blasphemy, but 'It is lucky for you that you brought a god on to my doorstep.' Samson does not comprehend at all, but Kotonu becomes agitated and begs Professor to explain. Professor refuses, saying 'Like you all I also wait...'

Professor tries to persuade Samson and Kotonu to form a syndicate, but the two young men do not see that Professor is not now talking of business but of the quest. And yet, in the external world, he is also trying to filch Samson and Kotonu's savings, for Professor is not a man to mean only one thing at a time. Integrity and guile coexist within him as naturally as the lamb and lion are said to lie down together in paradise. He fluctuates between despair and exultance. When Samson asks if he has any assets, Professor (in one of his up phases) replies confidently, 'Almost too much.' He points to his bundle of old papers and bills, for he believes that somewhere in there, in the rejected words, lies the Word, the Key, 'the moment of my rehabilitation'. Salubi brings him food which he gives away, saving only the old newspaper in which it was wrapped, and saying of the market foodseller:

> That woman of Tapa knows something, or else she is an
> unconscious medium. Oh God oh God, the enormity of
> hidden wisdoms—say the word in our time, O Lord, utter
> the hidden Word.

Poring over the old newspaper, Professor imagines he has found cabalistic signs, but Samson gently explains that he is actually looking at a football coupon, '...A cross here, or as the Tax Collector would say—Mr. Samson, his mark. And then a lot of O here and there. That is how to fill a football coupon.'

This is a most moving scene. Professor may be deluded and demented, but if he is, he is in company with most of mankind. Who has not felt the same thing—'Oh God oh God, the enormity of hidden wisdoms'—and with the same unspoken and yet clear recognition of the feeling's absurdity?

Kotonu is anxious about Murano again. Professor caustically says, 'What can happen to Murano? A shadow in the valley of the shadow of!' Professor begins to explain his own estrangement from the Church. He was sacked for blasphemy, after he had come to see that the puritanical preaching of the Church, and the 'holy war' against such shacks and bars as his present one, did not constitute the Word, as he had once thought. He finally realised that the Church had been a kind of spiritual prison for him. 'One day I thought, I have never really known what lies beyond that window.' His mind has been deeply affected by the Church's rejection of him, however, for 'They cast me from grace'. He seems to be torn between a disillusionment with Christianity and a need to be reinstated, received again into that community. Yet this need he feels to be hopeless. He believes that the window of the Church is kept closed, and he will not listen to Samson, who tells him the window is wide open.

It is not yet possible to see Professor's ultimate goal. In relation to the Church, he suffers some painful dichotomy of mind. It hurts him that they cast him out, yet it was really he himself who caused his break with the Church because he could no longer believe in the rigid over-simplified certainties that were taught there. Professor is seeking his own way. Sometimes he seems to be seeking it for his own redemption, while at other times, as when he speaks of the Church, he appears to long for the revelation of some indisputable Word so he can cast it in the astonished faces of his former Sunday school colleagues. His references are a constant mixture of the ancient religions and Christianity. He quotes fragments of the Bible— 'the valley of the shadow'—and uses Christian terminology—for example, being cast from grace. His evening ritual with the palm-wine is a caricature of Christian communion. Yet he is thoroughly aware of the old gods, and in the final playing out of the drama which Professor contrives or causes to happen, it is the god Ogun who figures most significantly.

The presence of Ogun has been gathering and strengthening throughout the play. There have been many references to him, such as Samson's frenzied plea for Kotonu to kill a dog because the dog is 'Ogun's meat'. Now, with Professor speaking like an Old Testament prophet— 'Even atonement wilts before the Word'—we are suddenly plunged into a flashback, the Festival of Ogun, where Kotonu veered his lorry accidentally into a masked dancer who was wearing the Ogun mask and was in a state of possession. Samson and Kotonu believed that the dancer was killed, and they were frantic with fear. The other masked dancers and followers were approaching, and would almost certainly have killed the driver who killed their god. Samson therefore persuaded Kotonu to put the mask on. They threw the body of the masquerade dancer into the back of the lorry, and Kotonu donned the mask. The dancers passed on without molesting the two, but Kotonu was half crazed with fear of the mask and the blood inside it.

The reason for Kotonu's terror of the road is now plain, for he is convinced that he will have to pay with his own life for what he has done. Kotonu does not yet know that the dancer did not die. Professor found him and nursed him until he was well. The man was, of course, Murano, but because he was run down when he was in a state of possession and *was* at that time actually the god himself, Murano has lost the power of speech. Murano's own self is elsewhere. He is still completely the god's creature, a being without a human mind. Professor has indicated as much when he said, 'They know what they are doing.' The gods are holding Murano in a state of hiatus. Although Murano is the key to the whole thing, it is still not clear what Professor hopes to gain from him. Murano seems to represent to Professor the chance of piercing the veil of the unknown and discovering the meaning which Professor has been pursuing, but we are not certain of the nature of this meaning, other than the fact that it concerns death.

Particulars Joe, a policeman, enters and asks Kotonu, 'Where were you the day of the Drivers' Festival? On the feast of Ogun the dog-eater. Where?' Professor asks casually, 'was that the day of the miracle, officer?' Particulars Joe replies, 'It was the day a god was abducted, Professor.'

The event for which the Professor has been waiting—the propitious moment for revelation—the moment of truth—is moving in upon the company. Say Tokyo Kid gives his version of the day of the Festival— 'Ogun came among us in possession'. Kotonu, agonised, tries to confess, but the gang loyally prevents Joe from hearing. They begin singing and drumming, for they realise the Ogun mask is here, in the Accident Supply Store, and they do not want the police or anyone else to know it. Joe learns of the mask, however, but when he reaches into the Store to find it, Samson and Say Tokyo and the others snatch it out and toss it from one to another finally, hiding it beneath Professor's chair. They further distract Joe by beginning to talk about Sergeant Burma, whom Joe knew in the war. Professor appears to regard Burma's death as a sacrifice to the Road, which more and more is equated with Ogun. This relationship between Ogun and the Road is confirmed when Professor asks Joe, 'May an ignorant man ask what god you pretend to worship?', and Joe replies, 'Same as the others, sir, the Road.'

Professor at this point is in a state of intense excitement and yet he is almost dazed. He knows that the finale is near, but he feels that something has gone wrong. He is speaking more and more strangely. He says that all he demands of his followers is 'your presence at evening communion, and the knowledge you afford me that your deaths will have no meaning'. He would, he scathingly remarks, 'live as hopefully among cattle, among hogs, among rams—.' He is not, however, simply ranting insanely. He is comparing the habitués of his flophouse to sacrificial animals who are not aware of their role. This is what stings him the most. He does not want them to alter their role; he only wants them to be aware of it.

Particulars Joe reveals that the 'man who was possessed at the Festival of Drivers was a palm-wine tapper by trade'. Say Tokyo Kid seems upset and surprised by this, and so do Samson and Kotonu. Professor says urgently, 'Be careful. If my enemies trouble me, I shall counter with a resurrection.'

Once again, there is a mingling of the old gods of Africa with the saviour and resurrection concepts of Christianity. This is not to say that the god raised from the dead is unique to Christianity, for of course the event occurs in different forms in many religions. But the word 'resurrection', seen against the background of Professor's former associations with the Church, makes it necessary to include Christianity in this drama of gods which Professor is about to attempt. In fact, whatever names they go by at any time in history or any place, God and the gods at this point seem in essence indistinguishable from one another. All of them—or One—are the keepers of a mystery, *mystery* in the religious sense. Professor is about to try to force fate, to turn the wheel his own way.

Murano enters at last, carrying a large gourd of palm-wine. When he sees the mask, his face works with an effort to remember. Kotonu pleads with Professor to explain whether Murano actually is the man he thought he killed. Now, finally, there is the full revelation of Professor's motives and hopes.

> So, surely Murano, crawling out of darkness, from the last
> suck of the throat of death, and Murano with the spirit of a god
> in him, for it came to the same thing, that I held a god captive,
> that his hands held out the day's communion! And should I not

hope, with him, to cheat, to anticipate the final confrontation, learning its nature, baring its skulking face, why may I not understand—?

He is determined, yet he is still uncertain. '...why may I not understand?' He suspects that he may not, that it cannot be given to him or to any man, yet he will go on. He cannot stop now in the staging of a resurrection. He takes Murano into the Accident Supply Store. When Murano emerges, it is as an *Egungun*. Murano is wearing the mask, and the state of possession has already begun. The company is terrified. Professor says, 'I must hope, even now. I cannot believe that death's revelation must be total, or not at all.'

But why does he say 'even now'? With some part of his mind, Professor knows that what he is attempting is—according to one set of concepts— impossible, and according to another set of concepts, taboo. For Professor is trying to gain the forbidden knowledge, to learn the essence and meaning of death, to know what only the dead and the gods can know, to find out the exact meaning of his own death.

This is dangerous ground. Perhaps he also hopes to restore Murano to himself, to break the hiatus and have Murano's soul returned. Perhaps he hopes, as well, to pierce Kotonu's fear and to restore him not only to life but also to a life prepared and even willing to be a sacrifice and to know the meaning of his own death. But the main impulse of Professor is simply to know, to discover, whatever it will prove to be. He reproaches his people for their fear, and tells them to drum. They do so, beating out the *agemo* rhythm appropriate to the state of possession.

The *Egungun* continues to dance, and the group becomes more and more agitated. Say Tokyo Kid asks, 'Do you want to go blind from things you shouldn't see?' It is always forbidden for anyone except the chief priest to know who dances under any particular mask. It is considered dangerous to go near an *Egungun*. It is unthinkable to stage a masked performance and to bring about a possession without the proper ritual, the right time, the sanctioned means, the priest's supervision. Say Tokyo is therefore desperately afraid. He considers this whole thing an act of sacrilege.

Professor, however, considers himself to be in a priestly role, in terms of the old gods, and in terms of Judæo-Christian concepts he sees himself in a role which can only be described as messianic. He has been oratorical before; he has spoken of omens and hidden meanings; he has sometimes appeared to rant. But never before has he lost sight of himself as a man, a fallible human. He may have been eccentric, but he was not mad. Now he appears to be disintegrating into actual madness. He has toyed with this project before;

he has considered it, perhaps dwelt on it in his imagination. But now he is committed to it, and that is a different thing. He says, 'I only hope, whoever it is, that you will not balk me, that you will not keep me waiting until I am beyond benefiting from our settlement—one must cheat fear by foreknowledge.' He lives with the fear not only of death but of the meaninglessness of death. He appears now to believe that his unquenchable desire to know death's meaning will require a human sacrifice. He feels that 'whoever it is' will be as aware as he himself is. Whoever it is will be honoured to be the sacrifice. Whoever it is who may be chosen, the person matters to Professor now not as a man with a name and a being but only as a candidate for sacrifice. Yet even in the horrifying aspects of his madness, Professor himself never ceases to exist for us as a man with a name and a being. He says, very movingly, 'I also feel at last a true excitement of the mind and spirit. As if that day has been lowered at last which I have long awaited. Surely I am not alone. If I am that, then I have wasted evenings of instruction on you.' Won't they ever understand? Won't they ever see what he is trying to do? He suspects and fears that they won't.

The *Egungun* becomes thoroughly possessed. In a scene of almost unbearable tension, Say Tokyo Kid, out of his own horror and fear, stabs Professor fatally. The *Egungun* picks up Say Tokyo and smashes him against a bench, killing him. The thugs and layabouts chant the Drivers' Dirge, while the mask spins and sinks and finally collapses. Is Murano now dead or is he restored to himself? Murano by this time is so thoroughly the god's being that it is impossible to imagine a man emerging—and he would have to do it himself, with no priest to ritualise and make possible any transition. His death seems an inevitability.

Professor has achieved death's revelation, but the price has been his own death, for those who seek to know the final mystery cannot go on living, and those who dare to meddle with the gods and God invariably pay with their lives.

Before he dies, Professor tells his people what little he has discovered, although his words are not going to be comprehended and are indeed only a broken series of words, for the final Word cannot be spoken or known— maybe does not even exist.

> Be like the road itself. Flatten your bellies with the hunger
> of an unpropitious day, power your hands with the knowledge
> of death...

Professor, at the end, is mad in a way that is universally comprehensible and for which no better term has ever been found than *hubris*, the self-pride of the man compelled to try to know what only the gods may know, to be in fact a god. And yet he has wanted so strongly to give them a meaning, his rejects of the road, and he has cared about them after his own fashion. At every point he has been prepared to do what practically nobody is prepared to do—to risk everything he has.

Soyinka's portrayal of character in this play—Professor, Kotonu, Samson, Say Tokyo Kid, Salubi, Particulars Joe—is of a very high order. They are all observably and movingly alive. And yet his exploration of the state of possession, his use of masks and drums, his inclusion of dirges—all these serve to make of the play an elaborate dance of death.

Soyinka uses three languages—Yoruba, for the dirges and praise songs; English, which is Professor's natural means of expression but is used with the other characters mainly when they are meant to be speaking in their own language, Yoruba; and pidgin English, which is used when the drivers and thugs are meant to be speaking English. Samson's speech, for example, can shift all the way from pidgin ('Lef' your load, I say lef' your dirty bundle. Lef am. All right I sorry I mo know say na your picken'), when he is addressing the lorry customers in a necessary *lingua franca*, to the pure and anguished 'Kill us a dog before the hungry god lies in wait and makes a substitute of me', which indicates that he is speaking in his own tongue.

The significance of the Ogun mask is revealed too slowly. Kotonu's despair and Professor's obsession, in the same way, are unfolded so gradually that it is difficult to hold one part of the puzzle in mind until the next comes along. These are, nevertheless, minor objections. *The Road* is Soyinka's most mature work so far. Its form shows greater control over his medium than is shown in *A Dance of the Forests*. He displays in *The Road* his usual ability to create living characters, but here they are more diverse and more deeply explored than anything he has previously attempted. The play gives a picture of some aspects of contemporary Nigeria, and it also looks searchingly at a theme which has no boundaries, the fact that man is the only animal who knows he must die. Man can bear to die, but not to die with a total lack of meaning. So we invent meanings, and believe in them even if they fall to pieces as we look at them.

The Interpreters

Soyinka's first novel is a work in which moments of pure comedy are skilfully blended with a scrutinising irony. The bizarre and the beautiful coexist in passages of description of forest and sea and city. Above all, living people inhabit the novel's pages. The interpreters are a group of young intellectuals, men who went to university together in Nigeria and then went away to England or America for further studies. Now they are back home and can meet together as a group once more, comparing reactions and opinions, testing themselves against the eyes and feelings of the others, protecting each other when they can and giving their affection or grief when they cannot. They are interpreting their society, but they are interpreting themselves as well, and each man's view turns both outward and inward.

Egbo is the grandson of an Ijaw chief who still rules piratically in the swamps. The young man is both appalled and fascinated by his blind grandfather, and this split feeling extends to his grandfather's realm, a little kingdom which could become Egbo's in time, if he wants it. Part of him rejects this easy miniature power, while with another part of himself he is drawn to take up the traditional role of prince, to assume his heritage and to cease any difficult thinking in broader terms. Egbo's parents—his missionary father and princess mother—were drowned in the creeks when he was a child, and the event haunts him still. He resents this presence of the past, and wants to rid himself of it, but no one's past is to be dismissed by an act of will. Egbo's first sexual experience has been with the beautiful and yet oddly lethargic prostitute, Simi, and when he comes back to Nigeria after his time abroad, he finds himself involved once more with her, almost against his own wish. After that first lovemaking, years before, Egbo spent a night in the forest near a railway bridge, disturbed by the not-yet-to-be-looked-at implications of manhood, afraid of gods both past and present, afraid of his future self. Survival of that night strengthened him, and now he still returns to the same place sometimes for peace and for reassurance about himself. Egbo feels that the other members of the group are busy achieving and doing, while he himself merely lives. He does his job at the Foreign Office, but it is not of real importance to him. In the forest he has the feeling once more that merely to live is reason enough. He does not have to prove his meaning as a man over and over again. Then one day he takes a girl to his forest, a university girl, almost anonymous. When he makes love to her he discovers she is a virgin, and the act in his mind seems to take on the aspect of a sacrifice to the old gods, and yet a sacrifice made willingly on her part and performed on his part with tenderness. When they leave one another, Egbo does not even know her name. Later, at a university party of horrifying vulgarity in the guise of propriety, Egbo learns that the girl is pregnant. He becomes concerned to find her again, but when finally his friend Bandele brings a note from her, Egbo is torn between the girl and Simi, as he has always been between the new Africa of the complex city and the old Africa of his neglected inheritance. In the end, we do not know which way Egbo will go in either situation, both of which demand from him the decision he is unwilling or unable to make. To him, his choice appears as 'a choice of drowning'.

Sagoe is a far-out journalist, wildly humourous, essentially depressed. When he returns to Nigeria he applies for a job on a local paper, only to find that he is expected to bribe the selection board. He has several encounters with Chief Winsala, an old rogue who first appears amusing to our eyes, then repulsive, then sad. Soyinka's portrayal of Winsala is splendid—the immense man with a booming voice, an extroverted personality and a cheerfully admitted lust which sends every young secretary and switchboard girl skittering for shelter. Later, when Winsala keeps ordering drinks which Sagoe will have to pay for, the appeal of the chief's personality begins to diminish, until gradually, seeing him shamelessly discussing what bribe would be appropriate for the job Sagoe wants, we begin to understand the world-weary corruption that lies underneath the jovial front. But Soyinka does not leave the portrayal here. Worse is to come. Sagoe discovers that Sir Derinola, the apparently incorruptible judge who is head of the selection board, is waiting outside in his car, waiting for Winsala, waiting because he himself cannot risk being seen to be involved with this petty bribe-taking, sending Chief Winsala to do the dirty work because Winsala's hands are not expected to be clean. Sagoe is repulsed and angry, but when he returns to the hotel bar and finds Chief Winsala foggily drunk and being abused by the steward because he cannot or will not pay for the liquor he has consumed, Sagoe is unexpectedly shaken by the sight. He is even more appalled when he sees that Sir Derinola has come into the hotel to see what has happened to Winsala.

> Beside the young palm shoot in a halved petrol drum stood
> Sir Derinola. And Sagoe was never never to forget the look upon
> his face. Beside the fright and his affronted dignity was marked
> the anguish of indecision. He had come up to see what caused
> the long delay and had entered at the start of the baiting. It was
> at first a strange kind of fascination, as if in Chief Winsala he
> saw his own fate, recognised the downward logic of the loss of
> self-respect... But above all, Sir Derinola was truly paralysed at
> the confrontation of a future image...

This scene, which was of course written long before the first army coup in 1966, seems to express the feelings of a great many intellectuals towards political corruption or the toleration of political corruption. Sagoe is shown perceiving both Chief Winsala and Sir Derinola from every angle, for the picture cannot be a simple one and the reaction cannot be unambiguous. Winsala is a buffoon. He is also a crook. He is also—and tragically—a man of Sagoe's father's generation, an elder suddenly caught out in his folly, caught like the Biblical Noah in the shame of his drunken exposure. Sir Derinola is a man of dignity, a dignity which was once real and is now a cloak, a man who prizes his reputation for an integrity which he no longer possesses. He is also unbearably frightened at the view of himself which he has caught from seeing Winsala in this state. Sagoe detests the situation but cannot endure the pain of the involved men. He tells the steward to put the drinks on his bill.

> He put his hand on Chief Winsala's shoulder. 'Shall we go sir?'
> He rose humbly, the bluff all gone out of him. Bandele had come
> to support the man on the other side but Sagoe steered him round
> suddenly. 'We'll take the other lift.' And with the corner of his eye
> he saw Sir Derinola suddenly released, turn away from them and
> scamper to the lift.

The real irony is that after this act of spontaneous salvation, Sagoe is presented by Sir Derinola with the job which he is now by no means certain he really wants. Sagoe takes the job, however, because he does not have any firm idea of what else to do, but he very quickly comes to realise that none of his stories which deal critically with social or political conditions will ever get printed. Sagoe takes refuge, predictably, in beer, and unpredictably in his theories of Voidante, the philosophy of shit, which he expounds hilariously and yet always with that underlying sense of depression which is Sagoe's fate. Soyinka allows himself to free-wheel here, and the result is a series of blows, digs and side-swipes at anything and everything he considers phoney. At one point, Sagoe describes how he tried in France to convert two hiking students to the Mysteries of Voidancy, and the consequent clash of intellects.

> For three days we were surfeited with Voidante dialectics.
> You are a bourgeois Voidante, they yelled—you know how
> the French love polemics—and I replied, and you are Voidante
> pseudo-negritudinists! You deviationist fools, can you not
> understand, atmosphere must be created as in a church?

Dehinwa, the only woman member of the interpreters, is engaged to Sagoe and impatiently but faithfully takes care of him after his more severe bouts with the bottle. Respectability is something Sagoe will never acquire, although his more fanciful flights against it (such as the time he finds himself throwing plastic fruit out of the window at an overpoweringly stuffy party because he is tormented by the thought—who on earth would want *plastic fruit?*) occur as accidentally and inevitably as the same sort of episode does to Herzog in Saul Bellow's novel. Sagoe, like Herzog, is fated to create havoc out of a painful need to reassert order, and to mock himself always just a little more than he mocks others.

Kola is an artist who is absorbed in painting a pantheon of the Yoruba gods. For this project some of the interpreters serve as models. Egbo is painted as Ogun, for example, the creative god, god of iron and war. Kola's role is mainly that of observer, until he finds himself taking the side of Monica, the English wife of Faseyi, a professor who lives in a state of constant worry over his wife's manners. Monica reacts to life simply, not because she does not grasp complexities but because she does, and for this reason Kola is attracted to her. Faseyi, who calls his mother 'Mummy', is capable of being thrown off-balance for a week because his wife appears at a university function minus the regulation white gloves. As with all the group, there is no final resolution at the end of the book, but Monica intends to leave her husband, and she and Kola can speak to one another with comprehension.

Of all the interpreters, Sekoni is probably the most moving because the most awkward and the most vulnerable. Nicknamed Sheikh by the group, Sekoni is an engineer who has come from Northern Nigeria. Because he is a Muslim who has married a Christian, he has been cast off by his family. When he returns home after his training abroad, he is filled with a brave and yet naïve eagerness to build something worth while. He does build—an experimental power station, only to discover that he is not to be allowed to complete it and that it will never be turned on. An uncompleted contract can be collected on, the same as a completed one, and it does not carry the political difficulties of persuading recalcitrant villagers to accept its newness. Sekoni's project never was taken seriously by the powers that be. It is conveniently condemned as unworkable, and Sekoni, at first unable to believe what has happened and then unable to face what he can no longer deny, suffers a mental breakdown. Later, when he is better, or reasonably better, he joins the group once more in their week-end nightclub rounds. They take great care of him, and listen while he tries, through a crippling stammer, to express his thoughts. After a pilgrimage both to Mecca and Jerusalem, the warring faiths within him become fused into faith itself. Following this experience, Sekoni finds his means of expression through sculpture. He does one carving, the

Wrestler, which Kola recognises with half-ashamed envy as a truly original work born of real inner necessity. But ultimately only one thing can happen to Sekoni, and it does. He is killed in a car accident, and a focal point of the novel is the group's unexpressed but always-felt mourning for him and for the waste that an unseeing society imposed on Sheikh's life.

Lasunwon, the lawyer, seems to exist on the edges of the group. Obtuse, never quite catching the point of any remark, failing miserably in tact, Lasunwon is almost a scapegoat, and the others seem to tolerate his presence only because of this role and at the same time to avoid their reasons for tolerating someone whom none of them really like.

With Bandele, the last member of the group, there is a feeling of hesitation. Who is Bandele? What is he? Tall, lank, the least talkative of all the interpreters, Bandele's presence nevertheless is felt throughout the entire novel as the strongest personality of all. It is always to Bandele that the others instinctively turn in moments of crisis. Bandele will know what to do. Some men are like this, not seeking leadership but finding it inescapable. Bandele teaches at Ibadan University, and leads his life with more calmness and poise than most people are capable of, but without ever drawing attention to this fact. In a sense, he is an idealised character, and yet his quality of wisdom is convincing. His personal relationships, if any, outside the group are never detailed. His mind is never broached. Yet he remains forcefully in the background, occasionally making a remark which shows how carefully he has been listening and assessing all the time. Bandele's hatred, like Sagoe's, is directed against the phoney, the hypocritical, and yet he never charges head on as Sagoe does. He knows the world cannot be changed overnight and perhaps cannot be changed at all. Only at the end of the novel, at a faculty party where the status-seekers have gathered to exchange platitudes amid plastic fruits and *bons mots*, does Bandele lash out. Egbo is there, and is forced to listen while a tittering doctor describes the student girl who has come to him, asking for an abortion. This is the girl whom Egbo half loves, and he acknowledges wholly within himself the fatherhood of her child. The doctor and others of the faculty make the chit-chatting kind of remarks that are always made in such circumstances—the younger generation is suffering from moral turpitude; why doesn't she go somewhere else—how dare she come here to plead for the vile deed to be done, although heaven knows it were better done. Bandele, fully cognisant of Egbo's anguish, seems to absorb into himself the total cruelty of the entire situation and to become one of the elders of Ogboni, the cult of Earth, the power that is said to have existed before the gods and before the law.

Bandele, old and immutable as the royal mothers of Benin throne, old and cruel as the Ogboni in conclave pronouncing the Word.

'I hope you all live to bury your daughters.'

Although the interpreters come together to compare and to sustain one another, their lives take separate courses until the group is half unwillingly pulled into contact with an evangelical cult led by an albino, who is known as Lazarus because he claims he once rose from the dead (and, interestingly enough, turned from black to albino in the process). He asks—commands, almost—that the group come to his church. This grotesque insinuation into their lives occurs just after Sheikh's death, and the interpreters, especially Bandele, find themselves wanting to go to the evangelist church, not for anything definite, but out of some kind of unhopeful hope. The scene in Lazarus's church is weird, for after the usual semihysterical hymns, a young thief appears as a replacement of a dead elder. The young man is called Noah, and Lazarus obviously has some power, almost a hypnotic power, over him. Kola is determined to paint the boy, in whose face he sees Esumare, the rainbow, link between earth and heaven.

After the strangely unnerving service, Kola and Egbo go back to bring Noah to Kola's studio. Separated accidentally from Kola, Egbo observes an exceedingly odd scene beside the night lagoon. Lazarus is putting Noah to some crucial test. Lazarus is in a canoe near shore, and beyond him the water is flaming from petrol which has been poured on it and set alight. Lazarus holds out his hand for Noah to step into the canoe and go through the flames—almost like God in Michelangelo's painting of the Creation, holding out His hand to Adam—and yet in this scene there is a sense of something being staged, forced falsely, men made to bear more symbolic weight than their frail humanity will stand. It is not the writer who has overladen his people, for the people have ceased to be his. It is Lazarus who is desperately attempting to stage some miracle both for his own sake and for the eyes of the faithful who are watching on the shore.

The drawback here is that we are not sufficiently allowed into Lazarus's thoughts, and so his purpose and intentions remain obscure. All we know for certain is that Noah, in this final test, disappoints Lazarus. At the last minute, Noah's nerve breaks and Lazarus's power over him cannot be maintained. The boy turns and runs. Egbo sees Lazarus as a defeated man and feels that 'he must keep the secret of this man's defeat'.

Kola and Egbo take Noah to Kola's studio, only for Kola to discover that the mystical meaning is not there after all. Kola sees that 'Noah was simply negative. The innocence of his face was unrelieved vacuity—' and that Noah has only been a puppet, manipulated by his master Lazarus. But when Lazarus comes looking for Noah, Kola in sudden inspiration paints Lazarus as Esumare. Lazarus says, 'I know the arithmetic of religion. The murderer is your future martyr, he is your most willing martyr.' Then, and most revealingly, he tells Kola, 'My true disciples are the thieves, the rejected of society.'

Lazarus, in showing his perception of the unconsciously strong self-destructive wish in murderers is also revealing its existence in himself. We are reminded of Demoke, in *A Dance of the Forests* and even more of Professor in *The Road*. Like Professor, Lazarus is half in love with easeful death, and wishes to stage a miracle which will reveal some of death's mystery to himself and to his disciples. Like Professor, also, Lazarus feels his role is to take the rejects of society and give their shoddy lives a meaning, and like Professor, his true danger is that he feels compelled to take upon himself the attributes of a messiah and even of a god, to deal in human lives as gamblers do in cards.

This messianic theme is not handled as effectively and dramatically here as it is in *The Road*. Lazarus is not nearly as complete a character as Professor, and not nearly enough of his intentions and hopes are shown. He remains vague, and his experiment with fire and water remains too unspecific. We are never told what he hopes to achieve by it. His disciples, too, do not come across as individuals, whereas Professor's disciples, the drivers and thugs, were all human persons speaking in their own right, speaking in voices which could never be mistaken for anyone else's voice. The boy Noah is similar in character to Murano the mute in *The Road*, for both seem to be agents of the god, but whereas Murano is the god's creature, with a mindless innocence, because he was run down by the lorry while in a state of possession, Noah's mind is simply 'a blank white sheet for accidental scribbles', a mind so dull that it is an easy prey for any master seeking a slave. Where Murano was caught in a nowhere between the human and the divine, Noah seems almost a zombie, a walking dead man.

In the end Noah is propelled towards a death which he could not have been alert enough even to suspect he wanted. In an implausible scene, Noah ends up at the apartment of Joe Golder, an American who is one-third Negro and in desperate search of the reassuring blackness which always eludes him. Joe is a homosexual, and when he makes amorous advances to Noah, the boy becomes panic-stricken and leaps off the balcony to his death.

The themes of messianic desire, the nature of death, the portion of death born into every soul, do not emerge as tellingly in this novel as they do in *The Road*, and yet in a sense the characters who act as protagonists in this ritual fencing with death are more sinister than their counterparts in *The Road*. Both Professor and Murano are characters with whom we can feel contact and sympathy. Noah and Lazarus—although they are admittedly less fully drawn characters—are altogether more ominous and frightening. Perhaps that was the intention. Perhaps Professor's ornate oratory and laughter-cloaked oddity are too appealing. Perhaps the dark side of the moon is not shown, in *The Road*, to be half dark enough.

The bridge appears throughout the novel as a recurring symbol. Sekoni is fascinated by the idea of a bridge, for as he says, 'a bridge also looks backward'. Any process of going forward must also take into account the past. The railway bridge, for Egbo, symbolises the bridge between childhood and manhood. And in the end, Kola paints Lazarus as the god Esumare, the rainbow, bridge between the human and the divine.

As in nearly everything that Soyinka has written, this novel combines social and psychological themes. The picture of Nigerian university life is lively and often searingly funny, akin in its iconoclastic humour to the early novels of Kingsley Amis in England and to Saul Bellow or Bernard Malamud in America.

Lazarus's cult seems to be almost a novel within a novel. It is interesting and even absorbing in itself, but it does not entirely belong to *The Interpreters*. It involves the group, but never deeply enough to make it an integral part of their story. It does, however, bring out once again the questions which occupy Soyinka the most.

What comes across best in this novel is the picture Soyinka draws of the interpreters themselves—Egbo, Sagoe, Kola, Sekoni, Bandele. Each man steps from the printed page with all the paradox and conflict and warmth of a living man. To have done this with five closely associated characters, and to have maintained unfailingly the uniqueness of each, is a remarkable achievement.

A few themes recur again and again, in varying forms, throughout all of Soyinka's work. One of these is the reinstatement of the old gods, especially Ogun, both in a traditional and a contemporary way—that is, as gods revealing themselves to men directly, and in a symbolic way as facets of the human personality which cannot be expressed in anything other than this essentially poetic manner.

In Soyinka's presentation of the conflict between the values of the old society and the new, he constantly attacks both and also constantly sees the value of both. He can offer a withering assessment of the ancient king, Mata Kharibu, in *A Dance of the Forests*, and he can point out the fallacies of the old religion, as he does in *The Swamp Dwellers*. In contrast, there is his affectionate treatment of Baroka, the old Bale, in *The Lion and the Jewel*, or the integrity of the Warrior in *A Dance of the Forests*. As far as the present is concerned, what appears in his work as a continuing anger is his dislike of the limited and stultified mission-school outlook, his hatred of corrupt politics, and his sardonic attitude towards the prim status-seeking within the universities. On the other hand, he provides a sympathetic and subtle characterisation of the present generation of intellectuals in *The Interpreters*. To Soyinka, the artist cannot be withdrawn or isolated—he is part of his society and may have to try to change it, but never easily, never without a deep and possibly self-protective scepticism.

Psychological or spiritual themes are as important to Soyinka as social ones. He explores the question of human sacrifice in much of his writing. *The Road* expresses the culmination, so far, of this exploration, in the way in which Professor wants his rejects of the road to live as potential and willing sacrifices to The Road, which is Ogun himself. The same theme appears in *The Strong Breed*, where Eman is drawn to offer himself, and the main inquiry of this play is into the differences between scapegoat and redeemer. In *A Dance of the Forests*, Oremole the apprentice does not actually want to die, but to some extent his act in mocking Demoke until the master-carver flings him from the treetop to his death is not only a human act of spite but also a religious one of fervour, performed on behalf of his god Oro.

The theme of sacrifice leads into the theme of martyrdom, which for Soyinka means the *chosen* death. It can be seen in *A Dance of the Forests*, in Demoke's death wish, the one aspect of himself which he is unable fully to face, and which is symbolically expressed by the Half Child, the *abiku*, the child born with death in its soul. The same theme can be seen in *The Road*, with Professor's desire to know his own death without dying, and his inevitable death caused by his determination to know beyond the limits of human knowledge. Again, in *The Strong Breed*, Eman not only fulfils his destiny and duty, but also is drawn to a death which he himself has chosen and yielded to. Noah, in *The Interpreters*, is a man nudged falsely into the role of saintly martyr by his master Lazarus, who has messianic tendencies himself but who is compelled to fulfil them through his manipulation of someone else's life. What comes out, again and again, in all these works, is the concept of a man *giving* his own death—giving his death in order to learn its nature, in order to defeat it and in order to prove stronger than the finality.

Surrounding this central desire to control death, there are other important characteristics exhibited by Soyinka's people in their dramatic ballet-like encounters with death, encounters which are as delicately precise and as ritualistic as a bull-fight. They wish not only to conquer death by somehow anticipating it and learning it. They also desire to impose a meaning on it, a meaning which may not intrinsically be there at all. The murderer and the martyred messiah interest Soyinka for exactly the same reason—both are drawn magnetically towards death, both are fascinated with its nature, both may desire their own deaths more than anything else, even though one appears only to want to kill and the other appears only to want to save.

The murderer, the scapegoat, the messiah—none of these, in Soyinka's writing, are seen as *them*. They are, undeniably, ourselves. If there is a core to his work, it is certainly this.

Soyinka's writing is life-filled, overflowing with energy, capable of realising human personalities and catching the sound of one particular voice, at times intensely comic, coloured with rhythm and dance, with drums and masquerade. But underneath, there is a concern with the inner territory of the spirit, a painful appraisal of the usually hidden parts of the mind. This strong undercurrent in his writing places him, ultimately, among the chroniclers of the areas of darkness within us all.

Rituals
of Destiny

John Pepper Clark

IT IS PERHAPS TOO EASY TO SEE in the plays of John Pepper Clark the influences of classical Greek drama, for these parallels are what first strike the European or American reader and play-goer—the formal tone, the role of the chorus, the importance of lineage themes, the curse laid on a family, the presence of a prophet or prophetess, the man caught in the millstone of the gods, the theme of incest.

Clark himself has denied that his sources are primarily Greek. If they are not Greek, what are they? There is a possibility that similarly structured societies tend to dwell upon similar questions in their literature. The world about which Sophocles and Euripides were writing was a tribal world, governed by gods, brooded over by ancestors. Precisely the same could be said of the traditional Ijaw society.

Even a superficial examination of Clark's background indicates that the Greek parallels in his plays may be traced equally well to West African sources. Clark, like Soyinka, has made extensive use of the culture and mythology of his own people. His use of this material has been conscious but not self-conscious. He explains his sources even less than Soyinka does, and his symbols are generally organic ones—that is, they grow naturally from the material and are not superimposed upon it. He has been influenced much less by contemporary international theatre than Soyinka has, and he knows much less about it than Soyinka does—to the detriment of his writing, for sometimes Clark's plays seem gauche or stiff as though the writer had been unable to visualise how the thing would be when it was actually performed. On the other hand, contemporary poetry in English has had a greater effect on him, for he is primarily a poet. His literary heritage is a broad one, therefore, and contains elements which at first seem worlds apart but which upon a closer examination turn out to have interesting similarities. Whether or not Clark's sources are ancient Greek or Ijaw does not, of course, in the end matter. The only thing that really matters is what he has done with whatever has come his way. Nevertheless, because the Greek parallels will be only too obvious to most readers, whereas the Ijaw sources will be less so, it may be worth while to look at Clark's background.

Born in 1935, John Pepper Clark is an Ijaw from the Delta region of Eastern Nigeria. He was educated at Government College, Warri, and then at the University of Ibadan, after which he did post-graduate studies at Princeton, U.S.A. This was followed by a year's research fellowship at the Institute of African Studies, Ibadan. Clark has published four plays. The first three, *Song of a Goat, The Masquerade* and *The Raft*, were brought out in a collection in 1964. *Ozidi*, a play based on an Ijaw epic, was published in 1966. He has also published *America, Their America* (1964), an account of his experiences in the U.S.A. His poetry has appeared in many journals and literary publications, including *Transition* and *Black Orpheus*. His play *Song of a Goat* was first performed in Ibadan in 1961. *Song of a Goat* and *The Masquerade* were both performed by the Eastern Nigeria Theatre Group at the Commonwealth Festival in London in 1965.

Ekine Drama

Clark's immediate background is the intellectual world of the universities. But his cultural roots go back to the Ijaw fishing villages of the mangrove swamps, and he has done a great deal of research into Ijaw masquerade drama.

The structure of the traditional Ijaw world, spiritually speaking, rests upon the ancestors and upon the village heroes who have mainly come in from the outside and have been innovators and bringers of change, and upon the water people—the gods and demi-gods who dwell in the swamps and creeks and who exercise a considerable influence over the lives of men. The Ijaw, perhaps more than any other people in Nigeria, have developed over the centuries a form of dramatic art which is religious in purpose but which has become weighted heavily on the side of skilful performance and artistic values. The Ekine society is a male cult of masqueraders. The aim of the Ekine performance is to entertain the community and to propitiate the water spirits. Each year a cycle of thirty to fifty plays is put on. The cycle begins with the Ekine members' visit to the Beach of the Water Spirits, far out in the creeks of the Niger Delta. The spirits are called in, and they return to the village with the men. At the end of the cycle, masks from each play perform in a single morning, all together, and then they go to the consecrated beach once more at the ebb of the tide, and the spirits are sent back to the creeks.

The themes of Ekine masquerade plays are social and religious, but no moral tone is conveyed. One popular theme is lineage problems. The characters are mainly types such as Ikaki, the amoral hypocrite, Ngbula the herbal doctor who imagines that people are talking maliciously about him, and Ijona, a self-pitying widow. The plays are performed by masked dancers, who are often possessed by the spirit of the mask. This state of trance enables a dancer to perform beyond his normal skill. No one, however, in Ekine drama could be open to the god unless his own talents had been developed to the utmost. The verbal forms of Ekine are relatively simple, but the drumming and dancing are complex to a degree. The dance expresses the content and theme, and the first requirement of a masquerade dancer is that he should be able to 'hear' the talking drums well. That is, he must understand the drum language and be able to translate it instantly and smoothly into the dance movements. The training of dancers begins when boys are very young, and there is a junior replica of the Ekine society, where youngsters learn the simpler dances but where the presence of the spirits is not requested. Ekine drama is highly formal, ritualistic, dependent upon the voices of the drums, yet also expecting the unexpected, the state in which the individual artist ceases to be himself and becomes the vessel of the god.

John Pepper Clark, unlike Soyinka, does not make much use of the drums and masks of traditional African drama, with one exception—his version of the Ijaw epic, *Ozidi*. Generally, he draws upon Ekine drama partly for its themes and partly for its formal and ritualistic tone.

Ijaw View of the Personality

According to traditional Ijaw belief, before a person is born, a part of his soul decides his destiny. There is also a village destiny. The ancestors and the gods continue to play a parental role, and the living, as in most tribal societies, remain in the role of children. This, obviously, creates irritations for the adults in a community, but it also provides emotional security, for a man is never utterly alone. An individual's fate is influenced not only by his conscious efforts but also by his lineage and by his *teme*, that part of his spirit which decided his fate before he was born and which will continue to live after his death. But—and here is the really essential difference between the deeply tribal outlook of the Ijaw and the deeply tribal outlook of the classical Greeks—according to the Ijaw, a man's destiny can be changed. With the proper rituals, his pre-natal wishes can be altered. Unlike Oedipus, or Antigone, or Agamemnon, his destiny is not inevitable.

The personality, in the Ijaw view, is layered, just as it is in the Freudian view. The *biomgbo* or personal soul, containing the individual's desires and feelings, corresponds to the conscious mind. The *teme* or steersman of the soul is comparable to the unconscious, whose aims are unknown to the conscious mind and often in diametrical opposition to it. If a man's fate is to be changed, however, it can be done only with the proper observance of rituals, not by the individual acting alone.

Song of a Goat

In this play, which is John Pepper Clark's best, the surface theme is that of impotence. Zifa, a poor fisherman, finds himself impotent after having fathered one child. He is extremely troubled, and so is his wife, Ebiere, who longs for more children. Ebiere goes to see the masseur, who in terms of Greek drama can be seen as a Tiresias figure, the seer, in this case not blind but crippled. In Ijaw terms the masseur assumes the role of priestly elder. The masseur tells Ebiere there is nothing wrong with her, and implants in her mind the suggestion that she should go to Tonye, Zifa's brother, to get a child. Ebiere rejects the suggestion vehemently, at least with her conscious mind. Zifa then comes to the masseur, who gives him the same advice. Zifa reacts violently, even though the masseur suggests that such things were not unheard of in an older society—that is, the ancestors would not disapprove, provided the proper rites were observed. Zifa's half-mad aunt, Orukorere, thinks she hears the cries of a goat being killed by a leopard. Zifa and the neighbours hush her, but her words seem like a prophecy of the downfall of Zifa's house.

> I must find him, the leopard
> That will devour my goat, I must
> Find him. Surely his footsteps will show
> Upon the mud? Surely those claws bloody
> From hunt of antelopes in the forest
> Will show in the sand?

Orukorere, in Ijaw terms, can be seen as a kind of priestess, given to prophesying. She was once chosen by the water spirits, and then became inordinately proud, so a spell was cast upon her that she would utter words which no one would comprehend. She is at times in a state of possession and conveys her terror and anxiety for Zifa and his house, saying that the cry of the goat is everywhere—the goat, symbol of sacrifice, whose voice no one else can hear. Orukorere can also, of course, be seen as a Cassandra figure, and this parallel seems a little too obvious to be entirely effective.

Ebiere grows more bitter, and then is gradually drawn towards Tonye, and their mock-play scuffling is half anger, half sexual attraction. Zifa begins to suspect his brother and his wife. Tortured as he is by the thought of his impotence, he can see no further than his own pain. Ebiere becomes pregnant by Tonye, and Zifa, now certain of her infidelity, determines to sacrifice a goat—to cleanse the compound of its evil, he says. But he is part of that evil, and this he cannot and will not see. His aunt tries to warn him, but he will not listen.

> *Zifa:*   ...You
> Said I should make sacrifice to the gods.
> These past several years we have none of us
> Followed your word. Being the elder,
> I agree, I am to blame for this. But now
> I obey you and will make instant
> Sacrifice to the gods.
> *Orukorere:* But you are
> As yet not cleansed, and for that matter all
> The concession is reeking with rot and
> Corruption.

Zifa:	In that case, it needs drastic
	Cleansing, which is what we shall now all perform.
Orukorere:	Be careful, son, and do nothing that is
	Rash. When the gods ask for blood it is
	Foolish to offer them oil.

Although he perhaps does not fully recognise it until the ritual has begun, Zifa wants to destroy his wife, Ebiere, and her unborn child, as well as his brother. He kills the goat, then thrusts its head into a cooking pot belonging to Ebiere. His desire is to break the womb. Ebiere, in a completely unverbal and unexternalised sense, knows exactly what he is doing, and when the earthen vessel breaks, she responds to his act of concealed hatred by beginning to miscarry. Zifa's unconscious destiny is bringing about the ruin of his house. Tonye, not only frightened by Zifa's anger but also appalled by what he himself has done, runs away, and before Zifa can reach him he has hanged himself. Zifa, in an agony of remorse, walks into the sea and drowns himself. When she learns of Zifa's death, Orukorere snatches up the oil lamp and smashes it.

> Take away
> The light. Will you take away your lamp?
> What, am I become so like a statue
> That discovered among ruins in
> The sun-set day, you wonder at
> Yet will not bow down to? I know
> I have lost both my face and limbs.
> Recognition therefore's become a thing
> For houseflies and bats, has it? I say
> Let there be no light again in this house.

In a sense, Zifa and Tonye and Ebiere are all three both the sacrificial victim, the goat, and the slayer or power of destruction, as visualised by Orukorere in the unseen presence of the leopard. Orukorere makes frequent reference to the goat and the leopard, and it is this conflict which symbolises the fall of Zifa's house. Zifa is the sacrifice because of his wife's desertion of him and because of the treachery of his brother. He is the destroyer because his self-pride makes him ignore Ebiere's need for children. He sees his impotence only in terms of his self and public image. Tonye is the destroyer because he takes Ebiere, yet he is also the sacrifice because she ruthlessly seduces him and thus severs him from his blood-brother Zifa. Ebiere is the destroyer because of her seduction of Tonye, but she is also the sacrifice because her own need for more children is so strong and is never really acknowledged by Zifa. So, in this play, we have a three-way conflict in which the roles of victim and destroyer are played by all against all.

Lineage is a common theme in Ekine drama, and Clark uses this familiar subject to good advantage. It is never the downfall of Zifa himself which is spoken about—always the downfall of Zifa's 'house'. The emphasis is always on something beyond the individual, and it gradually becomes plain that although Clark is using an ancient theme he is using it with a contemporary purpose, for the whole question of the individual is something that concerns him very much.

The subject of childlessness is, of course, completely universal, although it is worth noting that in many parts of West Africa not to have children is regarded not only as a grief but also a deep shame. Ebiere points up this traditional attitude:

> Custom dictates those who die childless
> Be cast out of the company of the fruitful whose
> Special grace is interment in the township.

The question of impotence and the fear of impotence is dealt with much more openly in *Song of a Goat* than it usually is in European or American literature. In most of the English-writing world, this theme is so taboo that it is most often dealt with not only obliquely but by a reversal, an exaggerated or fantasy-based boasting of sexual athleticism, such as that found in Norman Mailer's *An American Dream*. Zifa in contrast admits his anguish and also admits his terror of being mocked.

Zifa is a good and generous man, caught up in a situation beyond his control, and refusing all help. His intense rejection of any help, in fact, is what ultimately causes his own destruction. The masseur calls him 'A man deep and furious'. Tonye, the younger brother, is inexperienced at the beginning and in awe of Zifa. But after his affair with Ebiere, he no longer accepts his elder brother's status, and even goes so far as to sleep openly on Zifa's bed. In the end, however, he cannot bear this severance and it is the feeling of being cut off from those of his blood, just as much as his own guilt, which makes Tonye hang himself. Ebiere is an understandable and sympathetic character, with her overpowering need for children. Her increasing resentment blinds her, and she blames Zifa for what is not his fault. She rejects the masseur's suggestion that she should go to Tonye, but her subconscious mind never for an instant rejects this possibility. When, fatally, she takes matters into her own contriving, she tries to solve her dilemma without either family sanction or the sanction of gods and ancestors.

Orukorere is one of the most interesting characters in the play, seemingly mad to those around her because she expresses in symbols and poetic terms the compulsions which she feels to be at work destroying Zifa's lineage. She is a splendid and moving figure, for she sees more than any of them and is constantly hurt and even bewildered by their inability to see and by their treatment of her as a madwoman.

The neighbours play a role almost exactly like that of the chorus in a Greek drama. They provide a foreshadowing of events, they reveal relevant facts about Zifa's family ('A curse lies heavily upon it') and they describe the violent events which take place off-stage.

The curse on the house of Zifa is left curiously vague. The First Movement of the play reveals that Zifa's father had a curse on him and was buried ' in the evil grove', but the specific nature of his offence against the gods is never mentioned. The mysterious talk of a family curse seems extraneous to the play, almost as though it had been included to give an additional sinister effect. The thing which really brings about the tragedy is Zifa's attempt to deal with his fate absolutely alone.

The sacrifice scene is a travesty of the proper observances, and this is the key to the whole thing. Zifa performs the sacrifice before he himself is cleansed, and will not admit that he is in need of ritual cleansing. His rage against Tonye and Ebiere compels him to take the law into his own hands and even to do something which verges on witchcraft. When he pushes the goat's head into the earthen vessel, he begins by doing so with a murderous desire which is unconscious but which, in the performance of the act, becomes conscious.

The other two main characters are also compelled by their respective *temes* to fulfil their fates. A solution might have been found, but they have failed to try to find one within the framework of the total community, including the ancestors and the gods. Instead, they have all gone their uncompromisingly individual ways, thus ruining one another.

Both Zifa and Ebiere are portrayed with sympathy. Their individual needs are not denied. But in the end the individual cannot stand alone or act entirely alone. Without the observances which lessen his anguish and isolation, he blunders among his own compulsions and finds only disaster. The downfall of the house of Zifa is explainable both in psychological and in traditional religious terms, and the two sets of concepts now appear not to be so far apart, after all.

Although the obvious themes of *Song of a Goat* are those of lineage and of impotence, the underlying theme is that of the individual in relation to his society. John Pepper Clark seems to be trying to find some middle course between the lonely individualism of the Western world and the stultifying dependence of tribalism, some means of preserving the individual creative intelligence without totally sacrificing the isolation-breaking ties of tribe and the links with the ancestors. He does not suggest any easy way out of the maze in *Song of a Goat*, but he does point out the tragedy which occurs when a man's self-pride places him beyond help and beyond human contact.

This play lacks the saving humour found in Soyinka's work, and in consequence sometimes comes dangerously close to being pompous. In a context of high-flown oratory, a few unfortunate phrases such as 'instant sacrifice', reminiscent of coffee or American Zen, tend to arouse inappropriate laughter. In general, however, the language is spare and yet rich, full of poetic images drawn from the land and the creeks.

The Masquerade

In contrast to *Song of a Goat*, *The Masquerade* seems much too frail a craft to bear the weight of the tragedy with which it is overloaded. It begins well enough, with a beautiful young girl, Titi, walking on the beach with Tufa, the man she has agreed to marry. The scene is lightly and pleasantly done, although some of the phrases— 'Oh what magic moonlight!', for example— are little more than sentimental clichés.

Tufa is to marry Titi tomorrow. Titi's father, Diribi, and her mother, Umuko, are delighted that at last their fickle daughter has found herself such a presentable and well-to-do young man. The first real intimation of trouble comes at the wedding feast, when a group of celebrating villagers bursts in. Diribi, upset at this drunken intrusion (upset out of all proportion, in fact), threatens to throw them out. The villagers are offended, and reply with phrases which it is difficult to believe could ever be uttered by anyone:

> And what cassava, safely stacked by housewives
> In baskets, have we nibbled to merit
> This ejection?

One angry villager, having been struck by Diribi, insinuates that Tufa's past contains something shameful. It transpires that Tufa is actually Ebiere's son, by Tonye. Considering that Ebiere, in *Song of a Goat*, was said to have miscarried, this seems curious. In any event, Diribi is enraged to the point of verbal violence by this revelation. Even Umuko, Titi's mother, says, '...get out/Of my house, you masquerader.' Tufa, however, has been unaware himself of his family's curse. The framework of the masquerade, therefore, does not stand up well. Tufa is not a masquerader, but an innocent man caught up in a difficult situation not at all of his own making.

Titi decides to go with Tufa, declaring herself to be his wife and swearing she will stay with him whatever her father says. Diribi says of her that she has 'turned out worse than a harlot'. His rage grows, and he says the gods 'have not done right by me', even though he has done right by them and has never failed to make the proper offerings. Now the gods 'have let this bilge/come into my blood'. It is necessary to accept Diribi's strong feelings against Tufa. Where lineage is of the utmost importance, a man such as Tufa, born of an unsanctioned relationship which might have been regarded as incestuous, would have been intolerable to Diribi as son-in-law, especially as the curse on Tufa's family would be regarded as still being potentially dangerous. What is not well enough developed, however, is Diribi's feeling against his daughter. Titi has always been his favourite, and it is understandable that he should be enraged at the thought of her marrying someone whose heritage he regarded as tainted. But as the final scene opens, we discover that Diribi has killed his daughter. There has been no build-up, no conflict, no sense of Diribi's having been torn this way and that, no indication that some final unbearable word on her part bent his mind into madness.

In the most successful scene of the play, Titi's mother enters, now mad and holding in her arms a cat which she croons over, believing it to be her infant.

> ...oh my child, my peerless child, let
> Me set the cap proper on your brow. This way,
> Not so far back! But so, yes, so: now
> It's good, very good.

This is virtually the only time in the play when the tones of actual human speech are even approached.

Inevitably, Diribi appears, and it is clear that his mind, too, has been unhinged. Tufa leaps at him, and in the scuffle Diribi's gun goes off accidentally and Tufa is killed. One of the priests suggests putting Diribi in chains, but the other replies, 'What chains? For a cripple?'.

Song of a Goat and *The Masquerade* were performed by the Eastern Nigeria Theatre Group at the Commonwealth Festival in London in 1965. *Song of a Goat* came across as a taut, self-contained play, but the weaknesses of *The Masquerade* were even more apparent on the stage than they are on paper. The vast emotions which the play tries to conjure up seemed to collapse flimsily. The whole question of Tufa's undoubted innocence should, perhaps, have been explored more. Is it meant to be injustice on the part of the gods? Is it meant to underline life's irony? The writer does not say. The characters themselves seem hardly to be developed at all. Nothing is shown of Diribi, for example, except his initial happiness at the marriage and then his unalterable fury, a fury which appears exaggerated, too much bluster and too little convincing anguish.

The Raft

Four men are on a timber raft on a creek in the Niger Delta. They discover that the raft has become unmoored and they are adrift. At first their plight is annoying more than alarming, and they continue bickering among themselves in their accustomed manner. Kengide, who has never lived in a city, snipes jealously at Olotu, who has been to Lagos, Kano and Onitsha, while he himself has been 'just a wall-gecko gone grey at home'. Then Kengide puts a bowl into the water, and Ibobo notices that the bowl is spinning. Ogro, the fourth man, seems to know more about the creeks than the others, although they are always mocking him and calling him an idiot. When he sees the spinning bowl, he realises the raft is caught in 'the great Osikoboro whirlpool'. Olotu tries in a panic to put the raft free, but Ogro tells him the water is much too deep.

The raft remains fixed in the whirlpool, and ultimately breaks in two. One half carries away Olotu, who refuses to jump because he cannot bring himself to abandon the logs on which he has hoped to make a profit. Ogro says, 'Lord, Lord, he's adrift and lost!' And Kengide replies, 'We are all adrift....'

Ibobo tells Kengide he ought not to have stopped Ogro from trying to save Olotu—'You stood between him and his destiny.' Kengide angrily replies, 'Bile and bladder, I stood between the man and certain doom.' The two things are the same, clearly. Ogro's unconscious mind, his *teme*, the steersman of his soul, is propelling him towards the fulfilment of a destiny that is 'certain doom'.

A Niger Company steamship appears, and for a short time the four men believe they may be saved by this external agency, the Captain who possesses enormous power. But the steamship's crew and Captain do not appear to have noticed the drifting raft. Ogro cannot believe that salvation is not to be found there.

Back in my home town, the boys all swim
Far out to stream to board the boats as they pass
By, and the good people on deck help to haul
Us up the bows—

Having faith in the kind hands that will be outstretched to him, Ogro jumps off the raft— 'I'm coming out to you, my Captain!' He swims to the steamboat, only to have the people aboard beat his hands away, until he drops back and is mutilated to death 'in the mortal arms of that stern-wheeling engine'.

Now only Kengide and Ibobo are left. The raft drifts into sight of Burutu, a town whose lights fill the two men with excitement and longing hope. But a fog descends, and they find they have gone past Burutu. They shout, but no one hears.

Although the symbolism of this play is perhaps a little too obvious, it stands up quite well. The raft is never overloaded or made to bear too great a strain of meaning. The river, as life, is effective not chiefly because it is one of the most ancient of symbols (in fact, this probably diminishes its effectiveness) but because it is convincing on the level of physical reality, simply as a river. The raft is our uncertain selves, unmoored and adrift, and yet drawn into whirlpools which are at least partly of our own making. We fulfil our fates according to the inner forces which move us the most deeply, even though we may not be aware of the destinies which we have charted for ourselves. Olotu finds his death because he cannot relinquish the hope of money. Ogro is destroyed because he is too trusting in the kindness of others and in the power of an external God to deliver him—but also because his unconscious desire is to perish in the river. Kengide and Ibobo continue, lost and adrift, shouting into a fog which is so impenetrable that no one hears their voices. They are afraid to risk themselves in the dark water, the unknown, so the lighted places of which they dream will always remain just beyond their reach.

The main effectiveness of *The Raft*, however, lies not in its underlying meaning but in the picture it gives of the life of the creeks and swamps, set down lovingly and with the kind of close-up detail that shows a lifelong knowledge and an inner understanding of a place—the perils of the whirlpools, the eerie look of the shore lights, the constant living with the river so that the people seem as much creatures of the water as of the earth, the talk of fishing and of the town women and of the hard lot of the poor. In *The Raft*, Clark is content to write more simply and plainly than he does in *The Masquerade*, and the writing gains immeasurably in strength from the absence of embroidery.

Ozidi

Ozidi is based upon an Ijaw epic, one of the masquerade serial plays which were told in seven days, accompanied by dance, music and mime. Clark made tape-recordings of this masquerade series and also filmed it. He later did a translation of the entire epic into English. His own version is an adaptation which nevertheless adheres fairly closely to the original play cycle, at least in the action.

The series is in five parts, and the masquerade opens with an invocation to the water spirits. In the first scene, the elders of the ancient town of Orua are meeting to discuss choosing a new king. Within recent years, the kings of Orua have all died after a short reign. An elder suggests that they must discover the cause of the taint that lies on every occupant of the throne. But—and in this beginning is the end—this advice is overruled and ignored. The elders want Ozidi, the strongest warrior, to become king. Ozidi refuses, saying that he knows it is the turn of his house to provide a king, but he is the younger brother, and his elder brother, Temugedege, is an idiot. He declines on behalf of them both, but Temugedege suddenly appears and says he will accept the throne. Temugedege becomes king, but everyone knows this is a farce. Ozidi is furious that his brother has accepted the throne, and mocks Temugedege, who sees rulership only in terms of the slaves and fine women he will now own. Ozidi's comment carries a distinct ring of Zifa's words in *Song of a Goat*, in the expression of the curse upon a family:

> They say man is better than goat,
> But having you for brother I can now see
> The curse upon our house.

The villagers discuss the new king, in terms that are reminiscent of Orukorere in *Song of a Goat* warning Zifa that 'when the gods ask for blood it is foolish to offer them oil'.

> ...a god is
> A god once you make him so. After
> The ceremony, he ceases to be mere wood. Give him
> Palm oil then, and he'll insist on blood.

Irresponsibly the people of Orua have made a madman king. But sacred acts cannot be done lightly, and the gods are not mocked. The idiot king, having undergone the ceremonies of kingship, has become sacred, something more than himself.

It was this situation that Ozidi wanted to avoid, and now the elders are afraid of Ozidi's vengeance.

Constantly, throughout this drama, the imagery of sacrifice—of slayer and victim—is used, the same kind of imagery that is found in *Song of a Goat*. Here it is Ozidi who is described as the leopard.

> How shall we stop the leopard's left paw
> From falling on our necks?

Or,

> He'll tear us to pieces
> Like mere goats unless we do something at once.

Orea, Ozidi's wife, is the daughter of the seer-woman Oreame, and therefore has something of her mother's second sight. She warns Ozidi not to go out, but Ozidi goes and is killed. The elders bring his head to the king, as a cup for him to drink from. Temugedege, upon seeing his brother's head, falls into a fit and later runs away. Orea laments and tries to commit suicide, but is stopped by an old woman who says that Orea is carrying Ozidi's child and must live to bear it, for the son will avenge his father.

As Act Two opens, we learn that Orea has borne a son, whose birth (in the familiar manner of the heroic child in the legends of many cultures) was attended by storms and various upheavals of nature. The boy has been brought up by his mother and by his grandmother, the witch Oreame. Orea worries about her son, but Oreame says:

> Shame! Will you tie him
> To the hearth like a goat—my boy
> That is a leopard and must prowl?

Oreame is determined that the boy will avenge his father. She takes him to the village of Orua, and on the way he encounters the 'hill' masquerade, which is Oreame in another form, attempting to test his mettle. The boy is frightened, and Oreame, disappointed, assumes her own form and reassures him. Once again, however, she tests him by shouting that a leopard has attacked her. The boy flees. From this time forward, Oreame sets out to harden the boy's nerve and to prepare him for vengeance.

Ultimately, she takes him to the Old Man of the Forest—Bouakarakarabiri—who is a 'half human figure', a wizard who knows all the secrets of 'all life and leaves of the forest'. Oreame obtains from him a charm for the boy, a potion made of eagle, hornbill, lizard and monkey, which will enable him to experience the fury necessary for battle and will protect him against his enemies. Oreame, as a character, is very like Orukorere in *Song of a Goat*—she is intensely protective of the boy; she is a prophetess and seer. The difference is that Orukorere is merely a wise-woman, sometimes possessed but not herself using magic, whereas Oreame is a full-fledged witch, experienced in the occult.

Ozidi sets off with Orea and Oreame for the town of Orua. The elders of the town, led by Ofe, are terrified at the return of the son of Ozidi the First. One by one, the young Ozidi picks off his enemies until there are only a few left. The townspeople, like a chorus, beg Ofe to get rid of Ozidi before he destroys the whole town. They accuse Ofe and the elders of not having made the proper sacrifices to the gods and of not having the masquerades performed for the water spirits. At last Ofe is forced to deal with Ozidi alone. Ofe's own people are criticising him within the town, and outside the gates Oreame is taunting and Ozidi is challenging. Ofe meets Ozidi, who finally wins and cuts off Ofe's head, but after this act falls into a state of possession.

Ozidi's father has been avenged, but the young man cannot settle to a life of fishing and farming. He has been too well prepared to be a warrior and now he cannot lead an ordinary life. He longs for more fights, yet those men whose lives he has taken haunt his memory. He feels that he is cursed for despoiling the land. An old man, Ewiri, tells him that what he needs is a wife. But Ozidi is drawn into battle once more by a challenge from a seven-headed giant. With the help of Oreame's magic, Ozidi slays the giant, but before he dies, the giant says his sister will avenge him.

Here the play becomes truly macabre. Ozidi's fate seems to be forcing him on relentlessly, for Oreame, who more and more becomes a sinister figure, tells the young man to go to the giant's sister and kill her. He does go, accompanied by his grandmother, and finds that the woman is an ordinary decent person who is delighted at having at last borne a child after many years of childlessness. Oreame is not moved at all. She urges Ozidi on, even though he says 'I don't want to kill anybody again', and he kills both the woman and her child. His *teme* is leading him on to fulfil his inevitable and disastrous fate. His grandmother, the witch Oreame, seems like an externalisation of this side of his soul, and Ozidi himself says at one point:

> ...my grandmother, she is
> The sea that fills my stream.

Several interesting questions arise here. It is impossible to tell exactly how closely Clark has stuck to the Ijaw original, but both an Ijaw view of destiny and an outlook which owes much to contemporary psychology appear to be present. Ozidi longs for a woman, but he is a clumsy and tactless lover. He longs to stop killing, but he goes on killing. He is talented at only one thing—the dealing of death. With his conscious mind he wants to change his life entirely, but subconsciously he is still totally attached to the repetitive acts of death. In Ijaw terms, his personal soul wants peace and a life of work and family, but that part of his soul which decided his fate before he was born urges him irresistibly towards destruction. As with Zifa in *Song of a Goat*, there might be a way out, through the changing of his destiny by the proper ritual, but he does not seek it. Ozidi is terribly bound to his own course through the subtle bondage imposed upon him by his grandmother. The figure of Oreame is a decidedly dual one. She is the ancestress, and she both protects Ozidi and makes it impossible for him to change. He relies upon her, and calls upon her every time he is in trouble. Yet her protection is a deadly one, for it keeps him firmly and even obsessively within his own narrow groove.

This ambiguous nature of the ancestors is brought out in Ozidi's fight with Odogu, the man whose wife Ozidi tried to take. Odogu has a charm from the forest wizard as well, so the battle ends in stalemate. Odogu's mother is also a witch, and she turns up, along with Oreame. The two witches—in a scene of unparalleled grotesquerie—engage in a battle of power, turning themselves into fires and showers of sand. The conflict is broken by the entrance of the wizard, the Old Man of the Forest, who says that the one who wins will be the one who first fetches the magic leaf. It falls to Oreame to do so, and she rubs the leaf on Ozidi's eyes. Ozidi, strengthened, cuts down Odogu, but, blinded by the herb, he also cuts down his own grandmother. We can see here both the subconscious urge to be rid of her and the horror that such an act must impose upon the conscious mind. Ozidi, realising what he has done, and knowing Oreame is dying, becomes mad.

The ending of the masquerade is in a lower key entirely and is peopled by symbolic figures such as the Smallpox King, attended by his servants Cough, Cold and Fever. In a masked dance of great intricacy, these figures arrive as though on a barge. Ozidi is in a state of high fever. His mother says, 'You'll be the death of us all,' and Ozidi replies:

> There's nothing else
> I know how to do, is there?

He has recognised his own destiny but cannot combat it. He cannot die by war because he has been magically protected, but there is an inevitable flaw in the gods' protection of him. His destiny impelled him to live by the sword, even when with his conscious mind he desired to stop killing, but his death can only be achieved by disease.

In Clark's version of this Ijaw play sequence, the characters are very much more simplified than they are in *Song of a Goat*, but the same elements are present in the drama—the theme of lineage, the concern with blood honour, the curse laid on an entire house, the son obliged to act out a fate begun by his father, the destiny-deciding *teme* catapulting a man into situations not of his conscious choosing, the different parts of the individual soul working in opposition to one another. Clark's rendering of this Ijaw epic shows the complexity of his traditional sources and the ways in which he has drawn— in all his plays—upon forms and concepts of Ekine masquerade drama, extending these and using them as a means of expressing conflicts which are both contemporary and universal.

The plays of John Pepper Clark suffer in places from an insufficient knowledge of theatre. Too much action takes place off-stage, and there are too many speeches which are stilted, with feelings or even events being declaimed rather than actually happening. His style is effective when it is simplest and most unadorned, but he frequently gives way to the urge to be grandiose. His epic tone does not always succeed, for what once worked in terms of the heroic characters in masquerade dramas may not work in this present world. Perhaps men cannot any longer be cast in the heroic mould. But this does not mean that the past cannot be drawn upon. It *has* to be, in some ways, as Clark recognises, and it has to be changed as well, according to the writer's own outlook, as he also recognises.

The subject which concerns Clark most of all is that of destiny—how much the individual chooses his own fate and how much is decided for him by forces (external or internal) beyond his knowledge and control. Clark has not yet learned how to make every scene work on both a symbolic and a realistic level, nor does he have Soyinka's gift for creating character. But what he does have is a poetic fluency which, when it is going well, goes very well indeed, and an intense desire to enquire into the rituals of destiny.

The Thickets
of Our Separateness

Chinua Achebe

CHINUA ACHEBE'S CAREFUL AND CONFIDENT CRAFTSMANSHIP, his firm grasp of his material and his ability to create memorable and living characters place him among the best novelists now writing in any country in the English language. He not only gives a great many insights into Africa, past and present; he also explores man's difficulties in communicating with others, and at the same time he emphasises the continuing necessity to keep on attempting to speak with the only means at our disposal—words. There is about Achebe's writing a patient comprehension and a wisdom which are not often found anywhere.

Achebe has published four novels—*Things Fall Apart*, 1958, *No Longer at Ease*, 1960, *Arrow of God*, 1964, and *A Man of the People*, 1966.

Born in 1930 in the village of Ogidi, a few miles from the Niger River, Achebe belongs to the Ibo people, the largest tribal group in South-Eastern Nigeria. His was a Christian family, his father being one of the first Ibo mission teachers. But his grandfather was a grown man when the first missionaries came to Ogidi. Taking into consideration the memories of an older society which must have been passed on to him, Achebe's personal knowledge spans three different eras—the pre-mission and pre-colonial time when the old Ibo society was still firmly fixed, the mission-oriented era of his parents, and the quite different era, emancipated and yet troubled, of his own generation.

Achebe was educated at secondary school in his own area, and then at the University of Ibadan. In 1954 he began to work with the Nigerian Broadcasting Corporation, ultimately becoming Director of External Broadcasting. In 1966 he left radio work in order to devote more time to his writing.

In his novels, Achebe deals with the traditional society of the Ibo people, the reasons for its breakdown and the ways in which social changes have affected the lives of individual men. Although the Ibo number some five million people, they never had any central organisation or any kings. Their tribal set-up was markedly different from most tribal societies because of its individualism and its rejection of any inherited or hierarchical system of authority. The largest social unit was the village group, which might consist of half a dozen small villages. Disputes were settled by public meetings, and where a common agreement could not be reached, an oracle would be consulted or a decision given by a group of the ancestral masks. As everyone knew that the great carved masks with the striking and sometimes grotesque features were worn by men of the village, why not submit the question to the elders and simply leave it at that? The difference was that the judgement given by the ancestral masks was a judgement which had the sanction of the supernatural. Also, when the village elders assumed the masks, they became, in a way, different. They genuinely felt a connection with the dead; they believed the ancestors were speaking through them. And because they believed this, any individual vested interests which they might have had would at least have tended to be held in check.

The Ibo people's highly individualistic society may have developed partly for geographical reasons, for the Ibo lived in forests which were all but impenetrable, and each village was invisible to the next. Living thus enclosed, it is not surprising that the Ibo tended to be a tense, excitable and nervous people. In the old days only the trading between various markets and the practice of exogamy lessened the isolation of each village, for it was a custom that a man must seek his wife outside his own village, and each family therefore maintained ties with a few other villages.

The British administration in Nigeria met with considerable opposition for a long time from the Ibo people, whose natural resentment of foreign intrusion was heightened by the fact that the British system of courts and government-appointed chiefs went directly against Ibo social institutions.

Things Fall Apart

Achebe's first novel, *Things Fall Apart*, re-creates the first impact of European invasion upon the old Ibo society. Okonkwo is an important and respected man in Umuofia, in the days immediately prior to the European colonisation, that is, the late 1800's. He has been driven on to achievement by shame at his father's failure. His father, Unoka, was a gentle but irresponsible man who loved playing the flute but who could not succeed because he did not work hard enough and did not care enough about the values of his intensely competitive society, a society in which a livelihood was hard to get from the soil and the man of status was the man who had a flourishing yam crop. Unoka never took a title. Among the Ibo, to take a title—especially that of *ozo*—was a means of proving one's status within the community, for the title with its accompanying staff of office was bought at considerable expense from the closed group who already held titles. Although the Ibo did not have kings or chiefs, the establishment had worked out ways to perpetuate itself. Okonkwo has always tried twice as hard as most men, and has been renowned as a great wrestler. He has built his farm into a wealthy one, and has three wives and two titles. But he is a very severe man who cannot express his affection lest anyone think he is weak. His *chi* or personal god is said to be good—'But the Ibo people have a proverb that when a man says yes his *chi* says yes also.' Because of Okonkwo's determination he moulds his own fate—or for a time appears to.

The nine villages of Umuofia send Okonkwo as an emissary of war to a neighbouring village where an Umuofia woman has been killed. Okonkwo returns with two hostages, one a boy of fifteen, Ikemefuna, who is given by the elders into Okonkwo's care and goes to live in Okonkwo's compound. Okonkwo's son, Nwoye, becomes friends with the young stranger, and begins a relationship which will in the end change the whole course of Nwoye's life.

After Ikemefuna has been living in Okonkwo's compound for three years, the Oracle of the Hills and the Caves ordains the boy's death as a sacrifice to the gods. An elder advises Okonkwo to have nothing to do with the boy's death, because Ikemefuna calls Okonkwo 'father'. But when the village men reluctantly lead the boy along the forest path, Okonkwo is among them, and when the moment comes, Okonkwo is trapped by his own obsession, the need to appear absolutely strong. The death of Ikemefuna is one of the most moving passages in the novel. The boy has been told not that he is to be sacrificed but that he is being taken back home to his own village.

'Eze elina, elina!
    Sala
Eze ilikwa ya
Ikwaba akwa oligholi
Ebe Danda nechi eze
Ebe Uzuzu nete egwu
    Sala'

He sang it in his mind, and walked to its beat. If the song ended on his right foot, his mother was alive. If it ended on his left, she was dead. No, not dead, but ill. It ended on the right. She was alive and well. He sang the song again, and it ended on the left. But the second time did not count. The first voice gets to Chukwu, or God's house. That was a favourite saying of children. Ikemefuna felt like a child once more. It must be the thought of going home to his mother.

One of the men behind him cleared his throat. Ikemefuna looked back, and the man growled at him to go on and not stand looking back. The way he said it sent cold fear down Ikemefuna's back. His hands trembled vaguely on the black pot he carried. Why had Okonkwo withdrawn to the rear? Ikemefuna felt his legs melting under him. And he was afraid to look back.

As the man who had cleared his throat drew up and raised his matchet, Okonkwo looked away. He heard the blow. The pot fell and broke in the sand. He heard Ikemefuna cry, 'My father, they have killed me!' as he ran towards him. Dazed with fear, Okonkwo drew his matchet and cut him down. He was afraid of being thought weak.

Dazed with fear—in such a way can an appalling act take place. This may be the nature of many murders; it is certainly the nature of Okonkwo's. Okonkwo's tragedy is that he can never explain himself. There is never any human being who can understand his anguish over the death of Ikemefuna, and even if he might have lessened his pain by sharing it—with, for example, his close friend Obierika—Okonkwo's main flaw, the need to appear publicly strong and absolutely certain, prevents his ever bringing out his sorrow. His son Nwoye does not understand Okonkwo's motivations any more than Okonkwo understood those of Unoka, his father. Nwoye, in a tragic but inevitable pattern, becomes increasingly severed from Okonkwo and from his entire family. Obierika, Okonkwo's great friend, reproaches him for the death of Ikemefuna, but Okonkwo—needing to believe himself right, even against his own feelings, which he sternly casts aside—rejects the reproach and will not listen. Okonkwo is unable to accept the values of love and gentleness—he fears them too much, fears that they may weaken him in his own eyes and in the eyes of the community.

Yet Okonkwo is never presented as a man in whom warmth is lacking. The love and concern are there, but are held firmly suppressed. When Okonkwo's young daughter, Ezinma, becomes ill, he is so anxious and upset that he goes to the *obi* or hut of Ekwefi, the child's mother, and prepares medicine himself for the girl. Ezinma is feared to be an *ogbanje*, 'one of those wicked children who, when they died, entered their mothers' wombs to be born again'. This is comparable to the Yoruba *abiku*, the child born with death in its soul, and in a country in which infant mortality was so high, it is not surprising that this belief grew up—the children who died were always the same children, born again and again, fated to die again and again, eternal bringers of anguish to each new set of parents. Ezinma has survived to the age of ten, and Okonkwo and Ekwefi are beginning to hope she may mean to stay after all. When the child recovers from the illness, however, Okonkwo cannot show his emotion.

Ezeudu, one of the elders, dies—this was the same elder who warned Okonkwo not to have anything to do with Ikemefuna's death. At Ezeudu's funeral, Okonkwo's dane-gun goes off accidentally and kills the dead man's son. Because the killing of a clansman is a crime against the earth, Okonkwo is banished from Umuofia for seven years. The neighbours, including his friend Obierika, help him to pack during the night. But when dawn comes, they can no longer raise a hand to help him. They come back, like avenging furies compelled into this ritual destruction. They set fire to his houses and kill his animals, for they are 'cleansing the land which Okonkwo had polluted with the blood of a clansman'. They are acting correctly in their own eyes, and with every social sanction. Their feelings as individuals have become subservient to the group mystique. They are doing what is expected of them and what they expect of themselves.

Thus, through an accident, Okonkwo loses everything he has worked so hard to obtain. Yet—was it entirely an accident that the boy whom Okonkwo killed was the son of the elder whose warning to Okonkwo had once been fatally ignored? Achebe makes it possible to interpret Okonkwo's act in a variety of ways and to see his downfall as being at least partly caused by forces of destruction and fear within himself. Okonkwo, having moved to his mother's village, is in despair and feels that his *chi*—the god within—is to blame.

His life had been ruled by a great passion—to become one of the lords of the clan. That had been his life-spring. And he had all but achieved it. Then everything had been broken. He had been cast out of his clan like a fish on to a dry, sandy beach, panting. Clearly his personal god or *chi* was not made for greater things. A man could not rise beyond the destiny of his *chi*. The saying of the elders was not true—that if a man said yes his *chi* also affirmed. Here was a man whose *chi* said nay despite his own affirmation.

But Okonkwo may misunderstand his own deepest nature. In suppressing any gentleness and any acknowledgement of love, may he not have done some violence to himself? Far from Okonkwo saying *yes* while his *chi* said *no*, it may have been that the god within wanted to affirm the values of human contact, while Okonkwo out of fear and out of anxiety about the community's appraisal of him, said his hidden *no*.

The whole question of the *chi* is one which comes into much of Achebe's writing, and perhaps it is worth while to try to see what the *chi* is. The Ibo have many gods, and the Supreme Being is Chukwu. Apart from the whole pantheon of gods, however, is the *chi*, which Margaret Green in *Ibo Village Affairs* (Frank Cass & Co., London, 1964) defines as 'the personal spirit which everyone has and which is in the nature both of a creating and a guardian spirit'. Some critics have described the *chi* as the 'Conscience' but this word—essentially Christian—does not seem very accurate. The term *chi* appears to be closer to a concept of the unconscious mind or perhaps to the Ijaw idea of the *teme*, the steersman of the soul, the deepest inner nature, the part of the human spirit that decides a man's fate before his birth. But where John Pepper Clark's Ijaw characters fulfil their violent destinies in ways which remain mysterious to themselves, and where Wole Soyinka's Yoruba characters are sometimes compelled to act in dark ways which may go contrary to their conscious desires, Achebe seems to be showing with the character of Okonkwo a man whose inner god prompts a gentleness which is always ignored. Okonkwo is constantly racked by anxiety, obsessed with his own publicly proclaimed strength and his own standing in the community. As such, he is a true representative of the Ibo of that period, living in villages which regarded one another with a mutual suspicion born of insecurity, a highly individualistic society which did not acknowledge inherited rulers but in which the wealthy became the virtual rulers. It hardly needs pointing out, however, that Okonkwo's spiritual afflictions are not limited to the Ibo society of the last century. Any city in America or Europe could provide Okonkwo's counterparts—a different language, a different background, a different way of earning one's living, a different set of beliefs, but the same anxieties which can cause a man to do violence to his own spirit.

When at last Okonkwo is able to return to Umuofia, he knows that the village will have changed but he does not realise quite how much. He has lost his place among the nine masked spirits, the *egwugwu* who wear the ancestral masks and act as a judicial council in cases which cannot be settled amicably by the councils of men. He has lost his chance to lead his people, and lost the years when he might have taken high titles. Nevertheless he plans to rebuild his compound and to initiate his sons into the *ozo* society, the members of which are the highest title-holders.

But Umuofia has changed beyond recognition. The new Christian mission has claimed many, including Okonkwo's son Nwoye. The government of the English is now established, and the court 'where the District Commissioners judged cases in ignorance'. Court messengers have been appointed to interpret and act as go-betweens, and although they are Africans and even Ibo, they are foreigners to Umuofia. The courts and the English district officers do not understand the status of the village elders and the men of title. Okonkwo is appalled. 'What is it that has happened to our people?' Obierika's reply sums up the cruel inevitability of the situation.

> 'The white man is very clever. He came quietly and peaceably with his religion. We were amused at his foolishness and allowed him to stay. Now he has won our brothers, and our clan can no longer act like one. He has put a knife on the things that held us together and we have fallen apart.'

Okonkwo's son Nwoye is now called Isaac. Achebe draws an unforced and unexplained but deeply ironic parallel here between Okonkwo and the Biblical patriarch Abraham, and the son Isaac who was once offered up as sacrifice, and we are reminded of the now shadowy figure of Okonkwo's other 'son', Ikemefuna, who was in fact sacrificed and whose death Okonkwo never recovered from and Nwoye never forgave.

The tension and misunderstanding mount. A mission convert tears off the mask of an ancestral spirit, exposing the human face and the man whose sacred duty it is to wear the mask and bear the possession by the spirit. This act, which amounts to the killing and defiling of an ancestral spirit, so infuriates the elders that they demand the mission head to leave. Acting out of his own very different concepts, not understanding their views any more than they understand his, the English missionary bravely refuses to go. The villagers then, completely understandably, burn the church. A number of the elders are arrested, among them Okonkwo. When finally they are released, after the village has paid a fine, they hold a meeting of all the men of the village. Once more the great rallying cry is heard—*Umuofia kwenu!* But the government court messengers arrive to break up the meeting. Okonkwo, his deep pride mingling with his desire to be strong and to be seen to be strong, draws his matchet and kills one of the messengers. But he knows that the days of his power and the days of Umuofia's power are over. He knows that Umuofia will not go to war against the strangers. He returns to his compound and hangs himself.

Suicide is an offence against the earth, and in a bitter scene Okonkwo's great friend Obierika has to ask the District Commissioner and his men to cut Okonkwo down and bury him, for he can only be buried by strangers. In a last passionate outcry, Obierika tries to express Okonkwo's tragedy.

> 'That was one of the greatest men in Umuofia. You drove him to kill himself; and now he will be buried like a dog—'

But the D.C. does not understand. He goes away thinking that Okonkwo's story may possibly make quite a good short paragraph in a book he is writing, entitled *The Pacification of the Primitive Tribes of the Lower Niger*.

In an article on Achebe's first two novels, in *Transition*, no. 13, 1964, Austin J. Shelton suggests that in a way it was Okonkwo himself who made things fall apart—as though Achebe were totally unaware of this interesting possibility. Shelton is of the opinion that 'Achebe makes a vainglorious attempt...to ascribe all the evils which occurred in Ibo society to the coming of the white men. But he stacks the cards in the novels, hinting here and there at the truth, yet not explaining fully the substratum of divine forces working to influence the characters. His own motives perhaps are linked with his patent desire to indicate that outsiders can never understand the works of Igbo-speaking writers (whose novels are in English)...'

In fact, Achebe specifically does not blame 'all the evils which occurred in Ibo society' on the white man. It is plain throughout *Things Fall Apart* that the tragedy of Okonkwo is due to pressures from within as well as from the outside. Okonkwo is a man who is very greatly damaged by the external circumstances of his life. He is also a man who commits violence against the god within. In the same way, the old Ibo society is destroyed, as Achebe makes quite clear, both by inner flaws and outer assaults.

The picture of Ibo village life in *Things Fall Apart* is splendidly realised, and each of the characters takes on a life of his own. There are no stereotypes. The relationship and conflict between the villagers and the missionaries is shown—probably for the first time—for the heartbreakingly complicated affair it must have been.

> 'You say that there is one supreme God who made heaven and earth,' said Akunna on one of Mr Brown's visits. 'We also believe in Him and call Him Chukwu. He made all the world and the other gods.'
>
> 'There are no other gods,' said Mr Brown. 'Chukwu is the only God and all others are false. You carve a piece of wood...and you call it a god. But it is still a piece of wood.'
>
> 'Yes,' said Akunna. 'It is indeed a piece of wood. The tree from which it came was made by Chukwu, as indeed all minor gods were. But He made them for His messengers so that we could approach Him through them...'

In a sense each man is right, but they understand one another scarcely at all. Naturally Achebe's sympathies are weighted on the side of his ancestors, for it was the Christian missions which came uninvited and which in the end managed to sever two entire generations of Africans from their past and to cause untold psychological harm. Nevertheless, Achebe never condemns Christianity and he does not even condemn individual missionaries. He recognises their devotion to their own beliefs, and their at times considerable courage. What he deplores is their total ignorance of the people to whom they were preaching, their uninformed assumption that Africans did not have any concept of God, and their lack of any self-knowledge which might have made them question something of their own motives in desiring to see themselves as bringers of salvation.

Okonkwo remains, until his death, enclosed within his own fears and his unhappy desire for status. Nwoye turns into Isaac and is cut off for ever from his father. Neither can speak to the other with any words which will bridge their separation. The villagers and the missionaries impinge upon each other's lives, but there is no comprehension between them. Achebe portrays this failure of communication at both a personal and a social level, in a prose which is plain and spare and at all times informed with his keen sense of irony.

No Longer at Ease

With his second novel, *No Longer at Ease*, published in 1960, Achebe deals with contemporary Nigeria. Obi Okonkwo is the grandson of Okonkwo and the son of Isaac. Isaac has been for many years a catechist of the Church Missionary Society and has brought up his son Obi in the Christian faith. Isaac has lived courageously and with difficulty, but he has rejected everything of the old Africa, and has instead taken on a ready-made *persona*, given to him by the mission, a deeply (although unconsciously) anti-African attitude which makes him speak of the old Ibo society as 'the days of darkness'. Obi, who has gone to university in England, does not feel himself threatened by the traditions of the past. In some ways he feels closer to his grandfather than he does to his parents, although he does not understand, any more than Isaac does, what motivated Okonkwo in killing the boy Ikemefuna. To Obi it is an ancient story, however, and not one which troubles him, as it still troubles his father.

Although Obi is fond of his parents, they seem narrow and too rigid in their outlook. He feels distant from them, and yet he finds himself moved by the very ways in which they are old-fashioned—especially his mother, Hannah, who has tried so hard to live her life by the rules of Isaac's Bible, Hannah who once liked telling old Ibo tales to her children until Isaac instructed her that these were not fit subjects for a Christian home. Her entire life has had little enough of joy and more than enough duty. When Obi returns home, he sees the pattern of her life shown tangibly in her room.

> Mother's room…was full of mundane things. She had her box of clothes on a stool. On the other side of the room were pots of solid palm-oil with which she made black soap. The palm-oil was separated from the clothes by the whole length of the room, because, as she always said, clothes and oil were not kinsmen, and just as it was the duty of clothes to try and avoid oil it was also the duty of the oil to do everything to avoid clothes.
>
> Apart from these two, Mother's room also had such things as last year's coco yams, kola nuts preserved with banana leaves in empty oil pots, palm-ash preserved in an old cylindrical vessel which, as the older children told Obi, had once contained biscuits. In the second stage of its life it had served as a water vessel until it sprang about five leaks which had to be carefully covered with paper before it got its present job.
>
> As he looked at his mother on her bed, tears stood in Obi's eyes. She held out her hand to him and he took it—all bone and skin like a bat's wing.
>
> 'You did not see me when I was ill,' she said. 'Now I am as healthy as a young girl.' She laughed without mirth. 'You should have seen me three weeks ago. How is your work? Are Umuofia

people in Lagos all well? How is Joseph? His mother came to see me yesterday and I told her we were expecting you.'

Obi answered, 'They are well, yes, yes and yes.' But his heart all the while was bursting with grief.

Obi owes his education to a loan from the Umuofia Progressive Union, and when he goes to work for the civil service in Lagos he is determined to justify his village's faith in him. He is full of hopes and ideals, and is strict in his condemnation of the bribery which he sees taking place all around him. But the past and the present are fated to do battle in Obi's life, just as they did in the lives of his father and his grandfather, although in quite different ways. Obi finds that the girl he wants to marry is an *osu*. The *osu* once were religious slaves, dedicated to the service of a god. They were outcasts and were not allowed to marry the freeborn Ibo, who regarded them as 'holy and horrifying'. The caste has been abolished now, but the emotional feeling against the *osu* cannot be obliterated so quickly. The fact that Clara is a well-educated girl and a nurse makes no difference. Obi knows he can expect nothing but opposition from his parents. Obi's father is shocked and grieved at the thought of his son marrying Clara, even though he knows that the concept of *osu* goes against Christianity and all he has spent his life for. As for Obi's mother, she tells her son quite plainly that she will kill herself if he marries an *osu* girl.

Obi then discovers that Clara is pregnant. He is forced to borrow money, and Clara submits to an abortion. Afterwards she leaves Lagos, refusing to see Obi again. He knows he has failed her and failed himself, but he simply has not known how to cope with the forces which have torn him in so many different directions. Ironically enough, soon after Clara's departure Obi's mother dies. Even the anguish which he feels at his mother's death is overshadowed by the fact that he has to borrow money for her funeral and for the wake which the Umuofia Progressive Union, Lagos Branch, expects him to provide. Now deeply in debt, Obi feels himself to be utterly alone. Desperately, and with a mixture of cynicism and suppressed guilt, he begins to take bribes. He pays off his debts, but finally he is caught. At his trial, people wonder how such a fine and well-educated young man could have got himself into such a mess.

As usual with Achebe's writing, one has a sense of inevitability about the main character's life. Obi is not the strong character that his grandfather was, and his downfall is not portrayed in such deeply tragic terms as Okonkwo's, but Obi's situation is, if anything, more complicated than Okonkwo's. Obi is torn not between two worlds but among three. He yearns for the world of his grandfather, which he feels to have been at least firm in its own values, and yet it is a world he can never really know, for he did not even hear about it as a child from Okonkwo. He never knew his grandfather and he never knew the old Ibo society even from hearsay. It is a world he longs for almost in a fantasy manner, not for what it actually was but for what he would like it to have been. He rejects the narrow puritanical world of his parents with one part of his mind, and rejects the crippling customs such as ornate and costly funeral observances, but with another part of his mind he can never be free from the parents he cares about and the village which, however embarrassingly hearty and pompous the meetings of the Umuofia Progressive Union, did have enough concern for him to send him to university. As Achebe knows very well, the chains of external bondage can be broken more easily, in the end, than the chains of love. To become independent of a colonial power, or of any intolerable social authority, however difficult to accomplish, can ultimately be done by fighting that authority, whether physically or politically. But to achieve an inner independence—that is another thing entirely, and one which does not totally depend upon human desire or will. Obi wants desperately to be free of his parents' concepts, the vestigial traditions which still make them horrified at the thought of an *osu* girl in the family, the mission-given joylessness, the interpretation of respect toward one's own blood which dictates that a man must impoverish himself to put on a fine funeral for a parent. Obi disagrees with all these things. But he is still emotionally tied, and no one could claim he was wrong to be so. He loves his mother very much. He is painfully (and with unreasonable but unshakeable guilt) aware that her life has not been a happy one. What else could he possibly do, when she dies, but to give her the funeral which was expected of him and which, however emancipated, he expects of himself?

The third world with which Obi is involved is his own—the world of his contemporaries, people like Clara or his friend Joseph, who do not want to be bound by the past but who do not feel it incumbent upon them to reject all traditions indiscriminately, either. In Obi's case, however, the contemporaries with whom he has any real contact are too few, and he himself is not innerly certain enough. Achebe's conclusion— 'Everybody wondered why...' is as piercingly ironic as anything he has written. Whenever a man falls, people always wonder why, and in their very question is an unadmitted attempt to reassure themselves—there could not possibly go I. One of Achebe's skills as a novelist is that he can lead the reader into the life of another individual in such a way that the response must go even further than *There but for the grace of God go I*. Achebe does not spare us from the knowledge that Obi's dilemma, torn between what is expected of him and what he himself believes, bound by the subtle but inescapable chains of love, is in some way our own.

Arrow of God

Achebe's third novel, *Arrow of God*, in which he comes into full maturity as a novelist, is unquestionably his best, and is probably one of the best novels written anywhere in the past decade. Achebe has a finely balanced control over his material here, and yet his characters are never for an instant manipulated but always act out of their own inner necessities. He deals with a large number of characters, and yet none of them fail to come across as individuals, unique and irreplaceable. The paths of human communications here are almost unbearably tortuous, yet these impossibilities have been set down with an admirably plain clarity.

Published in 1964, *Arrow of God* deals with a situation of the early 1920's. Ulu is the guardian deity of the village of Umuaro, and Ezeulu is his priest. As the novel opens, Ezeulu is watching for the new moon, when he will announce the Yam Festival, after which the new yam crop may be eaten.

> Whenever Ezeulu considered the immensity of his power over the year and the crops and therefore over the people he wondered if it was real. It was true he named the day for the feast of the Pumpkin Leaves and for the New Yam feast; but he did not choose the day. He was merely a watchman....If he should refuse to name the day there would be no festival—no planting and no reaping. But could he refuse?...His mind persisted in trying to look too closely at the nature of his power.

The nature of his power. This is the central theme of *Arrow of God*—Ezeulu's testing of his own power and the power of his god, and his efforts to maintain his own and his god's authority in the face of village factions and of the mission and the British administration.

In a land dispute with a neighbouring village, Ezeulu advises his own village not to go to war because their claim is not a true one, and their guardian deity Ulu will not aid them in a 'war of blame'. But Umuaro does go to war, against their priest's advice. The fighting is stopped by the British, and at the investigation which follows Ezeulu gives evidence, saying that Umuaro ought not to have fought at all. For this he is praised by the District Officer, but some portions of his own village will never forgive him, for they believe he has taken the white man's side against his own clan. Ezeulu knows this was not his intention, but he cannot explain himself and indeed he is too proud to try.

The faction against Ezeulu gains fuel for its fire when the priest actually sends one of his sons to the mission school. In fact, Ezeulu is gravely apprehensive about the new religion and the new administration, and he believes that if any power is to be retained in the traditional hands, the sons of Umuaro will have to learn the white man's methods. Ezidemili, the python priest, who leads the opposition against Ezeulu, finds more cause for outcry when Ezeulu's mission-educated son, Oduche, almost causes the death of a sacred python. Oduche's teachers have misguidedly suggested that it would be a glorious act to kill the symbol of paganism. Oduche, frightened of his father's anger at this sacrilege and frightened also by the possible vengeance of gods in whom he does not believe, does not actually kill the python. Instead, he traps it and puts it in his wooden box.

> The python would die for lack of air, and he would be
> responsible for its death without being guilty of killing it.
> In the ambivalence of his present life his act seemed to him
> a very happy compromise.

Achebe's ability to reveal ambiguous human motives is nowhere more apparent than in his treatment of the boy Oduche, seeking to destroy the sacred python without killing it.

The loose system of social controls traditionally used by the Ibo did not suit the tidy-minded British, who wanted a man clearly in charge of each village. Indeed, without some well-defined system of local authority, the British felt much too insecure, for who were they to speak to if not a chief who could make decisions on behalf of all? The administration therefore set about the appointment of local chiefs, even though this institution went directly against Ibo custom. Achebe in *Arrow of God* follows the course of history with accuracy, and at the same time manages to confirm that fiction is a great deal more true than fact, for he shows events happening to actual persons and within actual persons, and this is something that few history books can do.

Word is sent to Ezeulu to appear before the District Officer. Ezeulu, conscious of the villagers' feeling that he has sided once before with the white men, refuses to go. But the opponents of Ezeulu in the village choose to interpret this refusal as cowardice. So he changes his mind and goes to the government settlement after all, only to find himself thrown into jail for his previous recalcitrance. When the government official finally chooses to see him, Ezeulu learns that the chieftainship of Umuaro is being offered to him. Proudly, angrily, and with an anguish which the English officer does not in the least perceive, Ezeulu, priest of Ulu, rejects this chieftainship sanctioned by strangers.

The young British official, disturbed almost to tears because in his ignorance he imagined he was offering something very alluring to Ezeulu, reacts angrily and puts the priest back in jail. How dare this old man make a fool of the administration? But it is not a proper-sounding charge to write down in the books—*this man embarrassed the government*—so after a while Ezeulu is set free, as suddenly (and to him, as mysteriously) as he was locked up. He has not suffered much physically, but emotionally he has suffered even more than he himself realises, for now his feeling against both the intrusive British and the opposing faction in his village is approaching madness. Umuaro, he reasons enclosedly, allowed him to be imprisoned. They did not rise up. Was this not a grievous wrong against the guardian deity whose priest he is? Ezeulu receives a revelation from his god, indicating that the opposition forces must be silenced forever.

> '*Ta! Nwanu!*' barked Ulu in his ear, as a spirit would in the ear of an impertinent human child. 'Who told you that this was your own fight?'
>
> Ezeulu trembled and said nothing.
>
> 'I say who told you that this was your own fight which you could arrange to suit you?…Go home and sleep and leave me to settle my quarrel with Idemili, who wants to destroy me so that his python may come to power. Now you tell me how it concerns you. I say go home and sleep. As for me and Idemili we shall fight to the finish; and whoever throws the other down will strip him of his anklet!'
>
> After that there was no more to be said… It was a fight of the gods. He was no more than an arrow in the bow of his god.

When Ezeulu was away in prison, he could not perform the ritual of eating the sacred yams. Until all the old yams chosen for this purpose have been eaten by the priest, the Yam Festival cannot be announced and the new yam crop may not be eaten by the people. Ezeulu decides to stand firm on this rite. He will not announce the harvest. He is at last testing the power of his god. Or is it the power of himself? He believes it is his god, but he doubts also. In the midst of the famine which occurs because of his decision, he cannot think of anything except his love for Umuaro and its people. But he has set his hand to this course, and now he cannot turn back. No one in Umuaro realises what he is going through.

> …the heaviest load was on Ezeulu's mind. He was used to loneliness. As Chief Priest he had always walked alone in front of

Umuaro. But without looking back he had always been able to hear their flute and song.... Never until now had he known the voices to die away altogether... With every passing day Umuaro became more and more an alien silence—the kind of silence which burnt a man's inside like the blue, quiet razor-edge of burning palm-nut shells....What troubled him most—and he alone seemed to be aware of it at present—was that the punishment was not for now alone but for all time.

Ezeulu sees only too clearly that he himself is somehow compulsively helping to destroy the very structure he wants to hold together. But he must chastise his people and bring them back to their god. At last the sacred yams are eaten, and with relief Ezeulu announces the New Yam Festival. Immediately, the funeral of an elder takes place, a funeral which has had to be delayed until the new yams could be sold and money raised for the sacrifice of a bull. One of Ezeulu's best-loved sons, the strong-willed and handsome Obika, is asked to don the ancestral mask and carry the spirit on its ritual journey through the forest so that the dead man may be at rest. Obika is the best runner in all Umuaro. But this night he has a severe fever. He does carry the spirit, however, and is possessed by it. He runs more swiftly and more surely than he has ever done before. But upon his return to Umuaro, strained far beyond his resources, Obika dies. This, for Ezeulu, is the end of his own life's course, the moment when he is told about the death of his son.

'What happened to him? Who did this? I said who?'
Ozumba began to explain but Ezeulu did not hear. The matchet fell from his hand and he slumped down on both knees beside the body. 'My son,' he cried. 'Ulu, were you there when this happened to me?'

Ezeulu's terrible cry is a familiar and a universal one—my God, my God, why hast Thou forsaken me? Obika's death seems like a cruel punishment in Ezeulu's eyes. How has he gone wrong? What has really happened? He does not know. Caught in the outer web of the white man's disruptions and the divided village, and in the inner web of pride and yet uncertainty, Ezeulu is now unable to grapple any longer with his life. He does not go mad violently. He becomes a senile old man, witless with grief. At the funeral of Obika he tries to help by taking up a broom—women's work—and sweeping the compound. Someone gently takes the broom from him and leads him back into his hut.

Ezeulu is a magnificent character, seen in all his aspects as a man and as a priest, splendid even in his isolating obsessions. He is one of the relatively few fictional characters about whom it can be said that once he has been encountered, he will never cease from inhabiting the mind.

Achebe's irony is used at full strength with the ending of *Arrow of God*, for it is the mission which benefits from Ezeulu's attempt to declare his god's power. When the yams were withheld from the people, some of the villagers went to the mission, where they were told that if they would adhere to the new religion, they might eat the new yams without fear. In their hunger many listened, and afterwards remained as converts. So in the end the old religion is broken, and what wisdom it possessed dies. The links with the past are now irretrievably destroyed and the identity of a people will only be regained slowly and painfully, through such men as Achebe himself, seeking to reassess his ancestral past and establish his relationship with it.

Achebe does not give any ready explanation or theory about the breakdown of Ibo society. He is much too accomplished a novelist for that. We experience the breakdown happening to various individuals. We not only believe in it. We are taken into it in the most direct and undeniable way.

The thing that emerges again and again in *Arrow of God* is the lack of contact between people—between the villagers and Ezeulu, Ezeulu and his sons, the sons with each other, Ezeulu and the British. Nothing is simplified. Nothing is expressed in terms of definition-making theories. Everything is very delicately probed, and the reader has a sense of constant contact with the characters.

The British are exposed to Achebe's biting irony, but even the worst of them are seen as real people, men with their own doubts and uncertainties, their own need to hear cheering words, their own fears which compel them to act stupidly or cruelly towards others. They have no right to be in Africa, but they are there, and given the circumstance of being there, they cannot act otherwise than they do. On his part, Ezeulu cannot act otherwise either. The greatest tragedy is that of man's lack of comprehension of the reality of others, his lack of comprehension of the validity of differences.

Underneath the restraint of this novel, there is an almost choking sense of rage and sorrow. Not that Achebe would have wanted the old Ibo society to go on unchanged, for he sees plainly the weaknesses within it. But the rage is because it broke the way it did, by the hands of strangers who had convinced themselves that they were bringing light to a dark place, and whose self-knowledge was so slight that they did not recognise the existence of darkness within themselves. The sorrow is for such a man as Ezeulu, broken by the violence of both the inner and the outer forces. Yet Achebe never allows his own emotions to sway the novel from its natural course. It is always the emotions of the characters which come across the most strongly, and because of this, the novel succeeds as few novels do.

Ezeulu, man and priest, god's man, like Oedipus and like Lear, has the power to reveal not only moving and terrifying aspects of himself, but moving and terrifying aspects of ourselves as well. 'No one knows the drum to which Ezeulu dances—'. At the deepest level, Achebe is talking about the individual living within his own skull.

A Man of the People

Achebe's fourth novel, *A Man of the People*, published in 1966, is a full-scale portrait of a crooked politician, seen through the increasingly disenchanted eyes of Odili, a young schoolteacher.

Chief the Honourable M.A. Nanga is 'the most approachable politician in the country', a real man of the people. Odili, to begin with, has mixed feelings about Nanga, who is a Minister in an inefficient and corrupt government. Odili is scornful of the chief but he also remembers his boyhood hero-worship of Nanga, in the days when Nanga was a village schoolteacher. He could not have been much of a teacher, for he is semi-literate, but this has not prevented his swift rise in politics. Nanga attached himself some years ago to a party whose brand of pop nationalism is summed up in the tone of their newspaper... 'Away with the damnable and expensive university education which only alienates an African from his rich and ancient culture and puts him above his people...' This bandwagon suited Nanga's talents and capabilities perfectly, and he is now, fittingly enough, Minister of Culture.

When Nanga goes to visit the school where Odili is teaching, he is given a regal reception. The village hunters' guild shoot off their old dane-guns. The Ego Women's Party turns up in new, brightly patterned cloths. There is a students' guard of honour. Odili is exceedingly critical and feels vastly superior to Nanga. Then the Minister recognises him and flatters him, and Odili feels himself succumbing to the charm of the man.

For Chief Nanga *is* charming. He makes jokes with everyone. He switches from high-flown oratory to pidgin English at precisely the most effective moment. He assures everyone of his honesty 'my motto is: Do the right and shame the Devil.' in such a way that Odili finds himself admiring Nanga's disarming shamelessness.

Odili is invited to visit Nanga, and agrees to go, having persuaded himself that this is all right. Odili happens to have mentioned to Nanga the scholarship he plans to apply for, and we watch Odili now telling himself that he does not intend to solicit the Minister's help, or even to accept it should it be offered. Achebe uses a first-person narrative in this novel with excellent effect. Odili has described himself as 'a person…who simply couldn't stoop to lick any Big Man's boots…', but it is plain that Odili is not to be taken entirely at his own evaluation. Achebe displays skill in making Odili reveal more to the reader than he knows about himself. 'I just didn't want anybody to think that Odili Samalu was capable of stooping to obtain a scholarship in any underhand way.' Chief Nanga comes alive through Odili's descriptions of him, but Odili himself comes through to the reader by the ways in which he lets drop aspects of his own character without realising he is doing it, in the self-justifying thoughts which show his uncertainty, in his pride and in his conflicting desires—the genuine and earnest desire to be honest and yet the understandable yearning for the fleshpots. He is an extremely appealing character, and he grows in strength and in his own perceptions as the novel progresses.

Odili's visit to Nanga is filled with scenes of pure hilarity, such as the time when Nanga takes Odili to the house of Chief Koko, Minister for Overseas Training.

> 'I no follow you black white-men for drink tea and coffee in the hot afternoon' said Chief Nanga. 'Whiskey and soda for me and for Mr Samalu.'
>
> Chief Koko explained that nothing warmed the belly like hot coffee and proceeded to take a loud and long sip followed by a satisfied Ahh! Then he practically dropped the cup and saucer on the drinks-table by his chair and jumped up as though a scorpion had stung him.
>
> 'They have killed me,' he wailed, wringing his hands, breathing hard and loud and rolling his eyes. Chief Nanga and I sprang up in alarm and asked together what had happened. But our host kept crying that *they* had killed him and they could now go and celebrate.
>
> 'What is it, S.I.?' asked Chief Nanga, putting an arm around the other's neck.
>
> 'They have poisoned my coffee,' he said, and broke down completely. Meanwhile the steward, hearing his master's cry, had rushed in.
>
> 'Who poisoned my coffee?' he asked.

'Not me—o!'

'Call the cook!' thundered the Minister. 'Call him here. I will kill him before I die. Go and bring him.'

'Me? Put poison for master? Nevertheless!' said the cook, side-stepping to avoid a heavy blow from the Minister. Then with a surprising presence of mind he saved himself... He made for the cup of coffee quickly, grabbed it and drank every drop. There was immediate silence.

The answer to the mystery is that the coffee is not Koko's usual Nescafé. It is OHMS—Our Home Made Stuff.

Odili learns that Nanga plans to take another wife, a well-educated 'parlour wife', for he considers Mrs Nanga too 'bush' to act as hostess at his parties. In fact Mrs Nanga is an honest, down-to-earth woman with no pretence. She sees straight through the phoniness of the high-level government cocktail parties, which she describes with accuracy as 'Nine pence talk and three pence food. *Hallo, hawa you. Nice to see you again.* All na lie lie.' Odili discovers, however, to his surprise, that he is 'simply hypnotised by the luxury of the great suite assigned to me'. He begins to see under the surface of the whole question of bribery and corruption, and to see that he himself is not quite so far above temptation as he once believed. He had condemned the corruption of government officials before, but without ever analysing it. He condemns it still, but with a growing understanding of its reasons.

A man who has just come in from the rain and dried his body and put on dry clothes is more reluctant to go out again than another who has been indoors all the time. The trouble with our new nation—as I saw it then lying on that bed—was that none of us had been indoors long enough to be able to say 'To hell with it'. We had all been in the rain together until yesterday. Then a handful of us—the smart and the lucky and hardly ever the best—had scrambled for the one shelter our former rulers left, and had taken it over and barricaded ourselves in.

Odili learns just how unscrupulous Nanga and his cohorts are. He had known before, but not really known. Now he finds out about the huge sums of money given to ministers by contractors in order to get road jobs, the size of the bribes taken by men like Nanga, the property and buildings acquired as part of the process of feathering the nest.

Odili is outraged, and yet he cannot help still being drawn to Nanga. Nanga's charm is not only real for Odili. Achebe makes the reader feel it, also, and he makes us recognise that the true danger of men like Nanga is not that they are monsters but that they demonstrably are not. It is this almost hypnotic warmth and humour of Nanga's that make him so irresistible to the people. His counterpart is familiar in American literature—the bluff, hearty, pocket-lining politician whose lack of integrity is winked at, almost approvingly, because he is so much one of the boys. The title of Achebe's novel is ironic in more ways than one. Nanga is known far and wide as a man of the people, but he is stealing a fortune from those same people. Yet, in an undeniable way, he actually *is* a man of the people. They love him. He can talk to them with an unerring instinct for knowing what they want most to hear. If this personal magnetism were missing, the cold greed which lies beneath might be more easily seen.

Odili has observed the greed and the dishonesty under Nanga's affability, but it is only when the young man joins a new political group that he begins to realise that fear and its constant attendant, brutality, are also component parts of the old chief's structure. Some of the young intellectuals have decided that they must try to fight the now-chaotic state of affairs to which the government has brought the country. With this end in mind, the Common People's Convention is formed. In the forthcoming elections, Odili finds himself running against Nanga. Nanga does not fight clean. His hired thugs make repeated attacks upon Odili, and when these fail to make the young man give up the contest, Nanga tries to buy him off. Odili goes on with the campaign. Nanga bribes the voters, spreads scurrilous lies about Odili and finally has the young man cruelly beaten up, having first personally begun the assault by slapping Odili in an hysterical outburst of pique and terror.

Achebe leads the reader so unobtrusively into Nanga's personality that it is almost with surprise, at this juncture, that we realise Nanga is no longer in any way a comic character, no longer even partially the rogue charmer he first seemed to be. We can see much more deeply now, and what we see is an aging man so tainted with his own dishonesties, so enraged and panic-stricken at the thought that his power is being questioned, that he is not now capable of any restraint. Nanga will grab everything he can, as fast and as much as he can. No amount of bribe money or crookedly acquired apartment blocks will ever satisfy him, for he has become insatiable. He will use any method in his politics—violence has become a necessity to him. The last mask has been stripped away.

Odili loses the election, which has been rigged. His friend Max, running against Chief Koko, is killed—run down by one of Koko's jeeps on the eve of the election.

Much has been written about the prophetic nature of this novel's ending. 'The rampaging bands of election thugs had caused so much unrest that our young Army officers seized the opportunity to take over.' *A Man of the People*—which was of course written many months previously—was published at approximately the same time as the first Army coup in Nigeria. In the astonishment at life's imitation of art, the ending itself did not at the time seem questionable, but now the coup in the novel appears slightly contrived. The fact that it actually happened this way in real life does not alter the impression that the novel ends rather too conveniently. No active revolutionary force is ever hinted at throughout the novel, and it is therefore hard not to see the final coup as a kind of *deus ex machina* brought in arbitrarily in order to provide a conclusion.

Chief Nanga has fallen, and his colleagues with him. They have—as Achebe says in the terms of a proverb—'taken enough for the owner to see'. But Achebe does not opt for any easy solution, for he knows there is none. In the days when the owner was the village, offences could be dealt with, for '...the village had a mind; it could say no to sacrilege.' Now the situation is very much more complex, for '...in the affairs of the nation there was no owner, the laws of the village became powerless.'

The character of Chief Nanga has strong similarities to Uncle Taiwo, the politician in Cyprian Ekwensi's *Jagua Nana*, and to Chief Winsala in Wole Soyinka's *The Interpreters*, but Achebe's portrayal of this type of politician is a more full and revealing one than either of these.

What begins as a comic novel ends as an incisive social satire, written in scalding prose, the purpose of which is to cauterise.

In *Commonwealth Literature* (ed. John Press, Heinemann, 1965) Chinua Achebe in an article on African writing quotes a new version written by a school child for an ending to a Hausa tale—'They all came and they lived happily together. He had several sons and daughters who grew up and helped in raising the standards of education in the country.' Achebe's comment is—'If you consider this ending a naïve anti-climax then you cannot know very much about Africa.' He, in company with most Nigerian writers of today, is definitely not disengaged from the events and questions of his society. He says of himself, in the same article, 'Here, then, is an adequate revolution for me to espouse—to help my society regain its belief in itself and put away the complexes of years of denigration and self-denigration.'

Several generations of people, like Isaac in *Things Fall Apart*, were caught in the break-up of the traditional society, with the advent of colonialism. Several generations, mission-educated, were given outsiders' views about their own gods and ancestors and history—views which were at best inadequate and at worst false. It is no wonder that writers such as Achebe have set out to correct this warped view of African history. But it is important to notice how Achebe goes about this process. He never idealises the older Ibo society. He never speaks of it in terms of 'customs'. His work does not include those explanatory asides that mark the work of some African writers who seek to exploit 'customs' in an almost gimmick-like way, as though writing anthropologically-inclined tourist brochures. Achebe's method is always the method of the genuine novelist. He portrays the Ibo society of the late 1800's in *Things Fall Apart* and then of the 1920's in *Arrow of God* by re-creating that society, re-creating it imaginatively, unsentimentally and in terms of people who are shown in all their perplexities and contradictions. This gift of character portrayal is Achebe's greatest talent, and in *Arrow of God*, for example, he can deal with an entire village—priest, elders, wives, children—and have every single character come to life as themselves. He never makes his characters speak; he listens to them.

Where he describes rituals, such as the *egwugwu*, the ancestral masks sitting in judgement over the snarled affairs of men, in *Things Fall Apart*, or the priest of Ulu purifying the entire community at the Feast of Pumpkin Leaves, in *Arrow of God*, he does so dramatically, by showing the event happening, by allowing the reader to enter. He never preaches or writes in the abstract. His descriptions of the rituals of the old religion are lighted from within by a deep understanding. Almost without realising it, we find that we understand at least some things which we did not understand before. We see the old religion not as a set of distant oddities, not as 'customs', but as faith, which is a very different thing.

Achebe may have in mind, primarily, as his audience, his own people. But to non-Africans his novels give a comprehensive and comprehending view of how things were and are from the inside.

In what may be termed his two historical novels—although neither is concerned entirely with a re-evaluation of history—Achebe pictures the life of the village with tremendous richness of detail. The markets are here, the children whining or singing beside the cooking fires while their mothers prepare the evening meal, the excitement of the wrestling matches or the festivals. The drums are always there, accompanying and interpreting, providing a commentary on the rituals, proclaiming all the happenings which touch the heart of the village. In *Things Fall Apart*, for example, there is a strikingly rhythmic description of the drums and cannons announcing a death.

> Go-di-di-go-go-di-go. Di-go-go-di-go. It was the *ekwe* talking to the clan. One of the things every man learned was the language of the hollowed-out wooden instrument. Diim! Diim! Diim! boomed the cannon at intervals.... The wailing of the women would not be heard beyond the village, but the *ekwe* carried the news to all the nine villages and even beyond. It began by naming the clan: *Umuofia obodo dike*, 'the land of the brave.' *Umuofia obodo dike! Umuofia obodo dike!* It said this over and over again, and as it dwelt on it, anxiety mounted in every heart that heaved on a bamboo bed that night. Then it went nearer and named the village: *Iguedo of the yellow grinding-stone!* It was Okonkwo's village. Again and again Iguedo was called and men waited breathlessly in all the nine villages. At last the man was named and the people sighed 'E-u-u, Ezeudu is dead.'

Beyond Achebe's portrayal of the old Ibo society or his portrayal of a contemporary society in the throes of transition, there is one theme which runs through everything he has written—human communication and the lack of it. He shows the impossibly complicated difficulties of one person speaking to another, attempting to make himself known to another, attempting to hear—really to hear—what another is saying. In his novels, we see man as a creature whose means of communication are both infinitely subtle and infinitely clumsy, a prey to invariable misunderstandings. Yet Achebe's writing also conveys the feeling that we must attempt to communicate, however imperfectly, if we are not to succumb to despair or madness. The words which are spoken are rarely the words which are heard, but we must go on speaking.

In Ibo villages, the men working on their farm plots in the midst of the rain forest often shout to one another—a reassurance, to make certain the other is still there, on the next cultivated patch, on the other side of the thick undergrowth. The writing of Chinua Achebe is like this. It seeks to send human voices through the thickets of our separateness.

A Twofold Forest

Amos Tutuola

Amos Tutuola's strangely poetic writing was quick to gain recognition in England and America, but in his own country it was at first widely criticised because of its bizarre use of English and because Tutuola was dealing with a past which many people were trying to forget, a past associated with the old gods and the spirits of forest and village, an ancestral past whose traditions for many of the present generation had lost their powers of reassurance while still retaining some powers of fear and threat. Nowadays Tutuola's work is recognised and admired by a whole generation of more sophisticated Nigerian writers, who no longer feel the need to deny their roots, but Tutuola has little in common with these young intellectuals either. His writing does not belong to any mainstream. It is neither contemporary nor traditional. It is, really, quite timeless and quite individual, although Tutuola has been greatly influenced by his Yoruba background.

Tutuola was born in 1920, into a Christian family, in the Yoruba city of Abeokuta. The Yoruba constitute the largest group in Western Nigeria. They were in the past both empire-builders (the medieval states of Ife, Benin and

Oyo were Yoruba domains) and artists whose wood carving and bronze casting were developed in the middle ages to a high art. Many Yoruba are now either Muslim or Christian, but the cults of the gods still survive, and the old religions combine, often weirdly, with Christian concepts in Tutuola's writing.

After only a few years' education, Tutuola became a coppersmith and then a messenger at the Labour Department in Lagos, which was the job he held when his first book was published. He later moved to Ibadan, where he now has a storekeeper's post with Radio Nigeria. He is in a sense an epic poet who as a man belongs nowhere, and this isolation is both his tragedy and his artistic strength.

Tutuola has written five books. His first, *The Palm-Wine Drinkard*, was published in 1952 and was the first novel written in English by a West African to gain world-wide attention. *My Life in the Bush of Ghosts* was published in 1954; *Simbi and the Satyr of the Dark Jungle* in 1955; *The Brave African Huntress* in 1958; and *Feather Woman of the Jungle* in 1962.

The Yoruba culture is rich in folk tales, stories of gods and spirits, talking animals, magic charms and powers, people who are transformed into gazelles or fish or birds. Tutuola draws deeply upon the folk tales and myths of his own people, using this material in a way that is strictly his own, sometimes taking snatches of Yoruba tales or characters from Yoruba mythology and recreating them in his own fantastic manner, sometimes combining past and present in such creatures as the Television-Handed Ghostess. He is able to use the Yoruba tales in a variety of ways because they are genuinely his, and often he does not seem to be using them consciously at all. They are simply his frame of reference, the terms in which he naturally tends to think. The tone of Tutuola's writing also resembles that of many Yoruba tales, for it is both humourous and poetic, and it fluctuates between a portrayal of beauty and lightness and a portrayal of grotesque ugliness.

The work of Tutuola has undoubtedly been influenced as well by the novels of D.O. Fagunwa, written in Yoruba. But whatever his sources, in his best work Tutuola makes something new from his material. He writes very much out of himself, and his writing stands alone, unrelated to any other Nigerian writing in English. There is a tremendous courage about the man, for he has been able to go on alone, remaining true to an inner sight which perceives both the dazzling multicoloured areas of dream and the appalling forests of nightmare.

The Palm-Wine Drinkard

Tutuola's first book is his masterpiece. It takes the form of an odyssey, a journey into the underworld which the hero undertakes in order to prove himself. It is really a journey of the spirit, in which the hero meets the monster-creations of his own mind, suffers torments, wins victories and finally returns to his own country, able now to rule it because of the wisdom his experiences have given him and because of the power he has gained through the terrors he has overcome. It is, of course, a classic journey, found in the mythologies of all cultures. It has been compared to Orpheus in the underworld, to Bunyan's *Pilgrim's Progress*, to Dante, to the journey of Odysseus. Gerald Moore, whose essay on Tutuola is the most complete and perceptive analysis to have been made so far, says that 'all his heroes or heroines follow out one variant or another of the cycle of the heroic monomyth, Departure—Initiation—Return' (*Seven African Writers*, Oxford Three Crowns, 1962, p. 44).

The opening of the story must surely be one of the most compelling ever written—apparently simple and yet involving the reader instantly.

> I was a palm-wine drinkard since I was a boy of ten years of age. I had no other work more than to drink palm-wine in my life. In those days we did not know other money, except COWRIES, so that everything was very cheap, and my father was the richest man in our town.

Tutuola's hero, the Drinkard, sets out to search for his dead palm-wine tapster, who dwells now in the Town of the Deads. He encounters an old man, really a god in disguise, who can tell him which way to go, but first he must perform certain feats. The Drinkard identifies himself to the old man as 'Father of gods who can do anything in this world'. He wins the first riddle-test easily, but then is asked to go and bring Death in a net. His arrival at Death's house is both macabre and humourous.

> When I reached his (Death's) house, he was not at home by that time, he was in his yam garden which was very close to his house, and I met a small rolling drum in his verandah, then it beat it to Death as a sign of salutation.

The Drinkard tricks Death and brings him to the old man. Death, however, escapes and so 'since the day that I had brought Death out from his house, he has no permanent place to dwell or stay, and we are hearing his name about in the world.'

Another feat which the Drinkard must accomplish is to rescue a girl who has been abducted. He discovers that the handsome man who took the girl away is actually, in Tutuola's splendid phrase, 'A Full-Bodied Gentleman Reduced To Head'—that is, a Skull who rents all the parts of his body in order to go to the market, and who, at the end of the day, returns everything to the rightful owners. When the Drinkard first sees the Skull, clad in borrowed parts, he admires and envies him.

> I could not blame the lady for following the Skull as a
> complete gentleman to his house at all. Because if I were a lady,
> no doubt I would follow him to wherever he would go, and still
> as I was a man I would jealous him more than that, because if this
> gentleman went to the battle field, surely, enemy would not kill
> him or capture him and if bombers saw him in a town which was
> to be bombed, they would not throw bombs on his presence, and
> if they did throw it, the bomb itself would not explode until this
> gentleman would leave that town, because of his beauty.

Tutuola's writing here achieves a delicate combination of humour and pathos, and a marvellously grotesque effect is gained from the juxtaposition of the mythical Skull with the modern bombers.

The Lady has been imprisoned by the Skull family, but the Drinkard finally rescues her and marries her. They have a fearful child, born from the mother's thumb, who consumes all the food and is uncontrollable. They burn their house in order to get rid of the infant, who is the manifestation of a malevolent and unearthly power, but the child rises from the ashes and follows them as 'the half-bodied baby'. Drum, Song and Dance finally rid the pair of the child, and the Drinkard and his wife set out once more in search of Deads' Town.

Along the road they meet numerous apparitions, and are tortured frequently. At Unreturnable Heaven's Town they are buried in pits up to their necks and are mercilessly flogged about the head. When they finally escape, bruised and exhausted, they discover the White Tree, where lives the Faithful Mother. This tree, in mythological terms, is the Tree of Life, and its goddess is the archetypal earth-mother. The travellers find shelter and are healed. But before they enter the tree, a curious thing occurs.

> Now by that time and before we entered inside the tree, we
> had 'sold our death' to somebody at the door for the sum of
> £70.18.6d and 'lent our fear' to somebody at the door as well on
> interest at £3.10.0. a month, so we did not care about death and
> we did not fear again.

At the end of their stay in the White Tree their fear is returned to them, for it was, after all, only on loan. But they have sold their death, so now we know that whatever else befalls the Drinkard, he will not die. As with so many heroic sagas the world over, Tutuola's hero wins his victories partly by luck, partly by cunning and courage, and partly by powerful magic aids. The next ordeal takes place in Red Town, where the Drinkard and his wife are captured and are almost sacrificed to the Red Fish.

> At the same time that the red fish appeared out, its head was just like a tortoise's head, but it was as big as an elephant's head and it had over 30 horns and large eyes which surrounded the head. All these horns were spread out as an umbrella. It could not walk but was only gliding on the ground like a snake and its body was just like a bat's body and covered with long red hair like strings. …All the eyes which surrounded its head were closing and opening at the same time as if a man was pressing a switch on and off.

This creature has been compared by critics to the monsters that inhabited the imaginations of such writers as Bunyan and Blake. The Red Fish, also, like so many of Tutuola's monsters, is reminiscent of the brilliant and terrifying visions of the Book of Revelation.

The Drinkard and his wife arrive at last at Deads' Town and find the palm-wine tapster, who tells them that deads can never live with alives and therefore they must return to the earthly world. The Drinkard does not go back without obtaining a prize, however, token of his successful completion of the journey. The tapster gives him a Magic Egg which will do anything the Drinkard wishes.

The return journey is filled with horrors, the worst of which is the meeting with hordes of ferocious dead babies. Their final encounter is with the Mountain Creatures, and Tutuola heads this episode strikingly— 'To See The Mountain Creatures Was Not Dangerous But To Dance With Them Was The Most Dangerous.' The Drinkard escapes by turning himself and his wife into a flat pebble and skipping across the river. Gerald Moore describes the river as the 'Return Threshold', which 'in accordance with all the rules of mythology the hero's pursuers can never cross'. (*Seven African Writers*, p. 48)

The hero finds upon his return that his own country is in the grip of a long famine. The Magic Egg then feeds the population, until it is accidentally broken. The Drinkard himself finally solves the situation by the diplomatic act of sending a sacrifice to Heaven. Heaven, thus recognised as superior to Earth, is appeased. Rain falls and the famine is over.

The conclusion of *The Palm-Wine Drinkard* has its sources in a Yoruba myth. In one version of the Yoruba tale it is the vulture, despised by all other birds, who volunteers to take the sacrifice to Heaven, but when he returns he finds that he is still shunned and outcast. In Tutuola's much more moving version, it is a slave who 'took the sacrifice to heaven for Heaven who was senior to Land...' and when he returns and seeks shelter from the rain which has now begun to fall, no one will permit him into their houses lest he carry them off to Heaven as he did the sacrifice.

Gerald Moore sees the slave as a human sacrifice, and he believes that the return of the slave is really the return of a ghost. He also sees the seniority of Heaven as an indication that '...from henceforth the supreme deity will be the male Sky God and not the old female Earth Goddess, protectress of matriarchy' (*Seven African Writers*, p. 48). Anne Tibble, in her *African/English Literature: A Survey and Anthology* (Peter Owen, 1965), points out that this interpretation will not quite do, because Tutuola specifically refers to Land as 'he', so that the deity of Heaven and the deity of Earth are both male. It is true that Tutuola does refer to Land as male; nevertheless, Moore's interpretation seems basically to be the right one. The Yoruba myth is paralleled in the myths of many cultures, for it represents a transfer of affiliation which did in fact take place in innumerable religions at one time or another—the decision that the heavenly deity was superior to the gods of earth. In many places this change took the form of a rendering of chief homage to a male deity—Our Father which art in heaven—instead of the earth mother with which most religions began, and this shift in emphasis often paralleled a similar social move away from matriarchy.

Whatever the ending contains, intentionally or unintentionally, Tutuola has completed his story not as a theologian but as an artist, with a strong sense of calm after a perilous journey.

My Life in the Bush of Ghosts

Tutuola's second book approaches and in some ways even surpasses *The Palm-Wine Drinkard* in the grotesque quality of its visions, although the work as a whole is not as powerful as the first. 'Bush', to a West African, means the rain-forest or what Europeans and Americans might call the jungle. 'Ghosts' in this book are not the spirits of dead persons, but rather spirits who have never lived as people but have always inhabited their own spirit world which coexists with ours.

The hero is lost from his home and enters the Bush of Ghosts as a boy of seven. He emerges as a man many years later. Gerald Moore sees the story as a kind of *rite de passage*, an initiation, and undoubtedly this is so. As well, however, the story is a journey into the depths of the subconscious. Tutuola may not have intended it to be this; indeed, if he had intended it, it probably would not have worked out that way, for this type of exploration has to be done out of necessity, not calculation. The book appears to be a painful setting down of the publicly suppressed areas of the mind. In this fictional guise, the forbidden can be looked at, and the horrifying or appalling side of the self can be brought into the open. The 'self' in this sense means all our selves, for although the forest looks (and is) different to every pair of eyes, it is there in varying shapes and forms for us all. Few are brave enough to look at it, and fewer still to record it.

It is a grim world we are shown here. There is an obsession with pain, flogging, humiliation, torture, excreta. The torments of the hero are feared but also masochistically sought. The image of the mother is an interesting and ambiguous one, for the boy keeps thinking of his own mother with warmth and affection, yet he encounters such repulsive mother-types as the Flash-Eyed Mother, whose entire attention, significantly enough, is taken up with the snarling and evil-looking infant heads which are sprouting all over her body, and who therefore neglects all her other ghost children, including the hero, who has been taken into the community as one of her family.

The boy, when he first enters the Bush of Ghosts, is lured with the smell of food by the Golden Ghost, the Copperish Ghost and the Silverish Ghost. When he manages to get away from them, he encounters the Smelling Ghost, who wears scorpions on his fingers as rings and whose body 'was full of excreta, urine, and also wet with the rotten blood of all the animals that he was killing for his food'. Moving on, the hero is turned into a cow and is nearly sacrificed to a god. Escaping, and regaining his own form, he runs into the Burglar Ghosts, who represent Tutuola's version of the Yoruba belief that some children are born again and again, and that the children who die in infancy are always the same group of children—the *abiku*, the child born with death in its soul, the same kind of child that appears in Wole Soyinka's *A Dance of the Forests*. In Tutuola's rendering of this belief, the 'born and die' children replace real children in the womb. All gifts which are made to them are stored away in the Bush of Ghosts. They rob their earthly parents and then return to ghost life to enjoy the loot.

The deep split in the mind between the old gods and the new is expressed poetically and with great power. Tutuola never in this book actually names the old Yoruba gods—in fact, he hardly ever refers to them as gods at all. The old gods inhabit his writing in the form of spirits and ghosts, and most of these are frightening—ghosts with no feet and arms; the Smelling Ghost who stinks of carrion and excreta; the sadistic River Ghosts who are also called the Sceptical Ghosts because they hate the heavenly God the most. The hero of the story fears all these ghosts very much indeed, yet he repeatedly seeks their company. He cannot get away from them. The attitudes to Christianity, as they appear in this book, are mixed, to say the least. The conflicts which are laid bare here are the same conflicts as those described by Achebe in *Things Fall Apart* and *Arrow of God*, but in the work of Tutuola the clash between religions is not being described as such and is perhaps not even recognised as such. It is brought out in quite a different way, in terms of the main character's suffering, a suffering which only if it is viewed very superficially can be believed in as being merely external adventure. The hero puts a yearning faith in the Christian God. He is always saying 'as God is so good—'. At one point he discovers his long-dead cousin in the tenth Town of Ghosts, and finds that the cousin has set up a mission. The mission sign—humourously and yet in a way almost heartbreakingly—reads, THE METHODIST CHURCH OF THE BUSH OF GHOSTS. Rarely has dichotomy been expressed in so few words.

The unacknowledged resentment against Christianity comes out almost with a sense of relief and release, like someone speaking a long-forbidden obscenity in order to break its haunting power. This resentment is perhaps not so very difficult to grasp, for it is directed against the religion which severed several generations of Africans from their own past. It appears in odd forms—sometimes by taking Christian rituals and turning them inside out or upside down.

> Rev. Devil was going to baptize me with fire and hot water as they were baptizing themselves there. When I was baptized on that day, I was crying loudly so that a person who is at a distance of two miles would not listen before hearing my voice, and within a few minutes every part of my body was scratched by this hot water and fire...
>
> After the baptism, then the same Rev. Devil preached again for a few minutes, while 'Traitor' read the lesson. All the members of this church were 'evil-doers'. They sang the song of evils with evils' melodious tune, then 'Judas' closed the service.

The old religions of Africa have combined with Christianity in some peculiar ways. The two have also clashed—and clashed tragically—within the individual minds of men. The whole story of this conflict is only now beginning to emerge clearly. A writer such as Achebe deals with it by trying to understand it and perceive it, by re-creating it within the personalities of his characters, characters who are not himself but who exist as themselves. This is the method of the novelist. Tutuola's method is poetic and intuitive. Here we get the conflict raw. Whether or not he means it to be there, it *is* there.

The hero marries a ghostess, and their wedding is marked by a weird humour, for at the reception the hero gets into trouble because he has 'mistakenly smashed a small ghost to death'. Soon he is on his way again, however, wandering to various ghost towns, being beaten, tortured and starved. He meets the Ugly Ghostess and is fascinated and morbidly attracted by her ugliness. He has a narrow escape from the Spider-eating Ghosts. He meets the Short Ghosts and their Flash-Eyed Mother, and when at last he disentangles himself from this dreadful matriarch, he meets and marries the Super-Lady, who first appears to him in the guise of an antelope. Their marriage is one of the few gentle episodes in the book, but he leaves her, ultimately, because they cannot agree on the upbringing of their child.

When the hero has been in the Bush of Ghosts for many years, he almost becomes a ghost himself. His will to return home is nearly destroyed, but he does finally return to earthly life when he receives an Invisible Magnetic Missive, for the appeal of his earthly family proves stronger than that of the ghostly world. He is enabled to return home through the power of the Television-Handed Ghostess, after he has healed her suppurating sore by medicine rather than the nauseating way she wanted, which was for him to lick it with his tongue for ten years.

The ending is enigmatic. 'This is what hatred did.' This conclusion does not seem to make sense in the external context, but it has specific meaning if it is viewed as another direct and indeed tragic statement from the inner world. *My Life in the Bush of Ghosts* is the work of someone who has walked in the pit of hell, and who has been courageous enough to open his eyes while he was there.

Simbi and the Satyr of the Dark Jungle

Tutuola's third book concerns the learning of wisdom through ordeal. It is not as strong a story as either *The Palm-Wine Drinkard* or *My Life in the Bush of Ghosts*, but much of it is written in a sprightly manner which is partly produced by the appearance of more conversation than the previous books contained.

Simbi is Tutuola's only book not written in the first person. He succeeds best with a first-person narration, as though he were able in this way to get inside the personality of the central character and to write with the unfailingly true sound of a human voice.

Simbi is the daughter of a wealthy woman. She is an only child and has been brought up in luxury. She is also naturally gifted, being a lovely girl and having a fine singing voice. But Simbi grows weary of her pleasant life, and longs to experience '...the "Poverty" and the "Punishment"'. She prays to know the meaning of poverty and punishment, and her dangerous prayer is quickly answered. She is kidnapped by Dogo, of Sinners' Town, 'the town in which only sinners and worshippers of gods were living.' The Christian concept here appears to contain a harsh dismissal of the old religion, yet the same dichotomy can be seen as in *My Life in the Bush of Ghosts*, for earlier Simbi consults the Ifa oracle and makes a sacrifice to enable her to pierce the secrets of poverty and punishment.

Simbi is taken by Dogo on the Path of Death, and she learns that he plans to sell her as a slave. She now has second thoughts about her desire to learn suffering, and pleads to be taken back to her mother. The conversation between Simbi and Dogo is both touching and humourous.

> 'Don't you know that it is entirely wrong and shameful to sell
> the daughter of a wealthy woman like me, and furthermore my
> mother has no other issue except I alone?'
> 'Of course, I don't know! and I don't want to know whether
> you are the daughter of a wealthy woman, just keep going to
> where I am going to sell you,' he replied so horribly that Simbi
> thought she had already dead.

Dogo sells Simbi as a slave, and she receives rough treatment. Finally she is put into a coffin and thrown in a river. She is discovered by fishermen and taken to Sinners' Town, where she becomes a slave again. She finds that four of her friends have also been kidnapped. The other girls bitterly resent the fact that Simbi chose to experience punishment. The girls manage to escape and go through grueling adventures on the Path of Death. Bako, the 'Terrible Siamese Twin', goes mad and beats the others again and again. Bako is later turned into a cockerel and is henceforth referred to as 'the cockish lady'.

Simbi's meeting with the Satyr of the Dark Jungle manages to combine the sinister with the absurd in the way that Tutuola does so well. The Satyr is as grim a monster as any Tutuola has ever described, and yet there is something appealing as well about this impenitent pessimist.

He was about ten feet tall and very strong, bold and vigorous.
His head was full of dirty long hairs and the hairs were full up
with refuses and dried leaves. The mouth was so large and wide
that it almost covered the nose. The eyes were so fearful that a
person could not be able to look at them for two times, especially
the powerful illumination they were bringing out always. He wore
plenty of ju-ju beads round his neck. The spiders' webs were
spread over his mouth and this showed that he had not eaten for
a long time. This Satyr was a pessimist, he was impatient and ill-
tempered, impenitent and noxious creature.

Simbi boasts of her powers, saying 'I can change myself to *Iro*—' but
breaking off in the middle of the word, for her friend Rali warns her not to let
the Satyr know her secret power. The Satyr therefore does not realise that
Simbi meant to say *ironi*, a water insect, and Simbi retains a power which will
enable her to defeat him in the end. But their final battle comes later, after
Simbi has become a woodcutter's wife and then a servant to an old woman
who gives her three gods. When she re-encounters the Satyr, he sets a tempting
trap for her—a huge Hall of Music, built entirely of live singing birds. The
descriptions of the Hall of Music, with its living walls of song, and of Simbi
dancing there, are among the most dazzling which Tutuola has ever written.

Those who were playing the instruments to the song of the
birds, were just in form of shadows of angels, and they were
seemed as if they were touched with hand perhaps the hand would
not hold or feel anything...

But Simbi begins to suspect that the music is unearthly, and she tries to
escape. A group of 'ultra-beautiful ladies' surrounds her and draws her into
their dance. She realises she is imprisoned in this glittering place. The frail
and deadly beauty of the Hall of Music becomes apparent when the Satyr
enters. He shackles Simbi to a rock and beats her with a cudgel of bones.
When he tires of the game, his people 'were beating her greedily with anything
they could find thereabouts'. Simbi overcomes the Satyr by changing herself
into a water insect and entering his nostril, where she stings him to death.

As with so much of Tutuola's work, under the lightness and humour,
under the descriptions of enchanted places, there lies the continuing theme of
pain, dreaded and yet sought.

The Brave African Huntress

Tutuola's fourth book is something of a disappointment. It is altogether thinner in texture, not so richly imaginative as his first three books, although there are flashes of the old style—for example, in chapter headings such as The Animal That Died But His Eyes Still Alive (the heroine prudently salvages the animal's skull with its glowing eyes and uses it as a night light), or in beautifully expressive phrases such as 'Whisperly the king spoke—'.

Adebisi, whose father was a renowned hunter, inherits his skills and puts them to use in going forth to rescue her four 'senior brothers' who are imprisoned in the Jungle of the Pigmies. Along the way, Adebisi has many adventures, including the time she becomes private barber to the King of Ibembe and discovers his secret—he has horns sprouting from his head. Adebisi attempts, in the age-old manner of African folk tales, to bury her knowledge of the king's secret by speaking it into a pit and ridding herself of it. But, in a passage reminiscent of Tutuola's best work, the pit grows 'two young curious trees' which are cut by a bugle blower and carved into a bugle. When the bugle is blown, it announces, 'The head of the King of Ibembe sprouts two horns! The two horns are thick and short!' In the ensuing riot, Adebisi flees and becomes lost, but luckily is able to find her way again with the help of her 'inherited ju-ju compass'.

Once Adebisi enters the Jungle of the Pigmies, the familiar pain images become increasingly frequent. The sadistic Pigmies laugh at the girl as they cut off one of her feet (which is later rejoined to her ankle by magical means). She is branded on the face with a red-hot iron. The people who are kept as slaves of the Pigmies live in a foully crowded and filthy hut, and the keepers wield 'uncountable of leather whips, dried long tails of big animals, long big bones of animals, clubs, cudgels, whips, etc.'. Adebisi ultimately triumphs over the Pigmies, sets the other captives free and finds her four brothers, but as in everything Tutuola has ever written, the goal of peace and fulfillment can only be reached by the path of 'endless punishments'.

As Gerald Moore points out, Tutuola's creatures in this book often have a European sound—elves, goblins, demons, imps, gnomes. Moore voices the hope that Tutuola will 'banish the goblins and gnomes back to the Northern forests where they belong' (*Seven African Writers*, p. 56). Fortunately, this is precisely what Tutuola does in his next book.

Feather Woman of the Jungle

Tutuola's debt to Yoruba folk tales and legends is perhaps a more self-conscious one in this book, but even when he is retelling a Yoruba story almost directly, he gives it his own interpretation and imparts to it his own style. *Feather Woman of the Jungle* takes the form of a series of stories told by an old chief about his lifetime's adventures. Divided in this way into ten night's 'entertainments', the book is more planned and formal than some of Tutuola's earlier writing, but this is not a disadvantage, for the form suits the material.

When the old chief was fifteen years old, he was 'very clever and fast enough', but he had not yet 'experienced the difficulties, hardship, punishments, risk, dangers, etc., of the adventures'. Once more, right from the beginning, we can see that the underlying theme is going to be similar to those of Tutuola's other books.

The hero and his brother Alabi set off in search of adventure and wealth. They meet the hideous Feather Woman, and the description of this creature indicates that Tutuola's imagination is as strong as it ever was.

> ...we were looking at her as she was wobbling towards us. When she was near us, we saw her clearly. Her body was downy but she wrapped herself from knees to waist with the skin of a tiger and the rest parts were soft feathers. The feathers were really grown out from her body except her head which had white thick hair. Her eyes were red and hollow with old age. Her breasts were hardly to see because soft feathers covered them. Almost all her teeth had fallen out so that made her mouth to be moving up and down always as if she was eating something in the mouth.

Tutuola's knack of using English in an original way is nowhere better illustrated than in the two brothers' reaction to the feather-covered witch.

> My junior brother looked at my eyes with fear instead to speak out to me and in return, I looked at the ground with the same fear instead to reply with mouth.

What Tutuola captures here is the living sound of the narrator's voice speaking in an English adapted and changed by the thought-patterns and constructions of Yoruba speech underneath. The result, as in so much of Tutuola's writing, is a phraseology which is both fresh and precise without in any sense straining to be either.

The two boys are taken prisoner by the Feather Woman. In front of her hut stand innumerable mud images. These images once were people, over whom the witch has cast her spell. The boys are warned not to take the cover off a magic pit or they will suffer the same fate as all the others. When their sister, Ashabi, turns up, however, she innocently lifts the cover of the pit and the two boys instantly turn to images. They are appalled to discover that although they cannot move, they can hear and feel. In the description of their plight, Tutuola seems to be giving symbolic expression to every inchoate human whose unspoken cries remain unheard. 'We were hearing whenever somebody talked but when we were talking people did not hear us.' The Feather Woman flays them until all her whips are torn in pieces, but whatever they suffer, they can communicate none of it.

Ashabi, the sister, becomes '...so leaned that bones were appearing on every part of her body. She was always lonely and casting down in every corner of the hut.' This spontaneous newness of language is one of Tutuola's gifts and shows why he is inimitable. The description of gauntness could hardly be more striking, and the inner state of mind is paralleled by the physical in the double connotation of 'casting down', for she both casts herself down literally and is cast down in spirit.

An old man tells Ashabi that she can save her brothers if she can refrain from speaking for two years. She must pretend to be dumb. It is difficult here to see the publishers' justification for printing Tutuola's manuscript errors of spelling. For pages and pages, 'dump' is used for 'dumb', and later on in the book, we get 'forg' for 'fog', just as in *The Brave African Huntress*, 'belonged' is given as 'blonged'. It would have been a great editorial mistake to alter any of Tutuola's imagery and phraseology, for the fact that his writing is not expressed in grammar-book English never mars and often immeasurably adds to its effectiveness in terms of what it is actually communicating, and communicating inventively. Spelling is an entirely different matter. Tutuola is certainly not the only writer who makes spelling mistakes. Everybody makes them. The correction of such errors is common editorial practice, and the fact that it has not been done here seems to give weight to the feeling that many West Africans have had about Tutuola's work—that it was read in Europe and America only so that its language could be ridiculed. Because this view is so far from the truth, it is a pity that Tutuola's publishers have allowed themselves, even unintentionally, to give credence to it. It is to be hoped that in future editions of Tutuola's work, the normal editorial services extended to other writers will not be withheld from him in any mistaken attempt to give his writing that false quaintness which is precisely what it does not, in itself, have.

When a hunter-prince enters the witch's compound, Ashabi pretends to be a mute. The prince wants to marry her, but she can make no reply. She cannot tell him about her brothers having been turned into images, for this is too complex to be communicated in sign language. The prince takes Ashabi away, and the brothers are left, not knowing where their sister is.

Ashabi gives birth to a child, and it is killed because the local custom is against a prince's marrying anyone who is mute. Ashabi's choice is an impossible one—if she speaks to save her child, her brothers will remain under the spell forever. She bears another child, and again it is killed. But when her third child is about to be killed, the two years have expired and Ashabi can speak. When she returns to the Feather Woman's dwelling, she finds that her brothers are once more in human form. Ashabi, closing her eyes against the danger, breaks the gigantic ostrich eggs in the magic pit, and immediately all spells are dissolved and the images regain their human shape, while the Feather Woman, in the classic manner of such tales, collapses and is defeated once and for all. The sense of release and joy makes the ending a delight to read: 'so the whole of us left the hut and were singing and dancing along on the road to the town of the hunting prince.'

Tutuola has a natural talent for titles which will immediately capture the imagination. The title of the third tale is The Treacherous Queen and the King in the Bush of Quietness. The hero hears of a town which has disappeared, leaving only 'a fearful quiet bush instead'. He sets out to find it, and comes to a deserted old palace. There is a lovely set-piece here—the carvings on the palace portico, the trees growing up through the crumbling walls, the old shrines of gods, the atmosphere of decay and fear.

The hero hears groaning from inside the ruins, and when he explores, he finds a man who has been severely whipped. Here, once more, we have that preoccupation with pain, especially flogging, which alternates in Tutuola's work with scenes of lightness and tenderness. This story is one of the most gruesome of all Tutuola's writing. The afflicted man used to be king, but when he killed his wife's lover, the queen-sorceress turned him into a great snake from the waist down. He is chained with a chain that reaches into the earth, and each night his wife comes and beats the snake half of his body. The hero hides in the grave where the sorceress long ago placed the dead lover, who has now become a skeleton. The woman arrives and beats the king, then makes her nightly pilgrimage to the tomb. The hero pretends to be her lover, returned to life, and says he will be allowed to stay with her only if she turns her husband back to his former self. She does so, and when she returns to the hero, he ties her up with rope and forces her to vomit out her supernatural power, which is in the form of a small white bird 'shaking like a chicken which was just hatched'.

Apart from the theme of suffering, this tale expresses the theme of the male subconscious fear of woman as an emasculating force, a creature both infinitely desirable and infinitely dangerous.

In the fourth entertainment, the hero has three dogs, Sweeper, Cutter and Swallower, who save him from a giantess. This part of the story is almost identical with the Yoruba tale of Iyabomba, the fierce mother of the forest, whose body was covered with hungry mouths, and of the hunter saved by the same three dogs.

Tutuola's hero is then taken prisoner by wild men who live in caves but who possess treasures of raw gold and coral. The scenes in the cave of the savage king are as grim as anything Tutuola has ever written. The king flogs the hero and also rides him like a horse (another recurring masochistic image) with a neck-rein which nearly chokes him. The horror here is derived partly from the specifically defined pain and partly from the grotesque elation of the scene.

> ...I hardly started to sing that song when he took part in it.
> When I sang it in tenor, he sang it in bass. When I sang it in bass,
> he sang it in treble with great joy. But I blamed myself at last to
> form that song, because it added to my punishment instead to
> lessen it. For as he was singing it with me, he was just doing as if
> he was crazy. He enjoyed it so much that he had lost all his senses
> at the same time and he was jumping up so highly that his head
> was striking the roof of that hole. And he rode me into the
> roughest part of the hole...

After this torture, the savage king falls asleep, exhausted and fulfilled. When he wakens, he again rides the hero, again nearly throttling him in the process. The three dogs finally come to the hero's rescue, and he is able to escape with much of the treasure. He is honoured by his village and is at peace with himself because he knows he is 'able to endure severe punishment'.

The fifth entertainment is From the Town of Famine to the Town of the Water People. The hero enters a famine-stricken town, where the king promises him great riches if he can obtain food. In search of palm-fruit, the hero takes a canoe down the river. He falls into the water and is pulled under by some mysterious agency and put into a glass coffin. The creature who has captured him has fish's skin from the waist down, scales instead of hair on his head, fins on his shoulders and the jaw of a fish. The water man takes the hero to the underwater city. Tutuola gives a wonderful description of the water queen's palace.

> The decorations on the walls were stuffed gold fishes, polished large sea shells, skulls of sea animals, etc, and every part of that walls was twinkling like stars. The seats were also stuffed fishes and were as fresh as if they were still alive.

The queen of the water people 'had a clear and lovely voice and her face always seemed as if she was kind and merciful'. This longing for tenderness is a theme which is very moving in Tutuola's work, seen in juxtaposition to the recurring patterns of compulsive suffering. The queen gives the hero a magic box which will feed the entire population. The hero takes it to the famine town, but it is stolen by marauders. He attempts to get a second box from the water queen, but the rules of myth are strong and inflexible—if the gift is not guarded properly, the second gift turns out, invariably, to be poisonous. The new box produces only vicious bees and wasps.

The Goddess of the Diamonds on the Mountain is the appealing title of the sixth tale. Here the hero meets the formidable goddess in a city abounding with diamonds. He is befriended by a girl, Sela, and together they escape, taking with them 'diamond blocks'. After many perils, they reach the hero's village and are married. The hero's father advises the young bride to be a 'stagnant wife', constant in time of trouble, and not a 'flowing away wife', who 'never drink the bitter tea with her husband except the sweet tea'.

Sela is spirited away by the goddess of the diamond mountain, and only in the last tale is the hero reunited with her, after he has had further adventures, including one trip to Ile-Ife and Ede, where he meets and pays homage to none less than Sango, god of thunder. The 'town of wealths' is finally reached, but the path is strewn with pain. All ends well, but as the old chief says in his parting words to his people, 'So it is very scarcely to go on a journey and return without punishments, hardships, etc., etc.'

Anne Tibble says that a 'motif or deeper level of *Feather Woman of the Jungle*.... is the ruthless, cool perseverance men need to obtain any of the good things from life. Some of these good things Tutuola makes very clear: they are wisdom, wealth, and a "stagnant wife"' (*African/English Literature*, p. 101). As well as this, and despite the frequently humourous tone of the surface, the main underlying theme is a masochistic one. For the story's hero the goal is to be achieved only through pain and humiliation, suffering which he is compelled to seek, not really for its own sake but in order that the enduring of it may permit the gates to be opened to the desired end. The 'town of wealths' is gained, but at a high price.

Amos Tutuola has a way of combining the macabre and the beautiful, the horrifying and the humourous, the familiar and the mysterious. One of the most impressive things about him when he is at his best is the vitality of his writing and the completely unstudied and casual way in which he makes his dramatic effects, as for example the scene in *The Palm-Wine Drinkard* in which the hero meets Drum, Song and Dance.

> Nobody could beat drum as 'Drum' could beat himself, nobody could sing as 'Song' could sing himself, and nobody could dance as 'Dance' could dance herself in this world. Who would challenge them? Nobody at all. ...When 'Drum' started to beat himself, all the people who had been dead for hundreds of years, rose up and came to witness 'Drum' when beating: and when 'Song' began to sing all domestic animals of that new town, bush animals with snakes etc., came out to see 'Song' personally, but when 'Dance' (that lady) started to dance the whole bush creatures, spirits, mountain creatures and also all the river creatures came to see who was dancing. When these three fellows started at the same time, the whole people of that new town, the whole people that rose up from the grave, animals, snakes, spirits and other nameless creatures, were dancing together.

For music, for rhythm, for a sense of life, for the vibrant sound of the story-teller's voice, that passage would be hard to beat.

Essentially, however, the themes are dark ones, themes which can in no sense be said to exclude any one of us. Anne Tibble sees the work of Tutuola as 'fine fairy tales as well as contriving to be something more, for boys and girls and grown-ups' (*African/English Literature*, p. 101). It is quite true that the magic is never a mock-up, never a sham—it is always the real thing. But if Tutuola's books are for children, it is only in the same way that *Gulliver's Travels* was once thought to be.

Tutuola's books are not really novels. They are episodic and they follow the classical lines of the sagas found in all cultures. He writes best when most intuitively and most intensely inward. His forests are certainly and in detail the outer ones but they are, as well, the forests of the mind, where the individual meets and grapples with the creatures of his own imagination. These creatures are aspects of himself, aspects of his response to the world into which he was born, the world to which he must continue to return if he is to live as a man.

Masks of the City

Cyprian Ekwensi

CYPRIAN EKWENSI'S WORLD is largely the city world of right-this-minute. His idiom is that of the city streets and the beat of the highlife music. His writing is full of events, narrated in a brisk and snappy style that owes much to journalism. Ekwensi constantly criticises the city for the greed, the impersonality, the lust and the corruption which he sees there. But his feelings are divided, for he loves the city as well, and his liveliest writing is of life in Lagos.

Sometimes Ekwensi's writing seems too moral and sermonising. Yet he is not a one-stance writer. He is able at one moment to take on a warning tone when speaking of the city's prostitutes and thugs, and the next moment to show a genuine compassion towards these lost and fallen, seeing them as victims of the city which they victimise. He is particularly sympathetic towards women, especially the young girls who go to the city hoping with shining *naïveté* that their lives will be one glorious dream, and who find that reality is not quite as they had imagined. In fact, Ekwensi's women come alive and step from the printed page much more often than his men do, and he has created a few really memorable women characters.

All but one of Ekwensi's novels take place mainly in the city, but in all there are country episodes, and Ekwensi shows an equal attachment to Northern Nigeria, with its mosques and walled cities and desert-like plains, and to Eastern Nigeria with its rain-forests and lush vegetation. In the same way, he is one of the few Nigerian writers who consistently brings into his writing people of all tribes. Indeed, in most of his novels, there is a strong undercurrent of anti-tribalism, which is not a desire to abolish cultural or religious differences, but rather a conviction that these differences can and must be accepted and lived with.

Ekwensi was born into an Ibo family in Minna, Northern Nigeria, in 1921. He went to college in Ibadan, and later in Ghana. He studied pharmacy in England, after which he taught biology and chemistry at a college near Lagos. He then joined the Nigerian Broadcasting Corporation and was Head of the Features Department when his first novel was published. He has worked as a journalist and has had articles published in magazines in Africa, America and England. He has written a number of easy-to-read stories, such as *An African Night's Entertainment*, for use in schools and in adult education.

He began fiction-writing with the type of popular stories known as 'Onitsha market books'. These paperbacks originated in the big market town of Onitsha and are still produced and sold there in huge quantities. Their general tone is both sentimental and highly moral, and in content they are similar to many American and English women's magazines, with Nigerian variations of the familiar mixture—how to get your man or your girl, how to behave acceptably in social situations, how to be desirable and charming, how to succeed in business, how not to offend your mother-in-law—all presented in action-filled fiction with flamboyant titles.

One of Ekwensi's first stories, published as an Onitsha market book, was called *Where Love Whispers*. Something of this sentimentality and superficiality can still be seen in his later books, although there is scarcely a trace of it in his best novels, *Jagua Nana* and *Iska*. Ekwensi has published five novels—*People of the City*, 1954; *Jagua Nana*, 1961; *Burning Grass*, 1962; *Beautiful Feathers*, 1963; and *Iska*, 1966; as well as a book of short stories, *Lokotown and Other Stories*, 1966.

People of the City

This novel made quite an initial impact, for it was the first truly contemporary novel by a West African to be widely read throughout the English-speaking world. In West Africa, of course, its effect was greatest, for a lot of young Africans felt that at last here was someone who really understood them and accepted the fact that the world of today was not the world of their parents.

People of the City is written in a fast-moving style which suits the subject perfectly. Parts of it are exciting, and the night-club and street scenes are well done. The construction of the novel is weak, however, and the plot diffuse. The writing tends to be too sentimental and banal, and the characters are generally stereotyped and unconvincing, although Sango, the hero, comes across reasonably well.

Amusa Sango is a crime reporter for the *West African Sensation*. He also leads a jazz band in The All Language Club. He lives in Molomo Street, where everyone knows everyone else's business. The city is not named, but is clearly Lagos. Sango becomes involved with a succession of girls—Aina, Beatrice, Elena, and the girl he finally marries, who is also and most confusingly called Beatrice.

Apart from his difficulties with the women in his life, Sango experiences a reversal of his luck. He is sacked from The All Language Club, because he has been playing election music for the opposite party to the one the club's owner supports. The city begins to devour him, as it has devoured so many.

If this novel had been less jittery in its plot, its effect would have been stronger. But the story leaps about spasmodically like a nervous cricket. Aina flashes in and out. Sango decides that he loves Beatrice for ever, but as his rivals are Lajide, his landlord, and Zamil, a rich Syrian trader, he does not stand much chance. When he meets Beatrice the Second, however, he knows instantly that she is the *one*. But perhaps he should marry Elena, his parents' choice for him.

And so it goes on. At one point, Bayo, Sango's friend, tries to elope with the sister of Zamil. The lovers are discovered and Zamil shoots both of them. An almost unbelievably melodramatic scene follows, with the lovers expiring in one another's arms and swan-songing in a highly unlikely manner— 'Embrace me, sweetheart, before I die.' Ekwensi has a real understanding of the city and its people; he is capable of describing them genuinely, without phonily inflated, operatic-type emotions. When he writes falsely, as in this ridiculous scene, it is irritating.

The scenes at The All Language Club are done energetically and with the mixture of disapproval and attraction which characterises all Ekwensi's city writing.

> By ten o'clock The All Language Club was full, and still more
> people came. They liked what the Club was trying to do.

No bars—social, colour, political or religious. There were two
bars, though, a snack bar, and one plentifully supplied with all
percentages of alcohol right up to a hundred.

Some people came because they liked Sango's music, or the
music of the Hot Cats Rhythm, or the Highlife drumming of the
unsophisticated Nigerian bands. They came in couples, they came
alone and unescorted and sat under the palm trees and smoked
and watched the bright lights.

Ekwensi's descriptions of the city girls also have this ambiguity of feeling,
which is partly a perception of the loneliness under some of the city's masks
and partly a faintly moral tone combined with its opposite, the desire to
acknowledge openly the undeniable attractions. Sango knows that the
brightness may conceal poverty and aloneness, yet he yearns after such girls.

This was a girl who belonged strictly to the city. Born in the
city. A primary education, perhaps the first four years at
secondary school; yet she knew all about Western sophistication—
make-up, cinema, jazz... This was the kind of girl whom Sango
knew would be content to walk her shoes thin in the air-
conditioned atmosphere of department stores, to hang about all
day in the foyer of hotels with not a penny in her handbag, rather
than live in the country and marry Papa's choice.

As she sat down, Sango put her age definitely at sixteen. Do
not be deceived by those perfectly mature breasts. Girls ripen
quickly in the city—the men are so impatient.

The city's atmosphere of exhilarating newness, with its undertones of
isolation and uncertainty, is portrayed well in *People of the City*, but the
novel is now of interest principally because it was the first of its kind. Its
weakness of organisation and frequent falsity of tone prevent its being
considered an important novel in itself.

Jagua Nana

Astonishingly, with Ekwensi's second novel, the sentimentality is gone and
the quick and easy journalistic clichés do not appear. Ekwensi is a long way
from being the best writer in Nigeria, but he has written one of the best single
novels to have come out of the whole of West Africa so far. In *Jagua Nana* he

has created a magnificent and fully alive character. Jagua is a Lagos prostitute of forty-five—ageing, worrying about ageing, terribly proud, proud of her body and looking after it with great skill and care, and also proud within herself. Jagua loves a man much younger than herself, Freddie Namme, and although she realises quite well that her passion for him is foolish, she is unable to stop. She is guided only by her emotions, and she escapes from all problems by dancing at her favourite haunt, The Tropicana Club.

Ekwensi's descriptions of the Tropicana are extremely effective. They are done always in relation to Jagua, so we see not only the club itself but the ways in which it has formed her, the ways in which it explains her.

> The Tropicana to her was a daily drug, a potent habit-forming brew. Like all the other women who came here, alone or with some man, Jagua was looking for the ray of hope. Something will happen tonight, this night, she always told herself.
>
> The music was tremendously rhythmic, coming from the bongo drums, and the bandleader, pointing his trumpet skywards, blew till the blisters on his lips widened and he wiped his lips and the sax snatched away the solo, distorting it. This was it, Jagua felt.

Freddie knows that Jagua is a prostitute, yet he can never bring himself to admit it. He resents her association with other men, yet he also resents the fact that she is trying to possess him and to make him some kind of insurance for her old age. He does not want her to leave him, yet he often wants to leave her. Jagua regards her profession calmly as a means of livelihood, but she is generally tactful where Freddie is concerned and tries to protect him from seeing her in the company of another man. She does not always succeed, and then she feels sorry for Freddie, but she shrugs it off, because after all she has to consider her career and her living. Ekwensi explores the relationship between the wor[l]dly-wise Jagua and the young impetuous Freddie with humour and tenderness.

Jagua gives Freddie money towards his education in England, and helps him to obtain his passport. Unfortunately, soon afterwards she catches Freddie with a girl, Nancy Oll, daughter of Jagua's old arch-enemy, Mama Oll. Jagua is semi-literate and speaks in pidgin English. When she is enraged her speech is as fiery as her actions.

> Jagua sprang at her. 'I goin' to teach you pepper! And you kin go and call you Mama too an' I will give am fire to chop!' Freddie scarcely saw the flash of her hand but he heard the smack and saw

Nancy wince and place a hand on her cheek. The two women clinched, and it was Nancy who screamed, 'Oh! …Freddie, she bite me! De witch woman bite me!'

Jagua tears up Freddie's passport, but later repents and once more assists him to make arrangements for going to England. Freddie by this time is in love with Nancy and yet is still attached to Jagua. Jagua has been unable to have children, and this is a real sorrow to her. She wants Freddie's child—and yet Freddie himself in a sense is her child. Their relationship is coming to its inevitable end, but this is something Jagua cannot accept.

Freddie—unforgivably—sets a trap for her. Jagua picks up a man, gets into the car beside him, and discovers that Freddie is in the back seat and has made a bet with this acquaintance of his who told him he knew Jagua's regular beat. Jagua is deeply humiliated. She finds it impossible to understand how Freddie could have done this to her. He has taken money from her, but he could not accept that he must never question where the money came from. Nevertheless, with all the cards clearly stacked against her, Jagua persists in believing that Freddie will marry her when he returns from England. In some ways she is intensely realistic, but where Freddie is concerned she remains deceived by her own impossible dreams of quiet domesticity.

While Freddie is away, Jagua goes to visit her family, for she is an Ibo from Eastern Nigeria, but she has lived in Lagos for ten years. The ways of the country are slow and strange to her now, and she is strange to her own people.

> In Ogabu the people tilled the soil and drank river water and ate yams and went to church but came home to worship their own family oracles. They believed that in a village where every man has his own yam plots, there is much happiness in the hearts of the men and the women and the children; but where it is only one man who has the yam plots there is nothing but anger and envy, and strife breaks out with little provocation. Jagua knew that the men thought only about the land and its products and the women helped them make the land more fruitful. So that her city ways became immediately incongruous. The film of make-up on her skin acquired an ashen pallor. The women fixed their eyes on the painted eyebrows and one child called out in Ibo, 'Mama! Her lips are running blood!' Jagua heard another woman say, 'She walks as if her bottom will drop off. I cannot understand what the girl has become.'

She also goes to Bagana to see Freddie's family, but to her dismay she finds Mama Oll and her daughter there already. Young Nancy is now accepted by the family as Freddie's fiancée. Jagua never acknowledges defeat, or at least not openly, but after a brief liaison with chief Ofubara, one of Freddie's uncles, she returns to Lagos. Drawn magnetically to trouble, Jagua gets involved with Dennis Odoma and his gang of thieves. Her luck begins to go down. She takes up with Rosa, a gentle young street-walker who keeps house for Jagua in exchange for a place to stay.

There is a resilient quality about Jagua. She keeps on rising matter-of-factly from her own calamities, however much fuss and drama she may make of them at the time. She keeps a keen eye on the main chance, and soon she becomes the mistress of Uncle Taiwo, a flashy and elderly politician. Uncle Taiwo beams with generosity and goodwill. His election promises are as loud and sensational as his clothes. There is a definite bawdy appeal about him, and he is utterly dishonest. This quality bothers Jagua not at all. She is not a politically-minded woman, although she helps Uncle Taiwo in his campaign and even—to her own surprise—makes an election speech to the market women.

Freddie, now back from England and married to Nancy, makes his reappearance as Uncle Taiwo's opponent in the election. Uncle Taiwo, suspecting, and quite rightly, that Jagua is playing a double game with himself and Freddie, has his hired thugs attack the young man. But something goes wrong. Instead of merely being beaten up, Freddie is accidentally killed. No one can prove anything, but Uncle Taiwo's reputation is severely tarnished. He loses the election, and flees out of fear of his own party's anger against him.

Jagua has lost both her lover and her protector. She moves with Rosa to a room in the Lagos slums, where she plies her trade. She is still fighting, but things have changed a lot since the days when she was first given the nickname of Jagua, after the Jaguar car, because of her sleekness and her style.

Ultimately she cannot hold out any longer. She goes back home to Ogabu. She is not quite finished yet, though. She has an affair with a Lagos man who happens to be passing through, and at last she conceives the child she has wanted for so long. Jagua thinks she will settle down now, but this is not to be her fate. The child lives for only a few days. For a long while she is bleak and empty, but finally the old vitality reasserts itself. When we last see her, Jagua is telling her friend Rosa about her plans.

> 'I just told Mama dat I goin' to Onitsha. I wan' to become
> proper merchant princess. I goin' to buy me own shop, and lorry,
> and employ me own driver. I goin' to face dis business serious.
> I sure dat God above goin' to bless me.'

The way in which she might be able to become in reality a merchant princess is that Uncle Taiwo left a brief-case with her when he bolted, and when Rosa arrives in Ogabu with news that Uncle Taiwo has been murdered (by his own party, for his failure, the gossip goes) Jagua opens the brief-case and finds it full of cash, prudently stashed away by Uncle Taiwo for the rainy day that did not arrive quite in the way he expected. This ending might be thought too convenient a solution, but in context it is perfectly plausible. The Uncle Taiwos of this world always make provision for their own downfall, and although he did not trust Jagua, there was no one else he trusted half as much. Jagua's final expression of hope would have had too sentimental a tinge if we were able to take her words at their face value. But it is impossible to believe them.

From everything that has ever happened to Jagua, it is only too apparent that the solid life of a market trader woman is not for her. It is easy to imagine her being drawn back to Lagos, staying on and on there until finally it is too late. But she will go down, when she does, like a ruined queen.

The other characters in the novel also come across well: young Nancy, innocent only on the surface, but underneath far more capable of getting what she really wants than Jagua is, because far less easily distracted or led by her emotions; Uncle Taiwo, jovial, crooked, by turns confident and frightened; Freddie Namme, despising Jagua, never seeing her true strength, yet never able to break finally with her.

Ekwensi's descriptions of the Lagos streets and night-clubs, of political campaigns and markets, of Ogabu and Bagana with their rural slowness and courtesy and a measure of integrity not found in the city—all these are done with assurance and authenticity, and Ekwensi allows them to register their own impressions without interference or sermonising.

Yet the novel remains Jagua's. Ekwensi portrays her in all her often-contradictory moods. She is sharp-witted and calculating, but totally without knowledge of cause and effect, able to bring off small triumphs splendidly, but never able to sort out her own life. She has a temper like red pepper, but she is capable of great affection. She can screech and claw like a she-eagle one moment, and the next moment be as generous with her money and herself as though her whole future were assured. She is tough, enduring, and completely without self-pity. She accepts the world as she finds it, seeing its meanness with an undeceived eye and enjoying its pleasures whenever she can. As a fictional character she will remain alive for a long time.

Burning Grass

The uneven quality of Ekwensi's writing is nowhere more apparent than in the fact that he followed *Jagua Nana* with a novel which from an outsider's point of view can only be termed a B-grade Western set in Northern Nigeria.

Burning Grass is a story of the Fulani, nomadic cattle-herding people, and it begins exceedingly well, by conjuring up in a few words the appearance and atmosphere of an entire area.

> When they begin to burn the grass in Northern Nigeria, it is time for the herdsmen to be moving the cattle southwards to the banks of the great river. And the hunters, lurking on the edge of the flames with dane gun, bow and arrow sniff the fumes and train their eyes to catch the faintest flicker of beasts hastening from their hiding places.
>
> It is time too for the harmattan to blow dust into eyes and teeth, to wrinkle the skin: the harmattan that leaves in its wake from Libya to Lagos a shroud of fog that veils the walls and trees like muslin on a sheikh.

That description could scarcely be better or more apt, but from there on the novel is unbroken melodrama all the way. The story concerns Mai Sunsaye, head of a family, who becomes infected (magically, it is implied) by the *sokugo*, the wandering sickness which dooms men to go on and on forever, never able to settle down. Mai Sunsaye has three sons, Jalla, Hodio and Rikku, and the four chase all over the plains and through the cities and villages of the north in a series of adventures which are so tangled that they become almost impossible to follow. Long-lost relatives, dark dungeons, a legendary 'woman in white' who wanders in the bush with white cattle, a devilish lady spy 'dressed in Oriental fashion', a beautiful young girl who is accompanied by a tame lion, a series of mad pursuits, a whirl of flying hooves and fisticuffs and burning huts—these are a few of the elements of *Burning Grass*.

In a typical scene, a duel takes place between Mai Sunsaye's son, Hodio, and the villain Shehu.

> ...Shehu, master of the girl Fatimeh, original cause of the split in the Sunsaye family. Hodio whipped out his dagger...

They do not, of course, merely fight. They snarl things like, 'Prepare now for the slow death of a thief!' or 'Come now and meet your doom!'

It is not really possible to assess this novel in the same way as Ekwensi's others, for *Burning Grass* is written in a spirit and vein similar to Ekwensi's adult-education books—an entertainment done in a style that would be locally acceptable to people whose acquaintance with contemporary novels would be nil, but whose knowledge of their own folk literature, transmitted from generation to generation by storytellers around the fire, would be extensive. It contains many of the qualities of traditional African tales—magical occurrences, mysterious and seductive women, acts of phenomenal heroism, swift-paced adventure. In this sense, *Burning Grass* is not so much a novel as a modern folktale. It belongs with Ekwensi's adult-education series, and probably ought not to have been given a wider publication.

Beautiful Feathers

Ekwensi's fourth novel belongs in the mainstream of his writing but it falls very far short of the standard he set himself in *Jagua Nana*. Ekwensi is rarely at his best in descriptions of political situations, and this novel is concerned almost totally with politics.

Wilson Iyari is a pharmacist in Lagos and is the new leader of the Nigerian Movement for African and Malagasy Solidarity.

The novel's title is taken from an Ibo proverb which says that a man not respected in his own house is like a bird with beautiful feathers—wonderful on the outside, but ordinary within—and this describes Wilson accurately enough. He is making progress with his political movement, but he has trouble at home. Yaniya, his wife, is angry at his neglect, real or imagined, and she makes his life miserable in every way she can—by refusing to cook his meals, by demanding that he give money to her no-good brother, by running around with other men.

Ekwensi concedes that Yaniya does have something of a case, but ninety-five per cent of the fault is presented as hers. Although the novel sometimes conveys the impression that Wilson's own excessive earnestness (for example, in calling his sons Lumumba and Jomo) is being satirised, the satire is so faint as to be timid, whereas the thundering denunciations of painted women toll like sermons.

Wilson's political feelings are described in flat and pamphlet-like terms:

> Wilson thought ahead and decided, the time has now come
> to organise something on a much wider scale. 'The word is
> "solidarity", and it has captured my imagination.'

His, maybe, but in this context, certainly not the reader's.

The scenes between Yaniya and her lover, Gadson Salifas, are more real and convincing. She cannot cease complaining petulantly about her husband, even when she is with Gadson—to his obvious boredom. She yearns for excitement, yet when the chance comes, she cannot help worrying about her children. Will they be all right in her absence? Will they get ill, she wonders guiltily, as a punishment for her? Ekwensi's portrayal of Yaniya in these scenes rings absolutely true. Yet there is something dubious in Gadson's lecturing of her.

> 'Much as I love you, Yaniya, I will tell you this. For men,
> this kind of love is an adventure. For women, it is sure to lead
> to something else. Something terrible...'

It seems improbable that Gadson would warn Yaniya in this fashion at the very moment when he hoped to take her to bed. The foreshadowing contained in the list of terrible things which may follow—separation, murder, the death of the children—is clumsy and too obvious, for indeed the youngest child does die of fever soon after Yaniya has decided to leave Wilson and has gone back to her father's home in the forest.

The development of Wilson's career follows a curious line. He is summoned to the Prime Minister's office and asked 'to be useful now, instead of criticising'. To which Wilson replies, a shade too readily, 'Yes, sir. I shall be willing to make any contribution in any way you want, sir.'

The P.M. then decides to send Wilson to Dakar to a conference on African Unity. If Ekwensi had intended this outcome to be ironic, that might be a different matter, both in terms of social satire and in terms of character portrayal. But a distinct impression is given not of irony but of depressing cosiness. Hurrah! Wilson is a member of the Establishment at last.

Vague phrase is piled upon vague phrase. 'This country is already on the path to uniting all other African countries' is one which now reads with a cruel unintentional irony.

The development of the characters' personal lives is scarcely less rosy-tinted. Yaniya decides to become an air hostess because 'My plane will crash, and when I die, Lum's life will have been avenged.' Fate is relieved, however, of the necessity for this extreme course, for Yaniya performs her act of expiation by saving Wilson from a would-be assassin and getting stabbed herself in the process. She recuperates, and 'it appeared they were all set for a new life...'

Beautiful Feathers seems to represent a desire to preach rather than any need to write a novel. The writing is stilted, stiffly bristling with maxims pertaining to the solid bourgeois virtues. Wilson speaks platitudes and is himself indistinguishable from them. While Yaniya takes on some degree of life early in the novel, she later becomes just as one-dimensional as Wilson. At one point, she even says to her erstwhile lover, 'All you wanted was my body, that's all.' This antique cliché would never have been possible with *Jagua Nana* and it contrasts oddly with the pride and real hurt in Jagua's voice the day she is turned away from Freddie's funeral.

> Awright, Nancy; I goin' to leave. But look all de people who love your Freddie! You know all of dem? Or you goin' to drive de ones you don' know? Your Freddie was a famous man who people love. If to say he livin', he for no drive me from his house.

In fact he might very well have driven her from his house, and Jagua knows it—the recognition is implicit in the way she says 'Your Freddie'. But she speaks out of her actual pain and so her speech may not be accurate but it is true. Yaniya, on the other hand, has become a cardboard figure speaking cardboard conventionalities.

Lokotown and Other Stories

These short stories give an interesting although superficial impression of Lagos life—the markets, the bars, Lokotown where the trainmen live. Although they have only recently been published as a collection, most of them read like Ekwensi's early stories. Their chief value now lies in the fact that some of them contain the origins of the later novels.

'Glittering City' concerns Fussy Joe, who is a trumpet-player with a jazz band. He is always in trouble with a shoal of women, and he is also an inveterate liar, often passing himself off as a reporter on the *West African Sensation*. This story may be the embryo of what later developed into *People of the City*.

Certain familiar places and people appear in these stories—Molomo Street, where Ekwensi's first novel is set, and Lajide, who is Sango's landlord in *People of the City*. In 'Fashion Girl', we see Jagua Nana in her younger days, when she first ran away from her husband and went to Accra for a while. We see her learning how to be chic, how to be 'Jagua', and we witness how she picks up her first protector.

> Jagua Nana settled back in the car and wondered whether that talk would end all her wanderings. Perhaps it would. Providing he did not stop her being Jagua, she would listen to him and perhaps even give her consent.

But her wandering was only beginning—just as perhaps the character was only beginning in Ekwensi's mind.

Iska

Once again, with Ekwensi's latest novel, it is apparent that the quality of his writing is uneven, but this time the change is all in the right direction. The tone of *Iska* is completely different from that of *Beautiful Feathers*. In *Iska* the outlook is sombre and the whole novel is pervaded with a sense of grief. The writing is plain and spare, with no exaggerations, none of the sentimentality that marred *Beautiful Feathers*, no false optimism or mock-ups of happy endings.

One of the main themes of *Iska* is tribalism, and the first part of the novel is concerned with the Ibo-Hausa riots in the north. This is the first novel to deal with the problem of the Ibo people living in Northern Nigeria among the Hausa and Fulani. It is right that it is Ekwensi who has written it, for he is himself an Ibo who was born and grew up in the north. He not only knows the situation—he is deeply involved in it. He is writing about something he really cares about, perhaps more than he has in any other novel. There is no room for gimmicks any more, no room for facile solutions. The result is a novel which is his best since *Jagua Nana* and perhaps in some ways his best so far.

Filia, the main character in *Iska*, does not quite reach the dimensions of Jagua, nor take on such a life of her own, although she is a subtly-drawn individual. The novel as a whole, however, is the most skilfully structured of all Ekwensi's books. The plot confusions and diversions are gone. The novel is both clear and complex. It follows inexorably the life of one character and, through her, the present terrible plight of the country itself.

Filia Enu is an Ibo girl, born and educated in the north. She marries Dan Kaybi, a Hausa, against the wishes of both families. Dan is killed in a tribal riot, although he himself has been very much against tribalism. The feelings of individuals are not taken into consideration in a mob situation.

Filia goes back to her parents' old home in Ogabu in Eastern Nigeria (the same place where Jagua originally came from) but she finds herself too restless and bored there. She goes to Lagos, where she becomes a model. She takes up with a young thug, Rayimi, who is the bodyguard of a politician, and she also becomes involved with Gadson Salifas (who was the lover of Yaniya in *Beautiful Feathers* and is now a considerably older and sadder man). The bright life of the city palls, and Filia becomes for a time attracted to a religious sect, the Prayer People, and its leader, Piska Dabra, but this too fails her when she discovers Dabra's corruption. She falls in love with a young journalist, Dapo Ladele, who is political correspondent for the *West African Sensation*, but he disillusions her when he takes on the editorship of a political paper although he knows the rottenness of his bosses. Her home in the north, the city's glamour, religion, politics, all have become bitter-tasting.

The characters in this novel *are* the themes, and the themes are given individual voices with each character. The different men in Filia's life represent different aspects of present-day Nigeria's upheaval, and yet this novel is emphatically not propaganda and its characters are never abstractions. Taken together, however, these men illustrate both the agony and the hope that Ekwensi feels towards his torn land.

Dan Kaybi, the handsome young Hausa man whom Filia marries, is progressive and anti-tribalist. Idealistic, a man of integrity, he is prepared to stand up for his principles of tribal equality, yet he is drawn into the violence he seeks to avoid, and in the end he has altered nothing.

Ekwensi does not present tribal riots in one-sided or simple terms. In one of the most moving scenes in the novel, Filia gains admission to the prison, by a few skilful lies, to see the man who killed her husband, the murderer whom she imagines must be brutal and cruelly cold. Her intention has been to vent her sorrow and anger on him. Instead, she finds a terror-stricken boy, horrified by what he has done, who weeps when he learns who she is.

Ekwensi seems to feel that the tension between Hausa and Ibo is at this point politically induced or at least severely aggravated by politics. The ordinary Hausa and Ibo, as individuals, do not, he thinks, hate one another. The ancient mistrust and the suspicion felt toward strangers lie deep under the surface, however, and these buried feelings can be brought out and fanned into flame.

> Normally, the Ibo man worked like a steam engine, multiplied like the guinea-pig, and effervesced with honesty. The Hausa man was tolerant, philosophical, accommodating, believing that whatever would be would be. Both had lived peacefully together

for a hundred years. Then came politics—the vulture's foot that spoils the stew.

Or, again:

Politicians fan it up and we, the stupid ones, begin quarrelling and killing ourselves. They fan it up and still remain friends.

The fathers of Dan and Filia, Musa Kaybe (Hausa), and Uzodike Enu (Ibo), represent the traditional tribal enmities. They are willing to live side by side, even to work together, but their conceptual backgrounds are different, their religions are different and they both stand absolutely opposed to intermarriage.

Musa Kaybe tells his son, 'Whatever you do, wherever you go, you are still a northerner. You are my son, and we come from Nupe land. Our kingdom was founded by Tsoede. We are masters of the River Niger'—the proud aristocratic voice of the Islamic north.

Filia's father, on the other hand, is no less proud of his own inheritance and his own achievements. He worked extremely hard in the north as a skilled miner and he prospered, but his heart remained in Ogabu, among his own people, and when he returned there, after retirement, he took an Ibo title and became a leader in the community. His son was killed in a tribal riot in the north, and Uzodike's suspicion of the Hausa hardened into unappeasable bitterness.

Both are terribly right, and terribly wrong. Both command our sympathies. This is the tragedy which Ekwensi makes us see.

In Lagos, the themes shift and alter. Gadson Salifas is a civil servant, suave, smooth-talking, wanting both a settled home life and a succession of pretty young girls as mistresses. Yet underneath he is uncertain, anxious about his job and about himself as a man. When he goes to a meeting of the Prayer People (in order to retrieve his wife who has fallen under the spell of the sect's leader) Gadson prays—absurdly and touchingly—that he may never lose his post in the Ministry and that he may achieve the expected increment. He tries to make love to Filia, fails, and begs her not to tell anyone of his inability. He is a well-educated man, a man who has risen in his work and who enjoys his social power, and yet in middle age he finds himself impotent, dispirited, empty.

Rayimi, the young thug, radiates sexuality. He is muscular, tough, a lithe, panther-like creature, smartly dressed in an American-style suit. He carries a clasp-knife and is always ready to attack instantly. Rayimi found nothing to do when he left school, and so he became a paid thug because the money was good. There is a coldness and cynicism about him. He knows he will probably die violently, but in the meantime he has the city life, the girls, and above all, the excitement of his chosen profession. He has a chilling desire to hurt and even to kill, and at the same time he lives in a kind of bewilderment, almost a stupor, which is not entirely explained by the hashish he often smokes. It is as though he himself were surprised by his own character and the violence of his life but could make no attempt to comprehend himself. Ekwensi presents Rayimi as a man who is both frightening and pathetic. No judgments are attempted. He is portrayed just as he is, one of the inevitable by-products of his era.

The politician Nafotim preaches tribalism, with no regard for the consequences, because he sees in this doctrine an easy popularity, a means of rousing the passions of the public and turning them to his own advantage. He is attractive personally, and like Chief Nanga in Achebe's *A Man of the People*, quite unscrupulous. Yet Ekwensi shows him as a man of genuine action as well, a person capable of achieving results which, whatever his motives, will benefit the people as a whole. Filia, observing him, remembers the words of the Prayer People's leader—'It's the politicians who bring all the trouble.' But she herself has sufficient insight to see as well that 'it was also the politicians who brought national pride and freedom.'

Piska Dabra, the messianic leader of the Prayer People, is bearded and gorgeously robed, the possessor of enormous presence and magnetism. He has an almost hypnotic effect on the faithful, most of whom are women. For a time, Filia is caught up in the semi-hysterical prayer meetings. But she discovers that Piska Dabra, like so many Bible-punchers of his ilk the world over, preaches ascetism and yet succumbs to the fleshpots himself. Filia also recognises something genuinely searching in his preaching, and she acknowledges the tremendous desire on the part of the Prayer People as a whole to find an answer to their needs in religion.

In a grotesque scene, Piska Dabra's mind cracks under the strain of his personal duality. He has a fit-like revelation, in which he predicts civil chaos. He then walks into the lagoon, where he has baptised so many believers, and drowns himself. Is it religion that has failed him, or has he failed religion? Ekwensi points out both possibilities in the character of this man who is both enchanter and would-be enchanted.

Dapo Ladele, the journalist, is Filia's final love. She recognises, soon after she meets Dapo, that he attracts her partly because he resembles Dan Kaybi. Dapo is an older Dan—just as intelligent, but not nearly so unrealistically idealistic. He is capable of corruption, and he comes to see that this is true of himself, just as it is true of all men. In a confused world, filled with ambiguities, he may be in the end a more effective and more honest man for this recognition.

Filia herself is a convent-educated girl who, when we first meet her, is naïvely eager for her life to begin. She does not at all realise the difficulties that will result from her marriage to Dan Kaybi. After his death, she is for a time in a state of shock, but when she has recovered to some extent, at least outwardly, she is determined to make something of her life. The city, however, has a deceptive glitter. Filia succeeds as a model but not, in her own eyes, as a woman. Her affair with Rayimi leaves her filled with self-disgust, and the city itself loses its allure as she comes to know it more deeply. Her disillusionment with Dapo is partly a disillusionment with herself and with the total situation— 'I feel like killing myself. I hate all this nonsense. And worse still, the sight of you. I hate to live in this era.'

Near the end of the novel Filia seems simply weary, exhausted with the battles which never end. She suffers a mental breakdown and disappears for days. When she returns, she is nearly naked and bleeding from head wounds. She tells a weird story of being abducted and beaten, but it is not certain whether this is fact or fantasy. She is taken to hospital, but she goes into a coma and dies.

Filia is an interesting contrast to Ekwensi's other most notable woman, Jagua. Filia does not have such an immediate appeal as the fiery and vital Jagua, but she is an extremely well-realised character. She is convincingly intelligent, gentle, somehow always a little uncertain despite her attractiveness. She also conveys an impression of fragility. Ultimately we learn from her mother that Filia as a child was suspected to be an *Ogbanje*, 'one who comes to this world again and again', or as the Yoruba say of the same type, whom they call *abiku*, 'the child born to die'.

'Iska' means wind, and this has been Filia's nickname in the north. She *is* like the wind. There is a hauntingly sad quality about her, as though she senses all along that her fate will be to die without having borne children or having had a home of her own. Yet in some ways she is Africa's wind of change as well, representing both hope and anguish.

Written with greater restraint than any of Ekwensi's previous novels, *Iska* is probably his most moving work. Filia does not give out sparks like Jagua, but the novel as a whole burns with the painful love of a country in which individuals are caught up in lunatic ferocities not of their own making, forced to make choices which no one should have to make—the cruel choices imposed by a situation perilously close to civil war.

Ekwensi is writing about events as they happen. He has always been a chronicler of right-now, and in this novel he reaches a new maturity in that role. Some day *Iska* will be read as an historical novel. But then, as now, it will present events as no textbook can—in terms of the truly felt pain of real people.

Other Voices

THE PRECEDING CHAPTERS have dealt only with those Nigerian writers who have produced a considerable body of work or at least several works of a high standard. Nigeria has many other writers as well. Some of these have produced plays and novels which are little more than faintly personalised arguments between old values and new, written in stiff and cliché-packed prose. Others, however, must be mentioned here, either for the promise contained in their early work or because they have produced one work of outstanding quality. One such writer, Gabriel Okara, has published only one novel, but has long been recognised as a leading poet in Nigeria. Another, T.M. Aluko, has been widely read in his own country but has not yet received the recognition abroad which he deserves. Writers such as Flora Nwapa and Elechi Amadi are only beginning but have produced excellent first novels. The existence of a number of young and worthwhile writers does seem to indicate that Nigerian writing is likely to be just as interesting in the next decade as it has been in the last.

T.M. Aluko

The main talent of T.M. Aluko is a subtle irony, an irony completely West African in tone, and although his novels contain many flaws, they are informed with a keen and analytical intelligence.

Aluko was born in 1918, and is a Yoruba. Educated in Nigeria and in London, he is a civil engineer and town planner. He has held many engineering posts in Nigeria, and in 1960 was appointed Director of Public Works for the Western Region. He now teaches at the University of Lagos. He has written a number of short stories, and has published three novels—*One Man, One Wife*, 1959, *One Man, One Matchet*, 1964, and *Kinsman and Foreman*, 1966.

Aluko's work as an engineer has enabled him to understand in profound detail the clash between cultures and the difficulties involved in social change. These are the chief themes in his novels. In *One Man, One Wife* Aluko portrays a village which is split into factions, often ludicrously, sometimes tragically. His social satire is deft, and it takes in every aspect of village life. The puritanical and limited outlook of the church is a favourite target, and the way in which some African pastors have dogmatically upheld the stiff morality of the Christian establishment in order to exalt their own status as the custodians of virtue. The old Africa is not spared, either, with its chiefs who voice both well-tried wisdom and inflexible ignorance (smallpox patients ought not be treated with modern medicine, lest the ancestors be offended). No element of the community is immune from Aluko's satirical voice. *One Man, One Wife* deals ostensibly with polygamy, but it deals with very much more. The plot is too laden and too confused, and the novel—all flesh and no skeleton—finally collapses. But it remains worthwhile for its living inhabitants—the feckless girl, Toro; her mother Ma Sheyi, left too young without a man, devoting her life to her daughter's life, but not without resentment; Grandma Gbemi, denying with prudent shrillness in the pastor's presence that she knows anything about the old gods, but remaining faithful to the strongest influence in her life, the god of smallpox, 'Shonponna M'Lord'; 'Bible' Jeremiah, described always as 'a saintly man', but contriving to inform against his friends whenever possible; 'Teacher' Royasin, the pillar of the Church who quite unintentionally falls from grace and becomes a public letter-writer, advertising himself as 'Friend of the Illiterate and Advocate of the Oppressed'; Bada, the priest of the smallpox god, who, in the final irony of the novel, himself dies of smallpox. These villagers of Isolo are portrayed lovingly, with all their concentration on gossip and triviality, all their infuriating irrationality and their continuing concern with the things which ultimately matter the most—children, and the onward-going of life under whatever circumstances.

One Man, One Matchet is a more ambitious novel than *One Man, One Wife*. The clash of concepts is once again the theme. This novel should be required reading for every European or American technician and teacher involved in aid schemes in Africa, as well as for every African government official dealing with development projects, for Aluko sees clearly the heart-breaking difficulties which such projects inevitably entail, and he manages to make comprehensible the genuinely held and diametrically opposed views of the old chiefs and the new young men of government. Aluko sets his story in 1947, and it centres around Udo Akpan, a university-educated Nigerian, recently appointed as a District Officer. The framework of the novel concerns a problem which has been a major one in West Africa for many years—the treatment of diseased cocoa trees. In the village of Ipaja the main crop is cocoa, and the disease of cocoa trees, swollen shoot, cannot be cured but can only be cut out, in order to prevent the diseased trees from infecting the healthy ones. How is it possible to convince the villagers, who view life in completely unscientific terms, that they must cut down the trees which are their source of income? Even with extremely careful explanation and a true understanding of the diversity of concepts, the task might be an impossible one. But the administration's way of handling the situation is far from being tactful or sufficiently informed. The Agricultural Officer is English; he speaks virtually no Yoruba and has no grasp at all of the villagers' outlook. He flatly announces that diseased trees will be cut out, and when he sees the people's indignation, he says plaintively to the District Officer, 'Can't these people see we're trying to help them?'

Playing upon the villagers' fear and dismay, a young nationalist, Benjamin Benjamin, insinuates himself as interpreter and 'political adviser' to the old chiefs and the Oba, or king, of Ipaja. The people, he claims, must not allow themselves to be told to cut out their cocoa trees merely in order to demonstrate the power of the white man. What the Ipaja villagers want is the piece of land which in a long-ago dispute went to the neighbouring village of Apeno, and it is this they should concentrate upon, not the insane matter of cutting their trees.

Udo Akpan, the new D.O., attempts to put into practice the government policy of cutting diseased trees, but he finds himself opposed at every turn by Benjamin Benjamin. The two in a sense fight for the soul of Ipaja, but it is not a neatly defined battle of saviour and devil, for Udo Akpan, although he is sincere and well-meaning and progressive, is also in some ways self-righteous and naïve, and Benjamin Benjamin, although he is crafty and quite unscrupulous in turning every event to his personal advantage, also believes passionately and pathetically in his own fantasy, a glorious future for Ipaja and himself.

Basically, however, there is no doubt whose side Aluko is on, as he shows Benjamin Benjamin's increasingly harmful hold over the villagers and the old Oba. A skilled orator, Benja-Benja (as he is known to the villagers) appears at meetings, nattily clad and impressive in sunglasses, and manages to throw all manner of red herrings in the way of the cocoa issue. The ancient land dispute is revived, even to the extent of setting up a Land Dispute Fund so that the case may be fought in court. The villagers, excited by Benjamin's speeches, pledge large sums of money which none of them can afford. In the heat of the moment, one man promises seventy-five pounds. He is a railway clerk, and his yearly salary is a hundred and twenty pounds. Aluko allows these ironies to make their own impact, without comment, but the whole matter of a strictly local patriotism, the way in which it is understandable and yet can be turned to a destructive purpose, is painfully clear. The petty pride, the jockeying for status in the matter of who will promise most money to the Fund, the pomposity and pretence, the parochial quality of thought— all these are brought out without the writer's ever despising his characters.

Aluko displays great talent in catching the individuals' voices and the general tone of village meetings—the Yoruba love of words, the lengthy speeches and interminable preliminary greetings, the unhurried way in which everyone is allowed his say and yet the way in which this age-old tribal method now impedes action.

Not satisfied with the Land Appeal Fund, Benjamin Benjamin next whips up the people's feelings against paying taxes. Udo Akpan, he claims, in attempting to make them pay taxes, is obviously in the pay of the enemy village of Apeno. The Oba of Ipaja, more and more bewildered, seeks and gets reassurance from Benjamin Benjamin, and out of his own inability to grapple with the situation, the old man leans more and more upon the young crook. A Tax Appeal Fund is started, with Benjamin putting in a padded expense account and being supplied with a car in order to campaign for the cause.

The government at last sends in teams of men to cut out the diseased trees. The aged Chief Momo, unable to grasp the fact that cocoa trees can actually have diseases, gathers his household and attacks the government men. For this, he gets three months in jail. The Momo Release Fund is set up by the tireless Benjamin, but when the saddened and broken old chief dies on the way to prison, the appeal is changed to the Momo Memorial Fund, and Benjamin delivers a funeral oration cribbed from the Gettysburg Address—

'...government of the people of Ipaja by the people of Ipaja for the people of Ipaja shall not perish from the earth.'

Some of these scenes are convulsively funny, and yet Aluko succeeds in conveying their underlying tragedy as well. Benjamin Benjamin, whirling around the countryside, campaigning for a host of causes and lining his own pockets the whole time, has to be laughed at, and yet it is an angry laughter, for he is bleeding the people who touchingly believe in him because he can read and write.

Udo Akpan ultimately begins an investigation into Benjamin's fund-raising activities. He discovers that many villagers have actually paid out more to the Tax Appeal Fund than they would have paid in taxes if they had met their original assessments without a murmur. Benjamin's accounts include many unexplained items such as 'preliminary expenses' which are euphemisms for theft. Benjamin is taken to court but has to be acquitted because of legal bungling, for the case has been brought under the wrong sections of the law.

The Ipaja people do not believe Benjamin has swindled them. To them he is now a local hero. In a flaming speech he tells them that Ipaja must fight for its rights, by which he means the right not to pay taxes and not to cut out diseased cocoa trees. His slogan is 'One man, one matchet, One woman, one stick, One child, one stone!' Not surprisingly, rioting begins. But the rioters get out of control and finally loot and destroy the house of Chief Olowokere, a rich transport owner who has been Benjamin's principal supporter. Olowokere, unable to bear this final revelation that there is no honour among thieves, shoots Benjamin dead and then shoots himself.

Udo Akpan is fully aware of the final irony. The government in two years was unable to do anything about Benjamin Benjamin. In the old days he would simply have vanished. But under 'British justice' he could operate with impunity until one of his own kind disposed of him. And now Olowokere is not even allowed to die. The self-inflicted wound was not a fatal one, so he is saved and cared for in order that he may be hanged. In disillusionment both with the administration and with the local situation, the young District Officer resigns.

Udo Akpan is portrayed with sympathy but with no attempt at idealisation. When he first arrives in Ipaja, he is determined to approach his duties 'in an essentially African way'. But the villagers do not accept him. They call him 'the black white man', and he is unable to get them to understand that if they want piped water and roads and a hospital they must pay taxes. They do not have any basic confidence that they themselves might ever be able to achieve these things, which seem totally mysterious and always to be brought in from the outside. Why, then, should they have to hand over their scant money? Payment, surely, is the government's business. Udo tries desperately hard to get across his own concepts, but he becomes disheartened at the enormous task of changing the ancient thought-patterns. He is impatient; he wants progress to be immediate. He recognises even in such ridiculous things as the Land Appeal Fund a genuine desire on the part of the villagers to contribute themselves to their own welfare, to do something for themselves, but his final discouraged comment is 'How can we make the whole thing operate with efficiency? How?'

Aluko is expert at describing the intricate plottings of local politics, and his dramatic irony in dealing with double-edged events is shown in such scenes as the occasion when Benjamin Benjamin and Olowokere visit Udo Akpan to plead for Olowokere's appointment to a local chieftaincy. Benjamin hands the D.O. an envelope, saying it contains 'some useful information about the Obanla chieftaincy and other matters'. Udo takes it innocently, but when the pair leaves, Olowokere expresses relief that the young official apparently accepted the bribe without question or without having them arrested. Benjamin agrees. In fact, however, the envelope contains exactly what Benjamin said it did. The money has gone towards Benjamin's personal fund.

The old Oba of Ipaja is a well-drawn character. Aluko shows how maddening it can be for men such as Udo Akpan to have to try to explain the workings of modern society to the Oba, whose views are those of centuries ago. Yet the old ruler cares genuinely about his people, and not all his proverbs are outdated, for some incorporate a timeless wisdom and a shrewd knowledge of human nature. He keeps faith with his people, his ancestors and his gods, but he is an easy prey for Benjamin Benjamin, for many of the old ways are totally inadequate in new situations and the old man realises it. He is confused, weary and very much afraid he will be exiled from the throne of his fathers. He does not see further than his own village, which is the world to him, not because he does not want to see further but because he quite literally cannot. Aluko treats this character with affection and with a sense of sadness, for the Oba is a good man whose time is past.

The Reverend Josiah Olaiya is another character who is movingly portrayed. Like the Oba, he is out of date. He attended the seminary a long time ago, and he does not really know what is going on in the world now. He is reminiscent of Isaac in Chinua Achebe's *No Longer at Ease*, for he also has a mission-made personality and his limited grasp of history does not include the tribal pre-Christian past. He is concerned with progress and yet uncertain of himself, standing respectably between two worlds, hoping no one will upset things too much, unable to face a future in which things will have to be upset before they can get better.

The ending, with Udo's resignation and his discussion of the country's problem with his successor, is flat and too theoretical. Nevertheless, for its incisive irony, perceptive social analysis and convincing character portrayals, *One Man, One Matchet* will remain worth reading for a long time to come.

Aluko's third novel, *Kinsman and Foreman*, deals with the same conflict of outlooks as *One Man, One Matchet*, but it does so from a different vantage point, for where one of Udo Akpan's main difficulties is that he is not trusted because he is not an Ipaja man, in *Kinsman and Foreman* the dilemma of the central character hinges on the fact that he goes to work in the town where he was born. Titus Oti, returning to Western Nigeria in 1950 from university in England as one of the first qualified Nigerian engineers, takes a post with the Public Works Department and finds that he is being sent to his own village. The problems of this situation prove to be intolerable. One of his employees is the foreman, Simeon, and Titus soon discovers the man's inefficiency and dishonesty. But Simeon is his kinsman, a remote cousin, and in the eyes of the extended family, Titus's superior. The elder of the family, Pa Joel, in a public ceremony welcomes Titus home and cautions him to take the advice of Simeon in all things. How can Titus then get rid of Simeon? His slightest criticism of the crooked foreman is treated as treachery by the entire family. Titus's mother finally tells him that it was Simeon who paid for the boy's final years at university, after the death of his father. She is not even aware that Simeon obtained his money in very questionable ways. All she sees is that he helped Titus, and Titus must not under any circumstances turn against him. The disparity between two ways of thinking and the emotional warfare which goes on in Titus himself are portrayed with all the analytical power which Aluko shows in *One Man, One Matchet*.

The ending displays Aluko's irony at its best. Simeon finally betrays himself in a public religious confession, made through his nervous adherence to the *Alasoteles*, who believe that the Day of Judgement is dawning that very morning. But when the frenzy is over and the world still goes on, Titus learns from a lawyer friend that anything said by Simeon that day will be termed religious hysteria and will not be taken as evidence against him. Simeon is transferred, but the same situation and the same misunderstandings are still there—no miracle is ever going to ease Titus's painfully difficult way.

The novel is much less complex in structure than Aluko's previous novels, and this is both an advantage and a disadvantage. The profusion of sub-plots does not appear here; there are no ambling diversions; the main theme is closely adhered to, and the novel gains in clarity from this increased organisation of material. Something of the fiery life and human chaos of the other two novels is missing, however, and although there are some fine scenes of litigation and harangue, and one splendid set-piece in which Titus encounters a colonial ghost in an old government rest-house, the writing does not have quite the verve and biting humour of the other novels.

Aluko's main concern in *Kinsman and Foreman*, as in so much of his writing, is to set down the ways in which the generations are apart, and to explore the almost impossible problems created by this enormous gap between a tribally oriented way of thought and an individually oriented, scientific way of thought. He never suggests that one is right and the other wrong, nor that all worth is on one side or another. His query is, rather—how can we go on somehow, without damaging one another irreparably? Aluko does not pretend to know the answers. But he asks some of the essential questions, and he looks unflinchingly at opposing conceptual areas which he knows deeply from the inside.

Elechi Amadi

Elechi Amadi's one novel, *The Concubine*, differs from most Nigerian novels in its setting, for it takes place entirely in the pre-colonial era. No European administrators or missionaries enter to disrupt the life of these Ibo villagers. The tribal system is still stable and capable of coping with its own disasters in its own way. Amadi tells the story wholly from the inside, never attempting to give a contemporary interpretation to events, but adhering meticulously to the concepts and life-view held by the people within the novel. This method gives *The Concubine* an unfaltering authenticity which in turn helps to extend the novel's meaning beyond any one culture, for Amadi's theme is man's struggle with fate itself, his perpetual attempt to placate and therefore to control his gods.

Born in 1934, Elechi Amadi grew up in Eastern Nigeria and was educated at Government College, Umuahia, and University College, Ibadan. As a Captain in the Nigerian Army, he was attached to the Military School, Zaria. He now teaches at the Anglican Grammar School, Igrito, Port Harcourt.

A beautiful young woman, Ihuoma, is the central character of *The Concubine*, yet the novel is not so much about her as about the effect she has upon the three men who involve themselves, at various times, with her life.

This effect is always an unintentional one, for Ihuoma, although far from being a passive woman, never attempts to influence or dominate others. She accepts her beauty calmly, but she does not use it as a weapon. She is surprised at the devotion she inspires, but it is not until nearly the end of the novel that either the reader or Ihuoma herself begins to suspect anything sinister in her attractiveness.

Ihuoma lives happily with her husband, Emenike, and their three children, until one day he is drawn unavoidably into a fight with his neighbour, Madume, who claims a piece of land which rightfully belongs to Emenike. In their wrestling bout, Emenike falls on a jagged tree stump and badly hurts his side. After a time, he appears to recover and goes with other men of the village to the forest shrine of Amadioha, god of thunder. There, in the eyes of the shrine's priest, Emenike reads his own death. When he dies shortly after, the villagers attribute it to internal damage done in his fight with Madume.

Madume represses his feelings of responsibility over Emenike's death, and once more attempts to take back the disputed piece of land, this time by threatening Ihuoma, who is trying to work the farm and keep her family together. Paradoxically, Madume also hopes eventually to take Ihuoma as his second wife. Ihuoma stands up to his threats, and when he makes advances to her, she rejects him sharply. In fury, Madume chops down some of her plantains, and in the process encounters a spitting cobra. With the snake's venom in his eyes Madume calls for the *dibia*, or medicine man, Anyika, but he refuses to treat him, saying that the event was clearly an act of the gods. In the divination, Anyika receives some intimation of the presence of the sea god, but he, like the other villagers, interprets Madume's misfortune as a punishment for violating Ihuoma's land. Madume goes blind, and unable to bear his helplessness, he hangs himself.

A young bachelor, Ekwueme, finds himself more and more drawn towards Ihuoma, and the novel traces the course of their slow and turbulent courtship. Ihuoma is attracted by him, but keeps on refusing him, partly because she cannot forget her dead husband and partly because Ekwueme has been engaged since childhood to a girl in a nearby village, and Ihuoma feels it would be an offence to the whole community if she were to marry Ekwueme instead.

Ekwueme finally allows himself to be persuaded into the arranged marriage, but his young wife, Ahurole, is given to sulking and tears, and Ekwueme does not know how to handle her and is not basically willing to try. He begins dropping by Ihuoma's compound and talking to her. Ekwueme is a trapper, but his chief interest lies in singing and flute-playing. He is gentle, has never been sufficiently certain of himself, and has been too dependent upon his mother, even into his adulthood. Ihuoma is his ideal woman, for she combines physical beauty with the reassuring and maternal qualities he longs for. When his wife discovers he has been seeing Ihuoma, however, she is enraged. She administers a love potion to Ekwueme, to bring him back. The drug is one which Ahurole's mother has obtained from a *dibia* in another village, for Anyika, the local medicine man, has refused to take any part in the business. Ekwueme, after taking the drug, falls ill. He has convulsions and then, nearly insane, he runs away into the forest. Ahurole, in terror at what she has done, returns to her parents' village.

Amadi describes fascinatingly the episode of Ekwueme's illness, for the drug has the effect of reversing his personality. He viciously resists the attempts of his friends to get him to go back home. Where he was once docile towards authority, he now pours out vituperation upon the elders. And where he was once reserved and shy in his expression of love towards Ihuoma, he now declares that he will not come down from the tree where he has ensconced himself unless Ihuoma appears. Ihuoma agrees to come, although she is understandably embarrassed by the scene. When Anyika, the *dibia*, has administered an antidote to the drug which poisoned the young man, Ekwueme recovers and is painfully ashamed of his actions when he was under the drug's influence.

Ihuoma continues to see him while he is convalescing, and gradually realises that she is in love with him. The growth of this relationship is portrayed with moving gentleness, for both Ekwueme and Ihuoma are almost afraid to believe in their own happiness.

At this point, when the two have decided to marry and when their respective families have accepted it, a terrifying obstacle appears. Anyika announces that his divinations have told him something which makes the marriage—or any marriage for Ihuoma—impossible. Ihuoma, beloved of the village, is also the beloved of the Sea King, and the god will kill any man who seeks to marry her. She could be a concubine, but never a wife. Now the villagers' minds go back to Emenike, who died a considerable time after he had appeared to recover from his wound, and to Madume, so strangely encountering the snake immediately after he had told Ihuoma he wanted to marry her.

At first Ekwueme can hardly believe the *dibia*, but he says he will marry Ihuoma even if it is true. Ihuoma herself does not know whether the revelation about her is true or not. If it is, she has been totally unaware of it. Old Anyika swears that nothing can be done, so in the timeless manner of humans, Ekwueme and his father seek the advice of another *dibia*. This one claims that the Sea King can be bound and rendered harmless, with the proper rituals and sacrifices. But—and only now does Amadi's theme become apparent—can a man bind the gods?

The concluding pages of the novel are a counterpoint, with the happiness of Ihuoma and Ekwueme rising and recurring, but always in the background there is the anxiety, the sense of having to get the sacrifice prepared quickly, the apprehension about the ritual which will have to be performed from a boat on the river, the domain of the Sea King rather than the province of men. Ekwueme, who cannot swim and who by now is certain that the Sea King will appear, does not make a secret of his fear. When his family seeks to hearten him, he says 'The trouble is that it is difficult to feel other people's fears.' It is to the credit of Amadi as a novelist that he accomplishes this most difficult thing, for the reader is made to feel the reality of Ekwueme's fear.

When nearly everything is ready, Ekwueme sends Ihuoma's young son out to shoot a lizard with his bow, for this is the last thing necessary for the sacrifice. Ekwueme steps outside the hut door just as the boy shoots at the lizards. The arrow pierces Ekwueme's chest, fatally wounding him.

The enigma remains. Amadi wisely refrains from pulling out a last-minute alternative explanation. The build-up of the novel has been slow and extremely careful. The first accident, and Emenike's death, is thought by the villagers mainly to have been a simple accident. The manner of Madume's death has more significance attached to it. Finally, after Anyika's revelation about Ihuoma, the death of Ekwueme has a kind of reverberance, a tragic inevitability. Ekwueme is bound to try to evade his fate, and he is also bound to fail, for he will encounter it in a form quite other than he anticipated.

The view of the gods, as it appears in this novel, has been held deliberately within the framework of the society about which Amadi is writing. Although his characters are presented in depth, with motivations which are always comprehensible, Amadi does not seek to provide psychological alternatives to the interpretation of the central conflict, which is between men and their fate as controlled by their deities. The gods are gods only; they are not complexes going by another name. And like the gods of ancient Greece, they are not presented as being just. They are neither good nor evil; they are merely powerful. The accidents in *The Concubine* are not Freudian ones, despite the fact that Ekwueme is shot by the son of the woman he hopes to marry. The boy has not seen Ekwueme—he has simply fired his arrow along the nearest wall, as Ekwueme advised him to do, in order to knock off any lizard perched there. Ekwueme has not sought death, for he did not know that the boy would be there at that precise moment. It is the same with the earlier deaths. Emenike did not seek the fight with Madume, and when he read his death in the priest's eyes, he felt a shuddering curiosity but no wish to die. Madume might have been his own cause of accident if the accident had been of a different nature, but he could scarcely have anticipated, even subconsciously, the presence of a spitting cobra.

Amadi goes even further than Chinua Achebe in portraying traditional religious concepts, for the Ibo society about which Achebe is writing was already affected and altered by life-views dissimilar to its own. Amadi's Ibo villages in *The Concubine* represent a society which had not yet fallen prey to self-doubts. Its gods could be cruel, but they were real, and they affected the lives of mortals in real and inexplicable ways. Strangely, what at first appears to be a limitation of the novel—the single viewpoint, as contrasted with Achebe's ability to grasp and convey a multiplicity of viewpoints—turns out to be a type of strength, for Amadi's effect ultimately depends upon the extent to which he can convey the gods as actual and potent. He is not writing primarily about people's relationships with one another, although these provide much of the novel's substance. The underlying theme is always man's fate, to what extent he can change it, and how he chooses to face the inevitable. In this respect, Amadi's writing has something in common with that of John Pepper Clark, who is also concerned with destiny in very similar ways.

Ihuoma herself, although she is the chief protagonist in *The Concubine*, remains to some extent mysterious, even to herself, and this is a necessary accompaniment of her unsought role as the beloved of a god. Amadi succeeds in portraying a woman who is good without being in the least self-consciously 'good'. Ihuoma is a strong-willed woman, determined to keep her farm going and to bring up her children well. She is extremely aware of the eyes of others, however, and if she has a weakness it is probably an exaggerated fear of authority—the very quality which Ekwueme himself has, and from which he seeks refuge with her. Ihuoma is intermittently aware of the dangers of her own desire to please the community.

> ...she began to loathe her so-called good manners. She became less delighted when people praised her. It was as though they were confining her to an ever-narrowing prison.

The Concubine contains some of the best descriptions of a village in all of Nigerian writing. Amadi deals with many aspects of village life—the work on the small farm plots; the festivals with the drumming and the constant exchange of gossip; the shrines in the shadow-filled forest; the funeral rites and the embarrassed inadequacy of friends trying to comfort Ihuoma in her widowhood; the singing of Ekwueme and his clownish friend Wakiri; the visits from hut to hut, accompanied by the talk about children and illness and scandal; the greetings so apparently simple and casually exchanged, yet so full of uncertainty, 'Let the day break'. Amadi's writing has an ease and gracefulness about it, and like Achebe, his portrayal of village life is always done through events happening to particular individuals, never in terms of generalities. He does not probe as deeply into personality as Achebe does, but he has the ability in a short space to make a character come to life, and he can pinpoint the quirks and preferences which mark one person out from another, even in trivial ways, such as Ihuoma saying to her mother, 'Don't make the soup too thick. I prefer rather light soup, as you know.' It is through this eye for detail that Amadi makes his people live. In a sense, the novel is slow-paced, for it takes on the pace of village life, but this never renders it dull, for the leisurely development of major events is surrounded and supported by constant activity at a seemingly less important level—seemingly, because in the end perhaps the back-and-forth visiting, the comforting of children who have fallen and hurt themselves, the necessary work and the coming of night, may be not the most transient but the most enduring aspects of life.

But Amadi's principal statement remains an undeniably tragic one. *The Concubine* expresses in admirably simple poetic prose the age-old conflict of man with his gods, his awe of them and at the same time his proud attempts to bind them, to make them do his will. Although Amadi differs sharply from Wole Soyinka in that *The Concubine* does not offer alternative and contemporary interpretations to the struggle between men and gods, he resembles Soyinka in another way, for most definitely neither writer is a liberal humanist. Amadi, like Soyinka, does not ever suggest that man is improving and will ultimately be able to direct wisely and knowingly every facet of his life. On the contrary, *The Concubine* expresses the mystery at the centre of being. Amadi's is an essentially sombre view of life, and his novel contains an acute awareness of fate's ironies, for at the exact moment when we think the prize is within our grasp, the gods cut the thread. This outlook is reminiscent of the references Achebe makes to Chukwu, the supreme God, who severs a man's life when it is sweetest to him.

Although Amadi's view of life is not an optimistic one, it is not a passively fatalistic one either. Ekwueme may be doomed by his love for Ihuoma, but he is not defeated by the gods. He does not become less than he is. Despite his previous timidity and his present fear, he declares that he will marry Ihuoma even if she is the beloved of the Sea King. He does not want to do battle with the gods, but when he is forced into this role he does not draw back. He goes on, only too aware of his vulnerable humanity, but stronger within himself than he has ever managed to be before. The victory, with Ekwueme's death, does not entirely belong to the gods.

Nkem Nwankwo

No Nigerian novel is completely without humour, but writers of light fiction as such are rare. Nkem Nwankwo, although he touches on themes that are serious, refuses to treat them seriously for more than a moment at a time. He relies instead on the portrayal of a genuinely comic character who, like all true clowns, is movingly and palpably human, never simply funny in a one-dimensional way.

Born in 1936, Nwankwo went to university in Nigeria and now teaches English at Ibadan Grammar School. *Danda* is his first novel, and was published in 1964. It has now been made into a musical and has been performed in Nigeria and at the Festival of Negro Arts in Dakar in 1966.

Although he is the son of a highly respected chief, Danda in the conventional view is not much good. His nickname is 'Rain', and it suits his musical wayward nature. He goes about in a cloak covered with small bells which proclaim his unpredictable presence, and he loves to dance, to gossip, to drink palm-wine with his irresponsible friends, and to make love—especially with the young wives of old men. The story's setting is an Ibo village, and Danda possesses none of the Ibo virtues. He is not thrifty and hard-working; he is not interested in accumulating wealth; he does not give respect to his elders; he is neither aggressive nor ambitious. He is, like Okonkwo's father Unoka in Achebe's novel, *Things Fall Apart*, fond of playing his flute on moonlit nights and much less fond of work during the sun-heavy days. But where Unoka is portrayed gravely by Achebe, and with gentle irony, Danda blows through the village like a disruptive wind, scandalising and delighting the inhabitants, according to their outlooks, for to some he is the epitome of the ruin to which the younger generation has descended, while to others he represents the triumphant rebel, always in trouble but always unrepentant, as they themselves more timidly would never dare to be. Danda is, in fact, the classic rebel of comedy. His battles against the rigid and stolid establishment are fought with the weapons of impudence, not anger, and liberation is achieved through laughter rather than painful struggle.

Araba, Danda's father, groans over his son's misdeeds and swears that Danda will be the death of him, but he tolerates Rain, nevertheless, and is perhaps even entertained and sustained by him, although the old man takes good care to conceal his affection with irritability. When finally Danda is brought to heel, at least temporarily, and shoved into marriage, and when a son— 'another Danda'—is born, Araba becomes a doting grandfather, making sure that the child is carried carefully by the young daughters and wives of the compound, commanding Danda's wife to let him see 'our man'. Nwankwo conveys the personality of the old man and this aspect of the life of an extended family group with a warmth that never degenerates into sentimentality.

Nwankwo's descriptions of other details of village life are done with this same blend of affection and detachment. He shows with particular vividness the meetings which take place in an Ibo village to decide every community issue—the violent arguments, the shouting, the prolonged introductory speeches, the conniving flattery and the subtle malice couched in politely oratorical terms.

When Danda almost joins the local Christian church, the novel comes close to a more pointed satire, but Nwankwo quite rightly does not allow any sense of duty or his own personal opinions to alter the natural structure and tone. Danda's ultimate defection is presented as lightly as his initial attraction to the mission, and the writer never unnecessarily underlines the implications. The mission followers, inflamed with faith but also with enormous intolerance and self-righteousness, have established the rule that when a villager shows his willingness to become Christian but subsequently fails to attend services, his household possessions will be confiscated by the believers. Danda, having apparently been converted, does not turn up for his own baptism. When the church stalwarts investigate, they find him at a festival for the old gods, dancing and celebrating. The priest tells him it is a deadly sin to drink palm-wine with 'spirit-worshippers'. Danda, astonished, says quite simply and devastatingly, 'Your word is bent, stretch it'. The mission man cannot stretch his word straight and clear; he does not know how. Instead he and his flock go to strip Danda's hut of its goods in punishment. But all they find is an old sleeping mat for, apart from his flute and cloak, this is all Danda owns. There are a few of the Christian virtues which Danda understands a good deal better than the Christians do.

He is definitely not a hero, however. Out of consideration for the ageing Araba, Danda belatedly agrees to have the tribal marks cut on his face so that he may at last become established in the community. But he does not go through with it. Just as the knife is about to descend, Danda leaps up and vanishes from the village. He is essentially an anti-hero, and perhaps this is why he is so comprehensible to our age.

When Araba dies, Danda suddenly reappears, apparently now willing to take on his responsibilities. But he takes them on in his own way. He enters the village, his belled cloak tinkling, and charms the villagers on to his side once more. He is still Rain. They will never make a solid citizen out of him.

Danda is in some ways a disjointed novel. Some of the chapters read as though they had been written as short stories and later linked, and Danda's escapades are often episodic, with little connection between them. But Danda himself is a vibrant and memorable character, and Nwankwo's energetic prose can bring to immediate life, in a few sentences, a whole environment:

> The scorch season was dying. The happiest time of the year, the season for feasts, when men and women laughed with all their teeth and little boys, their mouths oily oily, ran about the lanes blowing the crops of chicken to make balloons.

Flora Nwapa

Only one novel in Nigeria so far has been written by a woman, and this in itself provides a certain amount of guaranteed interest, but the writing of Flora Nwapa contains very much more than mere curiosity value, and her first novel is an accomplished one.

Flora Nwapa was born in 1931 in Eastern Nigeria. She was educated at the University of Ibadan and in Britain at the University of Edinburgh. She has held various administrative jobs in Nigerian universities and when her novel was published she was Assistant Registrar at the University of Lagos.

Efuru, published in 1966, is an account of a woman's life in an Ibo village. Efuru is an attractive and intelligent young woman who defies local custom when she marries, for she simply goes to Adizua's hut and refuses to worry about such matters as bride-price and the usual family-wide negotiations involved in marriage arrangements. This independence of mind characterises Efuru, for she decides she will not go with Adizua to work his farm, but will become a trader instead. Her business flourishes, and for a time she is happy, especially when, after several years of childlessness, she finally bears a daughter. But Adizua cannot tolerate indefinitely his wife's competence and her popularity in the village. He leaves her in order to seek reassurance with a woman of lesser talents. This is only the beginning of Efuru's sorrows, for soon her child dies. Efuru's second marriage works out no better than her first. Gilbert is an educated man, presumably more able to bear a wife who is intelligent, but once again the pattern repeats itself. He often acts cruelly or neglectfully, and then becomes ashamed and apologetic. They do not have children, and this is a great disappointment to Gilbert. Efuru herself feels it as a mark of her own failure. She begins having strange dreams about the goddess of the lake, and finally realises that she has been chosen to be a worshipper. But the goddess Uhamiri, although she is said to be beautiful and wealthy, has no children and many of her worshippers appear to be barren. Efuru gradually accepts this as her fate, but the gods have not yet finished tormenting her, for Gilbert disappears and when finally he turns up again, Efuru learns that he has been in jail. Efuru falls ill and a local gossip suggests that her illness represents the gods' punishment for adultery. Gilbert seizes almost eagerly upon this totally unfounded charge. Unable to stand Gilbert's mistrust, Efuru leaves him as soon as she has recovered, and returns to her father's house, where she began.

Efuru's story bears some resemblance to that of Ihuoma, in Amadi's *The Concubine*, for both are women of high character who suffer in ways which apparently have nothing to do with their own actions. Both are fated not to achieve the happiness they deserve, and both are unluckily connected with a deity in ways unsought by themselves. Amadi's novel, however, draws more clearly and uncompromisingly the picture of human beings at the uncertain mercy of an uncaring fate. Flora Nwapa, on the other hand, suggests several possibilities to explain Efuru's misfortunes. The fact that she has been chosen, or feels herself to have been chosen, by the lake goddess certainly has a good deal to do with Efuru's fate, but her *chi* or personal inward-dwelling god is also believed by the village women to have influenced her life for ill. Unlike Achebe in *Things Fall Apart*, Flora Nwapa does not attempt to explore deeply the nature of the *chi* or the extent to which people are compelled to seek courses which may be contrary to their conscious desires. The *chi* appears only as another possible explanation for the disastrously repetitive pattern of Efuru's life. A third explanation, one which is never made explicit but which is implicit in the novel's development, is that Efuru has at heart both a deep uncertainty about herself and an unacknowledged desire to be the dominant person in any relationship. She chooses men who are well aware of her beauty and her capabilities but who are far from being in themselves strong characters. She is an excellent wife—loving, patient, good-humoured, hardworking. She can even cook well. In a sense, she nearly kills her husbands with kindness. She never points out her own qualities, and in fact seems almost unaware of them, so she cannot even be accused of being self-righteous. If she had been stupid or malicious, even occasionally, her men might have found her easier to live with. But each marriage follows the same course. Despite Efuru's attractiveness, her husband before very long stops sleeping with her and then begins seeking another woman. Neither man is particularly talented or confident, and Efuru has some emasculating effect on both, although quite unwittingly. Efuru's tragedy is partly that she cannot permit herself the mistakes of ordinary people, and partly that she does not marry a man with enough inner assurance to be able to bear her intelligence and efficiency.

Yet Efuru is consistently an appealing character. Her goodness alienates her husbands but it does not alienate the reader. She has humour and warmth, and she is capable of gaiety. Her virtues have not made her dull. Flora Nwapa also enables the reader to see aspects of Efuru which neither Adizua nor Gilbert can see, for her uncertainties and self-doubts are plain, but she is careful not to display them to anyone except her women friends and relatives, never to her men.

Set in juxtaposition to the character of Efuru are two other women—Ossai, her first mother-in-law, and Ajanupu, her aunt by marriage. Both emerge as fully drawn fictional portraits. Ossai has had the same kind of trouble as Efuru, for her husband also left her, many years ago, but unlike Efuru, she has gained a morbid enjoyment from her martyrdom and has practically made a career out of suffering. Efuru is intensely aware of this aspect of Ossai, and she regards Ossai's whining self-pity as a kind of dreadful warning.

Ajanupu is possibly the strongest character in the novel. Frankly domineering and bossy, Ajanupu always has the answer for everything. Is a child sick? Ajanupu knows the cure. Is Efuru having trouble with her husband? Ajanupu can tell her exactly what to do. Her tongue is sharp and even insulting, but she is truly concerned about her friends and her family. Her kindness may be rough, but it is genuine. Like Efuru, she is a trader, but her methods are considerably harsher than those of the younger woman. The humour and vigour of her speech are caught perfectly in a scene in which she goes to a village woman to collect a debt.

> 'You are talking rubbish,' Ajanupu said. 'I have heard all these
> stories before. You go to the room and bring me five pounds.
> That's all I want. I won't go until you have given me that amount.
> I am not leaving your house if you give me four pounds, nineteen
> shillings, eleven pence half-penny. Do you hear?'

Efuru takes place almost totally within the minds and the society of women. The life of the village is described compassionately, and from the viewpoint of a participant rather than an observer, for Flora Nwapa never deals with 'customs' in any theoretical sense, nor is there ever the slightest trace of condescension in her writing. These women do not 'know book', but they have a firm grasp of reality and they possess both shrewdness and tenacity. Every aspect of this domain is shown—the genuine help given to daughters and friends in time of domestic trouble, the ingrown and damaging gossip, the worried consultations over the health of children, the training of the young in good manners, the hours spent in telling stories to the children, the continuing rhythms of work, the attempts to understand husbands and sons.

Flora Nwapa excels at catching the exact tone of these women's voices. Whether they are speaking malice or love, tenderness or anger, the words are not bound by their printed form, for they can be heard. The situations and concerns which they are expressing might be spoken, with local variations, by women living in any small community, for although Flora Nwapa's women belong in an Ibo village, they convey insights which are valid anywhere.

Onuora Nzekwu

Onuora Nzekwu has published three novels—*Wand of Noble Wood*, 1961, *Blade Among the Boys*, 1962, and *Highlife for Lizards*, 1965. He was born in 1928 and is an Ibo. After training as a teacher, he taught for nine years. He is now the editor of *Nigeria Magazine*.

Nzekwu's first two novels mainly concern the difficulties of a man caught between old values and new. In *Wand of Noble Wood*, Peter Obiesie becomes engaged to Nneka, who turns out to be under a curse which was long ago spitefully directed against her mother when she was pregnant with Nneka. Peter is appalled that such 'primitive beliefs' are taken seriously, but he agrees to go through a ritual in order to obtain Nneka's release. This is done, but shortly before the wedding is to take place, the girl dies in a mysterious and inexplicable way. Peter ultimately discovers that Nneka had a visitation from her dead mother, who told her that an essential part was left out of the revocation ceremony and that if the wedding went ahead, Peter would die. Nneka has therefore poisoned herself.

The attitude to magic and to the ancient gods in this novel is an exceedingly ambiguous one. Peter fluctuates between disapproval and belief, and it is from his uncertainty that the novel gains most of its effectiveness. In this way, the novel is reminiscent of Tutuola, whose work also reflects the battle of gods within a man's heart and mind. But Nzekwu never manages to set down this conflict in all its direct pain, as Tutuola does. Nzekwu is frequently distracted from real contact with his characters by his tendency to explain Ibo rituals and social forms in a stilted and textbook manner. When a West Indian girl asks the meaning of the *ofo* staff, she gets a veritable lecture. "'It is a short piece of stick...cut from the *ofo* plant (*Detarium senegalense*) which, when consecrated, is a symbol of authority....'" and so on. Marriage, according to the old standards and the new, is discussed thoroughly and sensibly, but always from the outside, a kind of formal argument rather than a true fictional creation of individual dilemmas.

Blade Among the Boys tells the story of an Ibo boy, born in Northern Nigeria, moving to the coast because of the death of his father, determined to go into the Church and finally failing to do so because of an involvement with a girl.

The standards which Nzekwu applies in this novel seem to be those of a generation ago. The boy, Patrick, fails to become a priest when he gets a girl pregnant. She is presented as a warm and intelligent person who loves Patrick. Yet their act—and it becomes precisely this, their ACT—is seen as a grim sin. Patrick is dismissed from the seminary, and the authorities wish him 'God's forgiveness and blessings'. The novel finally becomes a fairly confused lecture in mission morality, a bending to what must appear to those on the outside as an unjust and totally uncomprehending authority.

The traditional Ibo way of life is generally treated patronisingly. There are exceptions, however, in the form of one or two lively scenes, such as the one in which the ancestral masks have assembled in the village square, and all women have prudently gone indoors, when suddenly an English missionary lady heaves into sight, surrounded by a lot of little schoolgirls. The lady will not budge from her course and neither will the masqueraders. They feel insulted that she will not go away, and she feels insulted that they will not. Finally, in desperation, they pursue her. The little girls flee in all directions, shrieking, and the lady drops her dignity and sprints like a gazelle. It is regrettable that Nzekwu does not more often allow his characters simply to be, as he does in this scene.

Nzekwu's third novel, *Highlife for Lizards*, concerns a woman of great spirit and independence, Agom, and is the most successful of Nzekwu's writing. His picture of Agom is more fully drawn than anything else he has done, and local beliefs and rituals are handled with greater insight and sympathy than is shown in his previous novels.

Intelligent and passionate, Agom marries a man who is basically weaker than herself—a pattern which seems to be a recurring one in Nigerian fiction. She endures the marriage, but her husband Udezue is unable to do so, and he takes on another wife, the indolent Nwadi, whom he has known since childhood. As long as Nzekwu is talking about Agom and her life with her husband and the second wife, the writing is genuine and moving. But when Agom gets involved with leading the market women in an attempt to have piped water brought to the village, the novel declines in effectiveness. Women like Agom do get involved in the business of community progress; they do act politically. This process is a difficult one to convey without the novel's deteriorating into propaganda. Nzekwu has not managed to do it, but he has made a valiant attempt. *Highlife for Lizards* does not reach beyond its own time and place, but within those limits it creates several convincing characters and sets down dilemmas which are unquestionably real.

Gabriel Okara

Best known as a poet, Gabriel Okara has written one novel, *The Voice*, published in 1964. This is a short novel of considerable power, and its imagery and spareness of expression are reminiscent of poetry. It is certainly one of the most memorable novels to have come out of Nigeria.

Gabriel Okara was born in 1921, in the Ijaw country of the Niger Delta. He was educated at Government College, Umuahia, and now works for the Ministry of Information at Enugu in Eastern Nigeria. He has translated a good deal of Ijaw poetry, and his own poems have been published widely, both in Africa and in Europe and America.

The theme of *The Voice* is an individual's questioning of the established values, his need to relate the inner truth to the outer reality. A young man, Okolo (whose name means 'the voice') is in search of what he calls *it*—the truth, honesty, some genuine contact with others. He dares to question the existing order of things and to suggest that there is more in life than the circumscribed laws of the tribe. To the village chief and elders, Okolo represents a great threat, and they attempt to discredit him by calling him mad. Chief Izongo sends his messengers to tell Okolo to stop his search. When the young man refuses, they attack him and he flees. Unexpectedly, he finds shelter in the forest hut of Tuere, a woman who long ago was maliciously and ignorantly accused of being a witch and was driven from the village, a scapegoat for the villagers' fears.

Tuere understands Okolo's search, but tells him it is hopeless—'How do you expect to find *it* when everybody has locked up his insides?' But Okolo cannot stop. He allows himself to be taken back to the village, when Izongo's men threaten to burn Tuere's hut, but he continues to refuse to conform. He is therefore banished. The hypocritical Izongo tells the people what a favour he has done them. The flavour of Okara's writing—its accomplished simplicity, the precision of its imagery, its strong underlying sadness, is well illustrated in this passage.

> 'It was a great task I performed, my people. A great task in
> sending him away. A dangerous task, but it had to be done for the
> good of us all. Only a mad man looks for *it* in this turned world.
> We know not what *it* is. We do not want to know. Let us be as we
> are. We do not want our insides to be stirred like soup in a pot.
>
> 'Only one small thing more, before we drink the palmwine.
> Only one small thing more. It's a very soft thing, soft as water,
> softer than softness. I and the Elders here have decided not to
> allow Okolo to come back to this our town. If he shows his face
> in this town we shall send him, and any person like him, away for
> ever and ever. Do you to this agree?'
>
> Loud shouts of 'Yes! Yes!' came out from the throat of Amatu,
> led by the Elders. Shouts of 'Yes! Yes!' drowned Okolo's lone
> voice asking 'Is *it* here? Have you *it*? Is *it* here?' forever they
> thought, in their insides.
>
> Then, with smile, Izongo looked at the people and with a wave
> of the hand, the palmwine ordered around. And the people
> rejoiced, their insides like honey becoming, and drank and drank.

Okolo goes to the nearby town of Sologa on the mailboat, hoping to find there a few people who share his outlook. On the deck of the boat, a girl sits beside him and goes to sleep with her head on his shoulder. When it begins to rain, Okolo covers her head with his coat. The girl's future mother-in-law, who is accompanying her, promptly accuses Okolo of touching the girl and attempting to seduce her. Okolo denies the charge, and so does the girl, but no one will believe them.

In Sologa, Okolo finds that his reputation has preceded him. He is met by thugs, beaten, and thrown into a dark room. When he comes to, he finds human bones around him. He escapes and reports to the police. But the house where Okolo has been imprisoned belongs to 'a big man', so the police will not listen to Okolo.

The journey brings disillusionment after disillusionment, and Okolo is a pilgrim whose faith is sorely tried. He enters an eating house where the painted slogans on the walls are 'Let the spoilt world spoil' and 'Eat and drink O, die one day we go.' The people here tell him that the town is in the corrupt hands of the Big One, and beg Okolo to stay with them and forget his search. 'The people who have the sweetest insides are the think-nothing people.' But Okolo must continue to look for his own meaning. He is finally turned out of Sologa because of the episode on the boat, for the old woman reappears with her son and entire family, and swears that Okolo 'spoiled' the girl. He returns to his own village, drawn back because it is his home. This time, bitterly, he sits on the boat deck trying not to touch anybody.

> This little he had now learned. He smiled in his inside. But is it possible for your body not to touch another body, for your inside not to touch another inside, for good or for bad?

When Chief Izongo and the elders discover that Okolo has returned, they attack him. With Tuere he meets his inevitable death. The two are tied in a canoe and sent into a whirlpool, where they drown. But Okolo before his death has decided that his meaning is to try to plant *it* within people's hearts, and he leaves one disciple, Ukule, who says 'Your spoken words will not die.'

Anne Tibble, in *African/English Literature*, compares the theme of *The Voice* to that of Dostoevski's *The Idiot*. Okolo and Myshkin do have much in common. Both need to speak the heart's truth; both are rejected by the establishment in society; both possess qualities which could be called saintly. Gabriel Okara's character has a more limited range, for Okolo is shown only in one aspect, as truth-seeker and questioner, whereas the subtly terrifying thing about Myshkin is that he really is partially idiot as well as saint, and his character fluctuates before the reader's eyes. Okolo remains constant, with no suggestion that there may be another side to his personality.

Another comparison would be with Eman in Wole Soyinka's *The Strong Breed*. Both are men of compassion and perception who are martyred by communities who fail to understand them and who therefore fear them. But Eman is a more complex character than Okolo, for in some ways he seeks his own martyrdom and his death has implications of saviourhood in it—he offers himself in order to redeem all. In terms of Christian parallels, Eman is a Christ figure, whereas Okolo could be called a Jesus figure, the difference being one of emphasis. In the case of Okolo, the emphasis is upon his teacherhood, the fact that his 'spoken words' may plant some seed of truth and desire for truth. There is nothing messianic about him, nor is there any suggestion that his death will, in itself, achieve anything. It is the survival of his words and his faith which is important. He does not seek his martyrdom as Eman does, for although Okolo is drawn back to his village, it is because he feels some sense of mission there, the need to make his 'teaching words' heard among his own people, rather than any need to die.

In *The Voice*, Okara uses the constructions of the Ijaw language experimentally, rendering them into an English which in its less successful moments can appear strained ('Are you a stranger man be?'), but which at its best is capable of acute and vivid expression. 'His inside did not agree with him', for example, conveys split feelings in a strikingly accurate way. Through the use of Ijaw speech patterns, Okara also achieves a freshness of imagery—'This is rain's time but the eye of the day is cleaner than cleanliness.' In some of the descriptive passages, Ijaw rhythms combine with Okara's qualities as a poet to produce a highly effective prose-poetry.

> It was the day's ending and Okolo by a window stood. Okolo
> stood looking at the sun behind the tree tops falling. The river
> was flowing, reflecting the finishing sun, like a dying away
> memory. It was like an idol's face, no one knowing what is
> behind. Okolo at the palm trees looked. They were like women
> with hair hanging down, dancing, possessed. Egrets, like white
> flower petals strung slackly across the river, swaying up and down,
> were returning home.

Okara makes use of Ijaw proverbs and parables in an unforced and natural manner, never peppering his writing with them but introducing them occasionally when they express the moment as nothing else could. In the boat episode, when Okolo is accused of touching the girl, the boat's engine man speaks up in his defence, whereupon the old woman viciously parries with a proverb— 'If you a bird of the sky take and in front of a fowl roast, the fowl's head aches.'

Sources of imagery that lie with Ijaw mask drama can be seen in Okara's use of the leopard and goat symbols. The villagers, led by Izongo, get drunk and begin to work up their hatred against Okolo.

> Who is the leopard in town?
> > Izongo!
> > Izongo!
> And who is goat in town?
> > Oko-lo!
> > Oko-lo!

> Can goat fight leopard?
> No, no!

Their chant compares interestingly with John Pepper Clark's use of this imagery in *Song of a Goat*, where the leopard is the slayer and the goat the victim. Okara uses the symbols in much the same way, but extends them by double meanings, for the leopard to the chief and elders represents power and nobility and the goat represents weakness and stupidity, whereas the reader has been shown the symbols' other significance—the leopard is power spiritually fossilised and gone blind, and the goat is weakness only if non-violence and the humility of genuine enquiry are weak.

Although Okara makes use of traditional Ijaw forms of expression, he also incorporates contemporary imagery with no sense of jarring. Chief Izongo, for example, speaks 'with a stone voice and the words fell like gravel from a tipper', or the villagers are described as 'making wry faces like people taking nivaquine'.

Okara's novel employs the method of poetry to make one central statement which is expressed with both delicacy and strength. Although it is set within a tribal society, *The Voice* contains a voice which reaches out. Okolo, essentially, is a man anywhere who must continue to question every establishment which becomes rigid and which surrounds itself with bulwarks of pretence. He is a man who must try to discover life through his own eyes.

Epilogue

CHINUA ACHEBE, in an article on 'English and the African Writer' (*Transition*, no. 18), said: 'The African writer should aim to use English in a way that brings out his message best without altering the language to the extent that its value as a medium of international exchange will be lost. He should aim at fashioning out an English which is at once universal and able to carry his peculiar experience.'

This process of adaptation is very much what has been happening in Nigerian literature. Nigerian writers, it is true, have not been wildly experimental, stylistically speaking, perhaps because they intend to be heard as widely as possible. A broad communication of ideas is important to them, and so most of them have opted for clarity now, rather than gambling on a possible understanding of their work several generations hence. Nevertheless they have evolved forms of English capable of expressing both West African modes of thought and a West African idiom. Achebe himself has developed an irony with an enormous range of expression, all the way from gentleness to bitter anger, and his style is admirably suited both to his re-creating of the baffling intricacies of two cultures in conflict and to his underlying theme, man's general misunderstanding of man.

Soyinka's ability to translate into English words the rhythms and the beliefs of Yoruba drumming and mask dancing; J.P. Clark's terse and formal lines which are so effective in dealing with the rituals he is exploring; Okara's use of Ijaw speech patterns in order to create a prose which is also a kind of poetry; Ekwensi's knack of catching the tone of the city dweller's speech with its jazziness like highlife music; the precision of Aluko's writing when he mimics a newspaper article which is a hybrid English, combining Yoruba oratory with mission-school sloganising—all these are ways in which Nigerian writers have made of English a language which is specifically their own.

The best of these writers have also chosen themes which are at once universal and able to carry their particular experience. Certain themes recur throughout contemporary Nigerian writing. There is a strong desire to reassess the historical past, to revalue the life of the village and the traditional forms of society, to rediscover roots which were severed. Many Nigerian writers have been concerned with an attempt, both personal and general, to reunite with a past which was for several generations lost or despised. No writer of any quality has viewed the old Africa in an idealised way, but they have tried to regain what is rightfully theirs—a past composed of real and vulnerable people, their ancestors, not the figments of missionary and colonialist imaginations.

The colonialists, although they have been severely satirised, have actually received less attention from Nigerian writers than have the missionaries. Perhaps this is not so strange. Alien administrators disrupt and alter a man's way of life, but proselytisers are aiming at the very core of his being. The Christian missions, as they are shown in contemporary Nigerian writing, have much to answer for. Yet there are few writers who do not display some division of mind over this subject, and even fewer who do not give the missions credit for the one unquestionably good thing they did—the establishment of primary education on a wide scale. The whole question of the missions, as it appears and reappears throughout Nigerian writing, is one which before many more years will no doubt be a topic for theses in literature, for it will prove to be a fascinating and ambiguous study.

The most persistent theme in Nigerian writing of today is today itself. A society is changing so swiftly and so painfully that it is hard even to see what is happening, much less to understand it, to perceive cause and effect, and to maintain a sense of the individual under the deceptive mask of crowds. The attempt both to be involved with a society and to stand apart from it in order to be able to see it—this is the difficult role which Nigerian writers have taken on.

Social satire, extending all the way from lightly barbed comedy to Swiftian venom, has been employed against crooked politicians and gullible populace time and again, but this has never been done with any tribal bias. Nigeria's writers have all, in one way or another, drawn upon their particular backgrounds, for they have all been concerned with the beliefs, rituals and ways of life of their own people, but they have never made qualitative judgements, have never said Ibo ways are better than Yoruba ways, or vice versa. Their fictional characters, too, have seldom been involved in tribal rivalries. Tribal animosity as such is a theme which appears scarcely at all in the Nigerian writing of the past fifteen years.

All this has now been radically changed by history itself. The first novel to mark the change—and it will prove to be a significant novel—was Cyprian Ekwensi's *Iska*, which deals with the first of the Ibo-Hausa riots in the North. Since then the tribal lines have hardened and sharpened, and the whole question of the breakdown of communication between various tribal groups, notably the Eastern Ibo (many of whom settled in the North) and the Northern Hausa and Fulani, appears to be Nigeria's deepest dilemma at the moment, something which demands to be examined, to be looked at in all its terrifying complexity. Writers do not have solutions. All they have is the sight of their own eyes, and the stubbornness to refuse to think of people in terms of faceless masses. Ekwensi's *Iska* was the first, but it will almost certainly not be the last novel to enquire into the concepts behind inter-tribal mistrust and the individual agonies beneath the violence of surface events.

Inter-tribal antagonism is not the only aspect of tribalism which is likely to be examined by Nigerian writers in the next decade. 'Tribalism' is an ambiguous word, for in one context it can mean the placement of loyalty with one group in such a way that members of all groups are automatically excluded and are regarded with fear or suspicion, whereas in another context it can simply mean the life-outlook and the social controls commonly found in societies based upon the extended family group. It is in this latter sense that contemporary Nigerian writers have delved into and re-created the patterns of life of earlier generations. Again and again, the old forms of government are described, the pre-colonial forms which survived at a village level even when the Yoruba empires had fallen apart and when the Ibo, whose proud claim had once been that they had no kings, were forced by European administrators to accept a system of externally appointed chiefs. There is so far very little suggestion on the part of Nigerian novelists and dramatists that the old methods might have some bearing on today and tomorrow, but in contemporary writings these traditional ways of rulership can be seen to amount to one basic way.

Authority—an authority which carried with it a mystical quality and therefore a religious reinforcement—was usually vested in one man, the king or chief or, in the case of the loosely structured Ibo society, in a small group of elders and title-holders. But power was not held solely in these hands, for every significant or controversial issue was discussed in council, either a council of king and elders, or (in the case of the Ibo) a general council of elders and people. All points of view were heard. It was the right of anyone to speak his mind freely, and to be listened to, however lengthy or irrelevant his oration might be. The role of the authority figure, then, was to assess the general view and to present the gathering with a decision which would be more or less acceptable to all. The advantage of this council system was its fairness to all points of view; its disadvantage was its crippling slowness. The existence of an organised, continuing and nearly always implacable opposition, which forms the basis of European parliamentary democracy, was never a part of tribal governments. Neither was the equally European concept of a dictatorship in which no man, however venerable, might dare to raise his voice against the pre-decided views presented to him by a ruler. It seems obvious at this point in history that forms of government transplanted without adaptation from other cultures will be replaced, in Nigeria as in other African countries, with new forms which do not yet exist. These new systems will develop not chiefly through analysis but through need, and they will in all probability make use of concepts and structures inherited not only from colonial days but also from much further back.

What these methods of government will be, no one can at the moment say, and certainly no one on the outside can even hazard a guess as to what they *ought* to be, for we simply cannot know. The difficulties of adapting the social controls of the village to a national level are adumbrated in the last paragraph of Chinua Achebe's *A Man of the People*. 'The owner was the village, and the village had a mind; it could say no to sacrilege. But in the affairs of the nation there was no owner, the laws of the village became powerless.' But when new forms of government emerge, as they inevitably must, they will be in the first place peculiarly African, and in the second place they will be widely misunderstood by the outside world simply because they will not correspond recognisably to existing forms in other countries. It seems reasonable to predict that the evolution of new forms of government will be interpreted by Nigerian writers, both for their own people and for the rest of the world, in terms which will not be entirely uncritical and which will also not be abstract, for the best Nigerian writers have always presented social themes through characters who could not be summed up neatly, characters who remained specific and paradoxical, and therefore alive.

Much as they are caught up in immediate happenings, however, Nigerian novelists and dramatists have constantly expressed in their work themes which are not confined to one place or one time—the individual's effort to define himself, his need to come to terms with his ancestors and his gods, his uncertainties in relation to others, his conflicts in the face of his own opposed loyalties, the dichotomy of his longing for both peace and war, his perpetual battle to free himself from the fetters of the past and the compulsions of the present.

In just over fourteen years Nigerian writers have already built up a body of work which is of interest and value not only in Africa but everywhere in the world where there are people who find in literature one way of discovering more fully the reality of others and of exploring the mystery of themselves.

List of Works

1. **Wole Soyinka**

    Five plays. London, Oxford University Press, Three Crowns Books, 1964.
    (A Dance of the Forests; The Lion and the Jewel; The Swamp
    Dwellers; The Trials of Brother Jero; The Strong Breed).

    A Dance of the Forests. London, Oxford University Press, Three Crowns
    Books, 1963.

    The Lion and the Jewel. London, Oxford University Press, Three Crowns
    Books, 1963.

    The Road. London, Oxford University Press, Three Crowns Books, 1965.

    The Interpreters. London, André Deutsch, 1965.

2. **John Pepper Clark**

    Three Plays. London, Oxford University Press, Three Crowns Books, 1964.
    (Song of a Goat; The Masquerade; The Raft).

    Ozidi. London, Oxford University Press, Three Crowns Books, 1966.

3. Chinua Achebe

Things Fall Apart. London, Heinemann, 1958; Heinemann African
   Writers Series, 1962 (paperback).
No Longer at Ease. Heinemann African Writers Series, 1963.
Arrow of God. London, Heinemann, 1964; African Writers Series, 1965.
A Man of the People. London, Heinemann, 1966.

4. Amos Tutuola

The Palm-Wine Drinkard. London, Faber, 1952.
My Life in the Bush of Ghosts. London, Faber, 1954.
Simbi and the Satyr of the Dark Jungle. London, Faber, 1955.
The Brave African Huntress. London, Faber, 1958.
Feather Woman of the Jungle. London, Faber, 1962.

5. Cyprian Ekwensi

People of the City. London, Andrew Dakers, 1954; African Writers
   Series. London, Heinemann, 1963.
Jagua Nana. London, Hutchinson, 1961; Panther Books, 1963.
Burning Grass. African Writers Series. London, Heinemann, 1962.
Beautiful Feathers. London, Hutchinson, 1963.
Lokotown and Other Stories. African Writers Series. London,
   Heinemann, 1966.
Iska. London, Hutchinson, 1966.

6. T.M. Aluko

One Man, One Wife. Nigerian Printing & Publishing Co., 1959.
One Man, One Matchet. African Writers Series. London, Heinemann,
   1964.
Kinsman and Foreman. London, Heinemann, 1966.

Elechi Amadi
The Concubine. London, Heinemann, 1966.

Nkem Nwankwo
Danda. London, André Deutsch, 1964.

Flora Nwapa
Efuru. London, Heinemann, 1966.

Onuora Nzekwu

Wand of Noble Wood. London, Hutchinson, 1961.
Blade Among the Boys. London, Hutchinson, 1962; Arrow Books, 1964.
Highlife for Lizards. London, Hutchinson, 1964.

Gabriel Okara

The Voice. André Deutsch, 1964.

General Bibliography

ACHEBE, Chinua, 'English and the African Writer', *Transition*, Kampala, Uganda, no. 18, 1965.

BABALOLA, Adeboye, 'Ijala, the Traditional Poetry of Yoruba Hunters', *Black Orpheus*, Ibadan, Nigeria, no. 1, 1957.

BEIER, Ulli, 'Yoruba Woodcarving', *Black Orpheus*, no. 4, 1960.

— 'Myths of the Yoruba Creator God', *Black Orpheus*, no. 7, 1963.

— 'Ibo and Yoruba Art', *Black Orpheus*, no. 8, 1964.

— 'Review of A Dance of the Forests', *Black Orpheus*, no. 8, 1964.

— 'The Oba's Festival at Ondo', *Nigeria Magazine*, Lagos, no. 50, 1956.

— 'The Egungun Cult', *Nigeria Magazine*, no. 51, 1956.

— 'The Oshun Festival', *Nigeria Magazine*, no. 53, 1957.

— *Art in Nigeria*, 1960, London, Cambridge University Press, 1960.

Commonwealth Literature, ed. John Press, London, Heinemann, 1965.

FUJA, Abayomi, *Fourteen Hundred Cowries: Traditional Stories of the Yoruba*, London, Oxford U.P., 1962.

GLEASON, Judith, 'Out of the Irony of Words', *Transition*, no. 18, 1965.

GREEN, Margaret, *Ibo Village Affairs*, 2nd ed. London, Cass & Co., 1964.

HORTON, Robin, 'The Kalabari World View', *Africa*, Journal of the International African Institute, vol. no. 3, 1962.

— 'The Kalabari Ekine Society', *Africa*, vol. no. 2, 1963.

— 'Destiny and the Unconscious in West Africa', *Africa*, vol. xxxi, 1961.

LAPIDO, Duro, *Three Yoruba Plays*, trans. Ulli Beier. Mbari Publications, 1964.

LLOYD, P.C., 'Sacred Kingship among the Yoruba', *Africa*, vol. xxx, 1960.

MACLEAN, Una, 'Soyinka's International Drama', *Black Orpheus*, no. 15, 1964.

MBARI Club and LADIPO, Duro, *Nigeria Magazine*, Sept. 1963.

MOORE, Gerald, *Seven African Writers*, Oxford University, Three Crowns Books, 1962.

MORTON-WILLIAMS, Peter, 'Yoruba Responses to the Fear of Death', *Africa*, vol. xxx, 1960.

— 'The Yoruba Ogboni Cult', *Africa*, vol. xxx, 1960.

— 'Ogun Festival', ibid., no. 85, 1965.

MPHALELE, Ezekiel, *The African Image*, Faber, 1962.

SHELTON, Austin J., 'The Offended Chi in Achebe's Novels', *Transition*, no. 13, 1964.

SKINNER, Elliott P., 'Strangers in West African Societies', *Africa*, vol. no. 4, 1963.

TIBBLE, Anne, *African/English Literature: A Survey and Anthology*. Peter Owen, 1965.

WESTCOTT, Joan, 'Sculpture and Myths of Eshu-Elegba, the Yoruba Trickster', *Africa*, vol. no. 4, 1962.

Index

ANNOTATIONS

Frontispiece
Page 5: **"Christopher Okigbo"** (1932–1967) Poet, author of *Heavensgate* (Nigeria: MBARI Press, 1962), *Limits* (Nigeria: MBARI Press, 1964) and *Labyrinths, With Path of Thunder* (Africana, 1971) and coeditor of *Transition*, who rejected the perceived exclusivity of Negritude and was influenced by Ibo myths, American modernists, and his own education in Greek and Latin; killed in battle while a volunteer for the Biafran forces in August 1967. According to critic Paul Theroux, one can hear "three separate melodies" in Okigbo's poetry: "the music of youth, the clamour of passage (that is, growing up) and lastly, the sounds of thunder" ("Okigbo, Christopher," *Africana* 1456, "Okigbo, Christopher," *Contemporary Authors* 404–5).

Page 5: **"*Heavensgate*"** Poem in five parts: "I THE PASSAGE II INITIATIONS III WATERMAID IV LUSTRA V NEWCOMER" The lines employed as epigraph to *Long Drums and Cannons* occur at the end of Part IV LUSTRA (Christopher Okigbo, *Heavensgate*. Ibadan: MBARI Press, 1962). (This poem also appears in Christopher Okigbo, *Collected Poems*, London: Heinemann, 1986, 19–35).

191

Preface

Page 11, 2nd paragraph, 7th line: **"Ezekiel Mphalele"** (1919–) South African author who went into exile in 1957, living in Nigeria and the United States before returning to South Africa in 1977; editor of *Black Orpheus* and other periodicals; works include *Down Second Avenue* (1959) and the 1984 novel, *Father Come Home*; first name changed to "Es'kia" in 1997 ("Mphalele, Es'kia" 1356).

Page 11, 2nd paragraph, 7th line: **"Ronald Dathorne"** (1934–) Nigerian author and critic whose works include *African Literature in the Twentieth Century* (1976) (Parekh 132).

Page 11, 2nd paragraph, 8th line: **"MBARI writers' and artists' club"** Ibadan group formed in 1960, the year of Nigerian independence, including John Pepper Clark, Gerald Moore and Wole Soyinka, to develop "a nationalist culture using theatre and other arts" ("Nigeria" 221).

Page 12, 1st paragraph, 2nd line: **"concepts of negritude"** A literary movement of the 1940s and 1950s whose leading figures, Francophone writers Aimé Cesaire and Leopold Sedar Senghor, Leon Damas, and other African and Caribbean expatriates living in Paris, encouraged the development of African diasporic culture and identity by looking beyond colonial definitions and indictments in order to re-evaluate African history and by incorporating African values and traditions in contemporary writing in order to develop critiques of Western culture and instill a "desire for political freedom" in the reader (Nesbitt 1404–8, "Negritude" 583). They asserted a specific black African nature and psychology in reaction to the assimilationist policies of French colonial rule (Ashcroft 21–22).

Page 13, 3rd paragraph, 1st line: **"This book was written before the outbreak of civil war in Nigeria and the secession of Biafra."** Laurence completed the composition of *Long Drums and Cannons* on 2 May 1967; civil war broke out in Nigeria in January 1966 when Major Chukwuma Nzeogwu staged a coup in which the Prime Minister and other leaders were assassinated (Crowder 246).

Page 13, 4th paragraph, 4th line: **"Christopher Okigbo"** (1932–1967) Poet whose poem *Heavensgate* (Nigeria: MBARI Press, 1962) provided the epigraph and title for *Long Drums and Cannons*. SEE ANNOTATION TO PAGE 5.

ONE   Voices of Life, Dance of Death
       Wole Soyinka

Page 15, 1st paragraph, 7th line: "**has written one novel**" *The Interpreters* was Soyinka's first novel, published in 1965.

Page 15, 1st paragraph, 8th line: "**his major work so far**" Since the mid-1970s, essays on dramatic theory, memoirs, and a wide range of political writings have raised Soyinka's work beyond easy categorization. He has become as much an academic figure and cultural commentator as a dramatist.

Page 15, 2nd paragraph, 4th line: "**Six...have been published**" Most of these early plays are now available in print. SEE THE BIBLIOGRAPHICAL INFORMATION, 233–34.

Page 15, 2nd paragraph, 7th line: "**The 1960 Masks**" An English-language theatre company established in Ibadan in the year of Nigeria's independence; with its first production, Soyinka's *A Dance of the Forests*, "Nigerian theatre clearly had begun to use indigenous experiences—in this case Yoruba experiences—to comment on political developments and the future of the nation" ("Nigeria" 221).

Page 15, 2nd paragraph, 7th line: "**Orisun Theatre**" Ibadan theatre company founded by Wole Soyinka.

Page 16, 2nd paragraph, 1st line: "**Yoruba**" SEE 'YORUBA' IN THE GLOSSARY.

Page 16, 2nd paragraph, 1st line: "**Born in 1934 in Isara, Ijebo Remo**" Contrary to what Laurence writes, biographer Thomas Hayes locates the birth of Akiwande Oluwole Soyinka in the city of Abeokuta, Western Nigeria. John Thomas points out that Soyinka's family lived in the Ake quarter of the city, hence the name of Soyinka's 1981 memoir, *Ake: The Years of Childhood*.

Page 16, 2nd paragraph, 6th line: "**to do research in traditional African drama**" This research was funded by a Rockefeller Foundation award.

Page 16, 2nd paragraph, 9th line: "**University of Ibadan**" By the time *Drums* went to press, Soyinka had already been in prison for some months, charged with aiding the Biafran independence movement. This did not affect his post at the University of Ibadan, which he resumed upon his release and held until his resignation in 1971.

Page 16, 4th paragraph, 10th line: "**Brecht**", Bertolt (1898–1956) Celebrated German playwright attracted to Marxism and pacifism; Brecht's works include *Trommeln in der Nacht* (*Drums in the Night*, 1922), *Die Dreigroschenoper* (*The Threepenny Opera*, 1928), and *Mutter Courage und ihre Kinder* (*Mother*

Courage and Her Children, 1941); founder of the Berliner Ensemble at the Theater am Schiffbauerdam in 1949 (Matlaw 105–6).

Page 16, 4th paragraph, 10th line: "**Durrenmatt**", Friedrich (1921–) Swiss-born Durenmatt's plays and novels are often influenced by Kafka, Kierkegaard, Brecht, and Bosch, among others; his works include *Romulus der Grosse* (*Romulus the Great*, 1948), and *Der Meteor* (*The Meteor*, 1966) (Matlaw 223–24).

Page 16, 4th paragraph, 10th line: "**Arden**", John (1930–) English playwright whose ambiguous, perhaps "confused" plots often utilise elements of satire and farce to explore themes of corruption and other sociological concerns; Arden's works include *The Waters of Babylon* (1957), *Soldier, Soldier* (1960), and *Harold Muggins is a Martyr* (1968) (Matlaw 36–37).

Page 16, 3rd paragraph, last line: "**results are...electrifying**" The element of the universal in Soyinka's work certainly ought not to be discarded, but, for Soyinka, the dramatic fusion of contemporary settings and references with traditional myth and ritual also lays the groundwork for a crucial social critique of a specific time and place. For a contemporary view of Soyinka's dramatic technique and its sociopolitical aims, see Derek Wright, "Ritual and Revolution: Soyinka's Dramatic Theory" in *ARIEL: A Review of International English Literature* 23:1 (January 1992).

Page 17, 3rd paragraph, 1st line: "*Egungun*" SEE 'EGUNGUN' IN THE GLOSSARY.

Page 18, 2nd paragraph, 1st line: "*Ifa* society" SEE 'IFA' IN THE GLOSSARY.

Page 18, 4th paragraph, 6th line: "**ancestral spirit is believed...present**" The state of possession into which the *Egungun* dancer enters has not unremarkable connections with certain Western acting techniques. Constantin Stanislavski's language, in describing his now-famous technique, is very much the language of possession: "...the very best that can happen is to have the actor completely carried away by the play. Then regardless of his (*sic*) own will he *lives* the part, not noticing how he feels, not thinking about what he does..." (*An Actor Prepares* 13, my emphasis).

Page 19, 1st paragraph, 2nd line: "**Festival of Ogun**" SEE 'OGUN' IN GLOSSARY.

Page 19, 2nd paragraph, 4th line: "**J.B. Danquah**" (Joseph Kwame Kyeretwie Boakye) (1895–1965) Ghanian scholar, playwright, and statesman, Danquah's highly influential works include the plays *Nyankonsem* (1941) and *The Third Woman* (1943), as well as the nonfictional *Revelation of Culture in Ghana* (1961) and *The Akan Doctrine of God* (1944, 1968) (Herdeck 101).

Page 20, 1st paragraph, last line: "**Ogun's sacrificial animal**" For a comprehensive consideration of the role Soyinka carves for mythology in contemporary African writing, see his *Myth, Literature and the African World* (Cambridge UP, 1976). A recent application of his theories can be found in "The Postcolonial Tradition: The Archeology of African Knowledge" by Noureini Tidjani-Serpos, *Research in African Literatures* 27:1 (Spring 1996), as well as in "Black Drama and Revolutionary Consciousness: What a Difference a Difference Makes" by Floyd Gaffney, *Theatre Annual* 41 (1986). See also Wright, "Ritual and Revolution."

Page 20, 2nd paragraph, 8th line: "**Hubert Ogunde**" (1916–1990) The Yoruba founder of the African Music Research Party (1946), which inspired Kola Ogunmola, Duro Ladipo, and many others, Ogunde used theatrical forms to reveal problems within colonial administrations and other realms; he also founded the National Troupe in 1986 ("Nigeria" 221–22).

Page 20, 3rd paragraph, 2nd line: "**Duro Ladipo**" (1932–1975) A music teacher who encountered resistance upon introducing "pagan" instruments into church performances, Ladipo established the Duro Ladipo National Theatre, based in Oshogbo, in 1961; also an actor and composer, his works include *Oba Koso* (*The King Did Not Hang*) in 1964 and *Eda*, published in 1970 (Axworthy 204).

Page 21, 4th paragraph, 1st line: "**This…is Wole Soyinka's inheritance**" In 1977, Soyinka wrote his own 'folk' opera. *Opera Wonyosi* re-writes Brecht's *Threepenny Opera* as a satire of late 1970s Nigeria. Laurence chooses largely to ignore Soyinka's Western influences as she summarizes his background—undoubtedly a political move, part of her critical project to give maximum authority to his position as an *African* artist—but Brecht's legacy is crucial to a complete understanding of Soyinka's work. Soyinka's own dramatic theory echoes Brecht's conception of theatre as a forum for social critique, and many of the techniques that Brecht developed to distance his audiences critically from and sharpen their analytical faculties towards the action on stage inform Soyinka's plays. For more on these techniques, see *Brecht on Theatre: The Development of an Aesthetic*, translated by John Willett (London: Methuen, 1964). SEE ANNOTATION FOR 'BRECHT' FOR PAGE 16.

Page 21, 5th paragraph, title, "***The Lion and the Jewel***" Other critical discussions of this play include C.N. Ramachandran, "Structure Within Structure: An Analysis of Wole Soyinka's *The Lion and the Jewel*," *Journal of Commonwealth Literature* 25:1 (1990); P.D. Tripathi, "*The Lion and the Jewel*: A Comparative and

Thematic Study," *Ba Shiru: A Journal of African Languages and Literature* 11:1 (1980); and A. Mohmed, "*The Lion and the Jewel* Reconsidered: Observations on the Relationship Between Character and Language in the Play," *The Mirror* (1972).

Page 22, 1st paragraph, 15th line: "**the Sun King in France**" Another name for King Louis XIV of France (1638–1715), whose reign was marked by the flourishing of French art and numerous wars of expansion ("Louis XIV" 851).

Page 22, 2nd paragraph, 2nd line: "**not a girl to be ordered about**" Despite the potential contained in such a statement, one of the oddities of Laurence's text is its distinct lack of concern with women's issues. Ironically, Laurence's own fiction manifests far greater feminist anxieties than this, her most significant "critical" work. As will become clear in her analysis of *A Dance of the Forests*, she often allows moments of potential misogyny to pass without a word, revealing the degree to which her primary concerns in *Drums* are more broadly humanist than specifically "feminist," or even "postcolonial." For a discussion of gender issues in *The Lion and the Jewel*, see Mariene Ndiaye's "Female Stereotypes in Wole Soyinka's *The Strong Breed* and *The Lion and the Jewel*" in *Bridges: An African Journal of English Studies* 5 (1993).

Page 22, 3rd paragraph, 1st line: "**refuses to pay any bride-price**" SEE 'BRIDE-PRICE' IN THE GLOSSARY.

Page 25, top of the page, title, "*The Trials of Brother Jero*" Very little recent criticism deals with this text. Other perspectives include Bu-Buakei Jabbi, "The Form of Discovery in *The Trials of Brother Jero*," *Obsidian: Black Literature in Review* 2:3 (1976), and Richard Priebe, "Soyinka's Brother Jero: Prophet, Politician and Trickster," *Pan-African Journal* 4:4 (1971).

Page 25, 3rd paragraph, 9th line: "**speech...is handled with...the same authenticity**" Hayes would disagree. He argues that Soyinka's use of both formal and pidgin English in his plays provides for some rather "un-African" dialogue (Hayes 7), as it disregards the less formal vernacular in which many of Soyinka's characters might normally speak.

Page 26, 5th paragraph, 3rd line: "**Ijaw people**" SEE 'IJAW' IN GLOSSARY.

Page 28, top of page, title, "*The Strong Breed*" One of the most recent discussions of this play can be found in Mariene Ndiaye's 1993 essay. (SEE ANNOTATION FOR 'NOT A GIRL' FOR PAGE 22.) See also Lalova Lyonga, "The Theme of Sacrifice in Wole Soyinka's *The Strong Breed*," *Ngam* 1–2 (1977).

Page 30, new section, title, "*A Dance of the Forests*" This remains a very popular play for critical consideration. The journal *Commonwealth Essays and Studies* devoted a special issue to it in 1989, in which can be found articles as diverse as "Soyinka's Use of Yoruba Mythology in *A Dance of the Forests*" by Michel Fabre, "The Cosmic Framework of *A Dance of the Forests*" by Etienne Galle, and "Metatheatrical Strategy in *A Dance of the Forests*" by Jane Wilkinson. This special issue also contains a select bibliography. For a view of the play contemporary to *Drums*, see Ian Watson, "Soyinka's *A Dance of the Forests*," *Transition* 27 (1966).

Page 32, 2nd paragraph, 3rd line: "**The *Oro* cult**" SEE 'ORO' IN THE GLOSSARY.

Page 41, last paragraph, 5th line: "**mother did not worry unduly about him**" Laurence's working manuscript reveals an anxiety about this line: which was re-written several times. Her concern was justified: although this final version seeks to strike a balance between comic relief and effective description, it nevertheless clashes with her otherwise critical tone.

Page 41, last paragraph, 1st line: "*ibeji* **figure**" SEE 'IBEJI' IN THE GLOSSARY.

Page 44, 3rd paragraph, 3rd line: "**of his own heart**" After her conclusion, Laurence notes, "So many of its scenes—the masquerade, the conjuring up of the court of Mata Kharibu—would film marvelously well" (Laurence ts. ch. 1, 21).

Page 44, new section, title, "*The Road*" Like *A Dance of the Forests*, *The Road* remains quite popular within academic circles. An overview of recent criticism might include Russell McDougall, "Spatial Dynamics of Mask and Face in Soyinka's *The Road*," *The Contact and the Culmination* (Liege, Belgium: Liege Language and Literature, 1997); Charles Uji, "Soyinka's *The Road* as a Romantic Tragedy," *Research in Yoruba Language and Literature* 4 (1993); K.J. Phillips, "Exorcising Faustus from Africa: Wole Soyinka's *The Road*," *Comparative Literature Studies* 27:2 (1990); Denise Coussy, "Metaphors of Life and Death in *The Road* by Wole Soyinka," *Commonwealth Essays and Studies* 7:1 (1984); and Jeanne Dingome, "Soyinka's *The Road* as Ritual Drama," *Kunapipi* 2:1 (1980).

Page 45, 4th paragraph, 5th line: "**make it any less genuine**" is followed in the Laurence typescript by "I do not claim to understand the state of possession any more than I understand evangelists who speak in tongues, but these are phenomena which exist and are experienced by some people. I have never personally witnessed a Yoruba religious masquerade, but I have seen in Ghana a stoolbearer carrying the sacred blackened stool of the ancestors at the head of a festival procession, and it was absolutely clear that his state of trance was genuine" (2).

Page 45, 5th paragraph, 2nd line: "the rejects of the road" Echoes of
Beckett's *Waiting for Godot* have been heard throughout this play.
See Clive Probyn, "Waiting for the Word: Samuel Beckett and
Wole Soyinka," *ARIEL: A Review of International English
Literature* 12 (1981), and Elaine Fido, "*The Road* and Theatre of
the Absurd," *Caribbean Journal of African Studies* 1 (1978).

Page 51, 3rd paragraph, 6th line: "**Yoruba Ogboni society**" SEE 'OGBONI' IN
THE GLOSSARY.

Page 51, 4th complete paragraph, 9th line: "**not turn out as...expect them to
do**" In Laurence's typescript, this paragraph ends with a curious
reference to Voltaire: "All is *not* right in the best of all possible
worlds."

Page 55, 2nd paragraph, last line: "**it concerns death**" Laurence's typescript
includes Soyinka's own description of Murano's suspended state,
defined in a note for the producer, as "an arrest of time" or "a
visual suspension of death" (18).

Page 56, 4th paragraph, 11th line: "**to turn the wheel his own way**" is
followed by "We also suspect that he may be crushed by it" (20).

Page 57, 2nd paragraph, 1st line: "**Professor knows that what he is
attempting is...taboo**" In more ways than one: from the 16th
until the early 20th century, representing any religious person or
ritual on the stage in England was against the law, and until the
late 1960s "core" Biblical figures (including God) remained
banned. As a result, to this day anyone wishing to play God in an
English theatre can expect to meet with some form of resistance
(see John Elliott, *Playing God: Medieval Mysteries on the Modern
Stage* (U of Toronto P, 1989)). Whether or not this taboo applies
to non-Christian deities, *The Road* certainly breaks new
representational ground for the theatre in English.

Page 58, 2nd paragraph, 4th line: "**layabouts chant the Drivers' Dirge**"
"It's a long long road to heaven, / It's a long road to heaven,
Driver / Go easy a-ah go easy driver / It's a long, long road to
heaven / My Creator, be not harsh on me—" (23).

Page 59, new section, title, "*The Interpreters*" Recent academic work on
this novel includes Femi Abodunrin, "The Politics of Poetics of
Otherness: A Study of Wole Soyinka's *The Interpreters*," *Yearbook
of English Studies* 27 (1997); Anjali Roy and Viney Kirpal, "Men
as Archetypes: Characterization in Soyinka's Novels," *Modern
Fiction Studies* 37:3 (1991); Aminigo Ibitamuno, "Myth, the Main
Characters and Meaning in Wole Soyinka's *The Interpreters*,"
Literary Half-Yearly 32:2 (1991); Kofi Owusu, "Interpreting the
Interpreters: The Fictionality of Wole Soyinka's Fiction," *World
Literature Written in English* 27:2 (1987); and David Attwell,

"Wole Soyinka's *The Interpreters*: Suggestions on Context and History," *English in Africa* 8:1 (1981).

Page 59, 3rd paragraph, 8th line: "*lingua franca*" "a language adopted as a common language between speakers whose native languages are different" ("Lingua Franca" 833).

Page 59, 5th paragraph, 1st line: "**Soyinka's first novel**" Soyinka has written just one other novel, *Season of Anomy* (1973). He has commented that he does not consider himself a novelist, and the two novels he has produced have, in his opinion, come about largely "by accident" (see interview with Kreisler).

Page 60, 2nd paragraph, 1st line: "**Ijaw chief**" SEE 'IJAW' IN THE GLOSSARY.

Page 61, 2nd paragraph, 7th line: "**cheerfully admitted lust which sends every...girl skittering for shelter**" For more on the treatment of women in this novel, see Anny Claire Jaccard, "Portraits de Femmes dans *Les Interpretes* de Wole Soyinka," *Nouvelles du Sud* 2 (1985–86).

Page 63, 1st paragraph, 6th line: "**Herzog in Saul Bellow's novel**" Canadian-born author whose (often apocalyptic) works include the novels *The Victim* (1947) and *Herzog* (1964) and the 1994 nonfictional *It All Adds Up* (Drabble 86).

Page 64, 3rd paragraph, 6th line: "**Bandele teaches at Ibadan University**" As Soyinka did, while writing this novel. SEE ALSO 'IBADAN' IN THE GLOSSARY.

Page 64, 3rd paragraph, 2nd-last line: "**Ogboni, the cult of the Earth**" SEE 'OGBONI' IN THE GLOSSARY.

Page 65, 1st paragraph, 13th line: "**Esumare, the rainbow**" SEE 'ESUMARE' IN THE GLOSSARY.

Page 66, 2nd paragraph, 4th line: "**half in love with easeful death**" echoes the sixth stanza of Keats's melancholy "Ode to a Nightingale" (1820): "Darkling I listen; and for many a time / I have been half in love with easeful Death, / Called him soft names in many a musèd rhyme / To take into the air my quiet breath."

Page 67, 3rd paragraph, 4th line: "**Kingsley Amis**" (1922–) English novelist and poet whose works include *Lucky Jim* (1954), *That Uncertain Feeling* (1955), and *The Old Devils*, which won the Booker Prize in 1986 (Drabble 25).

Page 67, 3rd paragraph, last line: "**Saul Bellow**" (1915–) Novelist whose (often apocalyptic) works include *The Victim* (1947) and *Herzog* (1964) (Drabble 86).

Page 67, 3rd paragraph, last line: "**Bernard Malamud**" (1914–1986) American author best known for *The Fixer* (1967) and *A New Life* (1961) (Drabble 618).

Page 68, 1st paragraph, last line: "**self-protective skepticism**" Soyinka, in his
recent interview with Harry Kreisler, notes that he sees "no
division at all" between the artist and activist in himself. He also,
however, qualifies this statement by asserting that, in his view, not
all artists are activists, and he often wishes he were of that
"different kind."

Page 69, 4th paragraph, last line: "**the areas of darkness within us all**" The
conclusion in Laurence's typescript ends with "His spiritual
ancestor could have been the minstrel David, poet of the Psalms—
'Behold, Thou desirest truth in the inward parts, and in the hidden
part Thou shalt make me to know wisdom'" (14).

TWO Rituals of Destiny
John Pepper Clark

Page 71, 2nd paragraph, 1st line: "**denied that his sources are primarily
Greek**" When asked about his sources and influences in a 1962
interview with Lewis Nkosi, Clark acknowledged the influence of
the ancient Greek dramatists, but implied that critics have aligned
his plays too closely with Greek tragedy: "I suppose we've been
led on to believe that my work is derived from the Greek classics
because I use the chorus and I use one or two other things which
people imagine are the exclusive qualities of Greek tragedy," but
adds, "I think there is here this cultural coincidence. I rather
believe that people like Yeats are right who say that at bottom all
people are the same, all folklores, mythologies, spring from the
same sources" (64–65).

Page 71, 2nd paragraph, last line: "**traditional Ijaw society**" The Ijaw,
perhaps the oldest inhabitants of the territory, are the people of
the delta region of the great River Niger in Nigeria. See "Chapter
One: Clark's Nigeria" of Robert M. Wren's *J.P. Clark* for a
discussion of these people and the places about which Clark
writes. SEE ALSO 'IJAW' IN THE GLOSSARY.

Page 72, 2nd paragraph, 3rd line: "**University of Ibadan**" Clark completed
his formal education at University College, Ibadan, from which he
graduated in 1960 with a Bachelor of Arts in English with
honours. During his university years, Clark was cofounder and
first editor of and contributor to *The Horn*, a student poetry
journal featuring the work of several writers who would become
prominent figures in Nigerian literature (Okagbue 154; Wren
114). Clark also honed his skills as poet and playwright while a
student, writing *Song of a Goat* and *Poems* (containing several
poems he contributed to *The Horn*) during this time. SEE ALSO
'IBADAN' IN THE GLOSSARY.

Page 72, 2nd paragraph, 4th line: **"Princeton, U.S.A."** In recognition of his work as a feature writer and editor for the *Express* newspapers in Lagos, Clark was awarded a Parvin Fellowship (a scholarship designed to teach potential third-world leaders about American democracy) in 1962 to study at Princeton University—an experience he records in his satirical *America, Their America* (1964) (Wren 113). Although he was unsuccessful as a Parvin fellow, he was productive as a playwright, writing both *The Masquerade* and *The Raft* during his year in the United States.

Page 72, 2nd paragraph, 5th line: **"Institute of African Studies, Ibadan"** Clark researched traditional myths of the Ijaw people, including the Ozidi legend.

Page 72, 2nd paragraph, 6th line: **"*Song of a Goat, The Masquerade* and *The Raft*"** Laurence is referring here to *Three Plays* (1964).

Page 72, 2nd paragraph, 7th line: **"*Ozidi*"** Clark's research of the Ijaw Ozidi legend was a fifteen-year venture that produced the play *Ozidi* (1966), a film titled *Tides of the Delta: The Saga of Ozidi* (1975), and a translation of the epic, *The Ozidi Saga* (1977). For more on these works, see "The Ozidi Complex" in Wren's *J.P. Clark*.

Page 74, 1st paragraph, 7th line: **"*teme*"** (Wren discusses the Ijaw concept of *teme* in Chapter One of his biography *J.P. Clark*, defining it as "the 'personal god' who determines one's role and success in life" and who "sends the individual into the world with a mission" (10). He elaborates: "Before one's birth, *teme* makes an agreement with the supreme deity. This agreement determines the future life of the individual. A wise *teme*, of course, will make a good agreement; but, unfortunately, before birth the spirit is too young to bargain well, and may even be foolish. Thus one may be compelled throughout life to contend with the mistake of one's own personal god. It can be a heavy burden" (10).) SEE ALSO 'TEME' IN THE GLOSSARY.

Page 77, 4th paragraph, second last line: **"Norman Mailer"** (1923–) American-born author, Mailer's novels—including *The Naked and the Dead* (1948) and *An American Dream* (1965)—analyse "aspects of his times" particularly in the United States (Hart 406–7).

Page 78, 2nd paragraph, 1st line: **"The neighbours play a role"** In the typescript of *Long Drums and Cannons*, Laurence elaborates on the role of the neighbours: "This role is a natural and even inevitable one in African drama, or indeed in any society where a man does not live to himself but very much as part of a community. The tragedy here is that the neighbors are *only* a chorus—they do not really understand what is happening, nor can they help" (Laurence ts. ch. 2, 10).

Page 78, 3rd paragraph, 3rd line: "**the specific nature of his offence**"
Laurence speculates on this curse in the typescript: "The masseur
says that Zifa did his duty 'when you brought him back home
among his people. It may have been a bit early for one who died
of the white taint.' Is this a reference to leprosy? Whatever disease
it may have been, the villagers obviously feared the taint" (10).

Page 78, 4th paragraph, 1st line: "**The sacrifice scene is a travesty of proper
observances**" Laurence prefaces this statement, in the typescript,
with a discussion of previous criticism of the sacrifice scene: "*Song
of a Goat* has been criticised by Anthony Astrachan (*Black
Orpheus*, 16, Oct. 1964) for being 'a tragedy without a cause.'
Astrachan feels that what is missing from Clark's play is a sense of
inner development. An offense of Zifa's and one of his father's 'are
hinted at, but never given enough emphasis to bear the burden of
tragedy.' I cannot agree that this is a tragedy without a cause, nor
that it is a tragedy without *hubris*" (10).

Page 78, 5th paragraph, 1st line: "**The other two main characters are also
compelled…to fulfil their fates**" Because of this, Laurence believes
(as the typescript reveals) that "[t]his scene works extremely well,
both in psychological terms and in terms of Ijaw belief" (11).

Page 79, 1st paragraph, last line: "**beyond human contact**" Laurence adds,
in her typescript, "Zifa's blindness to his own faults—i.e., his
pride—makes the tragedy plausible and inevitable, despite a
certain tinge of melodrama in the off-stage hanging and drowning.
The violence of his symbolic act, in the sacrifice scene, is
completely realized on all levels. The violence can be felt in the
whole scene—it needs no explanations. In religious terms, it is a
violence done not only to Ebiere, but also to the gods, a truly
sacrilegious act" (12).

Page 79, 2nd paragraph, 5th line: "**the language is spare and yet rich**"
Laurence expands her assessment of Clark's style in the typescript:
"Expression is accurate and acute, never unnecessarily long, never
verbose, full of poetic images drawn from the land and the creeks.
The imagery is always suited to the subject. …Some of the
descriptions, such as a villager's description of Zifa's death, are
done with great simplicity and yet with a wealth of local detail
which gives an indelibly true impression" (12–13). Earlier,
Laurence expresses her annoyance with Clark's method of line
division: "I confess that I find John Pepper Clark's style of line-
division puzzling and at times irritating.… I can see no advantage
to this method of line break, which obviously isn't arbitrary but
seems so" (12).

Page 79, 3rd paragraph, 1st line: "*The Masquerade* seems much too frail a craft" In the typescript, Laurence adds, "The tragedy itself, so far from moving me to pity or terror or even dull nausea at the spilled gore, leaves me absolutely cold, because I did not believe in it for one minute" (13).

Page 79, 3rd paragraph, last line: "little more than sentimental clichés" In the typescript, Laurence writes, "the young lovers' pursuit of one another might be called charming, I suppose, although some of the lines of poetry strike my ears with the unmistakable clonk of corniness"; she adds, "It is only fair, however, to add that some of the descriptions in the scene are well done, when Clark forgets to try to make them fancy" (13).

Page 79, 4th paragraph, last line: "phrases which it is difficult to believe could ever be uttered" Laurence, in the typescript, declares, "Poetic license is all very well, but not at the total expense of plausible human speech" (14). "Let's not overdo it" (14) is crossed out.

Page 79, 5th paragraph, 2nd line: "Tufa is...Ebiere's son, by Tonye" "The curse on the house of Zifa has thus continued to the next generation," Laurence adds (14).

Page 80, 1st paragraph, 1st line: "Tufa...has been unaware...of his family's curse" "and of the snarled situation...which caused the death of both Tonye and Zifa. One may well question how it is that Orukorere, the prophetess, who is meant to have brought up Tufa, permitted him to remain in total ignorance and one may also wonder how the story reached Diribi's village at this particular moment" (14).

Page 80, 2nd paragraph, 14th line: "we discover that Diribi has killed his daughter" "Wham—just like that" (15). Clearly, Laurence, in revising her typescript, thought better of some of these initial visceral reactions.

Page 80, 2nd paragraph, last line: "bent his mind into madness" Noting that the village priests have called Diribi "overcome," Laurence adds, "So might he well-overcome, one hopes, not primarily, by the terrible nature of his act, but by its feeble implausibility. He is all melodramatic character here—he does not really exist" (15).

Page 80, 6th paragraph, 1st line: "*Song of a Goat* and *The Masquerade* were performed" The typescript reveals more explicitly that Laurence personally attended these two performances: "I saw both *Song of a Goat* and *The Masquerade* performed by the Eastern Nigeria Theatre Group at the Commonwealth Festival in London in 1965" (16).

Page 81, 1st paragraph, last line: "**too little convincing anguish**" Laurence's conclusion about the play is found in the typescript: "I have the feeling with this play that the whole thing is somehow embryonic and under-developed" (16).

Page 81, 2nd paragraph, 5th line: "**Lagos, Kano and Onitsha**" Nigerian cities. SEE EACH CITY IN THE GLOSSARY.

Page 81, 2nd paragraph, 11th line: "**Olutu tries...to put the raft free**" The typescript reads "punt the raft free" (16). "Punt" may, in fact, be the appropriate word here.

Page 82, 2nd paragraph, 1st line: "**Burutu**" a Nigerian city. SEE 'BURUTU' IN THE GLOSSARY.

Page 83, 1st paragraph, 1st line: "*Ozidi*" For a discussion of Clark's research of the Ijaw legend Ozidi and the Ozidi works that he produced, see Wren's "The Ozidi Saga" in his *J.P. Clark*. Wren concludes the chapter by praising Clark's vision and efforts: "In the play, the film, and the saga an indigenous African epic is preserved and re-created as no other has been. The re-creation is continually exciting, but, more important, it evokes an authentic African experience. The variety of forms provides an unprecedented sense of the whole. Nowhere else can the student, whether African or alien, find so rounded and fully dimensional a record of what is now a lost experience of epic" (126).

The typescript reveals that Laurence had privileged access to *Ozidi* in its pre-publication stage: "Although *Ozidi* has not yet been published, I have read it in manuscript" (Laurence ts. ch. 2, 20).

Page 83, 1st paragraph, 3rd line: "**and also filmed it**" Laurence is most likely referring here to *Tides of the Delta: The Saga of Ozidi*, the film which would be released in 1975. The film's commentary was provided by Clark and Frank Speed.

Page 83, 1st paragraph, 4th line: "**translation of the...epic into English**" Laurence is referring here to what would be published in 1977 as *The Ozidi Saga*—collected and translated by Clark from the Ijo recitation of the epic by poet Okabou Ojobolo.

Page 83, 2nd paragraph, 1st line: "**an invocation to the water spirits**" Laurence includes the invocation: "People of the sea, People of the sea/ Two times, three times, I call upon you" (20).

Page 86, 1st paragraph, 2nd line: "**both an Ijaw view of destiny and an outlook which owes much to contemporary psychology**" Laurence adds, "Indeed, Ozidi can be interpreted in both these ways—and as with *Song of a Goat*, the two conceptual forms in many ways seem similar" (25).

Page 87, 1st paragraph, 5th line: "**his death can only be achieved by disease**"
"Ozidi's death completes the fate of his lineage. He could not die
by war because he had been magically protected, but—like
Achilles—there was an inevitable flaw in the gods' protection of
him, for otherwise he would have been like a god himself, and this
the gods do not permit to mortals" (26).

Page 87, 2nd paragraph, 7th line: "**Clark's rendering of this Ijaw epic**"
"J.P. Clark's rendering of this Ijaw epic is of great interest, partly
because it points up the fact that his work owes more to Ijaw
tradition than it does to Greek classical drama" (27).

THREE The Thickets of Our Separateness
Chinua Achebe

Page 89, title: "**The Thickets of Our Separateness**" was also called "Words
Across Canyons" (Laurence ts. ch. 3, 1).

Page 89, 2nd paragraph, 1st line: "**Achebe has published four novels—**
Things Fall Apart*, 1958, *No Longer at Ease*, 1960, *Arrow of
***God*, 1964, and *A Man of the People*, 1966**" For a more current
compilation of Achebe's writing, SEE BIBLIOGRAPHICAL
INFORMATION, 242–43.

Page 90, 5th paragraph, 1st line: "**The British administration in
Nigeria...went directly against Ibo Social Institutions**" Britain's
imperial presence in (what is now) Nigeria began in 1903. The era
of British colonialism was marked by the arbitrary creation of
Nigeria from a vast number of cultural groups and political
systems. Under British rule, Nigeria was divided into three distinct
regions: the northern area (primarily Hausa-Muslim); the
southwest area, (primarily Yoruba-Muslim and Christian); and the
eastern area (primarily Ibo-Christian). During the decades of
British domination, northern Nigeria's groundnuts and cotton,
and southern Nigeria's cocoa, rubber, and palm oil were exported.
Parliamentary institutions—based on the British model—were
established in each of the three regions. Independence was granted
to Nigeria in 1960, after which the First Republic was plagued by
internal conflict and regional unrest. Civil war broke out in 1966
and eastern Nigeria—Biafra—seceded. After three years, Biafra
was reintegrated. Over the years since independence, the Nigerian
government has been overthrown by numerous military coups.
SEE ALSO "CIVIL WAR IN NIGERIA", 267–68.

Page 96, 3rd paragraph, 3rd line: "*The Pacification of the Primitive Tribes
of the Lower Niger*" In Laurence's typescript, this paragraph
concludes with the sentence, "Such is the death of a man" (11).

Page 96, 4th paragraph, last line: "**Igbo-speaking writers (whose novels are written in English)**" Laurence's reaction to Shelton's judgment is even stronger in her typescript: "I find this diatribe astonishing. I would [have] said that the last thing Achebe ever does is to blame 'all the evils which occurred in Ibo society' on the white man. Achebe is not a propagandist. He is a novelist, and that is a very different thing" (12).

Page 106, 2nd paragraph, last line: "**individual living within his own skull**" This section is concluded in the typescript with the declaration, "If this is not a great novel, then time will of course prove me wrong. But I would be willing to bet on it" (24). Time, of course, has proved Laurence right.

Page 107, 2nd paragraph, 2nd line: "**Minister for Overseas Training**" In the typescript, Laurence adds: "The way in which Achebe catches the tone of voice of Koko and Nanga is a delight" (26).

Page 110, 2nd paragraph, 5th line: "**same time as the first Army coup in Nigeria**" The first army coup in Nigeria took place in 1966, the same year that *Man of the People* was first published by Heinemann.

Page 110, 2nd paragraph, last line: "**provide a conclusion**" Laurence clarifies her statement by noting in the typescript, "I don't think it is necessarily the ending itself which is weak—it is, rather, the lack of foreshadowing" (30).

Page 112, 2nd paragraph, last line: "**'Ezeudu is dead'**" is followed by the statement, "Achebe's writing is unvarnished, free of verbiage or falsely inflated phrases. He writes absolutely straight with controlled intensity, with irony, and with wisdom" (33).

FOUR **A Twofold Forest**
Amos Tutuola

Page 113, 1st paragraph, 3rd line, "**criticised because of its bizarre use of English**" For example, Nigerian critic Babasola Johnson wrote in 1954 that *The Palm-Wine Drinkard* "should not have been published at all," for he claimed it was "bad enough to attempt an African narrative in 'good English' [but] worse to attempt it in Mr. Tutuola's strange lingo…" (Lindfors 331). The debate over Tutuola's unprecedented use of English became quite vitriolic. For a selection of these early, controversial reviews see Lindfors, *Critical Perspectives on Amos Tutuola* (1975).

Page 114, 5th paragraph, 1st line: "**influenced…by the novels of D.O. Fagunwa**" Daniel Olurunfemi Fagunwa (1910?–1963) was a Nigerian author and educator celebrated for his use of Yoruba folktales and language in his works, which include *The Forest of a*

Thousand Daemons: A Hunter's Saga (translated from Yoruba into English by Wole Soyinka), *Igbo Olodumare, Adiitu Olodumare,* and *Irek-Onibudo* ("Fagunwa, D.O." 148). In accord with Laurence's view, Bernth Lindfors limits Tutuola's debt to Fagunwa to the "overall structure and descriptive technique" rather than to "content" (Lindfors 310). Another more recent, complementary view holds that "Fagunwa has a strong urge for enlightenment, while Tutuola has practically none" (Beilis 451).

Page 117, 2nd paragraph, 2nd line: **"Bunyan"**, John (1629–1688) English preacher and author of such texts as *The Pilgrim's Progress* (1684) and *The Holy War* (1682) (Drabble 148).

Page 117, 2nd paragraph, 2nd line: **"Blake"**, William (1757–1827) English author, artist, and critic concerned with various kinds of mythologies and social values; works include *Songs of Innocence* (1789) and *Songs of Experience* (1794) (Drabble).

Page 118, 2nd paragraph, last line: **"similar social move away from matriarchy"** is followed by "It does occur to me, as well, however, that the delicate question of the sex of the deity may concern some African religions rather less than it apparently has done with the religion of Europe. Onyame, the supreme deity of the Akan, in Ghana, for example, is sometimes described as Father and sometimes as Mother. In other words, the supreme deity may be visualized as neither male nor female, but incorporating aspects of both. If this is so, the myth which Tutuola draws upon here may be mainly the symbolic expression of the initial recognition of a supreme deity who was unseen and whose powers extended over the very real but lesser gods of the earth, of whatever sex" (Laurence ts. ch. 4, 8).

Page 120, 2nd paragraph, 4th line: **"the religion which severed several generations of Africans from their own past."** Laurence would perhaps disagree with her contemporary, Harold R. Collins, who calls Tutuola's "syncretism," or "grafting of Western ways and gear into Yoruba folk myths (especially in the episodes involving the Super Lady and the Methodist Church of the Book of Ghosts) one of the most interesting aspects of his art. Tutuola's is one reasonable way, though of course not the only reasonable way, of relating to the African past" (93).

Page 125, 1st paragraph, last line: **"form suits the material"** is followed in the typescript by "In fact, this seems to me one of Tutuola's best books, although I do not think it quite reaches the standard of either *The Palm-Wine Drinkard* or *My Life in the B.O.G.*" (1)

Page 125, 7th paragraph, 4th line: **"a phraseology which is both fresh and precise"** Tutuola's language has been the subject of lively, indeed, incendiary debate. On page 113, Laurence says that Tutuola's writing was "criticised because of its bizarre use of English" in *The Palm-Wine Drinkard*. Opinions range from approbation to awe on the one hand, and from mild displeasure to abhorrence on the other. Included here are a few comments which correspond with Laurence's. O.R. Dathorne pronounces Tutuola's language "a sensible compromise, between raw pidgin (which would not be intelligible to European readers) and Standard English. [Tutuola] is a conscious craftsman " (98). Harold Collins affirms that "unlike grammarians, literary critics, especially connoisseurs of style, usually find Tutuola's language supple, forceful, graphic and straightforward" (96). Omolara Ogundipe-Leslie contends that "Tutuola becomes fluent, even eloquent, in a language of his own making" (153). Conversely, Abiola Irele submits that "the very pressure of the Yoruba language upon the particular idiom which Tutuola wrung out of the English language may have a fascination for some of his foreign readers, but it is not a satisfactorily creative tension between the two languages that it produces, but rather an imbalance, and a resultant break between the content of his work and its medium of expression which must be considered a serious shortcoming" (183).

Page 126, 3rd paragraph, 12th line: "**The correction of such errors is common editorial practice**" As a fiction writer herself, Laurence is understandably disturbed by the publisher's apparent disregard for spelling errors. Collins addresses editorial treatment at length; he reminds readers "how generally felicitous [Faber and Faber's] hands off policy has been" (109).

FIVE   Masks of the City
        Cyprian Ekwensi

Page 133, 1st paragraph, 2nd line: "**highlife music**" Dance music from Ghana and Eastern Nigeria, originating from the kpanlogo rhythm. SEE 'HIGHLIFE' IN THE GLOSSARY.

Page 133, 1st paragraph, 3rd line: "**style that owes much to journalism**" Ekwensi began working for the Nigerian Broadcasting Company in 1951 and has remained in media, in various capacities, since then (Emenyonu 1992). SEE BIOGRAPHICAL INFORMATION ON CYPRIAN EKWENSI.

Page 133, 1st paragraph, last line: "**liveliest writing is of life in Lagos**" Until 1991, Lagos was the federal capital of Nigeria. The city is Nigeria's largest, and one of the largest in sub-Saharan Africa. By 1975, the city of Abuja was being developed to replace Lagos as capital, due to the industrial pollution, slums and traffic congestion plaguing the city. Lagos sprawls over four islands which are connected by a network of bridges. The port of Lagos serves as the principal export outlet; the nation's road and railway network terminates in Lagos. The city is also a major educational and cultural centre. (*New Encyclopedia Britannica*). SEE 'LAGOS' IN THE GLOSSARY.

Page 133, 2nd paragraph, 2nd line: "**to take on a warning**" "and even condemnatory tone" (Laurence ts. ch. 5, 1).

Page 137, 1st paragraph, 4th line: "**Freddie Namme**" Laurence's typescript notest that "[Jagua] loves him partly as a son and partly as a lover" (6).

Page 137, 1st paragraph, 5th line: "**she is unable to stop**" In her typescript Laurence adds "She is a creature of paradox ... We see her fighting intently with Freddie, then humbling [*sic*] asking him to forgive her. We see her preening, dressing up to the nines, yawning through a British Council lecture to which Freddie has dragged her" (6).

Page 140, 5th paragraph, 1st line: "**Yet the novel remains Jagua's**" Laurence's typescript adds "Ekwensi portrays her in all her often-contradictory moods" (10).

Page 142, 1st paragraph, 2nd line: "'**Come now and meet your doom!**'" is followed by "When Hodio says 'Listen! I am Hodio, son of Sunsaye of the cattle Fulani...', one feels that the only possible response ought to be *Howdy, pardner*. Our hero, having overcome the bad guys in this encounter, stoically walks home (his horse is dead)" (12). The excision of such lively personal responses may have been the decision of Laurence's Macmillan editor, Alan Maclean.

Page 143, 7th paragraph, 3rd line: "'**Lum's life will have been avenged.**'" In her typescript, Laurence adds "Why she doesn't simply take two hundred codeine or slit her throat, I can't think" (14).

Page 145, 2nd paragraph of *Iska* section, 2nd line: "**Ibo-Hausa riots in the north**" In her typescript, Laurence adds "(which have grown very much worse, of course, since the novel was written)" (17).

Only three groups have attained ethnic majority status in their respective regions: Hausa-Fulani (north), Ibo (southeast), and the Yoruba (southwest). Political conflict between the Ibo and Hausa-Fulani in 1966 contributed to the formation of the Ibo secessionist state of Biafra in 1967. Ekwensi's support for the Ibo people and Biafra can be seen in his capacities as chairman for the Bureau for External Publicity and director for an independent Biafran radio station. SEE 'IBO' IN THE GLOSSARY.

Page 150, 1st paragraph, 3rd line "**Some day *Iska* will be read as an historical novel.**" As in so many other instances, Laurence's prediction proved correct.

SIX   Other Voices
Elechi Amadi
Page 162, 3rd paragraph, 6th line: "**and to bring up her children well**" is followed by "She is affectionate, and she conveys a capacity for sexual passion, although this is never explicitly stated" (Laurence ts. ch. 6, 6).

Gabriel Okara
Page 173, 3rd paragraph, 2nd line: "**Dostoevski**", Fyodor Mikhailovich (1821–1881) Highly influential Russian author whose experiments with character and narrative development probed religious, class and other issues; classic works include *Crime and Punishment* (1886), *The Idiot* (1868), and *The Brothers Karamazov* (1880) (Drabble 288–89).

Page 175, 3rd paragraph, last line: "**to discover life through his own eyes**" Laurence's typescript conclusion ends with "He is a man who must try to discover life through his own eyes and to speak his own truth." (After inserting the phrase "life through his own eyes," Laurence crossed out the final phrase, "according to the undeniable sight of his own eyes" (6).

EPILOGUE
Page 179, 2nd paragraph, 2nd line "**Swiftian**" Refers to writing style of Jonathan Swift (1667–1745), Dublin-born author of fiction, pamphlets, and other political writings, often marked by "ferocity and coarseness"; works include *Gulliver's Travels*, published in 1726 (Drabble 962–63).

Works Cited

Ashcroft, Bill, Gareth Griffiths and Helen Tiffin. *The Empire Writes Back*. London: Routledge, 1989.

Axworthy, Geoffrey. "Ladipo, Duro." *McGraw-Hill Encyclopedia of World Drama*. Ed. Stanley Hochman. Vol. 4. New York: McGraw-Hill Inc., 1984.

Beilis, Viktor. "Ghosts, People, and Books of Yorubaland." *Research in African Literatures* 18.4 (Winter 1987): 447–57.

Clark, J.P. Interview with Lewis Nkosi in September 1962. *African Writers Talking*. Ed. Dennis Duerden and Cosmo Pieterse. London, Ibadan, Nairobi: Heinemann, 1972. 62–67.

Collins, Harold R. *Amos Tutuola*. New York: Twayne Publishers, 1969.

Crowder, Michael. *The Story of Nigeria*. London: Faber and Faber, 1966.

Dathorne, O.R. "Amos Tutuola: The Nightmare of the Tribe." *Introduction to Nigerian Literature*. Ed. Bruce King. New York: Africana Publishers, 1972.

———. *African Literature in the Twentieth Century*. London: Heinemann, 1976 (originally published as *The Black Mind*, 1974).

Drabble, Margaret. *The Oxford Companion to English Literature*. Revised ed. Oxford, New York: Oxford UP, 1995.

Emenyonu, Ernest N. "Cyprian Ekwensi." *Dictionary of Literary Biography: Twentieth Century Caribbean and Black African Writers*. Ed. Bernth Lindfors and Reinhard Sander. Vol. 117. Detroit: Gale Research Inc., 1992.

"Fagunwa, D.O." *Contemporary Authors: A Bio-Bibliographical Guide to Current Writers in Fiction, General Non-Fiction, Poetry, Journalism, Drama, Motion Pictures, Television, and Other Fields*. Ed. Hal May. Vol. 116. Detroit: Gale Research Company, 1986. 148.

Hart, James D. *The Oxford Companion to American Literature*. With revisions and additions by Phillip W. Leininger. 6th ed. Oxford and New York: Oxford UP, 1995.

Hayes, Thomas. "The 1986 Nobel Prize In Literature." *The Dictionary of Literary Biography Yearbook: 1986*. Ed. J.M. Brook. Detroit: Bruccoli Clark Layman, 1986. 3–8.

Herdeck, Donald E. *African Authors: A Companion to Black African Writing. Vol. 1: 1300–1973*. 2nd ed. Washington, DC: Black Orpheus Press/INSCAPE, 1974.

Laurence, Margaret. *Long Drums and Cannons* Ed. Nora Foster Stovel. Edmonton: U of Alberta P, 2001.

———. Typescript for *Long Drums and Cannons*. (Pages are numbered chapter by chapter.)

Lindfors, Bernth. "Amos Tutuola: Debts and Assets." *Cahiers d'Etudes Africaines* 10 (1970): 306–34.

"Lingua Franca." *The Canadian Oxford Dictionary*. Oxford, Toronto, New York: Oxford UP Canada, 1998.

"Louis XIV." *The Canadian Oxford Dictionary*. Oxford, Toronto, New York: Oxford UP Canada, 1998.

Matlaw, Myron. *Modern World Drama: An Encyclopedia*. New York: E.P. Dutton and Co., Inc., 1972.

"Mphalele, Es'kia." *Africana: An Encyclopedia of the African and African-American Experience*. Ed. Kwame Anthony Appiah and Henry Louis Gates, Jr. New York: Basic Civitas, 1999.

"Negritude." *The New Encyclopedia Britannica*. Vol. 8. 15th ed. Chicago: Encyclopedia Britannica Inc., 1998.

Nesbitt, Nick. "Negritude." *Africana: An Encyclopedia of the African and African-American Experience*. Ed. Kwame Anthony Appiah and Henry Louis Gates, Jr. New York: Basic Civitas, 1999.

The New Encyclopedia Britannica. 15th ed. Chicago: Encyclopedia Britannica Inc., 1998.

"Nigeria." *The World Encyclopedia of Contemporary Theatre*. Ed. Don Rubin. Vol. 3. London: Routledge, 1997.

Ogundipe-Leslie, Omolara. "*The Palm-Wine Drinkard*: A Reassessment of Amos Tutuola." *Critical Perspectives on Amos Tutuola*. Ed. Bernth Lindfors. Washington: Three Continents, 1975. 145–54.

Okagbue, Osita. "John Pepper Clark." *African Writers*. Ed. C. Brian Cox. Vol. I. New York: Scribner's, 1997. 153–66.

"Okigbo, Christopher." *Africana: An Encyclopedia of the African and African-American Experience*. Ed. Kwame Anthony Appiah and Henry Louis Gates, Jr. New York: Basic Civitas, 1999.

"Okigbo, Christopher." *Contemporary Authors: A Bio-Bibliographical Guide to Current Writers in Fiction, General Non-Fiction, Poetry, Journalism, Drama, Motion Pictures, Television, and Other Fields*. Ed. Frances Carol Locher. Vol. 77–80. Detroit: Gale Research Company, 1979. 404–5.

Parekh, Pushpa Naidu and Siga Fatima Jagne, ed. *Postcolonial African Writers: A Bio-Bibliographical Sourcebook*. Westport, CT and London: Greenwood Press, 1998.

Stanislavski, Konstantin, *An Actor Prepares*, trans. by Elizabeth Reynolds. Hapgood, London: Eyre Methuen, 1980.

Wright, Derek, "Ritual and Revolution: Soyinka's Dramatic Theory," *ARIEL: A Review of International English Literature* 23:1 (January 1992).

Wren, Robert M. *J.P. Clark*. Boston: Twayne Publishers, 1984.

GLOSSARY

Abeokuta: southwestern Nigeria town founded c.1830 by the Yoruba (Room 11).

abiku: the Yoruba concept of "a child believed to be caught in a cycle of death and rebirth" (Aguiar 1456); "an evil spirit of the Yoruba who inhabits the body of a child. The child soon dies and the spirit reenters the mother's womb, to be born and die again" (Dalgish 4); a child who dies before reaching twelve years of age, as well as the spirit(s) who cause(s) the death (Ellis 112).

agemo: rhythm drummed during a Yoruba *Egungun* ceremony (Laurence 57).

Amadioha: Ibo god of thunder, lightning, and rain (Cole 16).

Apostolic Church, and Cherubim and Seraphim: "prayer and healing groups" formed by Yoruba Christians following the devastating influenza epidemic of 1918, when it was believed established mission churches were powerless over the disaster ("Nigeria: Indigenous Churches").

Bale: civil governor of a Yoruba town, town-quarter, village, or household (Ellis 166).

Benin: republic, formerly known as Dahomey; celebrated independence in 1960; bordered by the Atlantic Ocean, Burkina Faso, Niger, and Nigeria; capital Porto Novo; 1998 population estimate of 6,100,799 (Heath 221–22).

biomgbo: Ijaw concept of the "personal soul" (Laurence 74).

bride-price: part of pre-marital transactions in which financial payments and other services are rendered unto the bride's father and kin by the husband (Forde 77).

Burutu: Nigerian city south-west of Warri (*Times Atlas* 85).

chi: an Ibo "personal god...who determines one's fortune" (Dalgish 33); acquired by an individual at birth "through a pact which establishes his character and longevity" (Cole 15).

Chukwu: an Ibo deity worshipped as "the centre of the supreme Authority which controls the world" (Sawyerr 3); "one supreme God" with "an ever-immortal spirit" (Yakan 368).

Dakar: capital and largest city of Senegal, lying on Cape Verde, near the westernmost point of Africa; became the capital of French West Africa in 1902, and of Senegal upon independence in 1960; population of approximately two million in 1998; sites of interest include Goree Island, The French Cultural Center, and the Marche Sandaga; called "the Paris of West Africa" (Johnson 551).

dibia: a largely hereditary profession of Ibo men, whose work includes divination, the establishment of shrines, and application of herbal and other remedies (Cole 228, Forde 26).

Egungun: among the Yoruba, a "re-embodied ghost; ghost-mummer" (Fadipe 332); also powerful ancestral spirits (Sawyerr 2).

Egwugwu: nine masked Ibo spirits "who wear the ancestral masks and act as a judicial council in cases which cannot be settled amicably by the councils of men" (Laurence 95).

Ekine society: an often political Ijaw, or Ijo, society whose masquerades can also be both recreational and religious in purpose (Dalgish 49).

ekwe: "hollowed out wooden instrument" of the Ibo, used to send messages to other villages (Laurence 112).

Enugu: southern Nigerian city, founded in 1917, and the former capital of Biafra (Room 65).

Esumare: Yoruba concept of the rainbow, "link between earth and heaven" (Laurence 65).

Fulani: divided between *Fulani bororo* (pastoral) and *gida* (urban) groups, this tribe does not form a majority in any African country, but has formed communities across the continent; the group remains united by the Fulfude language and a strict devotion to Islamic tenets; having once obtained power through the nineteenth-century Sokoto Caliphate, the *Fulani gida* of Northern Nigeria have allied with the Hausa to form the Hausa-Fulani, the "effective ruling class" of the region (Oppong, "Fulani" 794, Yakan, "Fulani" 316–18).

Hausa: with over fifty million Hausa speakers, the northern group is Nigeria's largest; ethnic ties are maintained through strict patriarchal, patrilinear practices; successfully cultivating such cash crops as cotton and peanuts, the Hausa often dominate civilian and military governments as well (Nave, "Hausa" 942–43, Yakan, "Hausa" 350–53).

highlife: music which first evolved during the 1930s in the dancing clubs of British colonies along the West African coast, blending the "rhythms and melodies of the indigenous people, piano and hymn music of Christian missionaries, brass band and fife and drum music of military garrisons, and other sounds of Europe and the Americas surviving via radio and records" (Ampadu 70).

Ibadan: Nigeria's second-largest city, 1995 population approximately 1,295,000; modern history begins in 1829, with Yoruba settlements; local industries include Yoruba handicrafts, furniture and automobile manufacturing, and publishing; with Ibadan University (1948), the Agodi Gardens, and a branch of the National Archives, it is also a key intellectual centre of Nigeria (Bennett 987, Room 88).

ibeji: Yoruba sculpted figures representing the spirits of twins, presented to mothers at their children's birth (Dalgish 67).

Ibo: cultural achievements of the predominantly-eastern group include carving, metalwork, weaving, and elaborate spiritual ceremonies; traditional social structures were built around autonomous villages governed by elders, and in the late 1960s, faced with extreme acts of violence and other political threats, the Ibo attempted to form the independent state of Biafra (Johnson, "Igbo" 988, Yakan, "Igbo" 366–68).

Ifa: Yoruba divination cult "in which prophetic verses are matched to patterns of throws of palm nuts" and are interpreted by a priest (Dalgish 68); also used to identify the *orisha* who speaks through the process ("Ifa" 988).

Igrito: southern Nigerian settlement, near Port Harcourt (*Rand McNally* 22).

Ijaw: with approximately 400,000 members, the Ijaw are the tenth largest ethnic minority in Nigeria; though some precolonial kingdoms were established, villages were traditionally governed by councils of elders; concentrated along the Niger Delta, the main economic activity of the group continues to be fishing ("Ijaw" 989, Yakan, "Ijaw" 369–70).

ju-ju: a fetish, charm, incantation, or evil spirit (Daglish 76).

Kafanchan: central Nigerian city (*Times Atlas* 85).

Kano: city in the Hausa region of northern Nigeria (Grove 76).

Lagos: Nigeria's largest city and chief port, 1991 population estimated at 1,340,000; founded by the Yoruba in the fifteenth century, as a settlement known as Oko; capital of Lagos state until 1975 and the federal capital of Nigeria until 1991; home of the National Museum (1957), the University of Lagos (1962), and other institutions, it is the "industrial, commercial, administrative, financial and cultural heart of the country" (Burton 115–16, "Lagos" 101).

mammy wagons: a highly popular and economical form of transportation, usually in the style of the "customized Bedford lorry," first introduced to Ghana after World War II; one of the most striking and prominent features of the vehicles are their painted mottos, which address religious and other issues through such phrases as "Thank You, Miraculous Virgin," "Death of Mother is End of Family," and "Because of Money" (Lewis).

Mata Kharibu: Yoruba king ruling c.1000 CE (Laurence 37).

Minna: central Nigerian city; 1988 population 96,470 (*Rand McNally* 22, 216).

Niger River: the third largest river in Africa (flows for approximately 4180 kilometres), originating in Guinea and running east through Mali, Niger, and Nigeria, emptying into the Gulf of Guinea (Fay 1438).

Nupe land: kingdom founded north of the Niger in the fifteenth century by Tsoede, whose people "look toward the Igala state as the source of their migration" (Olaniyan 13).

oba: Yoruba chief or king (Dalgish 137, Nave, "Yoruba" 2035).

obi: among the Ibo, the hut of the head of a household (Dalgish 137–38).

ofo: "the most important 'medicinal' object in Ibo life," the *ofo* twigs are often "lumpy shapes encrusted with sacrificial offerings," and sometimes feature iron facial features and strips"; phallic in shape, *ofo* are bestowed upon senior sons and represent paternity, ancestral powers, and *Chukwu*'s truths (Cole 17).

Ogabu: Nigerian city.

ogbanje: like the Yoruba *abiku*, a child believed by the Ibo to die and return to its mother's womb to be reborn (Dalgish 138).

Ogboni: Yoruba society "composed of both religious and political leaders, devoted to the worship of the earth (Crowder 110).

Ogun: a many-faced Yoruba god of "hunting, iron, and warfare" (Barnes 2); described by Wole Soyinka as "god of creativity, guardian of the road, god of metallic lore and artistry. Explorer, hunter, god of war...custodian of the sacred oath" (Katran 1768).

Olorun: like the Ibo *Chukwu,* the supreme Yoruba deity, "He...'whose Being spreads over the the the extent of the earth, the Owner of a mat that is never folded up'" (Sawyerr 40).

Onitsha: southern Nigerian city; 1988 population 262,100 (*Rand McNally* 22, 217).

orishas: a pantheon of semi-independent Yoruba deities "capable of working their own will with or without propitiation...or supplication by human beings," and who visit the earth through ritually trained mediums, often presiding over festivals of song and dance (O'Connor 1463-66).

Oro: a Yoruba cult through which ancestral spirits "control and punish criminals and whose presence is known in the sound of the bull-roarer" (Pemberton 143).

osu: slave-like, "taboo persons" among the Ibo, dedicated to the service of the owner's cult, and who are socially irredeemable and "both feared and despised" (Forde 23).

Oyo: precolonial Yoruba kingdom at the peak of its power between approximately 1650 and 1750 CE; collapsed during the mid-1800s due to internal conflict and Fulani attacks, and fell under British rule in 1888 ("Oyo, Early Kingdom of" 1474); presently, southeastern Nigerian city, 1988 population 180,700 (*Rand McNally* 22, 217).

ozo: Ibo title system which "placed political, moral, and spiritual authority with groups of mature, relatively wealthy men" (Cole 4).

sokugo: "the wandering sickness which dooms men to go on and on forever, never able to settle down" (Laurence 141).

teme: similar to the Ibo *chi,* Ijaw concept of "the 'personal god' who determines one's role and success in life...[by making] an agreement with the supreme deity. ...A wise *teme*, of course, will make a good agreement; but, unfortunately, before birth the spirit is too young to bargain well, and may even be foolish. Thus one may be compelled throughout life to contend with the mistake of one's own personal god. It can be a heavy burden" (Wren 10).

Umuahia: Nigerian city with 1988 population of 46,370 (*Rand McNally* 217).

Warri: southern Nigerian city with 1988 population of 88,840 (*Rand McNally* 22, 217).

Yoruba: Concentrated in southwestern Nigeria, the Yoruba continue to develop unique practices essential to communal and national development: while "most Yoruba are either Christian or Muslim," traditional deities such as Ogun are still worshipped; thirteenth- and fourteenth century bronzes and sculptures created by the tribe are considered to be among the finest works of art produced in Africa, while contemporary artists such as Wole Soyinka continue to bring acclaim to the group; though the Oyo empire had crumbled by 1840, the southwestern cities of Lagos and Ibadan remain centres of political and cultural life in Nigeria (Nave, "Yoruba" 2035–36, Yakan, "Yoruba" 705–6).

Zaria: north-central Nigerian city and former state, founded by the Hausa c.1536; 1988 population 267,300 (*Rand McNally* 217, Room 208).

Works Cited

Aguiar, Marian. "Okri, Ben." *Africana: An Encyclopedia of the African and African-American Experience.* Ed. Kwame Anthony Appiah and Henry Louis Gates, Jr. New York: Basic Civitas, 1999.

Ampadu, Nama. "Dance the Highlife." *Breakout: Profiles in African Rhythm.* Ed. Gary Stewart. Chicago and London: U of Chicago P, 1992. 70-78.

Barnes, Sandra T. "The Many Faces of Ogun: Introduction to the First Edition." *Africa's Ogun: Old World and New.* Ed. Sandra T. Barnes. 2nd ed. Bloomington and Indianapolis: Indiana UP, 1997.

Bennett, Eric. "Ibadan." *Africana: An Encyclopedia of the African and African-American Experience.* Ed. Kwame Anthony Appiah and Henry Louis Gates, Jr. New York: Basic Civitas, 1999.

Burton, Andrew. "Lagos." *Africana: An Encyclopedia of the African and African-American Experience.* Ed. Kwame Anthony Appiah and Henry Louis Gates, Jr. New York: Basic Civitas, 1999.

Cole, Herbert M. and Chike C. Aniakor. *Igbo Arts: Community and Cosmos.* Foreword by Chinua Achebe. Los Angeles: Museum of Cultural History, University of California, 1984.

Crowder, Michael. *The Story of Nigeria.* London: Faber and Faber, 1966.

Dalgish, Gerard M. *A Dictionary of Africanisms: Contributions of Sub-Saharan Africa to the English Language.* Westport, CT and London: Greenwood Press, 1982.

Ellis, A.B. *The Yoruba-Speaking Peoples of the Slave Coast of West Africa.* 1894. Oosterhout, Neth.: Anthropological Publications, 1966.

Fay, Robert. "Niger River" *Africana: An Encyclopedia of the African and African-American Experience.* Ed. Kwame Anthony Appiah and Henry Louis Gates, Jr. New York: Basic Civitas, 1999.

Fadipe, N.A. *The Sociology of the Yoruba.* Ibadan: Ibadan UP, 1970.

Forde, Daryll and G.I. Jones. *The Ibo and Ibibio-Speaking Peoples of South-Eastern Nigeria.* London: International African Institute, 1950.

Grove, A.T. *The Changing Geography of Africa.* Oxford and New York: Oxford UP, 1989.

Heath, Elizabeth. "Benin." *Africana: An Encyclopedia of the African and African-American Experience.* Ed. Kwame Anthony Appiah and Henry Louis Gates, Jr. New York: Basic Civitas, 1999.

Herdeck, Donald E. *African Authors: A Companion to Black African Writing. Vol. 1: 1300-1973.* 2nd ed. Washington, DC: Black Orpheus Press/INSCAPE, 1974.

"Ifa." *Africana: An Encyclopedia of the African and African-American Experience.* Ed. Kwame Anthony Appiah and Henry Louis Gates, Jr. New York: Basic Civitas, 1999.

"Ijaw." *Africana: An Encyclopedia of the African and African-American Experience.* Ed. Kwame Anthony Appiah and Henry Louis Gates, Jr. New York: Basic Civitas, 1999.

Johnson, David P. Jr. "Igbo." *Africana: An Encyclopedia of the African and African-American Experience.* Ed. Kwame Anthony Appiah and Henry Louis Gates, Jr. New York: Basic Civitas, 1999.

Katrak, Ketu. "Wole Soyinka." *Africana: An Encyclopedia of the African and African-American Experience.* Ed. Kwame Anthony Appiah and Henry Louis Gates, Jr. New York: Basic Civitas, 1999.

"Lagos." *The New Encyclopedia Britannica.* Vol. 7. 15th ed. Chicago: Encyclopedia Britannica, Inc., 1998.

Laurence, Margaret. *Long Drums and Cannons: Nigerian dramatists and novelists 1952–1966.* Ed. Nora Foster Stovel. Edmonton: U of Alberta P, 2001.

Lewis, George H. "The Philosophy of the Street in Ghana: Mammy Wagons and Their Mottos—A Research Note." *Journal of Popular Culture* 32:1 (1998): 165-71.

Matlaw, Myron: *Modern World Drama: An Encyclopedia.* New York: E.P. Dutton and Co., Inc, 1972.

Nave, Ari. "Hausa." *Africana: An Encyclopedia of the African and African-American Experience.* Ed. Kwame Anthony Appiah and Henry Louis Gates, Jr. New York: Basic Civitas, 1999.

———. "Yoruba." *Africana: An Encyclopedia of the African and African-American Experience.* Ed. Kwame Anthony Appiah and Henry Louis Gates, Jr. New York: Basic Civitas, 1999.

Ndibe, Okey. "Nigeria." *Africana: An Encyclopedia of the African and African-American Experience.* Ed. Kwame Anthony Appiah and Henry Louis Gates, Jr. New York: Basic Civitas, 1999.

"Nigeria." *The World Encyclopedia of Contemporary Theatre.* Ed. Don Rubin. Vol. 3. London: Routledge, 1997.

"Nigeria: Indigenous Churches." *World Christian Encyclopedia: a Comprehensive Study of Churches and Religions in the Modern World, AD 1900-2000.* Ed. David B. Barrett. Nairobi: Oxford UP, 1982.

O'Connor, Kathleen. "Orishas." *Africana: An Encyclopedia of the African and African-American Experience*. Ed. Kwame Anthony Appiah and Henry Louis Gates, Jr. New York: Basic Civitas, 1999.

Olaniyan, Richard, ed. *Nigerian History and Culture*. London: Longman, 1985.

Oppong, Yaa Poukua Afriyie. "Fulani." *Africana: An Encyclopedia of the African and African-American Experience*. Ed. Kwame Anthony Appiah and Henry Louis Gates, Jr. New York: Basic Civitas, 1999.

"Oyo, Early Kingdom of." *Africana: An Encyclopedia of the African and African-American Experience*. Ed. Kwame Anthony Appiah and Henry Louis Gates, Jr. New York: Basic Civitas, 1999.

Parekh, Pushpa Naidu and Siga Fatima Jagne, ed. *Postcolonial African Writers: A Bio-Bibliographical Sourcebook*. Westport, CT and London: Greenwood Press, 1998.

Pemberton, John, III. "The Dreadful God and the Divine King." *Africa's Ogun: Old World and New*. Ed. Sandra T. Barnes. 2nd ed. Bloomington and Indianapolis: Indiana UP, 1997.

Rand McNally World Atlas. Chicago, New York, and San Francisco: Rand McNally & Company, 1988.

Room, Adrian. *African Placenames: Origins and Meanings of the Names for over 2000 Natural Features, Towns, Cities, Provinces, and Countries*. Jefferson, NC: McFarland, 1994.

Sawyerr, Harry. *God, Ancestor, or Creator?: Aspects of Traditional Belief in Ghana, Nigeria, and Sierra Leone*. London: Longman, 1970.

Sharp, Harold S. and Marjorie Z. *Index to Characters in the Performing Arts Part II – Operas and Musical Productions: M-Z and Symbols*. Metuchen, NJ: The Scarecrow Press, 1969.

The Times Atlas of the World. 10th Comprehensive ed. New York: Times Books, 1999.

Wren, Robert. *J.P. Clark*. Boston: Twayne Publishers, 1984.

Yakan, Mohammed Z. "Fulani." *Almanac of African Peoples and Nations*. New Brunswick, NJ and London: Transaction Publishers, 1999.

———. "Hausa." *Almanac of African Peoples and Nations*. New Brunswick, NJ and London: Transaction Publishers, 1999.

———. "Igbo." *Almanac of African Peoples and Nations*. New Brunswick, NJ and London: Transaction Publishers, 1999.

———. "Ijaw." *Almanac of African Peoples and Nations*. New Brunswick, NJ and London: Transaction Publishers, 1999.

———. "Yoruba." *Almanac of African Peoples and Nations*. New Brunswick, NJ and London: Transaction Publishers, 1999.

TRIBALISM AS US VERSUS THEM

Margaret Laurence

THIS ESSAY HAS NOT BEEN PUBLISHED BEFORE. IT IS A PAPER WHICH I GAVE IN January 1969, at the Institute of Commonwealth Studies, University of London, England. I had, several years before, become deeply involved in the study of Nigerian writing, and had, in 1968, published a book called LONG DRUMS AND CANNONS, a series of essays on contemporary Nigerian writers. The book was published during the Nigerian civil war, and when I was asked to give a paper at the Institute of Commonwealth Studies, I took the opportunity to update my thinking in view of the war, which was then still going on. Christopher Okigbo, one of Nigeria's best poets, had been killed fighting for Biafra. Wole Soyinka, one of the finest writers of this century, was in jail on the Federal side for having suggested that the war was tragically unnecessary. It seemed to me then, and it still does, that what was happening in Nigeria had a very deep relevance to the entire world, and that we must stop thinking, as humans, in terms of Them and Us, if we are to survive at all. Since the civil war, Soyinka has published several books, including one about his prison experiences, THE MAN DIED. Chinua Achebe, whom I met for the first time not long ago, and who is one of the best novelists now writing anywhere, told me that he had to try to write a novel which will encompass the war, a work of incredible pain for him. I have no doubt that he will write it. And we will have to try to learn from what he is telling us, because he knows, as John Donne knew centuries ago, that "No man is an Islande."

"Tribalism As Us Versus Them," originally presented by Margaret Laurence in January 1969, is published for the first time in this edition with the permission of Laurence's estate. The original paper resides in the York University Archives and Special Collections. Ed.

TRIBALISM AS US VERSUS THEM

Margaret Laurence

TRIBALISM WOULD SEEM TO BE CENTRAL TO THE PRESENT CIVIL WAR IN Nigeria and Biafra. How does tribalism appear in the writing of Nigerian novelists and dramatists in the period between 1952 and 1966, when Nigerian literature experienced a tremendous upsurge?

"Tribalism" may be seen in several ways. The word can mean "The group as *Us*"—that is, the social organization of an extended family group held together by a common lineage, language, religion, social mores and ethical values, or some combination of these. It can also mean "The group as *Us Versus Them*"—that is, the placement of loyalty with a group in such a way that other groups are automatically excluded and are regarded with fear, suspicion or hostility. A possible variant, although unfortunately uncommon anywhere in the world of today, would of course be "*Us In Relation To Them*"—that is, a situation in which certain group loyalties and a sense of identity remain but where other groups are not felt as a threat or used as a scapegoat, so that relationships of mutual respect and varying degrees of closeness may be formed among members of different groups. One need hardly say that unless we as humankind can succeed in progressing towards this positive concept of *"Us In Relation To Them"*, both within our own cultures and countries, and in a world sense, then we will go the way of the dinosaurs.

The Group As Us

Although this aspect of tribalism has occupied a good deal of Nigerian writing in the past fifteen years, I intend to deal with it briefly. The scope of this paper does not permit my going into great detail about the various ways of life described in Nigerian writing, but perhaps several generalizations may be made. "The Groups As Us" has occurred in Nigerian writing as a description of many writers' own people, either at a present-day village level or as a re-creation of the society of several generations ago. The latter seems to have been done in order to re-establish a link with the ancestral roots and to restore a sense of value in the traditional African society and religions of the past, a sense of worth which was undermined by colonialism and the missions. This was the stated aim of Chinua Achebe when he spoke of "an adequate revolution for me to espouse—to help my society regain its belief in itself and to put away the years of denigration and self-denigration." (*Commonwealth Literature*, ed. John Press, Heinemann, 1965).

The treatment in fiction of this aspect of tribalism has been done more by Ibo writers than by any other. This may be because the younger writers have been influenced in this way by Achebe, or simply because there have been more Ibo writers in the past fifteen years than writers from any other tribe. The Ibo people are therefore known to us in greater social detail than any other tribe. They would appear also to have certain basic differences from the social organization of any other tribe, in that they never had a central authority—no chiefs or kings, and they tended to be more highly individuated than any other tribe, for individualism and individual enterprise were positive values at every level of social life, and, although there was a definite Establishment, it was not a hierarchical one nor an inherited one, the *ozo* staffs of office (which were Ibo titles, status symbols) being purchased by men who had accumulated enough wealth through their own enterprise to do so. Chinua Achebe has described Ibo life in the past, and at a village level, better than any other writer, for he is, to my mind, the best novelist writing in English in Africa today. From his writing, and from other Ibo writers such as Elechi Amadi, Nkem Nwankwo, Flora Nwapa, Onuora Nzekwu and Obi Egbuna, one gains a detailed picture of the people who lived in the forest-enclosed villages of Eastern Nigeria.

It is not possible to examine all the many tribes in Nigeria, nor have some been represented in writing in English so far. The way of life of the Ijaw people of the Niger Delta has been described by J.P. Clark in such plays as *Song of a Goat, The Raft* and *Ozidi,* by Gabriel Okara in his novel *The Voice,* and by the Yoruba writer Wole Soyinka in his play *The Swamp Dwellers,* although all these writers are dealing, as well, with themes which are universal. Soyinka is one of the few writers who has ventured to set some of his writing in backgrounds other than those of his own tribe.

The Yoruba people of Western Nigeria have been written about in vivid detail by T.M. Aluko, in such novels as *One Man, One Matchet,* and *One Man, One Wife,* although Aluko's main theme is always the clash between old and new values. In his plays Wole Soyinka has drawn upon the Yoruba traditional mask dramas of *Egungun,* a cult of the ancestors, and upon Yoruba praise songs, festival rituals, drumming, mythology and proverb. He is also much concerned with another aspect of the tribal past—the old gods, the *orisha.* Ogun, Yoruba god of war and iron, seems especially to fascinate him. It is clear from his writing that for many ordinary people among the Yoruba, whether Muslim or Christian, the old gods have long dwelt with the new in considerable compatibility. Soyinka seems to want to emphasize this fact, perhaps to drum it into the consciousness of the educated middle class who scorn or are ashamed of the gods of their grandfathers and their taxi-drivers. Soyinka seems to want to restore the sense of value of the old Yoruba religion, just as Achebe wants to restore his people's sense of the value of the past.

Ironically enough, to gain even a glimpse of the Hausa and Fulani of Northern Nigeria, through contemporary writing, it is necessary to turn to an Ibo writer, Cyprian Ekwensi, whose novel, *Burning Grass,* depicts the nomadic, aristocratic, highly conservative Muslim people of the north. As far as I know, no novel or play in English has yet been published by a writer from the Hausa or Fulani tribes, although very likely writing has been produced in their own tongues and possibly in Arabic as well.

The Group as "Us Versus Them"
and as "Us In Relation To Them"

How has the second aspect of tribalism appeared in contemporary Nigerian writing? Most Nigerian writers from 1952 to 1966 were concerned not only with the restoration of self-value through a re-honouring of the ancestors, but also with a present-day clash of old and new values, a subtle and ambiguous area, for neither "new" nor "old" are ever equated unequivocally with good. They were socially involved writers—they strongly criticized social and political corruption in a society which was in the throes of swift change and its attendant disturbances. Tribalism, or tribal antagonism, has had a considerable relation to Nigerian politics as such, but when we examine the fiction and drama of the past fifteen years it becomes plain that these writers seldom, if ever, dealt with the strictly tribal aspects of politics and social change.

T.M. Aluko, in his novel *One Man, One Matchet*, portrays with ironic humour the struggle between modern technological and scientific values and the old tribal values. The main character, Udo Ukpan, fresh to the civil service and armed with his university degree and his earnest idealism, is sent as District Officer to the village of Ipaja. He is shocked and hurt when he learns that villagers are calling him "the black whiteman." He tries to help the Agricultural Officer to persuade the people to cut down diseased cocoa trees, as this is the only known cure for "swollen shoot", but this method seems sheer lunacy to the villagers. In contrast to Udo, we have Benjamin Benjamin, the new slick type of semi-literate con man, who lines his own pockets by playing upon the villagers' anxieties and by turning every village faction against every other. The traditional values are illustrated by the old Oba or king of Ipaja, who cannot understand the methods and aims of a younger generation, but who is genuinely concerned about his people. Aluko is himself a civil engineer and so he knows the problems at firsthand. He writes out of his experience of Yoruba village life, because this is what is accessible to him, but he writes as a Nigerian, seeing the problems of Ipaja as relevant to the entire country.

In Wole Soyinka's novel, *The Interpreters*, the corrupt, pathetic and horrifying Chief Winsala accepts bribes, gets falling-down drunk in a hotel bar and refuses to pay his bill. He is observed and reluctantly rescued in this scene by the young journalist, Sagoe. Winsala, from his speech and the allusions he makes to the gods and proverbs, is plainly a Yoruba, but this is not the significant thing about him. The significant thing is that he is a Nigerian politician with power, and he is unfit to use that power.

The "interpreters" of Soyinka's novel, which was published in 1965, are a group of young intellectuals who went to university together in Nigeria and then to America or England for further studies. They are home again and meet as a strongly bonded group of friends. They are interpreters both of society and of themselves. They come from various tribes, but the fact of their tribal backgrounds does not appear to be important to their relationships with one another. Egbo is an Ijaw, the grandson of an old chief who still rules his tiny kingdom in the swamps of the Niger Delta. Egbo is torn between the old and the new, unable to want to do anything much in the new Nigeria, but unable also to return to his grandfather's dying way of life. Kola, an artist, [is] engaged in painting the entire pantheon of Yoruba gods. Bandele, a teacher, is also Yoruba, as is Sagoe the journalist. Sekoni, nicnamed Sheikh, comes from Northern Nigeria and is a Muslim who has married a Christian girl and who has, therefore, been outcast by his family.

Soyinka's social criticisms in this novel are general ones—they extend to the whole of Nigeria; they are not essentially tribal in nature. In fact, the world of *The Interpreters* seems similar to the way Lagos and Ibadan must have been in the early 1960's, for Soyinka, Achebe, J.P. Clark, Cyprian Ekwensi, Christopher Okigbo, and many others—men from many tribes, intellectuals who were engaged in teaching, journalism and broadcasting, as well as writing. All were highly critical of their country's flaws, but all apparently saw the country as a well-established entity, however arbitrarily its borders may have been drawn up in the colonial era. It may well be that these writers, very understandably, underestimated the terrifying potential power of that aspect of tribalism, the group as "Us Versus Them", which still existed, deep-rooted and persistent, as it does, I am afraid, in all countries, by whatever name it is known or whatever slogans it chooses.

The way in which Chinua Achebe portrays contemporary individual and social dilemmas is also free of inter-tribal antagonism. In *No Longer At Ease*, published in 1960, Obi Okonkwo returns to Nigeria after university in England, where his education has largely been paid for by the Umuofia Progressive Union, that is, his own villagers. The novel is the story of Obi's growing dismay with the corruption he finds in the new Nigeria, and his own ultimate giving in to this corruption, through the taking of bribes himself. In the end, Obi feels he has failed both the new world and the old, partly because of their incompatible demands upon him. The tribal aspect, however, is never emphasized. The details are Ibo in this case, but the battle between the old patterns and the new are seen by Obi, as by Achebe himself, in terms of a wider application, and indeed this wider application is both valid and necessary.

Achebe writes scathingly of political evils in *A Man of the People* published in 1966, just before the first Army coup, but he does not mention the tribe of the unscrupulous Chief Nanga, as indeed why should he? These issues went far beyond any one tribe, which was part of the writer's purpose, to show just that. He goes even further by setting his story in an unnamed and newly independent African country. He describes the final army coup at the end of the novel as the outcome of a situation in which the country had been increasingly the prey of marauding bands of thugs in the pay of politicians such as Nanga.

> The Army obliged us by staging a coup at that point and locking
> up every member of the government. The rampaging bands of
> election thugs had caused so much unrest and dislocation that our
> young Army officers seized the opportunity to take over.

The novel ends on a sombre note. The military government abolishes all political parties and announces that "they will remain abolished until the situation became more stabilized once more." Public opinion shifts with alarming ease to the side of the new rulers. Achebe, with his hard realism and his wisdom, is not much more hopeful of the new regime than he was of the old. Clearly, when the book was written, social disruption had reached a point where it was plain that some sort of coup or revolution was almost inevitable. But there is no suggestion in the novel that inter-tribal hatreds might prove to be the disaster which they soon became.

The novels of Cyprian Ekwensi are perhaps the most un-tribal of all. Ekwensi, an Ibo, was born and grew up in Northern Nigeria. Later he worked as a journalist and broadcaster in Lagos, and it is there that much of his writing is set. *People of the City* is the name of his first novel, and the title epitomizes most of Ekwensi's writing. In this novel, and in the subsequent *Jagua Nana*, he deals with the largely detribalized people of the city. He is often too moralizing for my tastes, and his writing tends to be plagued by journalistic clichés, but his nightclubs, politicians, taxi-drivers, good-time girls and jazz band artists, all convey a sense of the city itself, its excitement and tinsel splendours, its underlying loneliness.

Ekwensi for many years championed (and bravely) the cause of inter-tribalism. In *Beautiful Feathers*, his worst novel, he even goes so far as to make his chief character, Wilson Iyari, the leader of the Nigerian Movement For African And Malagasy Solidarity, and he is not being satirical, as Achebe or Soyinka would have been. Naive, certainly, but in some way reaching out towards a wider brotherhood.

One can only speculate why the themes of sharp social criticism and the clash of old and new values included almost no mention of inter-tribal animosity. This must have been the way the situation looked to the country's intellectuals at that time. They themselves had undoubtedly achieved, at least among themselves, the positive variant of "Us Versus Them", that is, "Us In Relation To Them", and could be, as indeed they were, close friends, like the "interpreters" of Soyinka's novel.

The only novel of this period which deals specifically with inter-tribal relationships and antagonisms is, oddly enough, Cyprian Ekwensi's *Iska*, written just after the first of the riots in the North, and published in 1966. Filia is an Ibo girl who married Dan Kaybi, a Hausa, against the wishes of both families. Dan is killed accidentally in a tribal riot, although he himself is opposed to any form of tribal violence. Ekwensi presents the tribal riots in terms of individuals as well as masses, and sees both sides.

The differences in outlook between the Hausa and the Ibo are pointed out skillfully through the characters of the fathers of Dan and Filia. Musa Kaybe [*sic*], the Hausa, tells his son: "We come from Nupe Land. We are the masters of the River Niger." His is the proud aristocratic voice of the Islamic North. Filia's father, an Ibo, has worked hard in the North as a miner and has prospered, but his heart remains in Ogabu, among his own people, and when he retires he returns there and buys an Ibo title, becoming a leader in the community. His values lie in individual labour, in trade, in the success symbols of his own people. Both men command our sympathies. Both are understandable. But in their bitterness, when the tribal riots hurt both their households, each seeks to blame all misfortunes upon the other side.

Ekwensi undoubtedly presents too simple a solution when he blames tribal animosities totally upon the politicians.

> Politicians fan it up and we, the stupid ones, begin quarreling and killing ourselves. They fan it up and remain friends.

And yet, simplistic though it may be, it does express some universal truth—ordinary people as pawns, played with in the chess game known as history, by those few who are addicts of power.

Perhaps the only Nigerian writer yet to have looked in depth at the heritage of tribal antagonism is Wole Soyinka, in his play *A Dance of the Forests*, although tribalism is only one of the destructive aspects of the past which he is talking about. The play's themes are bewilderingly profuse, but a main one is that of the recurring past. The "gathering of the tribes" is about to take place, that is, Independence, and the people have invited the dead to take part, hoping for representatives who will confirm the glory of the ancient lost empires. To their disappointment, the Dead Man and Dead Woman who turn up are anything but illustrious in appearance. They are shabby, uncertain, ill-spoken. But, having been conjured up, they refuse to go away. Demoke, the carver, who has just finished a splendid totem for the occasion, is led with Rola, the prostitute, and Adenebi, the crooked counsellor, into the forest by Forest Head, who turns out to be the chief deity. Forest Head wants to direct the humans towards a greater self-awareness, towards a freedom from fear and from the shackles of some aspects of the past. To this end, Soyinka produces in effect a play within a play, in which we go back in history to the court of Mata Kharibu, where all the present characters are seen to have had their historical counterparts. Forest Head wants the past to reveal itself in order to make the present see *itself* more plainly. Eshuoro, the spirit of destruction, attempts to foil this revelation, for he wants humans to remain forever enslaved in their own violence and ignorance. But the revelation does take place, and the Dead Man and Dead Woman, who have been scorned by the living, are seen to have been, in their historical roles, two of the few members of Mata Kharibu's court with any true integrity. The Dead Man, who was then a Warrior, refused to fight in an unjust war against another tribe. As his ancient warrior self, he says with a despair which strikes to the heart of the reader even more now than it must have done when this prophetic play was written: "Unborn generations will, as we have done, eat up one another."

In the dance of the Half-Child, the play's culmination, Soyinka gives a new significance to the *abiku*, the child born to die, the child born with death in its soul. It is a common belief among the Yoruba, as among many other West African peoples, that the children who die at birth are always the same children, fated never to remain with earthly parents but to be born and die again and again. Demoke, in the end, must choose whether to allow the Half-Child to remain on earth or to return it to the world of the dead. There are several interpretations of this scene. Personally, I believe that in her role as Ancestress, the Dead Woman wants to relinquish the child to the world of the living, to be rid of the burden of death-in-the-soul, and to have the living forced to acknowledge and take on responsibility for this part of themselves. Demoke, however, returns the child to the Dead Woman, and Eshuoro shouts in triumph. The past has revealed itself, and it has brought some knowledge but no final freedom. Demoke has faced in himself all he is capable of enduring. Rola and Adenebi have remained in ignorance, too fearful to look. The *abiku* will be born again and again. The destructive aspects of the past will continue to recur and our ancestors' blindness to be reborn in us. *Unless we learn.* We still have that option, or so I must believe.

Towards Some Future

One main thrust of contemporary Nigerian writing, then, has been the re-creation of the ancestral and traditional ways of life, not done didactically but rather out of the deep emotional need of these writers to rediscover their history and to proclaim their people's value. Another mainstream has been an incisive and passionate contemporary social criticism, a highly political writing which at its worst is polemic and at its best is irony and social satire of a very high order. It is not at all surprising that tribal antagonism was seriously underestimated by these writers during this period. The other themes were ever-present and paramount and enough to occupy their energies and talents, and they had, in their own lives, achieved a group loyalty which did not exclude their birth tribe but which was based upon their common trade as writers. When the open conflict began (and it was certainly economic and political as well as tribal) none of them stood aloof. They could not. They are deeply involved in the struggle—they aren't and never have been ivory-tower writers; the very phrase would probably be anathema to them. In the future, I believe, they will not cease from this same commitment, this same involvement, the business of examining their history, their place and their time, and transmuting it into literature.

It is surely right and fitting that we should honour our ancestors and our gods. Affiliations with and loyalties to a group are not necessarily negative—they can be positive, reassuring and creative, an extension of family, a sense of belonging. But when membership in any group (whether racial, religious, or nationalist) expresses itself in hatred towards all other groups, then the dark side of tribalism, perhaps the dark side of every human psyche, emerges and erupts. It is not sufficient and not useful to deny that this dark side exists. It exists, at least potentially, within all of us. What is necessary is to examine it, to try to understand it, and perhaps to begin thereby to overcome it and make it lose some of its threat. Nigerian writers at some point may be in a position to make this very difficult examination through the anguish of their own experience.

In a future which, at this point, does not seem foreseeable, writers in that part of Africa may find that one of their main areas of exploration will be the sources and causes of tribalism in its aspects of fear, hatred and ultimate violence. If so, they will be telling the rest of the world something about a subject which we, too, desperately need to understand better, for their dilemma is not theirs alone. It is very profoundly all mankind's.

APPENDICES

APPENDIX I
Bibliographical and Biographical Information on the Writers

WOLE SOYINKA
Bibliographical Information

Plays (initial dates indicate original performance, where known)
The Invention, 1955. Unpublished. First produced London, 1955.

The Swamp Dwellers, 1958. Published in *Three Plays* and *Five Plays*.

The Lion and the Jewel, 1959. London: Oxford University Press, 1962. Also in *Five Plays*.

The Trials of Brother Jero, 1960. London: Oxford University Press, 1969. Also in *Three Plays*, *Five Plays*, and *The Jero Plays*.

Three Plays. Ibadan: MBARI Publications, 1962.

The Strong Breed. Published in *Three Plays* and *Five Plays*.

A Dance of the Forests, 1960. London: Oxford University Press, 1962. Also in *Five Plays*.

Five Plays. London: Oxford University Press, 1964.

The Road, 1965. London: Oxford University Press, 1965.

The Detainee, 1965 (BBC radio play).

Kongi's Harvest, 1965. London: Oxford University Press, 1966.

Three Short Plays. London: Oxford University Press, 1969.

Madmen and Specialists, 1970. London: Methuen, 1971.

Before The Blackout. London: Orisun Acting Editions, 1971. Reprinted in *Camwood on the Leaves*. London: Methuen, 1973.

Before The Blackout. London: Methuen, 1973.

The Bacchae of Euripides, A Communion Rite, 1973. London: Methuen, 1973.

Camwood on the Leaves. London: Methuen, 1973. Reprinted in *Camwood on the Leaves* and *Before The Blackout*. London: Third Press, 1974.

The Jero Plays. London: Methuen, 1973.

Jero's Metamorphosis. London: Methuen, 1973. Also in *The Jero Plays*.

Collected Plays. London: Oxford University Press, vol. 1 1973, vol. 2 1974.

Death and the King's Horseman, 1976. London: Norton, 1975.

Opera Wonyosi, 1977. Bloomington: Indiana University Press, 1981.

A Play of Giants. London: Methuen, 1984.

Six Plays. London: Methuen, 1984.

Requiem for a Futurologist. London: Rex Collings, 1985.

A Scourge of Hyacinths. London: Methuen, 1991.

To Zia With Love. London: Methuen Drama, 1992.

The Beatification of Area Boy. London: Methuen Drama, 1995.

Novels
The Interpreters. London: Deutsch, 1965.

Season of Anomy. London: Rex Collings, 1973.

Poetry
Idanre and Other Poems. London: Methuen, 1967.

Poems from Prison. London: Rex Collings, 1969.

A Shuttle in the Crypt. London: Rex Collings, 1972.

Ogun Abibiman. London: Rex Collings, 1976.

Mandela's Earth and Other Poems. London: Methuen, 1990.

Early Poems. New York: Oxford University Press, 1998.

Autobiographies and Memoirs

The Man Died: Prison Notes of Wole Soyinka. New York: Harper, 1972.

Ake: The Years of Childhood. New York: Random House, 1981.

Isara: A Voyage Around "Essay." New York: Random House, 1989.

Ibadan: The Pekelemes Years (A Memoir). London: Methuen, 1994.

Editions and Translations

D.O. Fagunwa. *The Forest of a Thousand Daemons: A Hunter's Saga* (novel), Trans. W. Soyinka. London: Nelson, 1967.

Poems of Black Africa. Ed. W. Soyinka. London: Secker and Warburg, 1975.

Plays from the Third World: An Anthology. New York: Doubleday, 1971.

Essays and Other Writings

Palaver: Dramatic Discussion Starters From Africa. With Abbey Maine and Tesfaye Kabtihimar. New York: Friendship Press, 1971.

Myth, Literature and The African World. London: Cambridge University Press, 1976.

Art, Dialogue and Outrage: Essays on Literature and Culture. Ibadan: New Horn Press, 1988.

The Credo of Being and Nothingness. Ibadan: Spectrum Books Ltd., 1991.

The Open Sore of a Continent: A Personal Narrative of the Nigerian Crisis. New York: Oxford University Press, 1996.

The Burden of Memory, The Muse of Forgiveness. New York: Oxford University Press, 1999.

Biographical Information

Akinwande Oluwole Soyinka was born 13 July 1934 in Isara, Ijebu Remo, Western Nigeria, to Akinyoda and Eniloa Soyinka. Of a distinguished Yoruba family, his paternal grandfather was a local chieftain who administered a scarification rite of manhood, consecrating the boy to Ogun (god of metal, roads and both the creative and destructive essence), whom Soyinka calls his muse, while his father was a headmaster and school inspector in the Anglican schools at Abeokuta and his mother was a devout Christian—accounting for the traditional African and modern European strains in his work. He celebrates his childhood in an autobiography, *Ake: The Years of Childhood* (1981), followed by *Isara: A Voyage Around "Essay"* (1989), a biography of his father—nicknamed "Essay" for his initials "S.A" for Soditan Akinyoda— and *Ibadan* (1995), a memoir of the years 1946–1966, the period between the end of his childhood and the outbreak of civil war.

Educated at University College, Ibadan (1952–1954), and the University of Leeds (1954–1957), where he took an honours B.A., Soyinka was a play reader for the Royal Court Theatre, London, where his early plays, *The Swamp Dwellers* (1958), *The Lion and the Jewel* and *The Invention* (both 1959), were produced. Before departing for Britain, he published poems and short stories in *Black Orpheus* and produced his first play, *The Invention* (1955), a satire on apartheid policies. Subsequently, he served as editor of *Black Orpheus*, 1961–1964, and later of *Transition*, 1974–1976.

Soyinka returned to Nigeria in 1960, shortly after Nigeria gained independence, to a research fellowship in drama at the University of Ibadan, 1960–1961, that gave him opportunities to produce, direct and act in his own plays, including *A Dance of the Forests* (1960), a fantastical but satirical celebration of Nigerian independence based on Yoruba folklore and traditional mask drama.

Soyinka's first novel, *The Interpreters* (1965), capturing the idealism of a group of five young Nigerian intellectuals educated abroad and envisioning a new Africa and anticipating a new Biafra, marks the beginning of a more political position at the point when conflict was erupting.

Soyinka's academic intellectual life became radically politicized in 1965 when he hijacked a state-controlled radio station, holding up at gun-point broadcasters preparing to announce false election results provided by the governing party of the Western Region, which had failed to win re-election, forcing them to play, instead, a cassette that he had previously recorded giving the correct election results. Tried for armed robbery (with a maximum sentence of death), Soyinka was acquitted on a technicality, partly because Nigerian High Court judges were still independent officials in those days of pre-military rule.

Incarcerated without due legal process for conspiring to aid Biafran revolutionaries, by providing them with jet planes during the civil war, Soyinka served two years in prison, 1967–1969, much of it in solitary confinement in a four-by-eight-foot cell, his books and writing materials confiscated—an experience memorialized in *The Man Died: Prison Notes of Wole Soyinka* (1972), originally composed on scraps of toilet paper and cigarette packets (Thomas 3).

A different Soyinka emerged from that existential experience, and his post-prison writings exhibit a darker quality, including bleaker verse and prose in *Madmen and Specialists* (1970) and his second and more brooding novel, *Season of Anomy* (1973). Soyinka's scope broadened considerably after his confinement: he continued producing drama, but composed more political, academic, and polemical prose writings, such as *The Credo of Being and Nothingness* (1991) and *The Open Sore of a Continent: A Personal Narrative of the Nigerian Crisis* (1996).

After serving as Chair of Theatre Arts at the University of Ibadan, 1967–1971, and Professor of Drama, University of Ife, 1972, Soyinka took up a fellowship at Churchill College, University of Cambridge, 1973–1974, earning his doctorate at Leeds in 1973, and later returning to serve as Chair of Dramatic Arts, University of Ife, 1975–1985. There he resumed his play-writing career, notably in *Death and the King's Horseman*—a threnody memorializing his father who had recently died—which embodies his cultural philosophy, enunciated in *Myth, Literature and the African World* (1976), a cultural study analyzing the cross-fertilization of African and European aesthetics.

Soyinka has declared, "I have one abiding religion—human liberty" (Hayes 4). He views theatre as activism—art with transformative, even revo-lutionary, power. He managed his two community theatre companies—The 1960 Masks, reformed as the Orisun players in 1965—to stage "guerilla theatre" (Kreisler 3) in his fight for freedom. His best drama displays the "guerilla" spirit, forcing Yoruba traditions, Christian iconography and contemporary political issues into confrontation to speak to the social schiz-ophrenia of a people caught between the received traditions of ancestral heritage and the forced cultural experiences that are the by-product of a colo-nial régime. The result is a body of work which, in its very hybridity, mirrors the process of cultural negotiation which this schizophrenia demands, and responds metaphorically to its political consequences.

Soyinka's contribution to the world of letters was rewarded with a Nobel Prize for Literature in 1986, making him the first African to win that presti-gious award. Since then he has continued his distinguished academic career as visiting professor at Harvard, Cornell, Sheffield and Emory Universities, receiving an honorary doctorate from the latter in 1996 and a prestigious Chair, as well as honorary doctorates from Yale University and Leeds.

While Soyinka's drama constitutes a cultural force, his political activism continues to take a more practical form. Soyinka found his international voice in speaking for African reform and amnesty around the world—most recently in *The Burden of Memory, The Muse of Forgiveness*—a commitment that earned him the Prisoner of Conscience Prize from Amnesty International. In November 1994, General Sani Abacha, who seized power illegally in June, 1993, exiled Soyinka from Nigeria once again on the basis of his critiques of the military regime. In October, 1998, following the death of General

Abacha, Soyinka returned to Nigeria for the first time since his escape in 1994.* He was greeted with the jubilation of a nation and the hope among many that he will become Nigeria's next president, perhaps an indication that the writer whose politics are almost as famous as his drama may be due for another life-altering honour in the near future.

---

* Those interested can access the text of his speech on this occasion at www.mg.co.za, or contact the Johannesburg *Mail and Guardian* for a printed version.

Selected Bibliography

Hayes, Thomas. "The 1986 Nobel Prize in Literature." *The Dictionary of Literary Biography Yearbook: 1986*. Ed. J.M. Brook. Detroit: Bruccoli Clark Layman, 1986. 3–8. (Note that pages 8–18 contain the text of Soyinka's Nobel Lecture.)

Kreisler, Harry. "Writing, Theatre Arts, and Political Activism." Interview with Wole Soyinka. *Institute of International Studies*, UC Berkeley (16 April 1998): 7 pp. 6 Nov. 1998. Available at www.globetrotter.berkeley.edu/Elberg/Soyinka/soyinka-con1.html.

"Soyinka, Wole." *Contemporary Authors: New Revision Series*. Ed. Susan M. Trosky. Vol. 39. Detroit: Gale Research Inc., 1992.

"Soyinka, Wole." *The Oxford Companion to English Literature*. Fifth Edition. Ed. Margaret Drabble. Oxford: Oxford UP, 1985.

Thomas, John D. "A Dramatic Life." *Emory Magazine* (Spring 1997): 5 pp. 6 Nov. 1998. Available at www.cc.emory.edu./EMORY_MAGAZINE/spring97/wole.html.

"Wole Soyinka." *The Dictionary of Global Culture*. Ed. Kwame Anthony Appiah and Henry Louis Gates, Jr. New York: Vintage Books, Random House, 1999.

JOHN PEPPER CLARK
Bibliographical Information

Drama

Song of a Goat. Ibadan: MBARI, 1961.

Three Plays. London and Ibadan: Oxford University Press, 1964, 1970. Contains *Song of a Goat* [published previously by MBARI], *The Masquerade*, and *The Raft*.

Ozidi: A Play. London and Ibadan: Oxford University Press, 1966.

The Bikoroa Plays. Oxford: Oxford University Press, 1985. Contains *The Boat, The Return Home*, and *Full Circle*.

Poetry

Poems. Ibadan: MBARI, 1962.

A Reed in the Tide. London: Longman, 1965, 1970.

Casualties: Poems 1966–68. London: Longman, 1970; New York: Africana
Publishing Corporation (APC), 1970.

State of the Union. New York and London: Longman, 1985.

Mandela and Other Poems. Ikeja: Longman Nigeria, 1988.

Translation

The Ozidi Saga. Collected and trans. from the Ijo of Okabou Ojobolo.
Ibadan: Ibadan University Press and Oxford University Press, 1977.

Satire

America, Their America. London: Deutsch, 1964; London: Heinemann,
1968; New York: Africana Publishing Corporation (APC), 1969.

Criticism

The Example of Shakespeare: Critical Essays on African Literature. London:
Longman, 1970; Evanston, Ill.: Northwestern University Press, 1970.

The Hero as Villain. Lagos, Nigeria: University of Lagos Press, 1978.

Film

Tides of the Delta: The Saga of Ozidi. Commentary by J.P. Clark and Frank
Speed. Colour Film Services, 1975.

The Ozidi of Atazi. [Details Unknown]

The Ghost Town. [A documentary on Forcados]

Collected Works

A Decade of Tongues: Selected Poems, 1958–1968. London: Longman,
1981.

Collected Plays and Poems, 1958–1988. With an Introduction by Abiola
Irele. Washington, D.C.: Howard University Press, 1991.

Collected Poems, 1958–1988. With an Introduction by Abiola Irele.
Washington, D.C.: Howard University Press, 1991.

Biographical Information

Johnson Pepper Clark-Bekedermo was born 6 April 1935 in Kiagbodo,
Nigeria, to Clark Fudulu, an Ijaw tribal leader, and Poro Clark-Bekederema.
Educated at Government College, Ughelli, and at the University of Ibadan,
where he took a B.A. with honours in 1960, followed by a Parvin Fellowship
at Princeton, research fellowships at the Institute of African Studies, Ibadan,
1961–1962 and 1963–1964, and a research fellowship at the University of
Lagos, 1964–1966, he was appointed Professor of African Literature and

served as instructor in English at the University of Lagos, 1966–1985. In addition to his academic work, he served as information officer for the Nigerian Federal Government, 1960–1961, and as head of features and editorial writer for the Lagos *Daily Express*, 1961–1962. In addition to his publication of poetry and plays, he was founder and editor of *Horn*, a literary magazine, and co-editor of *Black Orpheus* from 1966 to 1975/76.

At the time of the original publication of *Long Drums and Cannons* in 1968, playwright, poet, and critic John Pepper Clark was establishing himself as one of Nigeria's most prolific and precocious writers. In addition to the four plays—*Song of a Goat* (1961), *The Masquerade* (1964), *The Raft* (1964) and *Ozidi* (1966)—that Laurence discusses, Clark had also published two volumes of poetry—*Poems* (1962) and *A Reed in the Tide* (1965)—as well as *America, Their America* (1964), a satirical account of his year in the United States. He was also emerging as an important researcher and scholar in the field of African Literature, undertaking a significant project researching traditional myths and legends of the Ijaw people. His attempt to record the Ijaw Ozidi legend in its entirety, which he began in 1963/4 as a Research Fellow at the Institute of African Studies in Ibadan, would continue for the next fifteen years and would result in not only the play *Ozidi* that Laurence examines, but also a film, *Tides of the Delta: The Saga of Ozidi* (1975), and a translation of the legend, *The Ozidi Saga* (1977). In addition to this Ozidi work, Clark also kept up his own original writing and went on to publish three more volumes of poetry, three more plays, and much literary criticism. Most notable among his works are *A Reed in the Tide*, which was the first volume of poetry by a black African to be published internationally; *America, Their America*, his controversial satire of American life, values, and manners; and his various Ozidi works, which Robert Wren, in his biography *J.P. Clark*, calls "a grand, if sometimes ambiguous, achievement" (126); and *State of the Union* (1985), which marks Clark's professional reassumption of his full name—John Pepper Clark-Bekederemo—which had been shortened for purposes of design on the cover of his first book.

John Pepper Clark's work in various areas has earned him international recognition. Along with fellow Nigerians, novelist Chinua Achebe and playwright Wole Soyinka, Clark is generally positioned in the first rank among British Commonwealth writers. As Laurence points out, Clark's literary influences are wide and his writing is informed by both Ijaw and Western Classical traditions. He has been very active in the field of African (and, specifically, Nigerian) Literature—his commitment to local literature demonstrated by his critical essays, his roles as founder and editor of *Horn*, a literary magazine, as a founding member of the Society of Nigerian Authors, and as co-editor (with Abiola Irele) of *Black Orpheus*, a literary magazine, from 1966 to 1975/76. True to his broader literary interests, Clark is also an active participant in international literary conferences.

Retired since 1980 from his position as English Professor and Department Head at the University of Lagos (where he began as a Lecturer in 1964), Clark now lives in Kiagbodo with his wife since 1964, Ebun Odutola, a professor at the University of Lagos, with whom he has three daughters and a son. Together, they started the PEC (Pepper and Ebun Clark) Repertory Theatre in Lagos in 1982, and Clark remains its artistic director.

Selected Bibliography

Clark, J.P. Interview with Lewis Nkosi in September 1962. *African Writers Talking*. Ed. Dennis Duerden and Cosmo Pieterse. London, Ibadan, Nairobi: Heinemann, 1972. 62–67.

"Clark, John Pepper." *Contemporary Authors: New Revision Series*. Ed. Daniel Jones and John D. Jorgenson. Vol. 72. Detroit: Gale Research Inc., 1998.

Gibbs, James. "Wole Soyinka." *Twentieth-Century Caribbean and Black African Writers*. Ed. Bernth Lindfors and Reinhard Sander. Detroit: Gale Research, 1992. 298–396.

Herdeck, Donald E. "Clark, John Pepper." *African Authors: A Companion to Black African Writing*. Vol. I: 1300–1973. Washington: Black Orpheus Press/Inscape, 1974.

Janheinz, Jahn, Ulla Schild, and Almut Nordmann. "Clark, John Pepper." *Who's Who in African Literature: Biographies, Works, Commentaries*. Tübingen, Germany: Horst Erdmann Verlag, 1972.

Okagbue, Osita. "John Pepper Clark." *African Writers*. Ed. C. Brian Cox. Vol I. New York: Scribner's, 1997. 153–66.

Wren, Robert M. *J.P. Clark*. Boston: Twayne Publishers, 1984.

———. "J.P. Clark." *Twentieth-Century Caribbean and Black African Writers*. Ed. Bernth Lindfors and Reinhard Sander. *Dictionary of Literary Biography*. 117. Detroit: Gale Research, 1992. 112–33.

Zell, Hans M., Carol Bundy, and Virginia Coulon, eds. "Clark, John Pepper." *A New Reader's Guide to African Literature*. 2nd ed. London: Heinemann, 1983.

CHINUA ACHEBE
Bibliographical Information
Novels
Things Fall Apart. London: Heinemann, 1958; New York: Astor-Honor, 1959.

No Longer At Ease. London: Heinemann, 1960; New York: Fawcett, 1960.

Arrow of God. London: Heinemann, 1964; New York: John Day, 1967.

A Man of the People. London: Heinemann, 1966; New York: John Day, 1967.

Anthills of the Savannah. New York: Anchor Books, 1988.

Poetry
Beware, Soul Brother and Other Poems. London: Heinemann; New York: Doubleday, 1972.

Christmas in Biafra and Other Poems. Garden City, NY: Doubleday, 1973.

(Editor with Dubem Okafor) *Don't Let Him Die: An Anthology of Memorial Poems for Christopher Okigbo*. Enugu: Fourth Dimension Publishers, 1978.

(Coeditor) *Aka Weta: An Anthology of Igbo Poetry*. Nsukka: Okike, 1982.

Short Stories
The Sacrificial Egg and Other Short Stories. Onitsha: Etudo, 1962.

Girls At War and Other Stories. London: Heinemann, 1972; Garden City, Conn.: Doubleday/Anchor, 1973.

(Editor with Innes) *The Heinemann Book of Contemporary African Short Stories*. London: Heinemann, 1992.

Juvenile
Chike and the River. Cambridge: Cambridge University Press, 1966.

The Flute. Enugu: Fourth Dimension, 1979.

The Drum: A Children's Story. Enugu: Fourth Dimension, 1979.

(With John Iroaganachi). *How the Leopard Got His Claws*. Nairobi: East African Educational Publishers, 1972; New York: The Third Press, 1973.

Articles, Essays and Miscellaneous Works
Morning Yet On Creation Day. London, Heinemann: 1975; Garden City, NY: Anchor Press, 1975.

The Trouble with Nigeria (essays). Enugu: Fourth Dimension, 1983.

Hopes and Impediments: Selected Essays. New York: Doubleday, 1988.

Home and Exile. Oxford and New York: Oxford University Press, 2000.

Books Edited
(With C.L. Innes). *African Short Stories*. London: Heinemann, 1985.

(et al.). *Beyond Hunger in Africa: Conventional Wisdom and a Vision of Africa in 2057*. London: Currey, 1990.

(With Dubem Okafor). *Don't Let Him Die: An Anthology of Memorial Poems for Christopher Okigbo*. Enugu: Fourth Dimension, 1978.

(With C.L. Innes). *The Heinemann Book of Contemporary African Short Stories*. London: Heinemann, 1992.

(et al.). *The Insider: Stories of War and Peace From Nigeria*. Enugu: Nwankwo-Ifejika, 1971.

(et al.). *Aka Weta: An Anthology of Igbo Poetry*. Nsukka: Okike, 1982.

Biographical Information

Since Margaret Laurence praised Chinua Achebe as one of the best novelists writing in English, Achebe's international reputation has steadily grown. Many critics over the years have come to consider him Nigeria's best novelist. Critic G.D. Killam observes that Achebe's "prose writing reflects three essential and related concerns: first, with the legacy of colonialism at both the individual and societal level; secondly, with the *fact* of English as a language of national and international exchange; thirdly, with the obligations and responsibilities of the writer both to the society in which he lives and to his art" (3). Achebe has been praised for his ability to mould both the novel form and the English language to suit his aesthetic and social objectives; "any good story, any good novel, should have a message, should have a purpose," Achebe observes.

Although Achebe has also published poetry, essays and short stories, he is best known for his novels (see bibliography). *Things Fall Apart* (1958) became, in 1964, the first novel by an African writer to be required reading for English-speaking secondary schools throughout Africa, was considered the first 'classic' from tropical Africa by critics at the time, and has since been translated into forty-five languages.

Two decades passed between Laurence's critique of *A Man of the People* (1966), and the publication of his fifth novel, *Anthills of the Savannah* (1988). This novel returns to the themes of independent Africa first addressed in his early novels. *Anthills of the Savannah* was well-received, earning Achebe a nomination for the Booker Prize, and further enhancing his reputation as an artist. Achebe's writings are considered to provide a significant, balanced examination of the forces at work in contemporary Africa.

Albert Chinualumogo Achebe was born on 16 November 1930, in Ogidi, a small Ibo village in the eastern part of Nigeria near the Niger River; the fifth of six children born to Janet Ileogbunam and Isaiah Okafo Achebe, a school teacher for the Church Missionary Society. Achebe was educated at a mission school and at the Government College in Umuahia, 1944–1947, and the University College in Ibadan, 1948–1953. Although he had intended to study medicine, he graduated from the University of London with a Bachelor of Arts degree in English in 1953.

After graduating and teaching briefly, Achebe secured a position in 1953 with the Nigerian Broadcasting Corporation in Lagos. In 1956 he studied broadcasting at the British Broadcasting Corporation in London. He worked in broadcasting until 1961, eventually earning the title of Director of External Broadcasting. His first novel, *Things Fall Apart*, was published in 1958.

Achebe traveled through East Africa on a Rockefeller Fellowship in 1960 and 1961; he visited Brazil, North America, and Britain on a UNESCO Fellowship in 1963. In 1966, when the persecution of Ibos in Nigeria (particularly in northern Nigeria) escalated, Achebe was forced to leave his job in Lagos and take his family back to their homeland, eastern Nigeria (Biafra). During the civil war of 1967–1969, Achebe became an official ambassador for Biafra. He went on numerous political missions to Europe and North America.

Many of Achebe's works have received literary awards and honours. *Things Fall Apart* (1958) was awarded the Margaret Wrong Memorial Prize; *No Longer At Ease* (1960) received the Nigerian Trophy for Literature; *Arrow of God* (1964) was the recipient of the New Statesman Jock Campbell Award; *Beware, Soul Brother and Other Poems* (1972 edition) won the inaugural Commonwealth Poetry Prize; *Anthills of the Savannah* (1988) was short-listed for the Booker Prize. Achebe himself has been the recipient of numerous honours and honorary degrees in North America and Britain.

Throughout his writing life, Achebe has implicitly and explicitly expressed strong opinions with regard to writers' social responsibilities. He has written works for children as well as adults. In the early 1970s, he—along with Christopher Okigbo—attempted to establish a publishing house in Nigeria; in 1971, he began editing the magazine *Okike: An African Journal of New Writing*. Achebe became Director of African Studies at the University of Nigeria, Enugu, in 1971. Until 1981, he acted as both Professor of English and head of the English Department at the University of Nigeria. From 1971 to 1976 and again from 1987 to 1988, Achebe has been a visiting professor at several American universities.

In 1990, a three-day symposium was held in Nsukka, Nigeria, to celebrate Achebe's sixtieth birthday. While returning to Lagos, en route to New York, Achebe was seriously injured in a car crash. Achebe recovered and continues to both write and lecture widely. His latest book, *Home and Exile*, based on three lectures he gave at Harvard University in 1998, was published in 2000. He lives with his wife Christiana Chinwe Okoli, whom he married in 1961, and has four children—Chinelo, Ikechukwu, Chidi and Nwando.

Selected Bibliography

"Achebe, Chinua." *Contemporary Authors: New Revision Series*. Ed. Pamela S. Dear. Vol. 47. Detroit: Gale Research Inc., 1995.

Ezenwa, Ohaeto. *Chinua Achebe: A Biography*. Bloomington: Indiana UP, 1997.

Feldman, Gayle. "Chinua Achebe: Views of Home From Afar." *Publishers Weekly*, July 3, 2000.

Hanna, S.J. "Achebe: A Bibliography." *Studies in Black Literature* 2:1 (1971): 20–21.

Herdeck, Donald. "Achebe, Chinua." *African Authors. A Companion to Black African Writing*, Volume I: 1300–1973. Washington, DC: Black Orpheus Press, 1973. 22–25.

Innes, C.L. and Bernth Lindfors, eds. *Critical Perspectives on Chinua Achebe*. Washington, D.C.: Three Continents Press, 1978.

Jahn, Janheinz, Ulla Schild and Almut Nordmann. "Achebe, Chinua." *Who's Who in African Literature: Biographies, Works, Commentaries*. Tübingen: Erdmann, 1972. 19–21.

Killam, G.D., *The Novels of Chinua Achebe*, Africana Publishing, 1969.

McDaniel, Richard B. "An Achebe Bibliography." *World Literature Written in English* 20 (1971): 15–24.

O., V.O. "Profile: The Man Who Looks Ahead." *Radio Times* (Lagos) March (1955): 14.

Severac, Alain. "Chinua Achebe: I. Notes biographiques; II. Bibliographie." *Annales de la faculté des lettres et sciences humaines*, Université de Dakar 2 (1972): 55–56.

Silver, Helene. "Biography: Chinua Achebe." *Africana Library Journal* 1:1 (1970): 18–22.

Wren, Robert M. *Achebe's World: The Historical and Cultural Context of the Novels of Chinua Achebe*. Washington, DC: Three Continents Press, 1980.

Zell, Hans, and Helene Silver. "Chinua Achebe." *A Reader's Guide to African Literature*. London: Heinemann; New York: Africana Publishing Corp., 1972. 117–19.

Amos Tutuola

Bibliographical Information

Novels

The Palm-Wine Drinkard and His Dead Palm-Wine Tapster in the Dead's Town. London: Faber, 1952.

My Life in the Bush of Ghosts. New York: Grove, 1954.

Simbi and the Satyr of the Dark Jungle. London: Faber, 1955.

The Brave African Huntress. New York: Grove, 1958.

Feather Woman of the Jungle. London: Faber, 1962.

Ajaiyi and His Inherited Poverty. London: Faber, 1967.

The Witch-Herbalist of the Remote Town. London: Faber, 1981.

The Wild Hunter in the Bush of the Ghosts. (facsimile of manuscript) Washington: Three Continents Press, 1982.

Pauper, Brawler and Slanderer. London: Faber, 1987.

Other Works

(Contributor) *Winds of Change: Modern Short Stories from Black Africa*. Longman, 1977.

Yoruba Folktales, 1986.

The Village Witch Doctor and Other Stories. London: Faber, 1990.

Biographical Information

Amos Tutuola's writing has been both greatly praised and criticized since the publication of the highly successful *The Palm-Wine Drinkard* in 1952. As Laurence observes in her discussion of Tutuola's first five books, Tutuola's genius lies in his ability to refashion and transform the traditional Yoruba folktales, which form the basis for his fantastical characters and plots, into his own unique stories. His unconventional use of the English language and adherence to the Yoruba oral tradition has garnered praise from critics outside Nigeria, and criticism within. Although critics are, in Charles Lawson's words, "a little less awed now than they were in the early 1950's," Tutuola's works continue to receive critical attention. When *The Witch-Herbalist of the Remote Town* was published in 1981, thirty years after his acclaimed *The Palm-Wine Drinkard*, it was widely reviewed. Critics observe that Tutuola's use of English has become more standard over the years, and opinions differ as to whether or not the strength of his imaginative constructions has waned.

Answering his interpreters' questions about how he began writing, Amos Tutuola replies:

when I was young I lived in the town while my parents lived in the village, and during the school holidays I went back to my parents. In the evening people will sit down and tell folk tales. From then I listened. But after a few months when I returned to the village I found that one of the story-tellers had died. Then I thought over it. Supposing the man should take all his stories with him. From that day I prepared myself that whenever I grow old I will start to write the stories down. (Obe Obe 1023)

While Tutuola explains his coming to writing as an epiphanic moment, he did not begin to write until he was well into his twenties. Born in 1920 into a Christian farming family in the Yoruba town of Abeokuta in Western Nigeria, Amos lived at home until the age of ten, when he attended the Salvation Army School of Abeokuta. The family's financial straits made it difficult for him to continue in school; it was therefore arranged that he work as a houseboy for his uncle's friend in exchange for tuition. Amos attended school until his father's death in 1939, at which point he tried farming (unsuccessfully), worked as a coppersmith, and then served in the Royal Air Force, 1943–1945. In 1947 he married Alake Victoria, with whom he had eight children. While working as a messenger at the Labour Department in Lagos in 1946, "bored and weary of time and clock-watching as he waited for errands, he reverted to his childhood habit of storytelling" (Collins 19). In 1952, *The Palm Wine Drinkard* was sent to Faber and Faber by a bookselling agency. Despite the remarkable success of this first publication, Amos did not intend to become a professional writer. However, financial pressures and the impetus born of his success combined to spur him to continue his craft. The author's prolific output—especially during the 1950s and 1960s, but continuing into the 1980s and 1990s—is a testament both to his need to write Yoruba tales and to his resilience in the face of fame, adoration, ridicule, and, finally, acceptance and respect.

Amos Tutuola died from hypertension and diabetes on the eighth of June, 1997.

Selected Bibliography

Adeyemi, Sola. "On a One Way Trip to the Deads' Town: A Tribute to Amos Tutuola." *USAfricaonline.com.* June 1998.

Baldwin, Claudia. *Nigerian Literature: A Bibliography of Criticism 1952–1976.* Boston: G.K. Hall & Co., 1980.

Beilis, Viktor. "Ghosts, People, and Books of Yorubaland." *Research in African Literatures* 18.4 (Winter 1987): 447–57.

Collins, Harold R. *Amos Tutuola*. New York: Twayne Publishers, 1969.

Dathorne, O.R. "Amos Tutuola: The Nightmare of the Tribe." *Introduction to Nigerian Literature*. Ed. Bruce King. New York: Africana Publishers, 1972. 64–76.

Ilesanmi, Obafemi. "The Folklore Fantasist." *West Africa* 3716 (1988): 2041–42.

Irele, Abiola. *The African Experience in Literature and Ideology*. 1981. Bloomington: Indiana UP, 1990.

Johnson, Babasola. Letter from Babasola Johnson (West Africa April 10, 1954). Lindfors, Bernth. *Critical Perspectives on Amos Tutuola*, 31–32.

Larson, Charles R. *The Emergence of African Fiction*. Revised ed. Bloomington: Indiana UP, 1972.

Lindfors, Bernth. "Amos Tutuola: Debts and Assets." *Cahiers d'Etudes Africaines* 10 (1970): 306–34.

———. "Amos Tutuola: Literary Syncretism and the Yoruba Folk Tradition." *European Language Writing in Sub-Saharan Africa*. Vol. 2. Ed. Albert S. Gerard. Budapest: Akademiai Kiado, 1986. 632–49.

———, ed. *Critical Perspectives on Amos Tutuola*. Washington: Three Continents, 1975.

———, ed. *Critical Perspectives on Nigerian Literatures*. Washington: Three Continents, 1976.

———. "Indigenizing British Language and Culture in Yorubaland." *Language and Literature in Multicultural Contexts*. Ed. Satendra Nanden. Foreword. James A. Maraj. Suva, Fiji: U of South Pacific P, 1983.

Obe Obe, Ad. "An Encounter with Amos Tutuola." *West Africa* 3482 (1984): 1022–23.

Ogundipe-Leslie, Omolara. "*The Palm-Wine Drinkard*: A Reassessment of Amos Tutuola." *Critical Perspectives on Amos Tutuola*. Ed. Bernth Lindfors. Washington: Three Continents, 1975. 145–54.

Osofisan, Femi and Bayo Williams. *The Genre of Prose Fiction: Two Complementary Views*. 4th Series, no. 3. Ife: U of Ife P, 1986.

Palmer, Eustace. "Twenty-five Years of Amos Tutuola." *International Fiction Review* 5 (1978): 15–24.

"Tutuola, Amos." *Contemporary Authors: New Revision Series*. Ed. Daniel Jones and John D. Jorgenson. Vol. 66. Detroit: Gale Research Inc., 1998.

Cyprian Ekwensi
Bibliographical Information
Novels
People of the City. London: Drakers, 1954.

Jagua Nana. London: Hutchinson, 1961.

Burning Grass. London: Heinemann, 1962.

Beautiful Feathers. London: Hutchinson, 1963.

Iska. London: Hutchinson, 1966.

Divided We Stand. Enugu: Fourth Dimension, 1980.

Jagua Nana's Daughter. Ibadan: Spectrum Books Ltd., 1986.

Stories
The Rainmaker and Other Stories. Lagos: African Universities Press, 1965.

Lokotown and Other Stories. London: Heinemann, 1966.

The Restless City and Christmas Gold, With Other Stories. London: Heinemann, 1975.

Juvenile
Ikolo the Wrestler and Other Ibo Tales. London: Nelson, 1947.

The Leopard's Claw. London: Longmans, Green, 1950.

The Passport of Mallam Ilia. Cambridge: Cambridge University Press, 1960.

The Drummer Boy. Cambridge: Cambridge University Press, 1960.

An African Night's Entertainment. Lagos: African Universities Press, 1962.

Yaba Roundabout Murder. Lagos: Tortoise Series, 1962.

The Great Elephant-Bird. London: Nelson, 1965.

The Boa Suitor. London: Nelson, 1966.

Juju Rock. Lagos: African Universities Press, 1966.

Trouble in Form Six. Cambridge: Cambridge University Press, 1966.

Coal Camp Boy. Ibadan: Longman, Nigeria, 1973.

Samankwe in the Strange Forest. Ibadan: Longman, Nigeria, 1973.

Samankwe and the Highway Robbers. London: Evans, 1975.

The Rainbow-Tinted Scarf and Other Stories. London: Evans, 1975.

The Masquerade. London: Heinemann, 1991.

Masquerade Time. London: Heinemann Educational Books, 1992.

King Forever! London: Heinemann Educational Books, 1992.

Editions
Festac Anthology of Nigerian Writing. Festac, 1977.

Other Works
When Love Whispers. Onitsha: Tabansi, 1947.

Survive the Peace. London: Heinemann, 1976.

Motherless Baby. Enugu: Fourth Dimension, 1980.

For a Roll of Parchment. Ibadan: Heinemann, 1986.

Jagua Nana's Daughter. Ibadan: Spectrum, 1987.

Behind the Convent Wall. 1987. Publication details unknown.

Gone to Mecca. Ibadan: Heinemann, 1991.

Biographical Information

Cyprian Ekwensi is considered by African critic Ernest N. Emenyonu to be the father of the modern Nigerian novel. In a career spanning over four decades, Ekwensi has published novels, short stories, plays, works for children, and essays, demonstrating his immense versatility as a writer. Despite criticism for producing overly sentimental and clichéd prose, Ekwensi remains popular because his writing vividly captures the changing face of a modernizing Africa. His indictment of the corruption of the people who frequent urban centres is central to most of his novels. He addresses themes such as love, infatuation, war, marriage, death, ritual sacrifice—not only in his novels, but also in numerous contributions to juvenile and popular literature. Ekwensi's diverse experiences have given him an opportunity to publish with blunt honesty those social injustices that have disturbed him over the years. *People of the City* (1954) was Ekwensi's first major novel. Although Ekwensi has written five novels, his second, *Jagua Nana* (1961), remains his most popular and highly praised.

Cyprian Ekwensi was born 26 September 1921, into an Ibo family in Minna, Nigeria. After obtaining a B.A. at Ibadan University, he continued his studies at the Chelsea School of Pharmacy in London and at the University of Iowa. Ekwensi combined his Arts and Science background as lecturer in Biology, Chemistry and English at Igbodi College in Lagos, 1947–1949, before lecturing at the School of Pharmacy in Lagos and working as pharmacist superintendent for Nigerian Medical Services, 1956–1957.

Ekwensi's writing career reflects his interest in Ibo-Hausa relations and the unstable political situation in Nigeria in the 1960s. During the Biafran Secession, 1967–1969, Ekwensi acted as chairman for the Bureau for External Publicity and as director for an independent Biafran radio station, traveling to the United States more than once to raise funds for Biafra and the station. He addresses this civil unrest in his novels *Beautiful Feathers* (1963), *Iska* (1966), *Survive the Peace* (1976) and *Divided We Stand* (1980).

Following the Biafran Secession, Ekwensi remained active in Nigerian publishing and business communities. He was managing director of the Star Printing and Publishing Company (1975–1979) and the Niger Eagle Publishing Company (1980–1981); he acted as a consultant to three Nigerian newspapers and held posts with the federal government in the areas of Information and Broadcasting. Ekwensi has continued to publish well into his seventies, including the 1986 release of a sequel to his acclaimed *Jagua Nana*, *Jagua Nana's Daughter*.

Married to Eunice Anyiwo, with whom he has five children, Ekwensi still lives in Nigeria.

Selected Bibliography

"Ekwensi, Cyprian." *Contemporary Authors: New Revision Series*. Ed. Susan M. Trosky. Vol. 42. Detroit: Gale Research Inc., 1994.

Emenyonu, Ernest N. "Cyprian Ekwensi." *Dictionary of Literary Biography: Twentieth Century Caribbean and Black African Writers*. Ed. Bernth Lindfors and Reinhard Sander. Vol. 117. Detroit: Gale Research Inc., 1992.

T.M. ALUKO
Bibliographical Information
Novels

One Man, One Wife. Lagos: Nigerian Printing and Publishing Co., 1959. Revised ed. London: Heinemann, 1967.

One Man, One Matchet. London: Heinemann, 1964.

Kinsman and Foreman. London: Heinemann, 1966.

Chief the Honourable Minister. London: Heinemann, 1970.

His Worshipful Majesty. London: Heinemann, c.1973.

Wrong Ones in the Dock. London: Heinemann, 1982.

State of Our Own: London: Heinemann, 1986.

Conduct Unbecoming. London: Heinemann, 1993.

Biographical Information

Although many critics consider T.M. Aluko to have made a key contribution to the development of modern Nigerian literature, the nature of his contribution remains controversial. Each of Aluko's eight novels is centrally concerned with Nigeria's social and cultural transformation. Two of the novels Laurence discusses—*One Man, One Matchet* (1964), and *Kinsman and Foreman* (1966), along with *Chief the Honourable Minister* (1970)—are considered his major works. *Chief the Honourable Minister*, which presents the break-up of the Nigerian civil service during the 1966 military coup, anticipates Aluko's move away from the comic satire of his major works towards the more somber, less hopeful tone of his later novels. According to many critics, his later novels—*His Worshipful Majesty* (1973), *Wrong Ones in the Dock* (1982), *State of Our Own* (1986) and *Conduct Unbecoming* (1993)—lack the vitality of the earlier works. Although Aluko incorporates themes that are common to the contemporary postcolonial literature of his nation, such as the clash between traditional and "modern" lifestyles, his comic approach to social problems and his use of satire have caused him to be strongly criticised by his more politically committed contemporaries.

Born a Yoruba on 14 June 1918, Timothy Mofolorunso Aluko studied civil engineering and town planning at the University of London from 1946 to 1950. He returned to Nigeria and was employed by the Public Works Department, of which he was later director, as district engineer in various western Nigerian localities and as town engineer for Lagos. In 1950, he married Janet Adebisi Fajemisin, with whom he has six children. From 1960–1966, Aluko was a senior lecturer at the University of Ibadan. From 1966–1978 he was a senior research fellow in municipal engineering at the University of Lagos, where he earned his Ph.D. in 1976. He has also worked as the State Commissioner for Finance in Ibadan (1971–1973), and he is currently a consulting engineer and writer in Lagos.

Selected Bibliography

Adamolekun, Ladipo. "T.M. Aluko." *Afriscope* 5.2 (1975): 57, 59.

"Aluko, T.M." *Contemporary Authors: New Revision Series*. Ed. Daniel Jones and John D. Jorgenson. Vol. 62. Detroit: Gale Research Inc., 1998.

Banjo, Ayo. "Language in Aluko: The Use of Colloquialisms, Nigerianisms." *Ba Shiru: A Journal of African Languages and Literature* 5.1 (1973): 59–69.

Carter, Donald. "Sympathy and Art: Novels and Short Stories." *African Literature Today* 5 (1971): 137–42.

Dzeagu, S.A. "T.M. Aluko as a Social Critic." *Legon Journal of the Humanities* 2 (1976): 28–41.

Kirpal, Viney. "The Structure of the Modern Nigerian Novel and the National Consciousness." *Modern Fiction Studies* 34.1 (1988): 45–54.

Lindfors, Bernth. "T.M. Aluko: Nigerian Satirist." *African Literature Today* 5 (1971): 41–53.

Ngugi, James. "Satire in Nigeria: Chinua Achebe, T.M. Aluko and Wole Soyinka." *Protest and Conflict in African Literature*. Ed. Cosmo Pieterse and Donald Munro. London, New York: Heinemann, Africana Publication Corp., 1969.

Ngwaba, Francis-E. "From the Artifice to Art: The Development of T.M. Aluko's Technique." *Literary Half Yearly* 23.1 (1982): 115–27.

———. "T.M. Aluko and the Theme of the Crisis of Acculturation." *Nsukka Studies in African Literature* 2.1 (1979): 3–11.

Omotoso, Kole. "Interview with T.M. Aluko." *Afriscope* 3.4 (1973): 51–52.

Osundare, Oluwaniyi. "Speech Narrative in Aluko: An Evaluative Stylistic Investigation." *Journal of Nigerian English Studies Association* 8.1 (1976): 33–39.

Palmer, Eustace Taiwo. "Development and Change in the Novels of T.M. Aluko." *World Literature Written in English* 15 (1976): 279–96.

Scott, Patrick. "A Biographical Approach to the Novels of T.M. Aluko." *When the Drumbeat Changes*. Ed. Carolyn Parker. Washington, D.C.: Three Continents, 1981. 215–39.

———. "The Cultural Significance of T.M. Aluko's Novels." *Bulletin of So. Association of Africanists* 7.1 (1979): 1–10.

———. "The Older Generation: T.M. Aluko and Gabriel Okara." *European-Language Writing in Sub-Saharan Africa*. Ed. Albert S. Gerard. Budapest: Akad. Kiado, 1986. 689–97.

Taiwo, Oladele. "T.M. Aluko: The Novelist and His Imagination." *Présence Africaine: Revue Culturelle du Monde Noir / Cultural Review of the Negro World* 90 (1974): 225–46.

ELECHI AMADI
Bibliographical Information
Novels
The Concubine. London: Heinemann, 1966.

The Great Ponds. London: Heinemann Educational, 1970.

The Slave. London: Heinemann, 1979.

Estrangement. London; Portsmouth, NH: Heinemann Educational, 1985.

Drama
Isiburu. London: Heinemann, 1973.

Peppersoup [and] *The Road to Ibadan*. Ibadan: Onibonoje Publishers, 1977.

Dancer of Johannesburg. Ibadan: Onibonoje Publishers, 1978.

Other Works

Okpukpe (prayerbook in Ikwerre). Port Harcourt: C.S.S. Printers, 1969.

Lkwukwo Eri (hymnbook in Ikwerre). Port Harcourt: C.S.S. Printers, 1969.

Sunset in Biafra: A Civil War Diary. London: Heinemann Educational, 1973.

"The Novel in Nigeria." *Afriscope* 4.11 (1974): 40–41, 43, 45 and *Oduma Magazine* 2.1 (1974): 33, 35–37.

Ethics in Nigerian Culture. Ibadan: Heinemann Educational, 1982.

Biographical Information

Elechi Amadi is considered one of the foremost chroniclers of the African village in fiction, drawing on his own upbringing in the rainforest belt of southeastern Nigeria. As Laurence observes in her discussion of his first novel, *The Concubine* (1966), Amadi's depictions of village life are considered unique in that he does not present explicit contrasts between the pre-colonial world and that which replaced it. Amadi sets later novels, such as *The Great Ponds* (1969) and *The Slave* (1979), in this same pre-colonial village environment. With the publication and production of the play *Isiburu* in 1973, Amadi made his debut as a dramatist; he has published four plays in total.

Born on 12 May 1934 in Aluu near Port Harcourt in Eastern Nigeria, Elechi Amadi graduated with a degree in mathematics and physics from University College, Ibadan, in 1959. He worked first as a land surveyor in Enugu, 1959–1960, then as a teacher in Nigerian schools, 1960–1963, and as headmaster, 1966–1967, and, subsequently, at an Anglican grammar school. In 1957, he married Dorah Nwonne Ohale, with whom he has eight children. During the Biafran War, Amadi was a member of the Federal army, and he recounts his war experiences in the autobiographical narrative *Sunset in Biafra: A Civil War Diary* (1973). After the war, Amadi served as administrative officer of the Rivers State Government's Ministry of Information, Port Harcourt, 1969–1983, and Commissioner of Education, 1987–1989, and Commissioner of Lands and Housing, 1989–1990. From 1984–1987 Amadi held the positions of Writer-in-Residence, Dean of Arts, and Director of General Studies at the Rivers State College of Education, where he has been Head of the Department of Literature since 1991.

Selected Bibliography

Aje, S. O. "Music and Dance as Metaphors of Language in Elechi Amadi's *The Concubine*." *Neohelicon: Acta Comparationis Litterarum Universarum* 16.2 (1989): 187–99.

"Amadi, Elechi." *Contemporary Authors: New Revision Series*. Ed. Daniel Jones and John D. Jorgenson. Vol. 63. Detroit: Gale Research Inc., 1998.

Banyiwa-Horne, Naana. "African Womanhood: The Contrasting Perspectives of Flora Nwapa's *Efuru* and Elechi Amadi's *The Concubine*." *Ngambika: Studies of Women in African Literature*. Ed. Carole Boyce Davies and Anne Adams Graves. Trenton, NJ: Africa World, 1986. 119–29.

Chandar, K.M. "Elechi Amadi's *The Concubine*." *Literary Half Yearly* 21.2 (1980): 123–33.

Finch, Geoffrey J. "Tragic Design in the Novels of Elechi Amadi." *Critique: Studies in Modern Fiction* 17.2 (1975): 5–16.

Ivker, Barry. "Elechi Amadi: An African Writer Between Two Worlds." *Phylon: The Atlanta University Review of Race and Culture* 33 (1972): 290–93.

Keo, Ebele. "African Aesthetics in Elechi Amadi's *The Slave*." *The Literary Criterion* 23.1–2 (1988): 143–53.

Kiema, Alfred. "The Fantastic Narrative in Elechi Amadi's Works: Narrating and Narrator." *Commonwealth Essays and Studies* 12.2 (1990): 86–90.

Moore, Gerald. "Dirges of the Delta." *Afriscope* 10.11 (1980): 23–25.

Niven, Alastair. "The Achievement of Elechi Amadi." *Common Wealth*. Ed. Anna Rutherford and A.N. Jeffares. Aarhus, Denmark: Akademisk Boghandel, 1972. 92–100.

———. "From Empire to Commonwealth: The Birth of Literature." *La Litterature et ses lieux de production*. Ed. A. Vermeylen. Louvain-la-Neuve; Paris: Fac. de Philos. et Lettres, U Catholique de Louvain, 1980. 27–40.

———. *A Critical View on Elechi Amadi's* The Concubine. London: Rex Collings, 1981.

Nwankwo, Chimalum. "The Metaphysical as Tangible Presence: Elechi Amadi." *Subjects Worthy of Fame: Essays on Commonwealth Literature in Honour of H.H. Anniah Gowda*. Ed. A.L. McLeod. New Delhi: Sterling, 1989. 88–96.

Ogundele, Wole. "Chance and Deterministic Irony in the Novels of Elechi Amadi." *World Literature Written in English* 28.2 (1988): 189–203.

Osundare, Niyi. "'As Grasshoppers to Wanton Boys': The Role of the Gods in the Novels of Elechi Amadi." *African Literature Today* 11 (1980): 97–109.

Palmer, Eustace. "Elechi Amadi and Flora Nwapa." *African Literature Today* 3.1. (1969): 56.

————. *An Introduction to the African Novel: A Critical Study of Twelve Books by Chinua Achebe, James Ngugi, Camara Laye, Elechi Amadi, Ayi Kwei Armah, Mongo Beti, and Gabriel Okara.* New York: Africana, 1972. London: Heinemann Educational, 1972.

"The Question of a Writer's Commitment: Two Points of View." *Kunapipi* 5.1 (1983): 35–48.

"Roadshow Back from Uganda." *Weekly Review* 30 Jan. 1981: 41.

Sample, Maxine. "In Another Life: The Refugee Phenomenon in Two Novels of the Nigerian Civil War." *Modern Fiction Studies* 37.3 (1991): 445–54.

Sarr, Ndiawar. "*The Concubine*: Roman sur la Societé Africaine Traditionnelle." *Université de Dakar Annales de la Faculte des Lettres and Sciences Humaines* 8 (1978): 139–52.

Vincent, Theophilus. *The Novel and Reality in Africa and America.* Lagos, Nigeria: U.S. Information Service and U of Lagos, 1974.

NKEM NWANKWO
Bibliographical Information
Novels
Danda. London: Collins Clear-Type Press, 1964.

My Mercedes is Bigger than Yours. London: Heinemann Educational, 1975.

Short Stories
Tales Out of School. Lagos: African Universities Press, 1965.

More Tales Out of School. Illust. Adebayo Ajayi. Lagos, Nigeria: African Universities Press, 1965.

Drama
Eroya. Ibadan, Nigeria: University College, 1963.

"Danda." (dramatised version of the novel). 1966. Produced in Dakar, Senegal.

Radio Plays, all produced by Nigeria Brodcasting Corporation:
"The Inheritors" (1964)

"Fire and Brimstone" (1965)

"In My Father's House" (1965)

"Full Circle" (1965)

"The Two Sisters" (1966)

"Who Gave Monkey Banana?" (1966)

"The Serpent in the Garden" (1966)

Other Works

"The Artist's Place in Modern African Society." *Ufahamu: Journal of the African Activist Association* 4.1 (1973): 7–9.

"Cultural Primitivism and Related Ideas in Jean Toomer's *Cane.*" *DAI* 43.8 (1983): 2669A.

Biographical Information

Nkem Nwankwo is known as a writer of short stories, novels, and drama. In an interview Nwankwo comments:

> I came of age at the highpoint of Nigerian nationalism, with the achievement of self-government. We were the inheritors of a brave new world rescued from the West. My first book responded to the mood of euphoria. My subsequent books have reflected the inevitable disillusionment with the gap between idyll and reality. (CA 1977)

Nwankwo was born in 1936 in Nawfia in what was then Nigeria's East-Central State. He studied English at University College, Ibadan, earning his B.A. in 1962 before working as an English teacher, radio producer, and journalist in Nigeria. Nwankwo fought with the Biafrans during the Nigerian civil war (1966–1969). "Out of tune" with post-war Nigeria and considering himself a "spiritual exile," he left Africa for the United States to take up a position as writer-in-residence and specialist in the African Studies Centre at Michigan State University in East Lansing, 1972–1973. After the publication of his second novel *My Mercedes is Bigger than Yours* (1975), Nwankwo enrolled in the comparative literature program at the University of Indiana at Bloomington, from which he received a Master's degree in 1976 and a doctorate in 1982. Nwankwo now holds the position of Professor in the Faculty of Languages, Literature, and Philosophy at Tennessee State University.

Selected Bibliography

Abrahams, Cecil. "No Longer at Ease." *Canadian Journal of African Studies/Revue Canadienne des Etudes Africaines* 14 (1980): 529–31.

Midiohuoan, Guy Ossito. "Nkem Nwankwo, *Ma Mercedes est plus grosse que la tienne.*" *Recherche, Pedagogie et Culture* 64 (1983): 78–80.

"Nwankwo, Nkem." *Contemporary Authors.* Ed. Jane A. Bowden. Vol. 65–68. Detroit: Gale Research Inc., 1977.

Okeke-Ezigbo, Emeka. "The Automobile as Erotic Bride: Nkem Nwankwo's *My Mercedes is Bigger Than Yours.*" *Critique: Studies in Contemporary Fiction* 24.4 (1984): 199–208.

FLORA NWAPA
Bibliographical Information
Novels
Efuru. London and Ibadan: Heinemann, 1966.

Idu. London: Heinemann, 1971.

Never Again. Enugu: Tana Press, 1975; Trenton, NJ: Africa World, 1992.

One is Enough. Enugu: Tana Press, 1982.

Women Are Different. Enugu: Tana Press, 1986; Trenton, NJ: Africa World, 1991.

Children's Fiction
Emeka – Driver's Guard. London: University of London Press, 1972.

My Animal Colouring Book. Nigeria: Flora Nwapa Books, 1977.

My Tana Colouring Book. Nigeria: Flora Nwapa Books, 1978.

Mammywater. Enugu: Tana Press, 1979.

Journey to Space. Enugu: Tana Press, 1980.

The Miracle Kittens. Enugu: Flora Nwapa Books, 1980.

The Adventures of Deke. Enugu: Flora Nwapa Books, 1982.

Stories
"The Campaigner." *The Insider: Stories of War and Peace from Nigeria.* Enugu: Nwankwo-Ifejika, 1971.

This is Lagos and Other Stories. Enugu: Tana Press, 1971; Trenton, New Jersey: Africa World, 1991.

Wives at War and Other Stories. Enugu: Tana Press, 1986; Trenton, New Jersey: Africa World, 1992.

Poems
Cassava Song and Rice Song. Enugu: Tana, 1986.

Biographical Information
With the publication of *Efuru* (1966), Flora Nwapa became Nigeria's first published female novelist in English. In her prolific writing career she went on to publish four more novels, numerous short stories and works for children. Of primary interest in Nwapa's work for adults is the depiction of Igbo women, whose internal strength and energy she celebrates. The transforma-

tion of women characters forms the centre of Nwapa's themes. In her earlier novels, *Efuru* (1966) and *Idu* (1971), this transformation occurs within a pre-colonial setting, involving women who move outside the traditions of Igbo society when its ideals of women's behaviour does not satisfy their social, economic and spiritual needs. In later novels, such as *One is Enough* (1986) and *Women are Different* (1986), the female characters leave the moral security of the village and meet the challenges of survival in Nigeria's fast-paced urban centres. The feminist slant of Nwapa's themes challenges the literary image of women created by her male contemporaries. "My interest," says Nwapa, "has been in both the rural and the urban woman in her quest for survival in a fast-changing world dominated by men" (CA 1994).

Florence Nwanzuruahu Nkiru Nwapa was born on 18 January 1931, in Oguta in Eastern Central State, Nigeria. She attended the University of Ibadan, where she obtained her Bachelor of Arts degree in 1957, and the University of Edinburgh, from which she received a Diploma of Education in 1958. When she returned to Nigeria, Nwapa held administrative positions in several educational institutions before the Nigerian civil war, after which she served as Minister of Health and Social Welfare (1970–1971) and Minister of Lands, Survey and Urban Development (1971–1974) in East-Central State (the former Biafra). In 1967, she married Gogo Nwakuche, with whom she had three children. After her retirement, she founded Tana Press in 1974 and Flora Nwapa Books in 1977. Nwapa was a visiting professor and lecturer at numerous colleges and universities in the U.S. and in Nigeria until her death in 1993.

Selected Bibliography

Achufusi, Ify-G. "Feminist Inclinations of Flora Nwapa." *African Literature Today* 19 (1994): 101–14.

Adeola, James, ed. *In Their Own Voice: African Women Writers Talk.* Portsmouth, NH: Heinemann, 1990.

———. "Idu, Flora Nwapa." *African Literature Today* 5 (1971): 150–53.

Andrade, Susan Z. "The Joys of Daughterhood: Gender, Nationalism, and the Making of Literary Tradition(s)." *Cultural Institutions of the Novel.* Ed. Deidre Lynch and William B. Warner. Durham, NC: Duke UP, 1996. 249–75.

———. "Rewriting History, Motherhood and Rebellion." *Research in African Literatures* 21.2 (1990): 91–110.

Banyiwa-Horne, Naana. "African Womanhood: The Contrasting Perspectives of Flora Nwapa's *Efuru* and Elechi Amadi's *The*

Concubine." Ngambika: Studies of Women in African Literature. Ed. Carole Boyce Davies and Anne Adams Graves. Trenton, NJ: Africa World, 1986. 119–29.

Berrian, Brenda. "African Women Seen in the Works of Flora Nwapa and Ama Ata Aidoo." *CLA Journal* 25.3 (1982): 331–39.

———. "Flora Nwapa (1931–1993): A Bibliography." *Research in African Literatures* 26.2 (1995): 124–29.

———. "The Reinvention of Woman Through Conversations and Humor in Flora Nwapa's *One Is Enough.*" *Research in African Literatures* 26.2 (1995): 53–67.

Conde, Maryse. "Three Female Writers in Modern Africa: Flora Nwapa, Ama Ata Aidoo and Grace Ogot." *Presence Africaine: Revue Culturelle du Monde Noir/Cultural Review of the Negro World* (7500) (1972): 82, 123–43.

Davies, Carole Boyce. "Motherhood in the Works of Male and Female Igbo Writers: Achebe, Emecheta, Nwapa and Nzekwu." *Ngambika: Studies of Women in African Literature.* Ed. Carole Boyce Davies and Anne Adams Graves. Trenton, NJ: Africa World, 1986. 241–56.

Duruoha, S. I. "The Language of Flora Nwapa's *Efuru* and *Idu*: A Study in Ambiguity." *Feminism and Black Women's Creative Writing: Theory, Practice, and Criticism.* Ed. Adebayo Aduke. Ibadan, Nigeria: AMD, 1996. 245.

Emenyonu, Ernest N. "Who Does Flora Nwapa Write For?" *African Literature Today* 7 (1975): 28–33.

Ezeigbo, Theordora Akachi. "Traditional Women's Institutions in Igbo Society: Implications for the Igbo Female Writer." *African Languages and Cultures* 3.2 (1990): 149–65.

Ezenwa, Ohaeto. "The Child Figures and Childhood Symbolisms in Flora Nwapa's Children's Fiction." *Research in African Literatures* 26.2 (1995): 68–79.

———. "The Notion of Fulfillment in Flora Nwapa's *Women Are Different.*" *Neohelicon: Acta Comparationis Litterarum Universarum.* 19:1 (1992): 323–33.

Githaiga, A. *Notes on Flora Nwapa's Efuru.* Nairobi: Heinemann, 1978.

Ikonne, Chidi. "The Society and Woman's Quest for Selfhood in Flora Nwapa's Early Novels." *Kunapipi* 6.1 (1984): 68–78.

Jell-Bahlsen, Sabine. "The Concept of Mammywater in Flora Nwapa's Novels." *Research in African Literatures* 26.2 (1995): 30–41.

Maja-Pearce, Adewale. "Flora Nwapa's *Efuru*: A Study in Misplaced Hostility." *World Literature Written in English* 25 (Spring 1985): 10–15.

Nichols, Lee. "Unpublished Interviews with Flora Nwapa." *ALA-Bulletin* 20.2 (1994): 26–36.

Nnaemeka, Obioma. "Feminism, Rebellious Women, and Cultural Boundaries: Rereading Flora Nwapa and Her Compatriots." *Research in African Literatures* 26.2 (1995): 80–113.

Nwapa, Flora. Interview. *African Woman* 10 (1977): 9.

———. "Flora Nwakuche, nee Nwapa, a Former Cabinet Minister and One of Africa's Leading Women Writers Talks to Austa Uwechue." *Africa Woman* 10 (1977): 8–10.

———. "The Poetics of Economic Independence for Female Empowerment: An Interview with Flora Nwapa." By Marie Umeh. *Research in African Literatures* 26.2 (1995): 22–29.

"Nwapa, Flora." *Contemporary Authors*. Ed. Donna Olendorf. Vol. 143. Detroit: Gale Research Inc., 1994.

Nwankwo, Chimalum. "The Igbo Word in Flora Nwapa's Craft." *Research in African Literatures* 26.2 (1995): 42–52.

Nzewi, Meki. "Ancestral Polyphony." *African Arts* 11.4 (1978): 92–94.

Ogunyemi, Chikwenye Okonjo. *African Wo/Man Palava: The Nigerian Novel by Women*. Chicago: U of Chicago P, 1996.

———. Introduction. "The Invalid, Dea(r)th, and the Author: The Case of Flora Nwapa, aka Professor (Mrs.) Flora Nwanzuruahu Nwakuche." *Research in African Literatures* 26.2 (1995): 1–16.

Ojo-Ade, Femi. "Women and the Nigerian Civil War: Buchi Emecheta and Flora Nwapa." *Etudes Germano-Africaines: Revue Annuelle de Germanistique-Africaine Jahresschrift fur Afrikanische-Germanistik Annual Review* 6 (1988). 75–86.

Palmer, Eustace. "Elechi Amadi and Flora Nwapa." *African Literature Today* 3.1. (1969): 56.

Perry, Alison. "Meeting Flora Nwapa." *West Africa* (1984).

Phillips, Maggi. "Engaging Dreams: Alternative Perspectives on Flora Nwapa, Buchi Emecheta, Ama Ata Aidoo, Bessie Head, and Tsitsi Dangarembga's Writing." *Research in African Literatures* 25.4 (1994): 89–103.

Sample, Maxine. "In Another Life: The Refugee Phenomenon in Two Novels of the Nigerian Civil War." *Modern Fiction Studies* 37:3 (1991): 445–54.

Schipper, Mineke. "Woman and Literature in Africa." *Unheard Words*. Ed. Mineke Schipper. London: Allison and Busby, 1984. 22–58.

Stratton, Florence. *Contemporary African Literature and the Politics of Gender*. London, New York: Routledge, 1994.

Umeh, Marie. "Signifyin(g) The Griottes: Flora Nwapa's Legacy of (Re)Vision and Voice." *Research in African Literatures* 26.2 (1995): 114–23.

———, ed. *Emerging Perspectives on Flora Nwapa: Critical and Theoretical Essays*. Trenton, NJ: Africa World Press, c.1998.

Wilentz, Gay. *Binding Cultures: Black Women Writers in Africa and the Diaspora*. Bloomington: Indiana UP, 1992.

———. "The Individual Voice in the Communal Chorus: The Possibility of Choice in Flora Nwapa's *Efuru*." *ACLALS-Bulletin* 7.4 (1986): 30–36.

Zongo, Opportune. "Rethinking African Literary Criticism: Obioma Nnaemeka." *Research in African Literatures* 27.2 (1996): 178–84.

ONUORA NZEKWU
Bibliographical Information
Novels

Wand of Noble Wood. London: Hutchinson, 1961.

Blade Among the Boys. London: Arrow Books, 1964.

Highlife for Lizards. London: Hutchinson, 1965.

Other Works

(And Crowder, Michael). *Eze Goes to School*. Illust. Adebayo Ajayi. Lagos, Nigeria: African Universities Press, 1963.

Biographical Information
Onuora Nzekwu's literary output ended after the publication of the three novels that Laurence discusses—*Wand of Noble Wood* (1961), *Blade Among the Boys* (1964), and *Highlife for Lizards* (1965). As Laurence observes, Nzekwu's work explores the clash between old and new values in Nigerian society.

Nzekwu was born an Ibo on 19 February 1928 in Kafanchan, northeastern Nigeria. He worked as a teacher for nine years before joining the staff of *Nigeria Magazine*, of which he was editor-in-chief from 1962–1966. Though he was a Biafran patriot, he worked in the Public Service both before and after the Nigerian civil war and is currently Deputy Director with the Federal Ministry of Information in Lagos.

Selected Bibliography
Davies, Carole Boyce. "Motherhood in the Works of Male and Female Igbo Writers: Achebe, Emecheta, Nwapa and Nzekwu." *Ngambika: Studies of*

Women in African Literature. Ed. Carole Boyce Davies and Anne Adams Graves. Trenton, NJ: Africa World, 1986. 241–56.

Killam, G.D. "The Novels of Onuora Nzekwu." *African Literature Today* 5 (1971): 21–40.

Lasker, Carroll and Kwaku Amoabeng. "Titles, Names and Themes in African Literature." *Queen's Quarterly* 91.2 (1984): 282–300.

Lindfors, Bernth. "The Africanization of Onuora Nzekwu." *Literary Half Yearly* 13.1 (1972): 93–103.

——. *Early Nigerian Literature.* New York: Africana, 1982.

Povey, John. "The Novels of Onuora Nzekwu." *Literature East and West* 12.1 (1968): 68–84.

Gabriel Okara
Bibliographical Information
Poetry
"Ogboinba: The Ijaw Creation Myth." *Black Orpheus* 2 (1958): 9–17.

"The Crooks." *Black Orpheus* 8 (1960): 6–8.

"Tobi." *Flamingo* 4.1 (1964): 29–31.

The Fisherman's Invocation. London: Heinemann, 1978; Benin City, Nigeria: Ethiope, 1979.

Novel
The Voice. London: F. Watts, 1964.

Other Works
"Nigeria: Zwischen den Sprache." *Gestalt und Gedanke: Ein Jahrbuch* 8 (1963): 178–85.

"African Speech...English Words." *African Writers on African Writing.* Ed. G.D. Killam. Evanston, IL: Northwestern University Press, 1973.

"Poetry and Oral English." *Journal of Nigerian English Studies Association* 8.1 (1976): 41–49.

"Towards the Evolution of an African Language for African Literature." *Chinua Achebe: A Celebration.* Ed. Kirsten Holst Petersen and Anna Rutherford. Oxford: Heinemann, 1990. 11–18.

Biographical Information

Gabriel Okara is known primarily as a writer of poetry. *The Voice* (1964), which Laurence discusses, is his only novel. In an interview, Okara explained the reason for which he is not widely published: during the Nigerian civil war, the manuscripts for many of his poems, as well as for for two completed novels, were destroyed. *The Voice*, his first published novel, received mixed reviews because of its experimental application of Ijaw syntax to the English language; *The Fisherman's Invocation*, however, was awarded the 1979 Commonwealth Poetry Prize.

The son of an Ijaw chief, Gabriel Okara was born at Bumoundi in the Niger delta on 24 April 1921. Educated at Government College, 1935–1941, Okara was a printer and bookbinder for Government Press, 1945–1954. He went to the United States to study journalism at Northwestern University, and, upon his return to Nigeria in the sixties, he took up the post of Information Officer for the Eastern Nigerian Government Service, 1964–1970. During the Nigerian civil war, he served as Director of the Cultural Affairs Division of the Biafran Ministry of Information and toured the United States with Chinua Achebe to promote the Biafran cause. After the war, Okara was Commissioner for Information and Broadcasting for the government of the Rivers state, 1971–1976, and was the founder and general manager of the Rivers State Government newspaper *The Nigerian Tide*. He is now Head of the Rivers State Cultural Centre. Married and divorced three times, he has two children.

Selected Bibliography

Anozie, Sunday O. "The Theme of Alienation and Commitment in Okara's *The Voice*." *Bulletin of the Association for African Literature in English* 3 (1965): 54–67.

Asein, Samuel O. "The Significance of Gabriel Okara as Poet." *New Literature Review* 11 (1982): 63–74.

Ashaolu, Albert Olu. "A Voice in the Wilderness: The Predicament of the Social Reformer in Okara's *The Voice*." *International Fiction Review* 6 (1979): 111–17.

Beckmann, Susan. "Gabriel Okara, The Fisherman's Invocation." *World Literature Written in English* 20.2 (1981): 230–35.

Desai, Gaurav. "English as an African Language." *English Today: The International Review of the English Language* 9.2 (1993): 4–11.

Echeruo, Michael J.C. "Gabriel Okara: A Poet and his Seasons." *World Literature Today: A Literary Quarterly of the University of Oklahoma* 66.3 (1992): 454–56.

———. "Gabriel Okara at 70: A Poet and His Seasons." *African Literature Association Bulletin* 17.3 (1994): 30–34.

Egudu, R.N. "A Study of Five of Gabriel Okara's Poems." *Okike* 13 (1979): 93–110.

Elimimian, Isaac I. "Language and Meaning in Gabriel Okara's Poetry." *College Language Association Journal* 33.3 (1995): 276–89.

Farid, Maher S. "Gabriel Okara, *The Voice.*" *Lotus: Afro-Asian Writing* 13 (1972): 180–83.

"Gabriel Okara." *Moto-Review of Contemporary African Literature* 9 (1974): 9.

Gingell, S.A. "His River's Complex Course: Reflections on Past, Present and Future in the Poetry of Gabriel Okara." *World Literature Written in English* 23.2 (1984): 284–97.

Iyasere, Solomon. "Narrative Techniques in Okara's *The Voice.*" *African Literature Today* 12 (1982): 5–21.

Ker, David I. *The African Novel and the Modernist Tradition.* New York: P. Lang, c.1997.

Kiema, Alfred. "L'Imaginaire et le Theme du Voyage dans *La Voix* de Gabriel Okara." *Bridges: An African Journal of English Studies / Revue Africaine d'Etudes Anglaises* 7 (1996): 29–44.

King, Bruce. "The Poetry of Gabriel Okara." *Chandrabhaga: A Magazine of World Writing* 2 (1979): 60–65.

Kirpal, Viney. "The Structure of the Modern Nigerian Novel and the National Consciousness." *Modern Fiction Studies* 34.1 (1988): 45–54.

Lindfors, Bernth. *Dem-Say: Interviews with Eight Nigerian Writers.* Austin: African & Afro-American Study and Research Center, 1974.

———. "Gabriel Okara: The Poet as Novelist." *Pan-African Journal* 4.4 (1971): 420–25.

Maduakor, Obi. "Gabriel Okara: Poet of the Mystic Inside." *World Literature Today: A Literary Quarterly of the University of Oklahoma* 61.1 (1987): 41–45.

———. "Myth and Mysticism in Gabriel Okara's *The Voice.*" *Commonwealth Essays and Studies* 15.2 (1993): 58–65.

Mamudu, Ayo. "Okara's Poetic Landscape." *Commonwealth Essays and Studies* 10.1 (1987): 111–18.

Moore, Gerald. "Dirges of the Delta." *Afriscope* 10.11 (1980): 23–25.

Njoroge, P.N. "Gabriel Okara: The Feeler of the Pulse of Africa's Soul." *Busara* 5.1 (1973): 48–56.

"Okara, Gabriel." *Contemporary Authors.* Ed. Frances C. Locher. Vol. 105. Detroit: Gale Research Inc., 1982.

Okara, Gabriel. "Interview with Gabriel Okara." By Bernth Lindfors. *World Literature Written in English* 12 (1973): 133–41.

———. "1983 Robert Wren Interview of Gabriel Okara." *African Literature Association Bulletin* 17.3 (1991): 35–36.

Okeke-Ezigbo, Emeka. "The 'Sharp and Sided Hail': Hopkins and His Nigerian Imitators and Detractors." *Hopkins among the Poets: Studies in Modern Responses to Gerard Manley Hopkins.* Ed. Richard F. Giles. Hamilton, Ont.: International Hopkins Assn., 1985. 114–23.

Ouedraogo, Amadou. "*The Voice*: Par-déla le réel, ou la quête de la totalité." *Commonwealth Essays and Studies* 16.2 (1993): 101–9.

Palmer, Eustace. *An Introduction to the African Novel: A Critical Study of Twelve Books by Chinua Achebe, James Ngugi, Camara Laye, Elechi Amadi, Ayi Kwei Armah, Mongo Beti, and Gabriel Okara.* New York: Africana, 1972. London: Heinemann Educational, 1972.

Petersen, Kirsten Holst. "Heterogeneous Worlds Yoked Violently Together: The Commonwealth Poetry Prize, 1979." *Kunapipi* 1.2 (1979): 155–58.

Roscoe, A. A. "Okara's Unheeded Voice: Explication and Defence." *Busara* 2.1 (1969): 16–22.

Scott, Patrick. "Gabriel Okara's *The Voice*: The Non-Ijo Reader and the Pragmatics of Translingualism." *Research in African Literatures* 21.3 (1990): 75–88.

———. "The Older Generation: T.M. Aluko and Gabriel Okara." *European-Language Writing in Sub-Saharan Africa.* Ed. Gerard-Albert-S. Budapest: Akad. Kiado, 1986. 689–97.

Vincent, Theophilus. *The Novel and Reality in Africa and America.* Lagos, Nigeria: U.S. Information Service and U of Lagos, 1974.

Webb, Hugh. "Allegory: Okara's *The Voice*." *English in Africa* 5.2 (1978): 66–73.

William, Catherine. "Decolonizing the Word: Language, Culture, and Self in the Works of Ngugi wa Thiong'o and Gabriel Okara." *Research in African Literatures* 22.4 (1991): 53–61.

Wright, Derek. "Ritual and Reality in Four West African Novelists." *The Literary Criterion* 21.3 (1986): 72–90.

———. "Ritual and Reality in the Novels of Wole Soyinka, Gabriel Okara and Kofi Awoonor." *Kunapipi* 9.1 (1987): 65–74.

APPENDIX II

Civil War in Nigeria, 1967–1970

Though *Long Drums and Cannons* was written before the outbreak of the Nigerian civil war (King 220–21), the struggle sometimes seems to loom over the text, its presence felt through numerous concerns and tensions explored by the Nigerian writers, as well as through the reader's awareness of its impending destruction. Declared independent on 1 October 1960, Nigeria was seen as "a potential middle-level economic power," even "the great hope of Africa" (Ndibe 1432, 1437), but conflicts quickly emerged: established tensions between the northern Hausa-Fulani, the western Yoruba, and the eastern Igbos were exacerbated as each group struggled for political supremacy; widespread poverty and labour issues went unresolved as government officials and other members of the élite used their positions for personal gain; elections in 1964 and 1965 were rigged (Arnold 194–95, Crowder 246, Ihonvbere 48). By November 1965, public distrust and dissatisfaction led to "a state of near anarchy," and, in January 1966, a group led by Major Chukwuma Nzeogwu staged a coup, during which the Prime Minister and other leaders were assassinated (Crowder 246). Soon after, power was seized by Major-General J.T. Aguyi-Ironsi, an Igbo leader who abolished federal structures and introduced the National Military Government (Arnold 195). However, changes implemented since the January coup failed to bring order to Nigeria, as anti-Igbo riots resulted in the deaths of hundreds of officers and civilians, as well as the assassination of Ironsi on 29 July (Arnold 195–96). Under the following head of state, Lt. Col. Yakubu Gowon, some attempts were made at regional reconciliation; however, Lt. Col. Chukwuemeka Odumegwu Ojukwu, the Eastern Region military governor, "would not be reconciled," and, during September 1966, between 10,000 and 30,000 Igbos were killed in northern demonstrations and riots, prompting the group's exodus from the north, west, and Lagos to the east (Arnold 196). Following attempts by Gowon to divide Nigeria into twelve states, Ojukwu announced the secession of the Eastern Region and the creation of the state of Biafra on 30 May 1967 (Arnold 196, Crowder 246). By July 1967, the federal and Biafran forces were, respectively, 40,000 and 25,000 strong; assistance from such ideologically—and economically-concerned nations as Britain, France, and the USSR also strengthened each side (Arnold 197). Throughout the conflict, gains were made by both armies. On a westward offensive, the

Biafran troops reached a point from which they could threaten Ibadan and Lagos by 17 August, and, on 29 September, a Biafran administrator declared the overrun midwestern territory an "independent and sovereign Republic of Benin" (Arnold 198). Federal superiority reasserted itself by May 1968, when Biafra's last port fell and supplies were effectively blockaded; an army of approximately 120,000 was raised for a final assault on Biafra in early January 1970 (Arnold 199–200). Biafra's surrender at this time brought an end to the thirty-month war, a struggle which resulted in the loss of nearly one million (mostly civilian) lives and marked the beginning of Nigeria's painful reconstruction (Ndibe 1436).

Works Cited

Arnold, Guy. *Historical Dictionary of Civil Wars in Africa*. Lanham, MD and London: The Scarecrow Press, 1999.

Crowder, Michael. "Nigeria." *The Cambridge Encyclopedia of Africa*. Ed. Roland Oliver and Michael Crowder. Cambridge: Cambridge UP, 1981.

Ihonvbere, Julius and Timothy Shaw. *Illusions of Power: Nigeria in Transition*. Trenton, NJ and Asmara, Eritrea: Africa World Press, 1998.

King, James. *The Life of Margaret Laurence*. Toronto: Alfred A. Knopf Canada, 1997.

Ndibe, Okey. "Nigeria." *Africana: An Encyclopedia of the African and African-American Experience*. Ed. Kwame Anthony Appiah and Henry Louis Gates, Jr. New York: Basic Civitas, 1999.

APPENDIX III

Ethnic Groups Discussed in *Long Drums and Cannons*

Whether working within pastoral (*Fulani bororo*) or more urban (*Fulani gida*) surroundings, the Fulani people play key roles in Nigerian affairs: though they do not form a majority in any country, Fulani communities can be found across Africa, from Senegal to the Central African Republic; the group remains united by the Fulfude language and a strict devotion to Islamic tenets; once powerful through such theocracies as the nineteenth-century Sokoto Caliphate, the *Fulani gida* of northern Nigeria have allied with the Hausa to form the Hausa-Fulani, "the effective ruling class" of the region (Oppong 794, Yakan 316–18).

Nigeria's largest ethnic group, the northern Hausa hold a considerable amount of influence over the nation: with over fifty million Hausa speakers, the language (part of the Chadic branch of the Afroasiatic language family) is the most widely spoken in Nigeria; ethnic ties are maintained through strict patriarchal, patrilinear practices, as well as an adherence to Islam by the majority; the Hausa have also remained strong since independence by cultivating such cash crops as cotton and peanuts, and by dominating civilian and military governments (Nave 942–43, Yakan 350–53).

The predominantly-eastern Igbo people possess a complex, sometimes controversial history: a tradition of cultural achievement has been established through carving, metalwork, and weaving, while religious ceremonies (blending Christian and traditional African beliefs, with an emphasis on the afterlife) are also elaborate; a focus on community life has spawned a range of societies concerned with public duties and projects; traditional social structures were built around autonomous villages governed by elders, and, in the 1960s, the Igbo, faced with extreme acts of violence and other political threats, attempted to form the independent state of Biafra (Johnson 988, Yakan 366–68).

Approximately 400,000 strong, the Ijaw are the tenth largest ethnic minority in Nigeria; though some precolonial kingdoms were established, villages were generally governed by councils of elders; concentrated along the Niger Delta, the main economic activity of the Ijaw continues to be fishing ("Ijaw" 989, Yakan 369–70).

Concentrated in southwestern Nigeria, the Yoruba continue to develop unique practices essential to communal and national development: while "most Yoruba are either Christian or Muslim," traditional African deities such as Ogun are still worshipped; bronzes and sculptures created by the Yoruba during the thirteenth and fourteenth centuries are considered to be among the finest works of art produced by Africa, while such contemporary artists as Wole Soyinka continue to bring attention and acclaim to the group; though the Oyo empire had crumbled by 1840, the southwestern cities of Lagos and Ibadan remain centres of Nigerian political and cultural life (Nave 2035–36, Yakan 705–6).

Works Cited

"Ijaw." *Africana: An Encyclopedia of the African and African-American Experience*. Ed. Kwame Anthony Appiah and Henry Louis Gates, Jr. New York: Basic Civitas, 1999.

Johnson, David P. Jr. "Igbo." *Africana: An Encyclopedia of the African and African-American Experience*. Ed. Kwame Anthony Appiah and Henry Louis Gates, Jr. New York: Basic Civitas, 1999.

Nave, Ari. "Hausa." *Africana: An Encyclopedia of the African and African-American Experience*. Ed. Kwame Anthony Appiah and Henry Louis Gates, Jr. New York: Basic Civitas, 1999.

———. "Yoruba." *Africana: An Encyclopedia of the African and African-American Experience*. Ed. Kwame Anthony Appiah and Henry Louis Gates, Jr. New York: Basic Civitas, 1999.

Oppong, Yaa Poukua Afriyie. "Fulani." *Africana: An Encyclopedia of the African and African-American Experience*. Ed. Kwame Anthony Appiah and Henry Louis Gates, Jr. New York: Basic Civitas, 1999.

Yakan, Mohammed Z. "Fulani." *Almanac of African Peoples and Nations*. New Brunswick, NJ and London: Transaction Publishers, 1999.

———. "Hausa." *Almanac of African Peoples and Nations*. New Brunswick, NJ and London: Transaction Publishers, 1999.

———. "Igbo." *Almanac of African Peoples and Nations*. New Brunswick, NJ and London: Transaction Publishers, 1999.

———. "Ijaw." *Almanac of African Peoples and Nations*. New Brunswick, NJ and London: Transaction Publishers, 1999.

———. "Yoruba." *Almanac of African Peoples and Nations*. New Brunswick, NJ and London: Transaction Publishers, 1999.